TRAVELERS' TALES
DESTINATION TITLES

TRAVELERS' TALES GUIDES

ITALY

TRUE STORIES OF LIFE
ON THE ROAD

Travelers' Tales Guides

ITALY

True Stories of Life on the Road

✦ ✦ ✦

Collected and Edited by

Anne Calcagno

Series Editors

James O'Reilly and Larry Habegger

Travelers' Tales

An Imprint of Solas House, Inc.

Palo Alto

Credits and copyright notices for the individual articles in this collection are
given starting on page 410.

We have made every effort to trace the ownership of all copyrighted material and
to secure permission from copyright holders. In the event of any question arising
as to the ownership of any material, we will be pleased to make the necessary
correction in future printings. Contact Travelers' Tales, Inc., 853 Alma Street, Palo
Alto, California 94301. www.travelerstales.com

Cover design: Michele Wetherbee
Interior design: Kathryn Heflin and Susan Bailey
Cover photograph: © Corbis
Illustrations: Nina Stewart
Maps: Keith Granger
Page layout: Cynthia Lamb, using the fonts Bembo and Boulevard

Library of Congress Cataloguing-in-Publication Data

Travelers' Tales Italy : true stories / edited by Anne Calgagno.
     p. cm. — (Travelers' Tales guides)
  Includes index.
  ISBN 1-885211-72-4
    1. Italy—Description and travel I. Title: Italy : true stories. II. Calgagno,
Anne. III. Series

DG430.2 .T73 2001
945—dc21   2001027972

First Edition
Printed in the United States
10 9

All travel is…the exploration of love.

—DUNCAN FALLOWELL,
To Noto or London to Sicily in a Ford

Table of Contents

Part Two
SOME THINGS TO DO

Part Three
GOING YOUR OWN WAY

Introduction: The Idea of Italy

JAN MORRIS

"Close your eyes and think of England" was the legendary wedding-night advice offered by Victorian mamas to their daughters. "Close your eyes and think of Italy" might seem more apposite nowadays, because to most of us the idea of Italy is at once soothing, rousing and romantic, if not actually aphrodisiac. However, it was not always so: Italy's reputation has fluctuated disconcertingly down the centuries, and only fairly recently has it settled into its present mould of cultivated and sexy excitement.

Of course the cultivated bit has always been there, if only in retrospect. For example, eighteenth-century gentlemen went on the Grand Tour to Italy because they knew that there was the very seat of beauty, art, and learning, inherited from classical times by way of the Renaissance. They did not expect much, though, of the contemporary Italian, except as a kind of foppish fashion model, and their fathers indeed were often taken aback to find their sons tainted by the educational experience with every kind of coxcomb tomfoolery.

Then again, in the first half of our own century, if Rome, Venice, Florence, and Naples still possessed their incomparable allure, to the world at large the Italian was certainly no mother's cynosure: unreliable, corrupt, at worst a gangster, at best a comic or sentimental buffoon, he seemed the epitome of dissolute Latinism. In American movies then, your standard Italian wore a ridiculous moustache and talked a particularly absurd variety of broken English, unless he was a Chicago gunman messily eating spaghetti and setting up murders: in the iconography of the cartoonist he was sometimes a fat restaurateur, sometimes a poisoner in the Medici mould.

Yet ever and again the idea of Italy has burst upon the rest of us in a glory of glamorous inspiration. In Victorian times it was briefly embodied in the idea of Garibaldi and Mazzini, terrific heroes of the Risorgimento, who represented to a whole generation the grandeur of national liberty. Between the world wars it was represented by opera singers and aristocratic racing drivers. Today— well, dear God, today, just consider the roster of Italians and Italianate influences which add up to that modern honeymoon exercise: football stars and Pavarotti, dress designers and saintly Popes, Ferraris, olive oil, Umberto Eco, delectable shoes and everything that goes with suavity, sophistication, winning touches of sharp practice, peasant authenticity, and lovingly attentive manners.

The thing about Italy is that, in reputation as in landscape, in the past as in the present, in the idea of it and in the hard fact, it is never dull. For a thousand years and more it has been one of the most interesting corners of the earth—not always admirable, but never boring. That young man returning from the Grand Tour may have shocked his pater with his long hair and affected manners, but he was certainly not more prosaic for the change: the daily nightmare that is contemporary Naples, congealed in petty crime amidst a more or less permanent grid-lock, is nevertheless full of endearing fascination; the generic Mafia Godfather is hardly *nice*, but he is certainly compelling.

For myself, I found myself seduced by the ambiguous Italian idea at the end of the second world war, when I set foot in Italy for the first time in my life. It was a moment of heavy slump in the Italian reputation. Not only had the Italians fought poorly in the war (except at sea or as partisans), for most of the time they had fought on the wrong side. They were tarred still with the unlovely brush of Fascism, and remembered as the bullying invaders of Abyssinia and Greece. They were endemically corrupt, notoriously bombastic.

Yet I very soon found that none of this truly represented the national character, as it stood in 1945. The Italians, I discovered, were far ahead of most of us in their contempt for the matter of war. If they had been gulled by Mussolini into unbecoming behaviour, it was only because of their native simplicity of the people— their fondness for show, their ardent response to rhetoric. If they had switched sides at an opportune moment, supporting first the

Nazis, then the Allies, it was because they had by then discovered in themselves a profound disillusionment with the cruder kinds of patriotism and nationalism, so rampant then among the warring nations. By the time I got there, ordinary people hardly cared whether they were dealing with soldiers of the Wernmacht, the Grenadier Guards, or the U.S. Marines. They had realized the fallibility in all of us, the distinction between us and our leaders, and the overriding truth that a man's a man for a' that.

Now, half a century later at the end of the millennium, the genius of Italy has come into synch, as it were, with the times. It is at home with the Zeitgeist. That wry cynical attitude to the ways of the great world is now common to all of us in the West—which of us would now blame the harmless common citizen for the actions of his Government? The showy raffishness that our grandparents tended to despise in the Italian character is now the universal rage. The Italian Black Economy, which grew directly out of the rampant wartime black market, is now almost a model of economic opportunism. The severe authority of London's Savile Row, once honoured by males on both sides of the Atlantic, has long since been superseded by the slick urbanity of Armani and his peers, and the cuisine of Italy, once snootily disregarded by gourmets, is now everyone's healthy ideal. Even the familiar neuroses of the Italians, their confusions of machismo and mother-complex, their self-conscious sexuality, their fondness for noise and show-off, have become part of all our psyches.

And today more than ever, in good times as in bad, the world recognizes in Italy an essential idea of beauty: beauty of landscape, beauty of learning, beauty of art, beauty of human romance and affection. All these responses, all these varied judgements, are expressed somewhere or other in the pages of this book. Go on darling, close your eyes and think of Italy, if only while you copulate with its seductive chapters.

Jan Morris has been wandering the world and writing about her experiences for more than 40 years. She is the author of numerous books and her essays on travel are classics of the genre. She lives in Wales, the only person in her postal code.

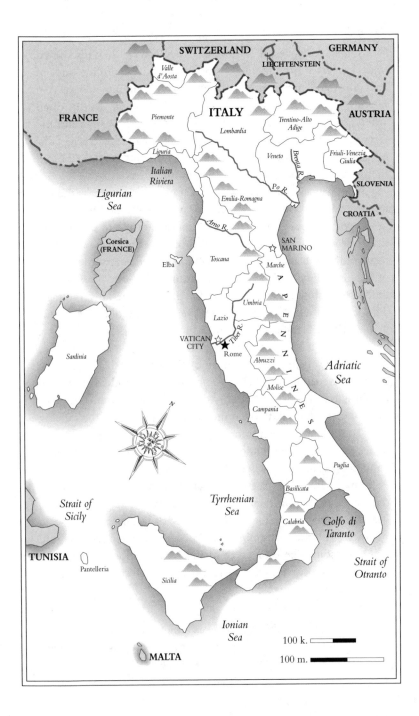

Editor's Preface

Before Italy was a journey of discovery it was home to me and thus unremarkable, a place lived in instinctively because my parents had brought me there at the age of four. I remained there until I flew back across the Atlantic to attend college, whereupon I first asked myself: Italy, unremarkable? My family had joined the tentative, though gradually more numerous, Americans who began in the 1960s to work in Italy. They were a significant reversal of the traditional exodus that had made the "Italian journey," that of Italians emigrating to America for work. In the 1960s, it was Italian-Americans, German-Americans, Jewish-Americans, and other Americans who arrived to this complex boot, this historical peninsula, to build subsidiary American companies (and then schools and services) in response to Italy's "economic miracle." I did not understand we had reversed the flow of emigration, but even as a small child I knew we had reached a place still reversed in time, a place where my mother no longer shopped at supermarkets but instead walked to an assortment of stores, such as the *frutteria, drogheria, tabaccheria, farmacia,* or *la latteria* where our milk bottles got refilled from large metal vats. This was milk that every Italian religiously boiled before consumption, and which brought my sister and me to tears when a grandmotherly babysitter refused to let us pour cold milk on our cereal. It was the country wherein my blond, athletic Oregonian mother always in slacks became a spectacle with entire busloads of people staring at us, shocked. Even girls my age only wore dresses, preferably made of blue wool, complemented by white knee socks, which fashion I came to slavishly revere as the standard of beauty.

Though these incidents are thirty-plus years old, Italian milk still tastes strange to an American child's palate (surely true for my two), and many an Italian girl continues to wear white knee socks and a dark wool dress for important occasions. In these travelers tales you will hear the amazement, surprise, frustration, and delight of travelers who have encountered Italy's time warp. It appears when Thomas Belmonte rounds a street in Naples to spot boys leaning as casually, as gracefully, as Etruscan statues. It resounds in James Gardner's walk through the Vatican's Hall of Maps—perhaps true inside all Italian museums—where the peninsula's City-States, agricultures, acqueducts, and flags remain forever ancient, and instantly vivid. Or it strikes us in Theresa Maggio's account of the yearly hand-to-hand slaughter of tuna caught during Favignana's *mattanza*, a ritual enacted today as it was at the start of the last millennium.

Italy is a country layered so densely and multiplicatively, contradicting itself always rather marvelously. I think all travelers go to Italy knowing this, yet it still surprises. We can't help ourselves from purchasing those postcards (why else would they appear for sale year after year?) that reveal a striped kitten sprawled luxuriously on the sunny marble base of an ancient Roman column. We must know how perfectly this *is* Italy; newness and antiquity melded with perfect casualness. We stamp home to our loved ones those ribald postcards of lovers kissing on the steps of a baroque basilica. In this country, the centuries-old *palazzo,* fountain, or church compete with the remarkable beauty and sexual charisma of the quite mortal Italian male or female. Should we study the region's art or the art of its life? As Libby Lubin points out, perhaps every cupola indicates that a woman's breasts (our own, Lucretia Borgia's, or the nursing Virgin Mary's?) are the merry measure of things Italian.

Thinking "Italy," one gathers Etruscan, Greek, Roman, Norman, Arab, German, French, Eritrean, Christian, Judaic history and more. The accounts by this book's travelers reveal so many strata in history, so many oppositions in time and belief. Think of young Romulus and Remus who spar to create Rome, a city which births a diversity of emperors, from the unstable Emperor Nero who allegedly conspired to burn the city down, to Emperor Marcus Aurelius who expanded the Roman Empire both morally and geographically. In time, Christianity blooms and, with it, important saints: Saint Ambrose, Saint Francis, Saint Agnes, Saint Teresa, and the many others who built churches and belief up and down the boot. Yet by the time Gian Lorenzo Bernini sculpts his magnificent Saint Teresa, her very ecstasy confirms the decadent Baroque. The Church is crumbling. From the rubble, Italy must fight for Unification. In 1870, she wins her definition as a country. In this sense, Italy is newer than the United States. Yet two World Wars were fought on this soil since then, yielding a fragmented Italy of sparring Fascists, Communists, Christian Democrats, Socialists, a country once held hostage by the Red Brigades, and lately resurrected by the ecological "Greens." We have to ask ourselves, which Italy are we talking about when we talk about Italy? The past is gone, but the pieces of time so ably remain.

This layering is what makes Italy so filling, as well as so confusing. Everywhere on aqueduct-fed Roman water mains and fountains the Latin initials S.P.Q.R still speak, as they did millennia ago: *Senatus Populusque Romanus* ("Belonging to the Roman People"). In this self-same Rome, nearly every bank (of the sort Natalia Galli discovered in Sicily) boasts a bullet-proof, computerized, futuristic, columnar entry.

Italian-Americans like Adria Bernardi, Fred Gardaphe, Don Gecewicz, or Vince Sturla reach Italy seeking their roots, toppling over cobblestones, hiking to festivals, marching with friends, researching street names. Others, like Robert Hellenga or Ivo John Lederer systematically relive critical historical moments: the flood of 1966 or the Allied freeing of Rome. Some travelers remain. Italy becomes home or at least an annual pilgrimage. Lisa St. Aubin de Terán, Barbara Grizzuti Harrison, Frances Mayes, Jan Morris, Tim Parks, Mary Taylor Simeti, and Matt Spender write lyrically of an Italy whose ancient landscape they resurrect into livable homes, keeping the old oil presses and vineyards while encountering new tax laws, maternity wards, schools, foods, holidays. Trey Ellis discovers the heightened visibility of a black man in Italy, while Henry

Alford watches the nomenclature of homosexuality pale through a shared intergenerational communion with Italy. Stanley Crouch highlights Italy's unexpected connection to southern black hospitality and jazz. Gary Paul Nabhan teaches how Italian polenta came from the New World's Native Americans.

Of course, there are those who come to Italy to seek their futures in the shape of a man or woman with whom to fall in love. This is the maddening country wherein magnified bottoms and breasts titillatingly preen on billboards everywhere. Sometimes, right above a sacred altar with a vase of lillies to the Virgin Mary. Italy is where feminists have fought some of their hardest battles. Until 1983, a woman could not impart her Italian citizenship to her child, independent of the nationality of the father. This was the father's right only. Yet, this is the country where a woman does not have to claim "disability" to receive maternity benefits, benefits which are far more generous than our allotted own. Here a woman gets pinched, fondled, whistled at, and followed with enraging blatantness. Yet she is also cajoled, revered, praised, and complimented with magical aplomb, delighted in for being a woman.

There are writers here who will please you, startle you, awaken you to the Italy you know but hopefully also to an Italy you have not yet discovered. Not all the writers are named in this preface, but each is lovingly gathered for your perusal. For my part, I came to Italy as a little girl and, three decades later, returned with my own little girl. What I was offered in love as a child, I watched her receive anew, in kisses, bites of ice cream, and compassion for her small tears and fears. For the Italy that grew me, and the Italy that nourishes all who cherish her embrace, I am ever grateful. These storytellers will tell you why.

—ANNE CALCAGNO

PART ONE

ESSENCE OF ITALY

THOM ELKJER

✦ ✦ ✦

A *Fiume* Runs Through It

In Italy, it is who you know that counts.

IN HIS CLASSIC BOOK *The Italians*, LUIGI BARZINI OBSERVES THAT
the basis of society in Italy is the family, not the law. This is because
in Italy, there is either no law at all, or so many that it's impossible
to sort out the tangled heap of overlapping jurisdictions. So you
call your brother, or your uncle, and he arranges things for you.
Americans, on the other hand, rely much more on their own initiative because there is usually a clear and stable structure for getting things done.

Barzini's analysis remained abstract for me until I began researching a novel set in Italy. The protagonist of the story goes fly
fishing there, which meant that I, diligent author, would have to do
the same. Before I left the states I talked to Graziano, a longtime
friend of mine living in the town of Vicenza, near Venice. He told
me not to worry, that all Italian rivers were public and there were
no special laws to be concerned about. I started packing.

I landed in Rome in late summer, when cleansing rain sepa-
rates the heat of the day from the cool of the evening. I checked
into my hotel, consulted the phone book, and looked for a sporting goods shop where I could get a fishing license. To my delight,
I saw that there was a new fly fishing shop only ten minutes away.

I looked at my watch and smiled. I might get to the river that very evening.

The shop owner spoke no English, but I had enough Italian to learn that the Fiume Velino, a good-sized river northeast of Rome, held fish year-round. But when I told the guy I wanted a fishing license, he looked confused. Perhaps you should go to the post office, he suggested. I explained more slowly that I wanted to fish not only in Lazio, but also in the north of Italy. He shrugged and suggested that I visit the Italian Department of Hunting and Fishing, somewhere on the via Nazionale. This made more sense, and I headed back to the hotel to look up the address. There I bumped into Giuseppe, the proprietor, while looking in the phone book.

"It is not in the interest of the government to help you," Giuseppe pointed out. "They do not even wish to help Italian people. Why will they want to help an American man to take their fish?"

"A friend of mine in Vicenza told me it was easy," I said.

"Is he close to you, your friend?"

"Like a brother," I said.

"Then go to your friend," Giuseppe said. "Not to the government."

I should have heard the echo of Barzini. But my entrepreneurial American ears were deaf to that kind of talk. "I can do this myself," I said, and dialed the number of the Department of Hunting and Fishing. After I explained what I wanted, I got a flurry of very fast Italian, the only words of which I understood were *ufficio postale*...post office.

I decided I must be using the wrong word for "license," because everyone thought I was asking for stamps. While I irritably looked through my dictionary, Giuseppe picked up the phone, hit the redial button, and got through to the same woman I had. They chatted merrily for ten minutes, evidently discovering they had several friends in common. Finally Giuseppe hung up.

"Did you find out where I should go?" I asked.

"Post office," he said. "There's one around the corner."

It took half a day and two visits to a nearby post office, but I eventually got a scrap of paper that allowed me to fish for three days in the state of Lazio. It cost more than a year's license in California, but I didn't care. I had successfully worked the system, or so I thought.

The next morning I drove out of Rome in my rented car and picked up the Velino River west of Rieti. From the highway I looked for good fishing spots. I could have arranged to have someone guide me to the best places to fish, but I had a map and a car and I had done this before, in the U.S. If you kept your eyes peeled and were willing to hike in from the highway, you found good places to fish. They seemed even better, of course, when you found them yourself.

The first place I stopped was lovely, the river curving through a sun-dappled valley dotted with farm houses and olive orchards. I spotted a small bridge from the highway and walked down to it through a grassy field, feeling like Nick Adams in Hemingway's story, *The Big Two Hearted River.* From the bridge I could see fish rising in the morning sun. I felt a congratulatory surge of self-reliance, and set to rigging my rod.

It was not until I looked behind me, preparatory to casting, that I saw the sign. In large red letters it said *divieto di pesca*. No fishing allowed. I lowered my rod and looked around. A man appeared in the doorway of a farmhouse a half-mile away, and he was looking right at me. I walked back up the hill to my car.

For the next eight hours I drove throughout the province of Rieti. Every time I stopped, I hiked farther to reach an even more remote location that was perfect for fishing. Every time there was a sign saying *divieto di pesca*. Each time I would think about ignoring the sign and fishing anyway. Then I would skulk back to the car. I might have been independent, but I couldn't break the rules.

A day later I left Rome and went north to Vicenza. When I told Graziano about my frustration in Lazio, he said he would introduce me to someone who could arrange everything to my satisfaction.

"I don't want to be a burden to anyone," I said quickly.

"Maurizio is like my own brother," Graziano said. "It is no problem."

After dinner that night we met Maurizio, who said he would be happy to take me fishing.

"But first you need a license," he pointed out.

"I'll go to the post office tomorrow morning," I said suavely.

"Do you want to go fishing, or do you want to mail a letter?" Graziano inquired politely.

"For the license," I said. "I go to the post office for the fishing license."

The two of them laughed uproariously, then Maurizio explained that it would be impossible for me to get the approvals I needed on my own. If I would give him my passport, he would return it to me the next afternoon with everything I needed.

He was as good as his word. What he put in my hand, however, hardly resembled the "license" I had gotten in Rome. There was a Venetian state booklet, which had to be filled in with the date, location, and number of fish each day; provincial stamps for the Vicenza region; and special riders for individual rivers. I noticed that my signature had been casually forged on each of these documents, and that together the fees totalled more than 200,000 lire. When I offered to reimburse Maurizio, he just smiled, exposing a mouthful of truly bad teeth, and said it had cost nothing.

There was a message in all this, but I couldn't put my finger on it. It appeared that the law was more complex in the north than in the south, but paradoxically it was also much easier to comply. How could that be?

Early next morning we drove up the Brenta River in a light rain. I dreamily envisioned hooking native trout in rustic streams, my fly rod bent double as I played a leaping four-pounder. So I was surprised when we pulled off under a freeway overpass that thundered with every passing truck. The river was a hundred feet wide and roared below high cliffs on the far side. You'd need a telephone pole and steel cable to fish water like this, I thought. It turned out I was not far wrong.

I got out of the car with my rod case in my hand, but Maurizio told me to put it away. "We will fish the historic Italian way," he said. With that he produced a pair of high-tech, carbon-composite telescoping fishing rods that extended 25 feet and weighed about ten pounds. The rods were made in Japan, which meant Italian history had some chapters I'd never read.

We did not even cast with these monster rods. The idea was to hang a worm about ten feet off the end of the rod, hold the rod out over the water so that the worm hung in the water, then wave the rod so the worm seemed to be borne downstream by the current. It seemed impossible that any self-respecting trout would fall for this gambit. I was just glad that no one I knew would ever see me: a confirmed catch-and-release wilderness fly fisherman, hauling trout out of a river next to a screaming highway, using live bait and less finesse than a behemoth on *All-Star Wrestling.*

Suddenly I felt a tug on my line. I lifted the rod and there was a foot-long trout hanging off the end of the line, squirming angrily. I thought it was a fluke until I put another worm in the water. I caught five fish in five minutes, and after that I didn't feel so religious. I lost track of everything but the fishing, until I heard a shout behind me. I turned and saw Graziano pointing to where lightning had just flashed against the far cliffs. I could not hear him above the roar of the river, so I shouted something in response and turned back to the water. More lightning struck, even closer. Another fish took my bait. This was great!

The next thing I knew, Maurizio was practically dragging me back up the bank and out of the river. He pointed out that I had been standing knee-deep in the water and holding a 25-foot carbon rod out in front of me during a lightning storm. I had to admit, it was a pretty good way to get electrocuted.

We repaired to a nearby bar to wait out the lightning. I was aglow with my success on the river, and asked about heading even higher up the valley, where the river was smaller and I could use my fly rod. It is difficult, Maurizio said, to get the authorization. I asked why. Had not Graziano said that all the water was public?

"The water, yes," Maurizio said. "The land, no."

"You mean all these licenses are no good?" I asked, holding up the papers Maurizio had secured for me.

"You must have all of them also," he said. "But higher up you must also know somebody who lives along the river. That is the final approval."

Now I understood why we had been fishing next to the highway. I also understood that the adventure I was having was not something I could have cooked up on my own, no matter how much independent initiative I displayed or how many laws I followed. I looked at Maurizio and Graziano and felt a wave of brotherly affection.

Suddenly Maurizio stood up and walked over to the pay phone on the wall. When he came back he picked up his cigarettes, which meant we were leaving.

"I remembered that my sister's husband knows a guy who lives quite high up the river," he said.

"Did you talk to the guy?" I asked. "Can we go?"

"I did not speak with him," Maurizio said. "But my sister's husband says this man is like a brother to him. It will be no problem."

Thom Elkjer is a freelance interviewer and scriptwriter whose work has appeared in print, on stage, in video, and in Travelers' Tales Paris *and* The Road Within. *He is also the author of* Hook, Line and Murder. *He and his suitcase live in Mill Valley, California. This story won the Travelers' Tales Italy writing contest.*

★

A few miles north of Rimini, on the coast road to Ravenna, I came to a trickle of summer water that was flowing under a bridge. Its name was the Rubicon. It was once the boundary between Cisalpine Gaul and Rome, and any general who crossed it with his army, without the permission of the Senate, was committing rebellion. Caesar crossed it because his spies had told him that his enemies in the capital were plotting his downfall, and he knew that he had to march on Rome or perish. It was the greatest gamble of his life and, as he ordered his legions to advance, it is said he remarked, like a true gambler, *Alea jacta est*—"the die is cast"—and ever since men have been casting their various dies and crossing their Rubicons.

—H. V. Morton, *A Traveller in Italy*

LIBBY LUBIN

✳ ✳ ✳

The Measure of All Things

The author reveals an Italian obsession.

FORGET THE FORUM, THE COLOSSEUM, OR ST. PETER'S. IN MY opinion the true symbol of Rome is the female breast. Not by chance, Rome's legendary founders, Romulus and Remus, were suckled by a mother with six teats, a she-wolf who found them nestled at the edge of the Tiber. Today, statues of the threesome adorn everything from bridges to fountains to sarcophagi. The six pendulous breasts are always prominently featured. America's founding hero chopped down a cherry tree. Rome's sucked milk.

Thus, even from ancient times, the city has been defined by the mound or the bump. First it was the seven hills so touted by Roman poets and historians. Since the Renaissance, it has been the dome, complete with nipple on top. No city anywhere can rival Rome for the sheer number of domes. From the moment Bramante, in the early 1500s, worked out his scheme for the little chapel called the Tempietto, domes began to pop up around town like mushrooms in a damp field.

Now, Rome's skyline is a pattern of breast-shaped domes in any number of colors and sizes. Indeed, breasts, the prototype of the dome, are so closely linked with the Roman concept of a church that when the 17th-century builders of Sant'Ignazio ran short of

9

funds, they painted on the ceiling an awe-inspiring *trompe l'œil* dome seemingly equal to, if not surpassing, that of St. Peter's. This was the Baroque's most outrageous, but certainly not only, instance of dome envy.

Rome's horizon notwithstanding, it is difficult to walk even a block without confronting at least several pairs of bona fide breasts. Newsstands are a sure bet. The otherwise respectable *L'Express*, an Italian equivalent of *Time* or *Newsweek*, always, regardless of current world crises, features a bare-breasted woman, or several, on its cover. Similarly, billboards, even those adjacent to the Vatican, frequently feature this favorite cross section of the female anatomy. Last summer, the city was wallpapered with a pair of well-formed, well-bronzed breasts. THESE WON'T FADE BY CHRISTMAS, the sign said. It was, of course, an ad for photographic film.

Italian television is likewise casual about breasts. Nudity banned from all but late-night cable at home is aired here in prime time. Most intriguing is the popular game show *Colpo Grosso*, in which ordinary housewives (or so they say) cheerfully strip down to pairs of sexy panties. The rules of the games are obscure, but the object is clear: to expose as much flesh as possible. Much of the action hinges around a slot machine. When tangerines come up, Miss Tangerine flips open her top to display a pair of ripe breasts within, one of which is adorned with an orange-sequined tangerine. Lest the show seem too provincial, a chorus line of young ladies, allegedly from around the world, parades past the cameras at various intervals. In turn, each Bettina, Carmen, and Monique takes the opportunity to disrobe, one article of clothing at a time. I wonder how these visitors from abroad describe their Italian television debuts to their parents back home.

Maybe they explain that, when in Rome, they do as the Romans. In the city of the breast, it all seems natural. At any rate, that's one rationale that occurred to me when a friend asked if I would model for her life-study drawing class. The class is made up of junior-year-abroad students from a small Catholic college in Texas. The week before, a muscle-bound Italian male had modeled for the class. He had offended half the class with his garlic breath and shocked the rest with his anatomy. My friend must have figured that I would be the perfect antidote. My breath is usually fresh, and, as a wife and mother, I would certainly put the class at ease.

Lest I appear immodest, I should explain my motives. First, the money was good for the two-and-a-half-hour class. But my reasons were not wholly venal. It was a novel experience, something I'd never consider doing in the small New England college town where my husband teaches art history. Were I to disrobe for a class at home, news would travel so quickly that within days I wouldn't be able to buy groceries without eliciting raised eyebrows from the checkout ladies.

But now, thanks to sabbatical leave and a fellowship, we're not in New England. We are foreigners in Rome and thus cloaked in anonymity: here today, gone tomorrow. This is my year to wear floppy hats and flowing scarves, to flirt with Italian men. Like Daisy Miller on her moonlit tryst in the Colosseum, I have been emboldened in so many small ways by the sensuality of *la dolce vita*.

Moreover, this is the city where, for hundreds of years, artists have come to paint and draw the nude. Since I can neither paint nor draw, modeling seemed a way I could connect to the process. Besides, I play a lot of tennis. I'm not in bad shape for a mother of two small children.

Perhaps to remind myself that this was all in the name of art, I visited the Borghese Museum the day before class. There I saw even more bare breasts than I'd passed at the Via Veneto newsstands

> *T*he University of Dallas, like many other schools, maintains a campus in Rome, a great jumping-off point for exploring the rest of Europe and North Africa. I received my first schooling there in the art of traveling on a shoestring. Had I known that modeling was an option I would have brought my G-string.
>
> ◆
>
> —Sean O'Reilly, "The Universal Primate Does Rome"

on the way over. There was naked Daphne, bare-breasted Venus, half-clad Persephone. I felt reassured, sort of. The nudity seemed like no big deal, but here in the land of the Baroque breast I suddenly realized that my own pair of domes might seem distinctly underdeveloped. Where was the cleavage?

When I arrived at the school the next day, I found it something of a disappointment after the Borghese. It was a nondescript brick and stone building on the outskirts of Rome. Inside, everything seemed appropriately institutional. The hallways were decorated with posters of Italian masterpieces. Botticelli's *Birth of Venus*, its heroine clad only in her windswept hair, greeted me as I entered the foyer. Imagine being born with a figure like that. Titian's honey-haired *Venus of Urbine*, reclining nude on pillows and cushions, gazed demurely at me from the stairwell. "Welcome to the club," she seemed to say.

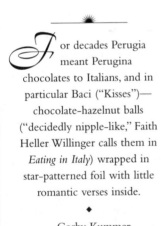

*F*or decades Perugia meant Perugina chocolates to Italians, and in particular Baci ("Kisses")— chocolate-hazelnut balls ("decidedly nipple-like," Faith Heller Willinger calls them in *Eating in Italy*) wrapped in star-patterned foil with little romantic verses inside.

◆

—Corby Kummer,
"Green-Hearted Italy,"
The Atlantic Monthly

The class numbered about a dozen. I'm used to college students. As I said, my husband teaches at a college, and I usually go to great lengths to cultivate a list of reliable baby-sitters. As one of the women in the class led me down a hallway to a bathroom where I could change, I was half tempted to ask if she was interested in baby-sitting. On second thought, I wasn't sure I wanted to get personal with these students.

I took off my clothes, slipped into the plaid woolen bathrobe I'd brought from home, and padded in my thongs back to the classroom. The students fell into silence as I entered. So here was the subject for the day. Where had she come from? What did she do when she wasn't naked in the classroom? As if to quell assumptions they might be formulating, I chatted with the teacher. "Let them know we're friends," I reasoned, "that I'm not a stray picked up along the Via Flaminia, where ladies of the night congregate beneath the bridge." I also made reference to my two children, as if childbirth would account for the anatomical differences between me and the girls on *Colpo Grosso*.

After a certain amount of paper shuffling, students settled into their chairs, anticipating the first pose. Despite a rather drafty classroom, I felt my face go hot and my skin flush as all eyes turned toward me.

There was no turning back now. *Sempre avanti*, I prodded myself. Always the first to jump off the dock, to reach the raft, to dive from the high board, I was known as a kid for my courage and foolhardiness. Slipping out of my bathrobe, however, was right up there with Glacier Lake in terms of chilling difficulty. But the longer one thinks, the harder it becomes. So, as nonchalantly as if I wore pajamas underneath, I shed my bathrobe, folded it on a chair, slipped out of my thongs, and got to work.

Never having modeled before, I cribbed my first pose from the Borghese Museum: beautiful Daphne, arms upraised, the moment before she becomes a laurel tree. The longer I held the pose the more ridiculous it seemed. What had I gotten myself into?

The poses progressed in quick succession: initially I held each for only a minute or two. I had to think fast. I borrowed extensively from the great nudes of Western art: a Sybil from the Sistine ceiling, an Ingres odalisque, Manet's picnicker on the grass. How handy to be married to an art historian. I thought it best to skip the wolf with six teats.

We moved to longer poses, five or ten minutes, then halfway through the session my friend called a break to discuss the students' efforts. I was disheartened to see my elegant poses rendered by the uncertain hand of undergraduates. With clumsy foreshortening and primitive proportions, some drawings were actually frightening. A pose I borrowed from Bernini had spawned a litter of bent elbows and stubby feet. Where was the sure line of Matisse, the sculptural shading of Renoir? And where, I wondered, was the cleavage? Had they no sense of imagination? In an odd way, I realized the students were exposing as much of their imperfections as I had of mine.

Back to work, I held the final pose for an hour, while the students drew in silence. They put the additional drawing time to good purpose. At the end of class, when they spread their work on the floor, I had a moment of *frisson* seeing my back rendered a dozen times over in a manner that actually seemed connected to that of the masters. It was clearly my back, my hips, even the mole on my shoulder blade. In that moment I experienced an uncanny sense of my own link to the great tradition of Western art. Sure, these were only undergraduates from Texas and I only a New England housewife, but, still, we were part of the process.

Artistic reveries aside, I didn't hesitate to pick up my pay when the day was done. My aching joints assured me that I had earned it. I nodded to Botticelli's *Venus* as I passed.

That afternoon I treated myself to a game of tennis on the fabulous red clay of Rome. I changed into tennis clothes, a wisp of a skirt cut twelve inches above the knee. It suddenly seemed modest. I stopped to pick up my opponent at his apartment. While waiting for him to change, I chatted with his wife, an art student. She was in the midst of sketching. My interest was piqued. She had just finished a minutely accurate rendering from a Raphael fresco and had turned to the at-home version of a life study class: an old *Playboy* spread of Brigitte Bardot at 40. My heart warmed, Brigitte Bardot looked great. So did the sketch.

Rome is a city that reveres beauty, both ancient and modern, and everything in between. And here, where every well wrought dome becomes a shrine, woman is indeed the measure of all things.

Libby Lubin lived in Italy for a year and travels there frequently when she is not writing.

⋆

I grew up with the conviction that Italians were decidedly more corpulent than Americans. At the sexy end of the spectrum were Loren and

Lollobrigida; in the middle was the Italian ur-mother of spaghetti ads, Mamma Mia; and at the far end loomed certain Fellini extras. The truth is, however, that after seven years of living in Italy I have seen very few overweight Italians. On the other hand, observing tour groups and looking around during my visits home to the States, I've seen ever more distinctly obese Americans, of all colors and creeds—including Italian-Americans, a fact that lays to rest any nature-versus-nurture questions.

—Andrea Lee, "Sit on It," *The New Yorker*

TIM PARKS

✦ ✦ ✦

Facciamo le Corna

*What happens if you stay, marry, and
have children with an Italian?*

CONTRARY TO POPULAR BELIEF, THE ITALIAN CHILD IS BORN NOT
into a splendid world of spontaneity, fun, and sensual delight, but
into a tight space of immense caution, inhibition, and a suffocating
awareness of everything, but everything, that can go wrong. Not to
mention how much it will all cost.

It was thus that I was persuaded, by solemn neighbors and employers, and of course my concerned father-in-law, that if I insisted
on having a second child (folly became madness when we arrived
at a third), the time had come for me to take the whole question
of insurance more seriously. My accountant agreed, remarking that
in terms of tax relief I would save only the equivalent of about
forty dollars a year by having another bundle of joy (there is no
Child Benefit in Italy). He pointed out the advantages of being
able to reduce my taxable income by the few million lire I would
pay into an insurance scheme, and he recommended, as Italians in
their eagerness to do favors always will, someone I could go to: an
agent, Ragionier Nascimbeni. Since *Nascimbeni* means "well born,"
I decided to take this as a good omen.

I telephoned Ragionier Nascimbeni. Generally, it is not easy to
make appointments in Italy, since it is important for the person of-

fering a service to appear to be extremely busy and hence successful. Any shortcomings in the service, in terms of slowness, will thus
seem to be a guarantee of its qualities. I have even had a courier
service in Verona tell me that they cannot come to pick up a package for forty-eight hours because they are so busy, and of course
they are so busy because they are so fast. It seems pointless arguing
with such logic. Nascimbeni, however, and to his immense credit,
must be one of the most amenable men in the world. He was extremely, yes, extremely busy, there was simply no point in my going
to his office, where he was "under an avalanche of work," but he
would come to our house immediately after he had finished for
the day. Yes, that very evening. Would nine-thirty be too late? I was
suitably impressed.

Ragionier Nascimbeni (*ragioniere* means accountant, or more
precisely, someone who has completed the kind of high school
that concentrates most of all on accountancy. It does not mean that
the person in question is a full-blooded accountant, since that
would entail a university degree, which would confer the more
enviable *Dottore*. *Ragioniere* is thus the least impressive of those titles—*Ingegnere*, *Avvocato*, *Architetto*, *Professore*, etc.—that Italians
like to place before their names to confer a little importance and
pomposity, in this case so little importance and so hollow a pomposity that one feels it might be wiser not to draw attention to the
fact at all).

Ragionier Nascimbeni arrives right on time. I buzz him in and
stand outside the door at the top of the marble stairs to guide him
to the right apartment. He comes up with an unusual clatter, a curious rolling gait. I watch with interest as he attacks the first flight,
disappears, then sways into view on the second. By the time I'm
face to face with him at the top of the fourth, I'm beginning to
appreciate why this man is genuinely so busy and successful in his
field: he is himself a walking advertisement for just how much can
go wrong in life, the perfect contradiction of the happy providence
suggested by his name. One look at Nascimbeni and you *know* you
need insurance. And perhaps he comes to your house, rather than
seeing you from behind his desk in town, just to remind you how

difficult it can be for a man to climb stairs, to cross a room, to find a comfortable chair....

I said "walking advertisement," but I should have said "lurching." Nascimbeni has the built-up show of the polio victim. He throws his limp leg forward, leaning on it only when it is rigidly straight, bringing round his good leg as rapidly as possible. The impression is of someone negotiating a ship's deck in a storm. His eyes behind thick glasses squint severely. Every few seconds he blows his nose, breathing hard.

"*Bella zona,*" he says automatically of the dusty street outside, "*bella palazzina, bell'appartamento. Molto bello.*" His voice is nasal, obstructed, adenoidal. We offer him the sofa, but he would prefer to sit at a table. His leg isn't comfortable on sofas. Not the right position. Then he must take notes, of course. Yes, the kitchen table is fine. "Many a family I go where the kitchen table is the only surface to write on," he laughs. No, he can't accept a coffee, his blood pressure is too high. Got to be careful. Had to have a bypass last year. Looking at him carefully, he doesn't look a day over forty. The baldness is premature.

"*Bene, allora?*" He has pulled out a notebook, a series of brochures, an impressive pocket calculator. He puts his hands together in a pantomime gesture of attentiveness. Every few seconds a tic obliges him to twist his neck to the right, together with a slight down-and-up rotation.

I explain that we are about to have our second child, and we thought...

"*Però!*" he exclaims, which is as much as to say, Who would have thought—what courage! "*Complimenti Signora,*" he adds to Rita, smiling generously and blowing his nose.

Then he begins to expound his various life insurance schemes. "The point is, hmm, with my still being so young, hmm that if," he hesitates, "if..." He hesitates again, he looks at me across the kitchen table, squinting, smiling, "Yes, if anything should, er, *happen* to you..." Immediately he says this, he lifts both hands from the table and makes two fists but with the forefinger and little fingers protruding and pointing upwards. "If anything should happen to you—*facciamo le corna*—it's likely to be an, er, accident—*facciamo le corna*—rather than, er, an illness. Isn't it?"

Facciamo le corna, literally translated "let's make the horns," refers to his gesture of the closed fists with pointing fingers at each side. For some reason, this is supposed to ward off evil luck. One might make it, for example, when seeing a hearse pass or contemplating the possibility of one's favorite soccer team losing a big match, or just at the mention, during dinner table conversations, of some normally unmentionable disease (pregnancy?). Ragionier Nascimbeni must combine expression and gesture, often simultaneous with the tic that twists his neck to one side, about a hundred times a day....

"Yes, I mean the most common cause of, er, yes, decease, among men of your age, is a road accident, *facciamo le corna.*"

And he does. The fingers point quite automatically but always eloquently from his two fists, accompanied by an apologetic smile. He is trying to explain to me, it seems, that it would be wise for me to take out a special kind of policy that would pay out very large amounts if *something happened to me*, above all in my car, and rather less, or at least in the early years, if I die a natural (that word again) death. But I am so mesmerized by his constant *corna* punching in the air across the table that I'm finding it hard to concentrate. Without thinking, I ask, "And do they pay out if it's the result of drinking?"

"What?"

"If I'm drinking and driving. Or, I don't know, if I didn't have my safety belt on and should have. Would they pay just the same?"

He looks at me with the concern of someone whose job is to be understanding but who finds this difficult when he hasn't understood. It's something to do with my being a foreigner perhaps. Then he gets it. He laughs. "For heaven's sake, nobody ever *checks* whether any body's been drinking and driving when there's an accident! *O Dio, no.*" Then he frowns. "Actually the insurance companies are presently taking the government to court precisely *because* they don't enforce the drunk driving law. But not so that they can avoid paying out. Oh, no no no, *per l'amore di Dio.* But because if the government did enforce the law, there would be fewer accidents, there would be fewer sad occasions on which they were obliged to pay out...."

"Ah."

"Now, where were we, yes, accidents. Hmm. Yes, so if, on the other hand," he picks up the thread, "if you should, er, be, er, be disabled in some way—*facciamo le corna,* then the…"

Smiling, Rita intervenes. He doesn't need to beat around the bush so much and keep making his *corna.* We know that insurance is about illness and death. We just want the appropriate coverage for the children. We're doing this for the children.

Ragionier Nascimbeni squints at her through thick glasses, then relaxes. He has a round, pleasant face, rounder still for that receding hairline. He seems relieved. There are many houses he goes to, he explains, where people actually get angry if he even uses the word death, because they think it can bring them bad luck. He blows his nose. It is almost the hardest part of his job, he says earnestly. Blowing his nose yet again,

---

*H*ere is another true story on the cultural effect of *facciamo le corna:* an Italian Professor was invited as a guest lecturer to the University of Texas which boasts the Texas Longhorns as its athletic team name. At the University, a friendly gesture of allegiance or greeting is the "longhorn" greeting: you hold your hand aloft with the middle and ring finger folded down, rearing the two "horns" of your pointer and little finger. This same gesture in Italy is one of the greatest insults a man can bestow on another man as it means *cornuto* or "cuckold." One only proffers this gesture in rage. As the Italian Professor appeared at the plane's exit door, a wild cheer met him, as well as over a hundred hands all jamming their "longhorns" at him. To the dismay of the welcoming students, he retreated back into the plane and refused to disembark.

◆

—AC

he apologizes that he suffers from allergies, against which, it seems, one cannot insure.

Much cheered by our non-superstitious attitude, he now proceeds more brutally. Yes, my most likely death would be in a car accident, though he can't imagine that I drink and drive, ha ha, hmm, anyway, no, in the event of such an accident, I, or rather, he laughs apologetically, no, my wife or children, would receive exactly, under this particular policy, four times the amount I would get by death from illness. Good. Well, if one accepts this kind of policy, there is no need for a medical. If one wants a larger amount for death by illness, then one has to accept a medical. He looks up sadly: "Not because we imagine you are trying to trick the company, already having an illness and not saying anything, but just in case, *facciamo le corna*, you have a condition without being aware of it."

Holding back my laughter, I ask him if he has children, and if so what provision he has made. I do this because an article in *Il Sole 24 Ore*, the financial paper, once suggested that the best way to deal with any investment or insurance agent is to ask them how they behave. They know all the best deals. Nascimbeni, however, shakes his head. He and his wife long ago decided that children were too risky a business. Too many things can happen. But having said this very solemnly, he suddenly becomes aware that it could be understood as foreseeing bad luck for ourselves. Rita comes to his rescue. "*Facciamo le corna,*" she says. Out spring her forefinger and little finger. I'm stifling laughter. And at exactly the same moment Michele begins to cry in the other room—furiously, a great bloodcurdling yell. Nascimbeni comes out with a nervous cough, as if to suggest that our irreverence might somehow be responsible. He blows his nose again, and, as my wife goes off to get the boy, begins to talk about a saving scheme for children. One of the major problems with children, and again he deprecates the fact that he always has to be imagining problems, is that when they get to eighteen or so, one has to pay for their university education, which could last what, five, six, even seven years, and then help them to set up home when they get married, buy an apartment, and so on. Well, by paying a fairly modest amount monthly into an entirely tax-free investment fund, one can be sure that come their eighteenth birthday...

"Nobody bought me an apartment," I remark. "We don't own this one."

"No, of course not, me neither." Nascimbeni twists his neck to one side and smiles. He looks about him, apparently appreciatively, at the window fittings, the quality of the tiles, the workmanship. "Perhaps you should buy it now. Or another apartment." He hesitates. "I mean home ownership is the only way really to insure yourself against, er, against the event of eviction, which with young children, of course, would be, er, disastrous. Anyway, if you did want to buy a house, I would certainly be willing to help you with the mortgage."

Rita walks through the room with Michele in her arms and takes him out through the French window onto the balcony. The cool evening air will calm him down. Outside on the street children are kicking a ball at each other, standing to one side every time a car races past. Not a situation, I imagine, that Nascimbeni would wish to contemplate. Except in business terms.

"And house insurance," the agent continues. "In fact, there's one very interesting policy that might be of use to you now, in the sense that it covers not only against damage to household belongings, but any damage your children might do to somebody else, or their property. Imagine, for example, that your little boy, when he's a bit older, were to push that basil plant off the balcony so it fell on somebody's head. They could then sue you for damages, something this policy would cover, and the wonderful thing about it is that the premium remains the same however many children you have, so..."

When he has gone, we roll about on the bed laughing and *facendo le corna* at all the possible things that could go wrong, a satellite falling on our apartment, the leaning Tower of Pisa collapsing precisely the day we go up, etc. Until it occurs to me that *fare le corna* can also mean to betray one's spouse (in the same way that, in Elizabethan English, horns were supposed to be visible, to the eye of faith, on a cuckold's forehead). *Facciamo le corna* could thus mean "let's betray your (or my) partner," and people here actually say: "Yes, so and so is away again, no doubt putting horns on her poor husband...." Though one could hardly accuse poor Nascimbeni of having meant this double entendre. On the other hand, it is an eventuality against which no meaningful insurance cover can be offered. As with almost all the serious things in life.

I remember some years later the shock of recognition when, upon warning young Michele that by the time we got to the *pasticceria* there might not be any chocolate croissants left, he raised his two chubby fists, shot out forefinger and pinkie, and earnestly declared, "*Facciamo le corna, Papà!*"

Tim Parks has won international acclaim for his work, including the Somerset Maugham, John Llewellyn Rhys, and Betty Trask awards. He is the author of several books including Italian Neighbors or, A Lapsed Anglo-Saxon in Verona; Goodness; Juggling the Stars; Family Planning; *and* Shear. *This story was excerpted from his book,* An Italian Education.

✳

The key to Italian family unity is the umbilical cord between the children, especially the son, and "mamma." This is never fully severed at birth and manifests itself in the most unlikely situations. While CNN was showing U.S. paratroopers heroically clambering ashore on the beach at Mogadishu to launch Operation Restore Hope in 1993, RAI showed Italian soldiers bidding farewell to their mothers at the airport. Mother and soldier were crying into each other's arms. Men bristling with automatic machine guns, bayonets, and pistols were screaming "Mamma!" No one was embarrassed.

The mamma even occupies a central role in Italian political science. The Christian Democratic Party was commonly referred to as the *Partito mamma*, the "mama Party." Most Italians, even sober-sounding newsreaders, do not talk about *la madre,* the mother, but *la mamma*: Mommy. Italian sociology has even invented an "ism" to describe the phenomenon: *mammismo*. The children, usually sons, who suffer from it are called *mammoni*. Since a whole generation of single children is currently coming of age, Italy with its very low birth rate is in danger of being swamped by selfish brats.
                    —Matt Frei, *Getting the Boot: Italy's Unfinished Revolution*

ANDREA LEE

* * *

Pornosaint of the Extinguished Lights

The life and death of Moana, a Diva of Porn,
reveals much about her countrymen.

MOST OF ITALY WAS IN MOURNING FOR WEEKS WHEN MOANA
Pozzi, the country's most famous porn star, died suddenly, of a liver
tumor, in mid-September [1994]. Ms. Pozzi, a phenomenally self-
possessed blonde, was 33 years old and for the last decade had been
a sort of erotic national monument. The announcement of her
death brought on an avalanche of testimonials in the press from
Italian artists, intellectuals, actors, and politicians, as well as from
thousands of fans who had devotedly packed theatres for her films
and live hard-core shows. "*Addio Moana, porno-diva intelligente*" was
a front-page headline in *La Stampa*. Inside, an entire page was dedicated to articles in which celebrities like the art critic and member of Parliament Vittorio Sgarbi, the actress and talk-show hostess
Cathérine Spaak, the film director Dino Risi, and the writer
Luciano De Crescenzo eulogized her beauty, wit, and high level of
culture (it is apparently true that her reading ranged from Edgar
Allan Poe to Marguerite Yourcenar) and the peculiar luminosity
she gave to a career about which there was nothing equivocal,
nothing sad, and nothing that did not seem the product of her own
free will. Not mentioned in the articles were the titles of her films,

which, like the star herself, lack any false modesty: *Moana—Deep Hole*, for instance.

Where but in Italy—where thousands of little sins of the flesh, duly confessed and pardoned, are woven into the fabric of daily life—would a hard-core actress have gained this kind of following? Daughter of a staunchly Catholic middle-class Genoese family (her father is a nuclear engineer) and product of an excellent education courtesy of the Ursuline sisters, Ms. Pozzi started out in a category much admired in Europe, a young woman from a good background—or, as Italians put it, *perbéne*. And at eighteen, with the forthrightness of a bourgeois girl dedicating herself to university studies, she set out to conquer the sex market. Tall and fair, in the Northern Italian manner, and with an amazing big body, whose rococo curves might in another context have been recorded by Titian or Veronese, she managed to exude a curious combination of carnality and respectability. Her dignified offstage deportment was such—she never used profanity or lost her temper with interviewers—that after her death a writer in the newsweekly *L'Espresso* described her as "the best-mannered of all Italians."

A few other Italian porn actresses—her colleague Cicciolina, for instance—were nearly as well known, but none were as well loved. Ms. Pozzi was interviewed on talk shows and featured in the news and women's magazines, and she performed in commercials for cars, cookies, chicken, and furniture. She was comfortably accessible, a household Lilith; at night, you could al-

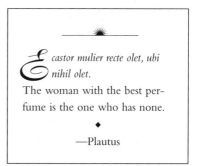

Ecastor mulier recte olet, ubi nihil olet.

The woman with the best perfume is the one who has none.

◆

—Plautus

most always catch a glimpse of her breasts and bottom by flipping through the channels, or, if not, you could call her recorded chat line. Fellini—student of the grotesque mythology of everyday Italian life—was a fan. Women, too, liked her. Young as she was, there was something reassuringly matronly about her, as there has been about all Italian female sex symbols. At the same time, she was smart enough to keep her work dirty. She declared that she had a natural taste for sin. Occasionally, she issued manifestos of turpitude that rang with Lawrencian grandiosity. "Pornography is the representation of our most intimate dreams, our most secret desires," she told a journalist. "Sex is also black, contorted, corrosive, it isn't always something sunny and joyous.... Obscenity is sublime."

Ms. Pozzi's death inspired in the Italian press an orgy of purple prose thick with Catholic imagery. "*Santa Moana Vergine*"—"St. Moana the Virgin"—was the title of a lead story in an issue of *L'Espresso* whose cover displayed a full-length photograph of the star wearing only red sequins and a halo. Inside, various journalists and *beaux esprits* earnestly discussed the de-facto canonization of the national bad girl. The intellectual columnist Roberto D'Agostino wrote, with deconstructionist prolixity, "The swift death of Moana has reversed the 'impure' dream of her into a 'chaste' need of her. Consequently, her image has been 're-virginized' in Catholic fashion, using the exact elements of the liturgy. And so we have the Pornosaint of the Extinguished Lights. And Holy Moana of the Sacred Taboo."

Rumors of a deathbed return to the faith, of the porno diva drawing her last breath clutching a pink rosary, led even the Church to pipe up. The Archbishop of Naples, in the all-important Mass in honor of San Gennaro, patron saint of the city, spoke feelingly of "that poor daughter" who demonstrated "how often faith dwells in the hearts of human beings like a spark under ashes." In the right-wing newspaper *Il Giornale*, the ultraconservative Catholic columnist Renato Farina wrote of Moana as a "little girl" who in her life made the mistake of "leaving the gate open."

In life and in death, Moana Pozzi touched a nerve of obsession for Italians in much the same way that on a far vaster scale the O.J. Simpson case has for Americans. In Italy, however, the collective dreams and nightmares simmering below the surface have to do with an age-old index of predictable theological conflict: Catholicism versus paganism; harlot goddesses versus the Virgin Mother of God; punishment versus forgiveness; the corruptible splendor of the body versus the immortal soul; the perplexing double nature of womankind.

Ms Pozzi's death at the height of her sinful splendor was a stroke of fate so clearly in tune with the traditional imagery that it sent shivers of emotion through the whole country. Meanwhile, the instructions she left for her demise break through the incense and the semiotics with a starkness that seems for an instant to reveal the real woman: no funeral, no photographs, no epitaph; a cremation, and her ashes to be scattered to the sea. There is something rather grand about this pitiless disposal of the body that brought her fame. It seems, at least, to negate the rumor of the pink rosary, and suggests instead a steely individualism that measured the real worth of fantasies, whether religious, romantic, or erotic; it reveals the person who once said she believed in God "*senza superstizione*"— without superstition—and who, whatever the priests may say, was never a victim. The single monument she set up herself has the mixture of kitsch and generosity that characterized her work: the continuation of her sex talk line, with the proceeds to be donated to cancer research. After that, with her usual good manners, she left the scene.

Andrea Lee is a staff writer with The New Yorker, *in which this piece originally appeared.*

✳

Most Italian men publicly touch their genitals at regular intervals, as though to check that they are still there. Carlo seemed to have been born with a premonition of loss, as one hand was permanently clamped on his trousers, checking and touching.

—Lisa St. Aubin de Terán, A Valley in Italy: The Many Seasons
of a Villa in Umbria

* ⋆ *

A Bank in Palermo

*Changing money is less a business transaction
and more an operatic scene.*

MY ELDERLY COUSIN, WITH WHOM I'VE BEEN STAYING IN Palermo, implied during lunch that if her helper Primo didn't escort me to the bank so that I could cash some traveler's checks...well, let's not even mention what might happen on the streets to a lone American female.

Primo and I trudge silently through loud traffic towards Il Banco di Santo Spirito. He gestures to a sliding glass door. We pass through three sets of them into a glass-walled antechamber. An armed guard on the other side demands that we hold up our ID cards to the window. When he buzzes us through he interrogates me: "What is the nature of your visit to the bank? How much in traveler's checks do you intend to exchange? How long do you plan to remain in Sicily? How long have you already been here? Do you like Palermo? Where did you learn to speak Italian? Were both of your parents Italian? Where are they now?"

He ushers us to an empty desk where we sit for ten minutes. No one shows up. The guard returns. "I don't know where he's gone. Give him a few minutes."

We wait twenty minutes more while various bank people stand

around smoking. Eventually the officer arrives, all smiles, shakes our hands and asks to examine my traveler's checks.

"Do I begin signing now?"

"No, you do that at the Cashier's window. But, *prego,* first you need to fill out these forms." Four pages of name, age, sex, local address, local phone number, passport number, intended length of stay and signature. Separate form for the amount I want exchanged—in triplicate. Primo sits placidly by.

Once the officer duly notates, stamps, and blesses this paperwork, he directs us to the Cashier's window. I join a clique of customers standing behind a red line painted on the floor. I receive overt, shameless, curious stares.

"How will I know when it's my turn?" I whisper to Primo seated on a bench a few paces away. "There's no order."

"Push. Don't let anyone get in your way."

That's one Mediterranean habit I can't adopt. Not that we even have a cashier to push for—the booth is empty. What gives with this crazy bank? And Primo willingly subjected himself to this ordeal, when he could be home tasting salsa, crushing oregano into it, or beating rugs instead.

"I think we should leave now. I could buy money at some exchange bureau. At least we won't lose the afternoon standing around."

"No!" He looks scandalized.

A uniformed man approaches, causing an excited buzz in the group. He stands ten feet away and throws a fistful of metal medallions at us. The men around me go crazy, lunging for the pieces clattering on the floor. I look to Primo. "What's going on?"

"Quick, quick, grab one," he cries, making a scooping motion. "Hurry."

I bend down to snatch up a tag that has rolled next to my shoe. It has "235" imprinted on it. The disk thrower retreats behind the Cashier's window.

"*Finalmente,*" I sigh to the man next to me.

"Don't be so sure," he retorts, "look at him."

I think it is important to be aware of how different cultures value or perceive their use of time. I was in the purchasing department of an American company; my job at that time was to buy computer parts from various companies. The parts would arrive and get boxed with other parts we had in house. It was pretty simple, I thought. You order a part, you specify the quantity and the date it is to arrive, it arrives and you are done with it. Well, I guess that is how it works in Japan, which seemed to always run like clockwork but...not in Italy. The parts from Italy kept coming in late and their quantity was never what was on my request form. So after a few shipments I called my counterparts in Rome and I asked is there a problem with your factory? They responded quite shocked: "A problem? What's the matter? So this week the shipment is late and maybe not enough. Next week it will come early and maybe we will give you a little more!"

◆

—Tracey Wilen,
"Italian Business Anecdotes"

The cashier has placed a Dagwood-sized hero sandwich on the counter before him. He removes his jacket, unfolds a white cloth napkin, tucks it under his chin, holds one end of the bursting *panino* to his mouth and starts to eat.

The crowd stirs angrily. "Hey, we've been waiting a long time now."

"Eat later, fool."

"Disgraceful. I'm in a rush, with my pregnant wife waiting inside the car at a red zone, and he has lunch."

"That does it. We're leaving," I announce. I'll pay more at some rip-off place. I don't intend to spend the whole afternoon waiting inside a bank.

Primo holds up his hands in prayer, imploring, "Pazienza." The cashier chews, swallows, selects a tag out of a pile next to his elbow and says into a microphone, "Seventy-three."

"But..." I turn to Primo.

After lucky seventy-three transacts his business, the cashier takes another big bite, picks another tag and calls out "Twelve." They're not even in numerical order? Too absurd. I walk over to my protector.

"*Andiamo,*" I bristle. "Let's go find something else. Honestly, I don't care if they charge me a big fee. It'd be worth it."

"You won't find one open now. They keep very irregular hours. Then you'll just have to come all the way downtown again later this afternoon. Stay." He holds up his palms again to placate me. "It's better." The soothing voice of Sicilian reason.

After a small geological eon passes, the cashier calls out "Two hundred thirty-five."

"That's me." I approach the window. The cashier speaks into a grill-like mouthpiece fixed into the glass partition, but I can barely hear him.

"It worked a minute ago," a voice behind me says.

"Do I sign now?" I push all the papers into the drawer. He reads them and says something.

"What?"

He reaches over to jiggle the microphone and broadcasts in a booming voice, "You would like two hundred and fifty American dollars exchanged, *signorina?*"

Oh that's just great. The exact amount I plan to walk out of the bank with has now become public information to the gathering of attentive men behind me. Primo teeters on the edge of the bench, his eyes bugging. "*Si,*" I mouth, keeping my head motionless.

After much studying, initialing and stapling of sheets, the cashier pushes his sandwich to the side. He orders me to sign over my traveler's checks. He counts out multi-colored fifty thousand lire notes, fanning them across the counter like a deck of cards. He switches to ten thousand and five thousand notes, tallying aloud in a singsong.

I glance behind me, and notice the gang counting with him, their lips moving. Primo, mortified, watches without blinking from the bench. The line painted on the floor means nothing—this has developed into a group endeavor.

The cashier stumbles over a bill, losing count. A voice behind me calls out, "No. That was two hundred eighty-five thousand..." The cashier wipes his mouth on the napkin still under his chin and begins again. This time everyone counts aloud. When the cashier has plunked down the last of the 500 lire pieces, the man at my back taps me on the shoulder reassuringly, "He got it right this time." The others nod. Primo springs to his feet. Everyone congratulates me as I push the money into the depths of my bag. Everyone knows I'm from Berkeley, California. Everyone knows I'm not married. I wave good-bye. They do the same. We've been through something important together. *Ciao, ciao, ciao.*

Natalie Galli is completing a non-fiction novel set in Sicily, an account of her search for France Viola, the first woman in the island's history to publicly refuse the tradition of forceable marriage. Her other work-in-progress, a children's book illustrated by her sister Crista Galli, is about a freewheeling cat in Southern Italy. Natalie lives in San Rafael, California.

★

I needed to get some cash, so I took advantage of the window of opportunity afforded between 3:45 and 4:15 p.m., the local concession to afternoon opening hours at my bank. As I approached the counter, however, I realized that there was something not quite right: the clerks were lounging just that much more than usual, their cigarettes dangling just that much more loosely from their lips. I made my request, handing over a check made out to myself, but the clerk smiled benignly and said, "I am sorry, miss, but we have run out of money."

I looked at him, uncomprehending, "You are kidding."

"Well, you see, the guy who comes to deliver our cash every day—you know, Giacomino, the one on the *motorino*—he didn't come today."

"What?"

"His moped delivery service is on strike today. Try to understand: we simply have no money today. Come back tomorrow, I think we'll be all right by then."

This, at the central branch of one of Italy's largest Rome banks.

—Claire Calcagno, "Rome, My City"

MARY TAYLOR SIMETI

✦ ✦ ✦

The Olive Harvest

An entire way of life is contained
in this small fruit.

THE MIRACLE OF WATER REPEATS ITSELF EACH AUTUMN. SICILY IS
green, intensely and springishly green all winter long, green in the
vineyards and the olive orchards where the grass grows wild, green
in the vegetable gardens where lettuce, spinach, chard, and cab-
bages will flourish throughout a the season, and green in my flower
beds, where the weeds, kept under control in the summer by sheet
composting and parsimonious watering, now leap into new vigor
and battle their way through a foot of mulch. Last summer's petu-
nias are still in bloom, and next spring's ranunculi and nasturtiums
are already sprouting their first leaves. This is heady stuff for my
northern blood, and my first steps when we arrive at Bosco each
Saturday are toward the garden, to see what has come up. Autumn
is a race: wait for the rains to soften up the earth for the plow, but
make haste before it is too late to sow the vegetables that will keep
us through the winter when the tomato vines, the peppers, and the
eggplants have given up.

As I work in my flower beds I can hear sounds of conversation
and laughter, punctuated by whacking noises, which drift down to
me from the olive grove. November is olive time, and the harvest
has begun. The harvesters spread nets out under the trees, pick

33

what they can reach from ladders, and beat the rest of the olives down by hitting the branches with canes. Even with the help of the nets it is backbreaking work; many of the olives were flung to the ground by the October storms, and the workers must gather them one by one as they crouch over the cold damp earth. Yet the olive harvest is one of the few occasions in the year when the women go out to work in the fields alongside the men; this unaccustomed company, in marked contrast to the normal routine of long and solitary hours behind plow or hoe, leavens the work, especially when the sunlight filters down through the branches and there is no wind to bite the groping fingers.

The olive harvest has a particular personal quality that the wine harvest has lost, now that most of the growers confer their grapes to the big cooperative wineries. Olive oil is the soul of Sicilian cooking; butter and other vegetable oils are a recent introduction, whereas olive oil has traditionally been used for everything: eaten raw on pasta, salads, and boiled vegetables; used to fry fish or sweet fritters and doughnuts; as a cure for squeaking hinges; or beaten up with lemon juice and rubbed into chapped hands.

I was startled and slightly revolted the first time I saw Tonino [the author's husband] rub olive oil onto his skin, for somehow I had never quite focused in on the fact that the oil with which all those classical Greek athletes massaged themselves was the same that I was accustomed to eating on my salad. And yet it would appear that in antiquity, olive oil was prized above all for cosmetic purposes: Psalm 104 speaks of "wine that maketh glad the heart of man, and oil to make his face shine, and bread which strengtheneth man's heart." The oil from the sacred olive groves of Athene was perfumed with volatile oils and awarded to the victors in the Panathenaic contests.

It was the Greek colonizers who brought cuttings of cultivated olives with them to graft onto the wild oleasters of Sicily, and the Sicilian today preserves the greatest respect for this mainstay of his household and goes to great effort and expense to insure his family their year's supply of good, unadulterated oil, preferably gown on trees he knows and processed in a trustworthy press.

Small farmers usually have a few trees, enough for family needs, while even the bigger producers in this area, which do not specialize in olive growing, still operate very much at a personal level and sell their excess production to friends and relatives. It is common for peasants who own no olive trees to sharecrop someone else's, thus buying their annual supply with a few days' work, a habit that persists even when they have become prosperous enough to have acquired their own land.

It is not enough to know which trees your olive oil comes from, unless you also know where and how it has been pressed. Most presses are fairly small family affairs, with

> The olive, in the western world, followed the progress of peace, of which it was considered as the symbol. Two centuries after the foundation of Rome, both Italy and Africa were strangers to that useful plant; it was naturalized in those countries; and at length carried into the heart of Spain and Gaul.
>
> ◆
>
> —Edward Gibbon, *The Decline and Fall of the Roman Empire.*

five or six men working the machinery, located in barns in the countryside or, more commonly nowadays, in warehouses on the edge of town. We have our own, a country press that was started by my husband's eldest brother, Stefano, shortly before his death, and has been kept going mostly through inertia and the good offices of a friend who is willing to run it for us: "This way I know what oil I'm getting."

The building is big and rambling, typical of the farmhouses around the Gulf of Castellammare, although "farmhouses" is a misleading term, since they are more like minor fortresses, a series of large one- or two-storied buildings with storage, stables, and workers' quarters on the ground floor, and the apartments of the *padrone* on the *piano nobile* above, with a balcony from which he could keep a watchful eye on the doings down below. In the course of time the buildings have reached out to embrace a courtyard from which a big gate with enormous iron doors heavy with irons and padlocks gives guarded access to the outside world. Both our house at Bosco and the house at Finocchio where the oil press is located follow this pattern. Finocchio, which is the bigger of the two, belonged to three brothers who divided it up among themselves, and the share that went to Tonino's grandfather and now belongs to his brother Turi includes the oil press on the ground floor and upstairs a tiny apartment, two rooms and an alcove for the bed, plus half the courtyard. The apartment, now completely abandoned, was never used except during the olive harvest: my in-laws would stay there in aid and comfort of Stefano while the press was running, and indeed my widowed mother-in-law gave up going out there for "the season" only when she turned eighty.

I had my unforgettable first view of Finocchio only a few days after I arrived in Sicily. The Dolci Center organized a symposium on irrigation in a town on the southern coast of the island, and it was there that I met Tonino. (Only years after we were married did I learn that his presence there was neither professional nor fortuitous: in a period in which Sicilian girls were still very strictly chaperoned, the foreign girls who came to the Center were hotly contended, and Tonino decided to get first crack, much to the chagrin of the Partinicotti, who lamented that Alcamo got more than its fair share.) Tonino had arranged with the friend who was giving us a ride home to be dropped off at Finocchio, where we arrived at dusk only to find the great gate locked and bolted. Stefano had gone to Alcamo and had locked his parents in for safekeeping, which surprised nobody but me. It was apparently unremarkable that one should have to scale the wall to get home. I learned later that there were bandits operating in that area then, the "gang of Highway 113," and for the first few years that I knew Tonino we never traveled the road between Partinico and Alcamo without first emptying our pockets and hiding our cash in my bra.

The olive is a capricious tree: for every year that it bears a heavy load it takes a couple of years off to rest. In the lean years the press opens for only a short time, operating on and off as the meager harvest dribbles in. But in the good years it will open for *I Morti* and keep going until Christmas, often working round the clock. Finocchio is alive and humming then, the courtyard choked with tractors, cars, and trucks, with brown gunnysacks of olives piled up in the bins along the wall, and with groups of men, peasant and landowner alike dressed in rubber boots and *coppola*, the flat golf cap that in various tweeds (and black for mourning) is the most common note in any

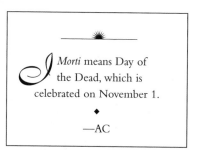

I Morti means Day of the Dead, which is celebrated on November 1.

—AC

southern Italian street. It would be unthinkable for anyone to leave his olives at the press and go home until it was time to come and pick up the oil. The journey from tree to oil jar must be accomplished under the *padrone's* eye to insure that no olives are exchanged or subtracted, nothing added. And so while the olive sacks stand in line, their owners gossip, play a hand of *scopa*, stretch their legs along the dirt road that leads to the highway, or catch a nap in their cars.

They are attentive when their turn comes, however, adjusting with the utmost precision the great brass weights on the scale where the olives are weighed and following the olives around the big barn as they pass from machine to machine. The sacks are emptied onto rollers that separate out the bitter-tasting twigs and leaves and carry the olives through a spray of water and into a mill that gives them a first coarse chopping. From there they pass into an enormous steel bowl in which two giant stone wheels, perhaps five feet in diameter and two feet thick, revolve in opposite directions as they rotate in a hypnotic and inexorable dance that grinds the olives, pits and all, to a smooth paste. This is squeezed out in a glistening pale brown ribbon onto woven wire disks, which are piled one upon another on wheeled dollies, interspaced with heavy steel disks, and rolled into the presses where they are slowly compressed so that the juice runs out, like maple syrup running down the sides of a stack of pancakes. The juice goes from the presses through the centrifuge and comes out in a thin stream of cloudy green oil, ready to be funneled into plastic jugs and loaded into the cars.

The steady grinding of the great wheels, the whirr of the presses, and the clanking of the steel disks drown out all but the loudest conversations. An invisible brush has painted every surface, each machine, each wall tile and bench with a thin patina of oil, and the workmen place their feet warily on the slippery floor. The very air is permeated with the smell of the new oil, which clings to one's clothes and vies with the perfume of the jasmine vine on the courtyard wall. Strong and harsh and ever so slightly bitter, but with all the flavor and the color of the olive intact, Sicilian olive oil is a far cry from the pale insipid stuff that is exported to the States, and a slice of freshly baked Sicilian bread, sprinkled with oil and salt and preferably still hot from an oven that has been fired with almond shells, would beat ambrosia any day. To eat it with the first oil of the new crop assumes the solemnity of a ritual. One November

---

*I*t is futile to pretend I am looking at something else. In fact, I am doing my best to gaze as deeply as I can into the crevice of a single olive blossom. There must be hundreds of thousands of these tiny flowers, falling all over themselves among the silver leaves of a single small tree. Too many for one tree to bear, they gather in heaps beneath the twisted branches, clusters so thick on the top of the low stone wall, all the breeze can do is blow them back and forth across each other, the way a larger wind can do no more with sand than allow it to build and dissolve and rebuild itself into dunes. I have a single olive flower in my palm. I mean I had one. Now the breeze has it, and I will never catch another. The whole mile of this mountain road high above tiny golden Gargnano gleams right now in a momentary noon of olive flowers, and I am the only darkness alive in the Alps.

◆

—James Wright,
The Shape of Light

my husband and I happened to drop by the house of a peasant who worked for us just as his wife was taking the week's supply of homemade bread out of the oven. She made us the present of a loaf; Tonino whipped off his sweater, wrapped it carefully around the bread, shoved me and the bread in the car, and made for Finocchio at breakneck speed to get to some new oil before the bread had cooled off.

It is satisfying to see that Francesco and Natalia, despite intimate acquaintance with potato chips, ice cream cones, and all the other enticements that their father's wartime childhood lacked, still have the greatest appreciation for these rituals. Francesco ends every meal, no matter how fancy or filling, with bread and oil, a sort of cork to insure that there are no air bubbles from which horrible hunger pangs might spring, and both children depend on bread and oil to get them from one meal to the next.

Mary Taylor Simeti was born and raised in New York City. In 1962 she went to Sicily, where she married and raised two children. She is also the author of Pomp and Sustenance: Twenty-five Centuries of Sicilian Food *and, with Maria Grammatico,* Bitter Almonds: Recollections and Recipes from a Sicilian Girlhood. *This piece was excerpted from her book,* On Persephone's Island.

✳

As a psychological case, Sicily is a sado-masochistic manic-depressive. Its own torturer and victim. Up and down, up and down. Sicilians feel exposed and claustrophobic simultaneously. Their exposure inclines them to machismo, i.e. overt power signalling, and their claustrophobia induces a rich vein of melancholy. Nothing moderate can survive here. They are alive to the immediate and they distrust the immediate. They are tough, put their backs into work as if their very soul depended on it. Then they drop it and do something else, distracted from their purpose by what someone else is doing—or thought to be doing. They cannot concentrate because they cannot abstract themselves. Life adheres round personalities, not ideas.

Sicilians love food, money, death and sex in that order. Their diet, though under pressure of debasement from international consumerism, is the most intelligent and nutritious in the world. They love to eat food in gangs. Money and death have been dealt with. Sex—by which I mean sex and sexual love, all the paraphernalia of physical congress. For Sicilians, chaste love is something to do with priests, Church, Virgin Mary, not anything to do with reality. For Sicilians, love is always erotic—is sexual love, even though the sexual expression may often be—usually is—thwarted. They like to make love and to talk love but to fall in love, oh dear, this is a problem for the men because to fall in love is to leak power. The enclosed self is strong, they believe. The revealed self is weak. Christians believe this too—that sexual love reduces one's ability to love God. In Sicily, God is the Self.

—Duncan Fallowell, *To Noto or London to Sicily in a Ford*

CLARA HEMPHILL

✦ ✦ ✦

Baby's a Bonus

Consider your child a goodwill passport.

ROME'S NO. 64 BUS IS FAMOUS FOR PICKPOCKETS AND BOTTOM-pinchers who torment unsuspecting tourists en route from the Vatican to the central train station. Well-heeled Romans avoid it at all costs. But when my husband and I squashed our way onto that overstuffed sardine can of a vehicle during our two-week Italian vacation last year, we were greeted like royalty. Or to be more precise, our five-month-old baby, strapped to Rob's chest in a cloth carrier and crying, was given the royal treatment.

"Oh, look! It's a baby! *Un bambino!*" a man shouted, fanning us with his hands to cool off little Max, as precious to him, it seemed, as to us. "Give them room! *Un po' di aria!* Please!" Our fellow passengers parted to make room for us, squashing even farther into the bowels of the bus to give us a little air. Max started to gurgle contentedly.

If you want first-class service in Italy, travel with a baby. People will bend over backwards to help you out and amuse your baby while you eat, sightsee or cope with trains and buses. Everywhere we went Max was treated like a new-found treasure, an unexpected bonus who immeasurably brightened the lives of strangers who had the good fortune to have him drool on them. At home in New

York, a baby in public is barely tolerated. In Italy, we discovered, a baby is a blessing to be welcomed, not a problem to be solved.

The year before Max was born, fearful that having a child would bring our globe-trotting to an end, Rob and I had arranged a triathlon of the least baby-friendly adventures we could imagine: camping in the Andes, paddling a canoe through the Amazon rain forest and sailing around the Galapagos Islands. We were sure we were about to be condemned to house arrest with only PBS wildlife documentaries and travel catalogs to satisfy our wanderlust.

It hadn't occurred to us that a baby might actually be a plus on a trip—that we might make more friends, get better service and see more (or at least different) sights with a child in tow than by ourselves. But so it went in Italy. Strangers routinely stopped us to strike up conversations. When Rob sat on a chunk of marble in the Circus Maximus in Rome to give Max a bottle, the two of them were surrounded by young women *oohing* and *ahhing*. Twice, in museums as we stared at paintings of the Madonna and Child, strangers actually called us *la Sacra Famiglia,* the Holy Family. And Max was clearly king of kings.

What a change from New York City, where a baby is considered a private indulgence. Have a baby if you insist, our society seems to say, but don't expect any help from the rest of us. What else can explain the meanness of the Frick Museum, where

---

*P*regnancy makes for an odd kind of calling card; there is, it seems, an international language of reproduction. We would have roamed the mammoth, two-story Florence produce market under any circumstances. But this time, the woman who sold the meaty, purple *dorone* cherries tucked an extra handful into our bag, for free—and then, having done her bit on the eating-for-two front, reached over, laughing, to pat the hidden beneficiary of her largesse.

◆

—Karen Stabiner, "The Last Waltz," *Travel & Leisure*

children under ten are summarily banned? Or the restaurants, chi-chi and not so chi-chi, that ban strollers?

In Italy, on the other hand, having a baby is considered a contribution to the commonweal, the nation's future and, as such, deserving of society's support. It comes not only in terms of government help—like paid maternity leave, subsidized day care and shortened workdays for nursing mothers—but also in the attitudes of shopkeepers, bus drivers, museum curators, anyone you're likely to run into.

"Has he eaten?" a busty, cheerful woman wearing a big apron asked, pointing at Max as we entered a neighborhood restaurant in a working-class section of Florence. She was clearly ready to leap to Max' defense if we dared deny him sustenance. I thought, "What about us?" But that was not, I sensed, an appropriate reply. So we accepted a mashed banana for Max and *ribollito*, a soup of beans, bread and spinach, for us. We were sorry, for his sake, that he was too small to appreciate more exotic cuisine.

Even at fancier restaurants we were welcomed with Max in tow. Late one evening at a small elegant restaurant in Pienza, an idyllic jewel of a Renaissance town in Tuscany, Max slept peacefully in his car seat while we ate. At lunch in a restaurant in the old Jewish ghetto in Rome, Max cried miserably as we took turns eating and rocking him. But the waiters were always tolerant, even indulgent.

Nobody blinked when I breast-fed Max, which was a good thing since he was hungry all the time. I tucked his little head discretely under the enormously baggy sweater I wore constantly. When we were stuck in traffic in taxis, I leaned over and nursed him strapped into his little car seat. I nursed him in the Sistine Chapel while I gazed up at the frescoes. I nursed him in front of Michelangelo's *David* in Florence. The only drawback: occasionally he'd get hungry in front of lesser works of art, and I'd be stuck looking at a one-star painting for a 30-minute feeding.

Our itinerary was somewhat determined by Max' unpredictable tastes. He didn't like Raphael, for some reason, so we moved quickly through the Raphael rooms at the Vatican rather than listen to him scream; Max loved Paolo Uccello's famous painting of a battle scene at the Uffizi, so we lingered. His favorite thing in Italy? The roar of motorbikes and garbage trucks. He would flap his hands in excitement as they went by. So we watched a lot of traffic. We drove a lot, too. Going from Pienza to Florence in a rented car, we stopped at medieval hill towns along the way, disturbing Max from his nap each time. By the time we got to Florence, we were all tired and cranky. Despite my brilliant navigating, we ended up in one gridlocked corner after another, circling but not quite reaching our hotel because of a maze of one-way streets.

After we swore at each other for an hour, Rob leapt out of the car and took Max with him to walk to the hotel. (There, Rob told me later, the bellman acted as if it was a pleasure to set up a crib for Max.) Meanwhile, I took the wheel. Desperate to ditch the car and unable to find a parking space, I finally took the car to the rental office and said I would pay any sum to be rid of it then and there rather than drive it back to Rome. For a price, the rental office took it off my hands.

We returned to Rome by train—a much more pleasant alternative. On the train a yuppie businessman took off his watch to let Max chew on it and made silly faces to amuse him as we dozed.

Clara Hemphill is a staff writer for Newsday *and the author of* Family Vacations.

★

Yep, I was pregnant. The worst of it was in Rome. Through the generosity of a friend, we were put up in a room on an empty floor of a hospital run by Little Sisters of the Poor. We had lots of privacy, including our own hospital beds. My husband had even more privacy, as he toured the sights alone. It was appropriate that we were in a hospital, as I needed to lay in bed most of the day. And it was so convenient to have a pregnancy test done "in house." We celebrated when a little white envelope was slipped under our door, with the result, *"positivo."*

—Angelique Syversen, quoted in *Gutsy Mamas: Travel Tips and Wisdom for Mothers on the Road* by Marybeth Bond

JONATHAN KEATES

✦ ✦ ✦

Five Ways of Escape

A train station is a microcosm of Italy.

MILAN, WHAT IS MORE, HAS A RAILWAY STATION. ACTUALLY IT IS not a railway station, but *the* railway station. There are other stations in Milan—sixteen to be precise, not to speak of an entire underground system—but Milano Centrale is The One, ultimate in the majesty of its affirmations, in its profligate splendour of revealed possibility, in its eternal defiance of all those curmudgeonly, mean-spirited, joyless, inhuman, godforsaken community-haters who tell us that train travel is dead and that our aspirations should soar no higher than the private car.

Milano Centrale sets at nought such banal individualism. Its monstrousness reduces human self-consequence to something quintessentially ephemeral. Its scale is so huge, the terms on which it engages with our experience so apparently limitless, that it does not especially care whether we get to the end of our ticket queues, whether (a frequent dilemma, this, in Italy) we have the correct sprinkling of small coins to please the philosophically glum clerks at the windows, or whether we shall catch the train with whose existence the capricious indicator board at the entrance to the platforms persists in teasing us.

For sheer moral education there are few places like it on earth.

It forces an existential crisis on the traveller by the tricks it plays with the rhetoric of architecture. The spaces within its great sequence of booking halls are anarchic in their immensity; whole villages might be crammed into them without squalor or discomfort. Stairs and escalators hurl you up into the realm of an unknown actuality, but even these seem emblematic, ghastly metaphors of ill-judged optimism. For halfway up is a little set of marble terraces, on whose stone benches sit or lie those who, for whatever reason, have abandoned the delusive ascent. The poorest of poor students, with grubby feet and matted hair, their lean bodies burned black, their eyes as visionary with hunger and thirst as those of desert hermits, sprawl beside Calabrian families picnicking off peppery sausage and coarse bread washed down with swigs of wine dark as cuttlefish ink. Pink-shouldered northern girls from a country where the sun is a cheese tied up in a muslin bag scribble their postcards next to snoring nondescripts wrapped in clothes whose true shapes and colours vanished aeons ago. These are the sirens and lotus-eaters and Circean beasts of Milano Centrale, wheedling you to turn back, not to bother with the hopeless business of going on.

They are right, or course, for at the head of the stairs, in the vast grey gallery, with its coffered ceiling and mosaic floor, a man might comfortably pass the remainder of his life. There's a kind of malaise bred in railway stations—and, I grudgingly concede, at airports—which makes you terrified of leaving them for fear of the complexities lying in ambush beyond. Thus, I am convinced, there must be a kind of alternative parasitic community living in Milan station which manages to avoid every attempt by the authorities to dislodge it, perhaps not unlike those peasant families whom Tsar Alexander II discovered existing, complete with their cows, in the attics of the Winter Palace in Saint Petersburg.

Why should anybody want to get out? There are two cafés, five bookstalls, a shop selling designer clothes, a bank and a chemist's and an exceedingly smart lavatory. There are a chapel and waxwork museum and one of those admirable Italian institutions known as *albergo diurno,* in which the traveller, on payment of a modest fee, may take a shower, have a bath, lie down for an hour or two, get his shoes shined and his hair cut and generally be made presentable to the world. And there is the cavernously dismal cafeteria, almost always empty except for an unshaven Sicilian, a bag lady in animated conversation with herself, and me, which serves the very worst food in Italy.

Buildings like this induce a kind of insanity. It was erected under fascism, a fact which no sensitive observer can ignore, even without the lectors' axes and gung-ho cracker-mottoes of Mussolinian wisdom which adorned it in the bad old times. Inherent in all political ideologies is a lethal element of fatuity which has much to do with the absence, in most politicians, of any redeeming sense of the ridiculous. Among the many reasons why Italians have not yet managed to come to terms with the experience of fascism must surely be a simple embarrassment of the barking absurdity of it all; considered in this light, Milano Centrale, as an essay in crushing, get-this, look-at-me triumphalism, is devastatingly silly. Its mock-Roman bas-reliefs (including a *Rape of the Sabines* which expresses everything meant by the Italian word *convincente*—rather more than just "convincing"), its cliffs of marble and granite and basalt, its great mottled plains of tessellated paving, have the imbecile musclebound grotesqueness of some steroid-popping Mister Universe.

It is this sense of exaggerated contour, of unsustainable weights and unbridgeable gulfs, which must in the end impel the traveller towards escape. The intrinsic romance of the place lies in the drama of release in which it encourages one to take part. To anybody with the merest jot of an associative faculty, the names on the yellow *Partenze* lists are instant spurs to a restless imagination. Suddenly you are Byron's Childe Harold or his musical alter ego Berlioz's Harold in Italy, or you are the wandering Goethe of Tischbein's splendid portrait—"I slipped out of Carlsbad at three in the morning"—or the President de Brosses or Augustus J.C. Hare or Corot or Claude or anybody else who has imbued themselves memorably in the experience of Italy, and here at once for the taking are the great reverberative toponyms: Venice, Florence,

Padua, Vicenza, Genoa, Turin, Rome, Naples, even the promise of distant Sicily.

The anticipation gets still headier once you buy the floppy red-and-green *Orario Generale,* the seasonal Bradshaw of Italy, its cover patchworked with squares of advertising: *"Hotel Cristallo, Udine, tutti i conforts, a 150 metri dalla Stazione Ferroviaria," "Hotel Mediterraneo, Brindisi, 69 camere tutte con bagno e aria condizionata," "Pescara è bella con la sua provincia, Mare, Monti, Arte, Terme."* Pescara isn't actually a very interesting town, though Gabriele D'Annunzio was born there, but the *Orario Generale* has the sort of talismanic potency that makes you prepared to accept such bland assertions at their face value.

I am, for whatever reason, addicted to directories. Almanacs, gazetteers and catalogues induce a strange ecstasy, and their parades of impacted fact, so far from deadening the imagination, open up rainbow clouds of fantasy. Thus it is with the *Orario Generale.* Its introductory rubric of little hieroglyphs—a pair of hammers for trains running only on workdays, a Maltese cross for Sunday services, a bed with pillows for wagons-lits, a bed without pillows for couchettes and so on—and its skeleton maps of the entire Italian railway system are clues to a perpetual romance of movement, chance and destiny.

The very sound of these places, cheek by jowl in the timetable, is enough to drive you mad. From sober-sided Alessandria on its marshy plain beside the Tanaro in eastern Piedmont, you'll take, maybe, the little second-class-only *locale* to Cavallermaggiore, stopping at Cantalupo, Carentino, Castelnuovo Belbo, Incisa Scapaccino, Calamandrana, Castagnole Lanze and Pocapaglia. From Aulla, at the head of the Garfagnana on the northern frontiers of Tuscany, you will come down among the swift-flowing streams and steep-hung chestnut forests towards Lucca and Pisa via Pallerone, Serricciolo, Villetta San Romano, Pontescosi, Fosciandora, Ghivizzano and Calavorno. And between Bologna and the Adriatic coast, even though you're panting to get to Ancona, you will not greatly mind halting at Mirandola, Forlimpopoli, Gambettola, Montemarciano and Palombina.

It doesn't honestly matter that any of these may be the dumps and armpits of the world, that, even as your fancy toys with their names, Calamandrana, Fosciandora and Forlimpopoli may be the dire provincial instruments of torture and suppression which frustrate or destroy potential genius. "I might have been a fine poet if I hadn't spent all my life in Pallerone," "I wanted to go to university but I stayed in Pocapaglia," "There just weren't any nuclear physicists in Gambettola." Gray's "Elegy" says it all for such places, but their sound is only the more romantic for that.

At its most practical and gritty and of-the-earth-earthy, the *Orario Generale* is an act of faith. It proclaims a belief in the railway not simply as a rapid and convenient mode of getting from one point to another but as the ultimate means of unifying a traditional fissiparous nation. When trains first arrived in Italy (the earliest ran from Naples southwards to the port of Grantatello on the coastal flank of Vesuvius: the line was opened in 1839), they were viewed by certain of the more reactionary rulers as harbingers of revolution. So dire did they seem to Pope Gregory XVI, an ex-monk to whom the least hint of technological progress was anathema, that he forbade the construction of a rail network anywhere in the Papal States. Travellers from the Grand Duchy of Tuscany or the Austrian provinces of Venetia and Lombardy got accustomed to the symbolically retrograde step of bundling into horse-drawn diligences as soon as they crossed the frontier.

So the train, for better or worse, contributed its share to the Risorgimento, and continues to insist on bringing Italians, however reluctantly, together. Railway journeys in Italy are not, as with us in England, a penitential experience designed to make us all travel nose-to-tail in automobiles along endless motorways. Italians love their cars—nobody in Italy walks anywhere if they can possibly avoid doing so—but they will take the train almost as readily, since it is generously subsidized, clean, fast, cheap and, for the most part, punctual.

Yet there is another, deeper, more aboriginally instinctive reason why trains and station platforms in Italy are always crowded. It is because of the Italian horror of solitude, the absolute negation, implicit in the forms and constructs of Italian social life, of the principle of living to oneself. Hardly anyone in this country is without somebody else with whom to share their existence. The unmarried do not, as in northern Europe or America, move away from their families at the earliest opportunity, but remain tied to them in perpetuity, suffering the crotchets and caprices of domineering parents from whose surveillance death alone releases them, as nurses, servants and unpaid companions. The tyranny of family life in small apartments proscribes individualism, annihilates outline and perspective. Without secrets, without worlds apart, without moments of determined solitariness, the grain and colour of personality are rubbed away. Maybe this explains the essentially flavourless and superficial nature of so much Italian conversation.

Much will compensate, however, for such a willing forfeiture of liberty. There is always somebody to talk to, there is a small domestic universe whose incidental problems and vicissitudes are sufficient to beguile your curiosity or engage your sympathy, and above all there is Mamma in the kitchen. Given any number of factors now instigating an insidious but perceptible change in the quality of modern Italian life, it is debatable how long it will be before Mamma and her culinary works are swept clean away, but for the time being she and her cooking are among the most notable determinants of Italian existence. Is it any accident that of the three most significant objects of furniture in the Italian household, the television (perpetually on but rarely attended to), the *letto matrimoniale* or double bed, and the dining table, the last should be the most important? By the way, it is nearly always round or oval, since mealtime chat among Italians must be general rather than one-to-one.

This inbred gregariousness extends into the wider reaches of society. It is by now something of a cliché, those classic *punti d'incontro,* meeting places where hank upon hank of talk is painstakingly unwound. If you sit and watch Italians carefully by the hour, you will notice how seldom they are voluntarily alone. Every Italian boy, for example, has his best mate, his mucker, his chum, with whom he goes about. The warmth and closeness between them is unembarrassed, they touch, embrace and walk arm-in-arm without that pathological awkwardness which compromises such relationships in England. In middle age they will simply turn into the paunchy, dewlapped, prosperous-looking men you see ambling in pairs, very, very slowly, along Italian streets, "developing" a conversation with the aid of a remarkable lexicon of emphatic gesture. No meaningful segment of their lives will ever be conducted in solitude.

Railway stations encourage this communal feeling. At any decent-sized staging post along the lines criss-crossing the peninsula, you will find people simply mooching about in the station. They may include the usual complement of hustlers, whores and pushers, there will be the odd vagrant or harmless lunatic, and nowadays their number is likely to be leavened by the despised and freely maligned *Gastarbeiter* population of Senegalese, Tunisians and others, known with slighting jocosity as *"Vu cumprà"* from a southern dialect expression meaning "Do you want to buy?" But there will also be those for whom a drink or a sandwich or a paper or a chinwag or just half an hour spent lounging on a bench to take the weight off provides an excuse for sharing the easy camaraderie of the buffet and the booking hall.

It is on the train, however, that this instinctive sociability and companionableness most obviously take over. The English notion of hiding behind a newspaper in the ghastly apprehension that somebody might actually engage you in conversation is shot to pieces as soon as you clamber into the carriage. You have reclaimed your cases from the plug-ugly blue-overalled bruisers in the Left Luggage, and you have providently invested in a *cestino di viaggio*, the little lunch bag sold from the platform refreshment trolleys, with its foil-wrapped wing of chicken, its packet of crackers and cheese, its rather elderly roll and cardboard-textured apple, which is one of the great institutions of Italian rail travel. Two willowy German girls with plaits and sleeveless vests have asked your help in heaving up after them a pair of gigantic rucksacks like Christian's burden in *The Pilgrim's Progress*, and a nun has enlisted your aid in perching her plastic grip on the luggage rack.

Perhaps you are honestly not disposed to talk, perhaps your interest in the *Politica interna* pages of *La Repubblica* is genuine. But you should never count on being left alone.

You will certainly not be ignored merely because you are foreign. Recent years have somewhat reduced the rampant xenophilia which used to characterize Italians, but the impulse towards courteous interrogation of the stranger (provided he or she is not an African) is still strong. From the initial questions about your destination and why you speak such good Italian (I always fall for that one), it is a short step to a series of variants on standard themes. The British royal family is a favourite topic, especially with readers of gossipy pictorial magazines like *Gente* and *Oggi*.

> *I*taly is well deserving the character it has acquired of being the Garden of Europe - and of being likewise the abode of poverty, villainy - filth and extortion. A Traveller pays dearly for the intellectual pleasures it furnishes, by suffering from bad accommodations in dirty inns - from the impositions of innkeepers servants & c - from wretched carriages, roguish drivers, corrupt custom house officers in short a combination of rogues of every class.
>
> ◆
>
> —Washington Irving, "Nineteenth Century," *Journal*, 22 April 1805

Best loved of all by the compartment conversationalist is the nature of Italy as seen through a stranger's eyes. There are times when it would be nice simply to say "*molto bella*" and leave it at that, but the shrewder of your interlocutors won't let go so easily. At first it always looks as if the Italians possess a rare genius for self-criticism, unlike, say, the insufferably bumptious French or the smug, sanctimonious Germans. The plausible introductory litany of national denigration—"we're really a disgraceful people," "part of the Third World," "lacking in order and discipline," "absolutely childish"— should deceive nobody however. Underneath all these disclaimers, the Italians like being Italian, relishing the apparently uncomplicated cosiness and tranquil prosperity of their lives, and feeling entirely at home with the most openly corrupt and ineffectual governmental system among those of the seven major economic powers. They envy the Germans because they are more "serious" (*serio* is an adjective of almost magical ambiguity, variously meaning "earnest" or "boring"), the French because they are cultivated, and the Americans for their cultural imperialism. They utterly detest the Swiss because, as they will delphically inform you, "they're Swiss." As for the English, they are liked for all the wrong reasons by the crypto-fascists who read *Il Giornale* and the stuffy, *bien-pensant* conservatives who take *La Stampa*, and for all the right ones by that tiny group of literate, cosmopolitan intellectuals who embody rational opinion in the Italian media.

This and much more you will be told on the train and, should it be one of the old-style compartment carriages, others will be tempted to put in their respective oars. These free-for-alls are often so enjoyable that after a while the last thing you want to do is to sink back into a corner with a book. Now and then, however, you may find yourself marooned next to the kind of garrulous autocrat who inspires a hankering for the spiritual comforts of La Trappe. I retain a nightmarish recollection of a journey on a jam-packed train from Florence to Rome (a good three hours by the ordinary express) which was tyrannized over by an old woman with a silent daughter in tow. From Figline to Arezzo, from Terontola to Orvieto, Orte and beyond, she maintained an unbroken flow of chatter so relentless in its vacuousness that the rest of us began perceptibly to falter under its deadening impact. We could not pretend to sleep or look out of the window, though it probably would not have mattered to her had we done so, since her remarks were hardly calculated to elicit any kind of worthwhile coherent response. Now and then one of us would throw a hopeless glance towards the corridor, only to see it pressed tight with schoolkids and soldiers, so that even the ticket inspector with his loud "*Permesso-o-o*" had difficulty in clearing a passage.

On went the dreary recital, engulfing the compartment like the noxious, petrifying mud of Herculaneum. We heard about her recipe for apple tart, the knitting pattern she had started out of *Mani di Fata*, the friend of hers from Prato who was having problems over naming a dog and the *bonbonniére* she had been given at a smart christening at Calenzano. The heartrending loveliness of Umbria and northern Latium, which makes this one of the most visually stimulating of all Italian train rides, flashed past us with a tantalizing irrelevance, and the silent daughter sat smirking enigmatically, as though she knew a thing or two but was damned if she was going to tell. When at last the express pulled into Roma Termini and we jerked ourselves out of this ignoble paralysis to get our cases off the racks, the old woman crowned her despotic triumph with a wondrous piece of insolence: "Well," said she, beaming at us all, "it's been really interesting listening to you. Other people lead such fascinating lives, don't they?"

What most struck me about this episode, in retrospect, was the extraordinary good manners of everyone concerned. There is rudeness in Italy as anywhere else—Florentine bank clerks, Venetian waiters, nearly all Romans are past masters of it—but the Italians are still the most naturally civil and gentle people on earth. The rhetoric of courtesy is everywhere, in the decorous appeals and injunctions of public notices, in the verb forms and vocabulary of those with whom you deal in shops and offices, a ghostly yet still vivid flourish from the age of Castiglione and Della Casa, when Italy taught politeness to the world.

Such glimpses of Italians being themselves are part of the pleasure of riding the railways, denied to the Cipriani-Harry's Bar-Excelsior-champagne cocktail-private beach tourist, whose sense of real life (which he or she may not want in any case) won't extend far beyond porters, maids and receptionists. From the train, whether it is the souped-up, air-conditioned "Eurocity" flier, or the trundling rustic *trenino* with slatted wooden benches for seats, you learn to read and interpret a country and its people.

You understand immediately the significance of personal cleanliness in Italy. Those yards upon yards of laundry festooning the streets in small villages and the suburbs of great cities are there not as gala decoration or in order to lend a "characteristic," "suggestive" appearance to some photogenic backdrop, but as evidence of the paramount importance of washing in the culture of the nation. Whoever saw a blouse, a teeshirt, a skirt or a pair of trousers on an Italian that was not ironed and pressed to a flawless miracle? Their hair is perfectly cut and brushed and shampooed, their teeth are white and strong, their skins are unblemished, even a pair of spectacles somehow renders them good-looking rather than drawing attention to myopia.

Above all they don't smell, unless it be of detergent, deodorant or scent. They have not yet reached that dubious stage of evolution at which bathing and daily changes of clothes are deemed too bourgeois to be taken seriously. Recall, in contrast, the feculent reek of a crowded English train, with its rancid compound of dried urine, old sweat, beer, tobacco, halitosis and the stale malodorousness of clothes worn many times

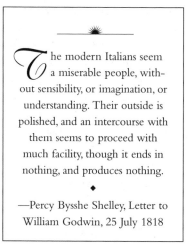

The modern Italians seem a miserable people, without sensibility, or imagination, or understanding. Their outside is polished, and an intercourse with them seems to proceed with much facility, though it ends in nothing, and produces nothing.

◆

—Percy Bysshe Shelley, Letter to William Godwin, 25 July 1818

too often. Brits at large in Italy shame their native country in many ways—by their surly, boozy pugnacity, by their stingy nitpicking over bills and prices, by their arrogant assumption that they ought not to be expected to know a word of Italian—but in nothing so much as by their shambling, tawdry, dingy, unwashed, unbrushed, reachmedown scruffiness.

For by these tokens you are judged in Italy. The grease-spot on your shirt, the smear on your collar, the crumpled look of your coat, even a hole in the sole of your shoe, counts far more gravely against you than the most obvious flaws in your moral and spiritual constitution. This truth was brought home to me once in Padua, where I effected what I thought would be the ideal introduction of two friends to each other. One was an eminent English writer, versatile, cosmopolitan, intellectually gifted and notable for the self-advertising sloppiness of his clothes. The other was a charmingly absentminded, ferociously brilliant Italian professor of comparative literature. We sat at a marble-topped table in the Caffé Pedrocchi, one of the monumental cafés of Italy like the Greco at Rome or Florian's at Venice, lined with empire mirrors and velvet banquettes on which plots political and operatic had been devised during the heady days of the Risorgimento, and drank delicious grogs while the mist gathered in the streets of that peculiarly somber city.

The pair seemed to get on famously. Perhaps discoursing, however rustily, in a language not his own made the Englishman forget to adopt that habitual just-an-ornery bloke pose of the average British literary man, while the Italian let go altogether of the awestruck pomposity with which distinguished cultural figures are usually engaged in Italy, and the two of them rattled along together as my heart could have wished.

Later I asked each of them independently what impression they had gained of one another. "He's nice, isn't he?" said the writer. "Not at all the kind of person who judges by appearances." It was just as well that I did not repeat this assessment to my Italian friend, whose response I ought in any case to have predicted. He was, as it turned out, quite beside himself with irritation, and, as was his custom when agitated, he insisted on addressing me in English. "Your friend, who you say is a famous writer?" he cried. "Listen, I ask you this question. How can a famous writer walk in the street with no strings to his shoes? But how can he do that? No strings! *Porca miseria!*"

What happens in a country where people get indignant about a writer's shoe-laces is that you begin to worry about such things to a degree you never supposed possible. What also happens is that you start to notice how much is lost by worrying about shoe-laces. In this respect one of the crucially instructive moments in an Italian train journey is the point when the train slows down and enters a station. As the crowd on the platform surges towards the carriages, you are ideally placed to see a lump of compressed Italy in all its unadorned normality, and the sight will tell you a thing or two.

Many of them are beautiful, heart-stoppingly, mouth-wateringly jealous-makingly stunning, with their sun-straightened limbs, long eyelashes, thickly-clustered hair and insouciant grace of posture. Their clothes fit their bodies, and the colours have been selected and matched with that visual awareness which is a birthright with them all. They have looked carefully in a thousand mirrors to ensure a perfect harmony between themselves and the things they wear. They have not had to think about this. And their shoe-laces are impeccably tied.

Yet in essence how boring, how utterly lifeless is this perfection, how lacking in the merest spark of singularity! Look into their soft, coffee-brown eyes or at their generously-curved mouths, and find not a hint of restlessness, animation, violence, bitterness, ecstasy, poetry or desire. They are people about whom nobody could ever write a novel, for the simple reason that their outwardness proclaims no in-

*I*t is impossible for anyone to be as fastidiously dressed as a Milanese matron with the means to regard convention (shoving toward the *prosciutto crudo*, never a hair out of place). It is possible to tell how old the average Milanese woman is from her back: by the time she is of a certain age, she is doomed to silk foulard and pearls forever; you cannot have your hair dyed aubergine unless you are under thirty—no respectable hairdresser would abet you in this folly. When you shop, the impeccability of Milanese ladies makes you feel—until you've learned the lessons, the measurements, the anomalies, the protocol—like a gawky American behemoth steering through an unmarked obstacle course. You can also— and sometimes simultaneously— feel invisible, as failure to observe protocol leads to your being completely disregarded.

◆

—Barbara Grizzuti Harrison,
Italian Days

wardness. There is no difference between them, only an abiding fear of distinction.

Extravagant generalizations of this sort nurture the odd grain of truth. What the sight of such platform crowds most potently discloses is the extraordinary power of convention in Italy, the thoroughgoing, unshakeable conservatism of a people whose favourite delusion is that they are not bound by tradition. Every age, every caste here has its uniform. The smart elderly woman going to the opera in January and February will always wear a fur. The businessman or senior professional employee will don, in early summer, a blue shirt. No young girl is without her fall of Botticelli curls, no boy without his ice-blue jeans and thick-soled docksiders. When the mode alters, everyone moves in step. None of them will ever dress for themselves, indulge a freak or a quirk or a caprice of personality, "do a number" "make a statement." There is bags of fashion, barely a hint of style. So far from being disgusted at the notion of belonging to a crowd, they are frightened in case it should not include them. Protective mimicry ensures survival.

Such are the cohesiveness and universality of Italian railway life that it might be possible to construct a sociology for the nation on the basis of a perpetual train journey. Since all rationalizations are inherently bogus, your ride along the tracks will perhaps guarantee you no more than a specious wisdom and a false security. Outside the station, across the peripheric boulevards, beyond the municipal flowerbeds, the taxi rank and the bus terminus, lies a world immediate, grown-up, resistant to simple answers, from which, once entered, you may never return.

Jonathan Keates is the author of two novels and reviews regularly for The Observer, The Independent, *and* The Times Literary Supplement. *His novel,* Allegro Postillions, *won the James Tait Black and Hawthornden Prizes. He has been working on a book about the life of Stendhal and a new collection of short stories.*

★

If anyone who had known Lombardy centuries ago could see it today, nothing would surprise him more than the absence of boats and sails.

Until modern times the towns and cities of the Po Valley were connected by an intricate system of waterways which transformed the large towns into inland ports. Shakespeare was aware that in his time one could go by ship from Milan to the Adriatic, and from Verona by canal barge and river boat to Milan. Throughout the Middle Ages the cargoes of Venice were delivered on the quaysides of Milan, Verona, Mantua, and Ferrara, and barges unloaded stone for the building of Milan's cathedral on the site in the centre of the city. There was even a time when Milan ranked as a naval power and maintained a fleet of warships that challenged the galleys of Venice.

The river and canal traffic gave a distinctive flavour to life in Lombardy. The inns were full of boatmen who possessed the inherited knowledge of those who for centuries had humoured a dangerous river. Many early travel writers describe the silence and ease of gliding through Lombardy by barge and boat. The regularity and safety with which cargoes could be delivered had an effect upon the civilization of the Renaissance: there were no oceans to cross, no pirates to fear, no mountain passes, no bandits or highwaymen; and the city states of the Po Valley were the first to receive the spices, the embroideries, and the Greek manuscripts from the East.

Scarcely a trace of this system of communications exists today.

—H.V. Morton, *A Traveller in Italy*

* * *

Venice Again

La Serenissima mirrors the labyrinth
of the human heart.

VENICE SEDUCED ME BEFORE THE WATER TAXI CROSSED THE lagoon from Aeroporto Marco Polo. Dazzled by the light, the water, the famous silhouettes assuming their fantastic shapes through the early morning mist, I surrendered to the city at first sight.

On my honeymoon, I wondered if this meant I was unfaithful.

Questions of fidelity seemed unimportant once we reached the small landing dock of the Hotel Monaco e Grand Canal. The youngest porter had stolen his face from a coin. The concierge's deep eyes had winked at years of assignations. I wondered what the wind had done to my hair and smiled at my husband.

We walked through the cool dark of the lobby and upstairs to the room we'd booked months in advance. When the requested room with a view mysteriously lacked said promised view, the hotel manager smoothly floated us down several corridors and into the luxurious excess of a small suite overlooking the Grand Canal. Patterned silk covered the walls. Brocade lined the drawers in the dressers and secretary. Each ornate piece of furniture embraced inset over overlay. The almost garish chandelier clamored we might want to reconsider a visit to the island of Murano.

Both the sitting room and bedroom had two tall windows, with sheer fabric ballooning off the elaborate curtain rods. The view through these windows erased all the lavish textures and colors of the rooms.

For the first time in my life, I saw more than I had dreamed of. Books, movies, paintings, hours of fantasizing—nothing had prepared me. Dark *gondole* were moored right below our windows. Five thousand shades of color, blues and greens whose names I didn't know, rippled across the canal. The gentle curves of the Salute on the canal's far side turned every twentieth century building into a Lego construction. Even the garbage barges looked glamorous.

The bedroom had two *matrimoniales*, double beds with seductively painted headboards and lush linens. At first reluctant to abandon the view from the windows, I learned the pleasures of watching reflected light cavort on a ceiling. The best cities embrace their visitors.

The hundreds of bewildered tourists clogging San Marco our first evening in Venice ridiculed my hopes that a late October visit might avoid the crowds.

Proust didn't complain about the crowds in Venice. Then again, whoever swarmed his path probably didn't wear plastic gondolier hats or garishly printed t-shirts. It's also difficult to imagine Henry James stopping in the middle of the plaza, arms extended in full crucifixion pose, silently bedecked with birds.

La Serenissima was unusually warm that October. Most of the crisp fall clothing I'd packed was far too heavy for the humid heat. The lightest weight clothes in my luggage were two simple long dresses, one cotton and one silk. I fantasized about Fortuny, alternated the two dresses, and softened both gowns with constant wear. The soft swishings of long skirts seemed the only proper response to the constant murmurings of the canals. Raising my hem to climb a flight of stairs or avoid a puddle in Piazza San Marco returned me to a grace I didn't know I'd fallen from.

Except for the three creamy vintage nightgowns packed in whispering tissue, nothing I owned seemed worthy to be called a trousseau. I craved silk lingerie, hand-stitched by nuns, with lace intricate enough to blind a novice. I wanted hand-made shoes, soft leather to cradle my feet and flirt with the cobblestones. Longing for enough hair to sweep into a luxuriantly demure chignon, I searched my luggage for hatboxes full of large-brimmed creations. Despite the perpetual inadequacies of my wardrobe, I never wore jeans in Venice. It would have seemed like blasphemy.

The later the hour, the more deserted the streets, or at least their Venetian versions. In daylight, we toured the Accademia, admired all the riches of San Marco, visited everything we'd planned on.

Sightseeing during the day, a honeymoon's late-afternoon naps, leisurely marble baths, Cinzano on the hotel's terrace, and dinners that lasted hours—nothing gave me as much pleasure as our late-night walks.

We really saw Venice at night, wandering for hours without guidebooks. Never with a specific destination, we followed the patterns of light and dark, twisting through the labyrinths beyond the Grand Canal. There were treasures in the shadows, portraits in the rare unshuttered windows. The narrower and darker the alley, the more it lured us. Even the deadends offered rewards,

My Claudia, let us live and love!
Give not the half of a brass farthing
for scandal talked by grim old men.
Suns disappear and again return—
when our brief light burns down and dies
darkness remains and an endless sleep.
So kiss me now a thousand times,
kiss me a hundred, a thousand more,
again a hundred and a thousand.
Then when we come to thousands of thousands,
lose the account, forget the sum.
Envious people could injure us
if they but knew of our million kisses.

◆

—Horace (65–68 B.C.)

some tiny detail on a building's exterior that needed to be admired at rest. We walked at night to avoid the crowds, yet more souls crowded the most deserted *calle* than have ever scrambled onto a rush hour subway. Time twisted and curved around us in the dark, and the twentieth century trembled in surrender. The past was almost visible in the city of reflections, as if the air were a mirror too. More complicated, more evanescent than ghosts, other feet stepped across the cobblestones, other shadows disappeared into darkened doorways. Hidden eyes watched even the most stolen of kisses.

It was impossible for us to walk alone. There is no virgin territory in Venice.

When an unexpected streetlamp threw our shadows into high relief across an alley wall, my resolutely modern husband claimed to want a costume to match the silhouette of my long dress. He described a plumed hat, high boots, and a sweeping cape. I felt the cape brush my right shoulder.

My sense of direction is infamous. In twenty years of living in New York City, I never did master the fastest route to the airport. I can get lost, quite easily, on the freeways surrounding my current home city.

I never lost my way in Venice. Never.

I cannot explain the familiarity I felt in this most mysterious of cities, how I always seemed to know my way there, how my steps took us unhesitatingly through the most circuitous of routes. Discovering new wonders on each walk, I marvelled at my lack of surprise and insisted on a knowledge I couldn't explain when it was time to head to our grand and temporary home.

Bemused and unwilling to argue, my husband followed as I infallibly led us back to the hotel at the end of each night's excursion. He asked each night how I'd known the way. Never a believer in past lives, I joked about trails of biscotti crumbs, luck, and fate.

My husband died four years after our honeymoon, his body swamped by a disease more insidious than millennia of erosion. We never returned to Italy together and his death was not in Venice.

I still take pleasure in imagining him there. He wanders the back alleys, looks for his wavering reflection in the small canal below an ancient footbridge, waits to hear the rustle of my skirts. He never liked to be alone.

Maureen Anne Jennings contributed to and edited Cartwheels on the Faultline *and* Saltwater, Sweetwater. *Her work has also appeared in* The Dickens. *She is currently writing her second mystery and a book about Proust. She wishes she were in Venice right now.*

★

On my first trip to Venice, I remember sitting in the Piazzetta reading Byron, amazed to be just a stone's throw from the place that inspired these words:

> *I stood in Venice, on the "Bridge of Sighs;"*
> *A Palace and a prison on each hand:*
> *I saw from out the wave her structures rise*
> *As from the stroke of the Enchanter's wand!*
> *A thousand Years their cloudy wings expand*
> *Around me, and a dying Glory smiles*
> *O'er the far times, when many a subject land*
> *Looked to the winged Lion's marble piles,*
> *Where Venice sat in state, throned on her hundred isles!*

And then a very Venetian thing happened. A young man, attracted by my dreamy expression, the poetry I was reading, the notebook, or something sensual in the ancient stones themselves, came up to me bearing a bunch of violets. He was a tourist, too, a Chinese doctor from Australia, and he was shy—not the sort of person who accosts American college girls with violets. As we spent the day touring the palaces, the works of art, I realized that only Venice could have released him from his shyness. Venice does that to people. Just as it releases their longings, it also allows unpredictable things to happen.

—Erica Jong, "Venice: A City of Love and Death,"
The New York Times

ROBERT HELLENGA

* * *

Imagining the Flood

The effects of a natural and cultural disaster
are still visible in Florence.

IN THE FALL OF 1984 MY OLDEST DAUGHTER RETURNED TO
Florence, where our family had recently spent a year, to do the last
year of Italian high school with her former classmates at Liceo
Morgani; and I started to write a novel—*The Sixteen Pleasures*—
about a young woman who goes off by herself to Florence. My
heroine, some ten years older than my daughter, was a book con-
servator at the Newberry Library in Chicago. The devastating
flood of November 1966 turned out to be just the excuse she
needed to slough off her old life, which was on hold, and seek a
new one in Italy.

My heroine was not alone. Thousands of young people from
around the world converged on Florence to offer their services.
Known as *angeli del fango*, or mud angels, they went down into the
cellars of the city and carried out buckets of oily mud that had
been deposited by the Arno. In the cellars of the Biblioteca
Nazionale they had to wear gas masks because of the poisonous
fumes given off by sewage and by the decomposing leather bind-
ings of the books; but they rescued thousands and thousands of
books and documents, which were perhaps the most serious casualties of the flood. In 1989, as I was finishing my book, I returned

to Florence myself, though unlike the mud angels, I didn't sleep in an old railroad car behind the station; nor did I survive on army rations provided by the government.

Most visitors to Florence will have difficulty, as I did, imagining the flood. In summer the Arno is often reduced to a trickle that one might easily ford; and even in November—the most dangerous month—it generally flows along quite comfortably between its stone embankments, under the famous bridges that link the downtown and the Oltarno (other side of the Arno): the Ponte alle Grazie, the Ponte Vecchio, the Ponte Santa Trinita, and the Ponte alla Carraia. Books and newspapers tell us, nonetheless, that in November 1966, within a period of forty-eight hours almost nineteen inches of rain fell on the city and on the surrounding hills, which gathered the water and funneled it into the tributaries of the Arno, and into the Arno itself, faster than it could be discharged. And eyewitness accounts tell us that the water was twenty feet deep in Piazza Santa Croce; that it came roaring through the narrow streets in the city center at thirty-five miles per hour.

In writing about the flood I relied heavily on these eyewitness accounts and on photos in the *National Geographic* (July 1967) and in various Italian books. But I also spent some time standing on

---

My room at the inn looked out on the river and was flooded all day with sunshine. There was an absurd orange-colored paper on the walls; the Arno, of a hue not altogether different, flowed beneath. All this brightness and yellowness was a perpetual delight; it was a part of that indefinably charming color which Florence always seems to wear as you look up and down at it from the river, and from the bridges and quays. This is the kind of grave radiance—a harmony of high tints—which I scarce know how to describe.

◆

—Henry James,
The Italian Hours (1909)

the Ponte Vecchio, which spans the Arno at its narrowest point. The first bridge of record at this location, a wooden footbridge constructed in 972 on stone pilasters, was damaged by a flood in 1117, reconstructed in stone, and ultimately destroyed by the great flood of 1333, which is commemorated by a stone plaque under the sundial that rests on a small column near the center of the bridge. The present bridge, which was built in 1345, has survived countless minor floods, and several major ones: in 1557, in 1844, but it barely survived the flood of 1966. As the site of some of the most dramatic moments of the flood it's a good place to exercise one's imagination.

If you had been the night watchman on the Ponte Vecchio on the night of November 3, 1966, you would not have known that 40 miles up river, in the hills of the Pratomagno, where the Arno rises, the sluice gates at the Penna reservoir, which was completely full, had been opened sometime in the early evening, and that the river was already out of control—flowing over the top of the dam as well as through the sluice gates. Nor would you have known that at about nine o'clock the water had reached the Levane dam, 35 miles up river, and that the gates had been opened because the dam was threatening to give way completely. The flood water was on its way. At one o'clock on the morning of the 4th, you would not have known that the river had already overflowed just east of Florence. But you would have seen with your own eyes that the river was rising dangerously, and you would have begun to telephone your employers, the gold and silver merchants whose shops line the bridge, as they have since the end of the 16th century. You would have seen your employers trying to salvage what they could of their stock in the driving rain; you would have seen them taunted by not-so-innocent bystanders who had gathered, perhaps to watch the bridge collapse; you would have heard the *carabinieri*, who had been summoned to the scene, decline to warn the city on the grounds that they had no orders.

By 3:30 a.m. the bridge was in danger. The river was only one meter below the high point of the arches, which were becoming clogged by debris that included trees, automobiles, oil drums, and dead animals (including a cow). As the pressure on the bridge increased, the water rose up over the bridge itself, destroying the shops, which exploded like bombs. Salvage work became impossible; the bridge was closed off. Later that morning, however, another drama was enacted on the upper level of the bridge, which was still accessible—the Vasari Corridor, built in 1564 so that the Grand Duke Cosimo I could walk from the Palazzo della Signoria to the Pitti Palace without going out into the public streets. Between nine and ten o'clock in the morning, officials from various agencies risked their lives to rescue the world's finest collection of self-portraits, including paintings by Filippo Lippi, Raphael, Titian, Rubens, Rembrandt, David, Corot, Ingres, and Delacroix.

If you stand by the bust of Benvenuto Cellini, in the center of the bridge, and look down river, towards the Ponte Santa Trinita, you will see, on your right, one of the places where the Arno first found its way into the streets of the city, at about 5:30 in the morning, overflowing and eventually destroying the concrete

> *T*he plain on both sides of the Arno which is today the site of the city of Florence was said by Livy to have been so marshy in antique times as to have impeded Hannibal during his march on Rome, and according to Florentine legend it took Hercules himself (whose effigy appears in one of the ancient seals of the city) to drain the swamp and make possible the founding of a settlement. The plain has had to be kept drained ever since, and, even so, the Arno has frequently flooded over into it; there have been about sixty floods of various degrees of gravity since the twelfth century, the worst until now having been those of 1333 and 1844. The summer tourist, who often sees the Arno at Florence as a stony riverbed, can scarcely be expected to imagine its sinister potentialities.
>
> ◆
>
> —Francis Steegmuller,
> *Stories and True Stories*

embankment along the Lungarno Acciaioli. If you walk up river from the bridge, past the Uffizi, you will come to the Lungarno alle Grazie, just past the Ponte alle Grazie. Here, at about the same time, the Arno overflowed both banks, flowing down the narrow streets that lead into Piazza Santa Croce, which, because it is the lowest area of the city, was the hardest hit in terms of works of art, and in terms of human suffering.

Millions of books and documents stored in the basement of the Biblioteca Nazionale, adjacent to Santa Croce (and to the river), were submerged in oily mud; the water covered the tombs in the church and stained the frescoes by Giotto in the Peruzzi Chapel. And Cimabue's famous crucifix, in the Museum of Santa Croce, was destroyed beyond hope of restoration, despite heroic attempts by the monks to salvage even the smallest bits of gold and flecks of paint from the oily muck that remained when the water had subsided. In the words of Sir Kenneth Clark (in *The Nude*) the Cimabue crucifix marked a return, after the middle ages, to a conception of the human body as "a controlled and canonized vehicle of the divine." Some people were impatient with Cimabue, however, especially in the Santa Croce quarter, the quarter of the *popolo minuto*, the little people, the artisans—leather workers, furniture makers and restorers, antique dealers—many of whom lost all their possessions, not only their homes, but their tools as well. The high water marks for the floods of 1557 and 1966, which can be seen above your head on the north side of the *piazza* (just around the corner from the Via Verdi) are astonishing.

The city center, though slightly higher than Santa Croce, was also devastated. The mass of water entering the city along the Lungarno Acciaioli and the Lungarno alle Grazie converged on the center—the old Roman city, which had its center in Piazza Republica, and which stands out clearly on the map because the streets run at right angles to each others—at approximately 35 miles per hour, completely covering the Michelangelo sculptures on the ground floor of the Bargello and ripping off five of the Ghiberti panels on the famous "Gates of Paradise" doors on the Baptistry. Ultimately it extended as far north as San Marco and the

Archeological Museum, where many Etruscan artifacts were damaged or destroyed.

Thirty years later the panels from the Baptistry have been moved to safety in the Museum of the Duomo; the damaged Cimabue crucifix is now suspended on chains from the ceiling in the Santa Croce museum so that it can be raised in case of another flood; the state archives have been moved from the basement of the Uffizi to Piazza Beccaria; frescoes have been restored or in some cases even removed from walls that had begun to disintegrate; hundreds of paintings and thousands of books and manuscripts have been expertly restored; the shops in Piazza Santa Croce do a brisk business all year long, and it's always difficult to find a place to stand on the Ponte Vecchio. What did it all mean?

In *The Sixteen Pleasures*, my heroine's Italian lover is one of the officials who risks his life to save the portraits in the Vasari Corridor. (I first read about him in the *National Geographic*.) Lingering for a moment, after the paintings have been carried to safety, he reflects on the scene below him, imagining that this is what it will be like at the end of the world. A natural disaster, yes— what the insurance companies call an act of God—but also the result of human stupidity: for building in the flood plain in the first place; for crowding the river; for failing to create a flood control plan, though Leonardo drew up a proposal for one in the 16th century; for failing to install an early warning system. Afterwards, he thinks, there will be a great flurry of activity; existing government agencies will be reorganized and new ones will be formed; commissions will be created to study the problem. And yet nothing will be done: there will be no flood control plan; there will be no warning system; precious books and documents will still be stored in basements near the river, just as they have been for years. And yet as he feels the bridge trembling beneath him he is strangely elated, as if the bridge were a stallion and he a great warrior astride it. His own instinct for happiness speaks to him of great acts of charity and kindness and selflessness; it speaks to him of natural enemies—priests and communists and *carabinieri* and *commercianti*—working together to alleviate suffering; it speaks to him of advances in the science of book and art conservation. In spite of the disaster, or perhaps because of it, he's having a good time.

For me, as a writer of fiction, the flood poses a problem that I have never quite resolved. On the one hand, for my American heroine and her Italian lover (and for the mud angels) the flood was the adventure of a lifetime. On the other hand, I continue to wonder about the natives, people who experienced the flood not imaginatively but at first hand, people who had to live in Florence after the mud angels had gone home. Surely the flood was one of the defining moments of their lives too, but was it *the adventure of a lifetime*, or was it simply a *disgrazia*, a disaster?

On the 30th anniversary of the flood, I decided to ask. I asked Franco Cipriani, who helped clean the mud out of the Museum of Santa Croce, where the Cimabue crucifix had been lifted out of the mud and placed on sawhorses; I asked Franco's friend Fabrizio Papini, who worked with him; I asked Signora Valastro, whose husband—an army captain—helped provision the mud angels; and I asked a shopkeeper in Santa Croce, Signor Giorgi, whose family business ("artistic objects in wood") was destroyed. My daughter, who was with me in Florence, also asked her friends and their parents. The results of this informal survey, though statistically insignificant, made me feel that I had not been too far off the mark when I granted Dottor Postiglione (my heroine's Italian lover) a certain degree of optimism. Like Dottor Postiglione, the people I talked to spoke of order rising out of chaos—not the kind of order that is imposed from without, but the kind of order that anarchists dream of: spontaneous and unpremeditated, natural rather than artificial; they spoke of the hard hearts of the Florentines being genuinely touched by the sheer numbers of young people who came to help; and they all agreed that the citizens of Florence, who seldom speak well of each other, worked together on this occasion for the greater good.

Robert Hellenga is the author of The Sixteen Pleasures *and his new novel,* The Fall of the Sparrow, *is about the bombing of the train station in Bologna in 1980.*

★

I had never known Florence more herself, or in other words more at-taching, than I found her for a week in that brilliant October. She sat in the sunshine beside her yellow river like the little treasure-city she has al-ways seemed, without commerce, without other industry than the man-ufacture of mosaic paperweights and alabaster Cupids, without actuality or energy or earnestness or any of those rugged virtues which in most cases are deemed indispensable for civic cohesion; with nothing but the little unaugmented stock of her medieval memories, her tender-colored mountains, her churches and palaces, pictures and statues.

—Henry James, *The Italian Hours* (1909)

BARBARA GRIZZUTI HARRISON

✱ ✱ ✱

My Roman Intimacies

The Eternal City is just that.

I LOVE ROME. I LOVE EVEN THE WAY THE CAR HUGS THE ROAD AS I am driven from the airport to the center city. There is a reassuringly symbiotic relationship between the vehicle and the surface on which we are traveling. The basic compact of the Roman taxi driver—unlike taxi drivers in my own city, New York, who see the road as conquerable space and enemy—is with the ground beneath us; and if, as a consequence, he is placed in conflict with other vehicles (if he finds himself in an *incidenza*, or, worse, a *coincidenza*), he will handle it judiciously—operatically, perhaps, but judiciously. For in Rome—the city of sensation—drama and prudence are remarkably united, held in a high and beautiful tension from which derive Roman pragmatism and sophistication, as well as that heightened awareness of the quotidian that is Rome's abiding gift to its citizens (who never tire of their city) and to its visitors, who, if they are open to experience, will find themselves, as Goethe did and Henry James did and I did born again into the shining appreciation of the moment.

The brakes grip concisely. The blood of charioteers courses through the veins of Roman drivers. And, indeed, we are passing the ruins of the Circus Maximus, in which, at the height of its

imperial magnificence, 250,000 Romans urged their favorite charioteers on to victory.

Broken and forbidding, set like a row of monstrous decayed
teeth in green gardens between the Aventine and Palantine hills,
these ruins are not what I come again to Rome to see. They are
not lovable (and you are likely to be suckered there; at the
Colosseum it is impossible, as it is nowhere else in Rome, to find
an honest taxi driver, or, for that matter, to find a taxi at all). And
the Forum, a bleached boneyard of antiquity, is not lovable:
"Time," said Pope Pius II, "has ruined all; ivy covers the walls that
once were clothed with tapestries and golden draperies; thorns and
scrub flourish where once sat purple-clad tribunes, and snakes in-
fest the queen's chambers." These ruins fill me with forebodings.
They say: the known world can end, the race ends in silence and
the grave, the racer's sweat and pleasure are folly, we make our final
bed on stone.

But before these thoughts become bloated we round a corner
and we are in the Rome of all delight, the Rome where past and
present are sweetly contiguous, the Rome which is mother to us
and in which we are nourished with the conviction that we are
part of a continuum. In the layered city of visible history, where
nothing is ever lost, man counts for something. Bodies count.
Poetry counts. The transcendental is at hand. A gesture counts.

Here on the bank of the Tiber is the endearingly circular
Temple of the Vestal Virgins; small, its dimension are instantly ap-
prehensible. (But it's wrongly named: the ruin of the actual Temple
of the Vestal Virgins is in the Forum, surrounded by yellow roses
that feed, one is tempted to believe, on the ashes of those vestals
who broke their vows of chastity and were buried alive; this temple by the Tiber is whole, and very pretty.) Here, too, is the four-
square Temple of Manly Fortune, solemn and sturdy. The two
form an essay in complementariness. And here—up these flights of
steps to a comfortable and elegant eminence—is Michelangelo's
Capitol, the Piazza del Campidoglio. And here is the thirteenth-
century church of Santa Maria d'Aracoeli—brown brick, simple,
severe, nothing gratuitous to mar its beauty—up to which, on their

knees, the pious climb: more than 120 steps they climb, still thanking God for having spared Rome from a plague in the fourteenth century. The small, moving bunches—black against the cypress, umbrella pines, and Roman sky—are a living enactment of the medieval belief that life is a series of ladders by which one ascends into light and glory and the presence of God.

And here is Rome's "wedding cake," the silly and bombastic and very white Vittorio Emanuele Monument, so much decried it is like an overgrown naughty child perversely soliciting affection and attention—which it succeeds, on account of its large and orienting *thereness*, in getting. One forgives it its impertinence and grows quite fond of it.

We have passed, by now, along the Tiber, the church of Santa Maria in Cosmedin, which some consider the most charming in Rome. On its porch sits the large stone Bocca della Verità, the mouth into which, legend says, one with a lie on his conscience must not, on pain of dismemberment, place a hand. (It was probably a Roman sewer cover, a manhole, which in no way diminishes its theatrical, childlike, fun-fair appeal.) And we have passed the balcony from which Mussolini—indiscriminate excavator of ruins and lover of all that was imperial, dominant, intimidating, and colossal—ranted. And so, too, have we passed the Teatro di Marcello (the baby Colosseum, it is sometimes called), the oldest continuously inhabited building in the world. In its apartments are hanging gardens; in its honeycombed labyrinths hid enemies of the Third Reich.

All this—the ancient, the medieval, the Renaissance, the Baroque—we have passed in far less time than it takes to tell of it. And yet one is not conscious of an indigestion of impressions. One is conscious only of Rome's generosity.

Freud, who wished to die in Rome, said that the human mind resembled this city, built, or superimposed, upon all the cities that ever stood where it now stands; all of them preserved as memory is preserved. The unconscious, like the underground river of Rome, flows through the cellars of the mind; as in Rome, the excavated past flows through the present. Perhaps it is because Rome resembles the structures of the mind that we feel, provided we relax into it, such an immediate and easeful affinity with landscape, people and stone—an intimacy that is like foreknowledge.

The streets leading to my *piazza*—the Piazza della Rotonda (Pantheon square)—are like a funnel delivering mechanical sight-seers from the Piazza Navona to the Pantheon, where, herded hot and cranky they will take in a Sight, and like good children learning lessons, move on. Goal-oriented and determined, they have much in common with visitors to Milan, mecca for lovers of that which is fashionable, brilliant, and brittle. Those who admire Milan, and those for whom shopping is all, think Rome's a waste. Milan has Industry! Design! (For the mechanical sightseers, Rome has Monuments! Ruins!) Nothing happens in Rome, the Milanese say. Life happens in Rome, the Romans say. Precarious, sweet, volatile, absurd, but most of all abundant, life.

Rome turns us from technology to humanity. Rome calls us to happiness. Rome cannot be learned by rote. It is absorbed through the pores.

"Abbasso Milano!" my taxi driver shouts. *"Viva Roma!"* In Milan, he says, they care only for work. In Rome, he says they care for food, for love, for pleasure. It's a cliché, and all around us (we're driving through traffic that gives anarchy a good name) drivers and car-imperiled pedestrians stop to form a chorus echoing my driver: *"Viva Roma!"*

From my window, I see the world. A *piazza* is a theater, a domestic enclosure, a living room, a town hall, a village.

I'm staying at the Albergo del Sole, a handsome, dignified building that has served as a hotel since at least the early part of the

> *I* love language, that soft bastard Latin,
> Which melts like kisses from a female mouth.
> And sounds as if it had been writ on satin,
> With syllables which breathe of the sweet South.
>
> ◆
>
> —Lord Byron, *Beppo,* 1818

sixteenth century. The poet Ariosto dined here, and centuries later—although the passing of a century is but an intake of breath in Rome, and a decade but the blink of an eye—Sartre lived here, and wrote, as I do now, in an enclosed roof garden where a peculiar silence reigns.

My room looks out onto the Pantheon, a perfect building that encapsulates perfect space. The ground of the *piazza* dips slightly to meet it. The buildings on either side—burnt orange, bitter yellow, rosy gray—curve gently away from it, as if in deference to its absolute perfection. Buildings have moral force and meaning in Rome, where there is nothing abstract about space.

The bold, raggedy boys who sit on the steps of the Renaissance fountain say (sounding oddly Garboesque), "I want to kiss your ass." This is addressed to the world at large. One of them wears a black t-shirt on which are printed the vague but ominous words YOU WILL BE LIKE THE OTHERS. A family of Gypsies prowls, begging.

There is, nevertheless, an ineffable sweetness in the air.

A hag, bent over, toothless (I have seen her before, in times past: she is a witch), approaches me: *"Giornalista,"* she says, conspiratorially. She is a witch: she has no purpose but to establish the fact of her knowing that which she cannot be expected reasonably to know.

Scaffolding and netting obscure all but six of the sixteen monolithic granite columns that support the porch of the magnificent building. (Half of Rome is *in restauro* half of the time; or, as Nancy Mitford has one of her characters say, "Abroad is always closed.") I am obscurely pleased by this state of affairs: I like a fly in the ointment of my happiness. Inside the Pantheon (the inside is a treat I have been reserving, as so much of the enjoyment of Rome lies in precisely calibrated anticipation and postponement) there is joy. The joy one experiences here cannot be accounted for by individual architectural facts alone. The diameter of the dome (stripped centuries ago, without diminution of glory, of its gilded bronze) is equal to the height of the building. Larger than that of St. Peter's, the dome *is* the Pantheon. This building, which is all center, and which I sometimes think is both culmination and progenitor of all the buildings on earth, is cave and womb—an absolutely safe and sheltering space. One cannot experience vertigo or uncertainty of movement or of purpose here.

In the center of the coffered dome is the oculus, the enormous round opening through which light enters and nourishes stone. I once, to my immense surprise, heard a priest mutter to himself, as clouds drifted in a sea of seeing blue: "The eye of the great white whale." What could he have meant? To look up and into that aperture is like looking into the eye of God.

Outside, on the Pantheon's facade, there is graffiti: ACID HOUSE: PORCO DIO: BUSH GO NEW YORK. An urban blight like the algae that bloom putridly on the Adriatic lagoons of Venice. On the *piazza*, a leaflet urging the legalization of drugs is thrust into my hands: "Aggression and blood on the streets, the ferocious hand of the Mafia in politics, in the economy…. This is the consequence not of drugs but of prohibition," it says. Blood on the streets. This is the twilight of the civilized world.

At four in the morning I awaken to a bruised purple sky. The *piazza* is empty. Floodlights illuminate the Pantheon; in the fountain before it, dolphins spew Nile-green water. The elegant, cozy, and gay houses surrounding the *piazza* are softly lit by lanterns; behind their sagging shutters is the faint answering gleam of chandeliers (the secret life of houses). In the *piazza*, the tables and chairs and potted plants of the cafés stand untroubled. Dawn comes with theatrical brushstrokes to the sloping and projecting roofs, the prickly antennas, the verandas and terraces with their pots of geraniums and trailing broad beans and tomatoes and wild mint. With a discreet rumbling of gates, the newsstand opens—though it will be hours before the first paper is sold. The streets are swept and washed. A young African rounds the corner and, without breaking stride, enters a café and begins to set up the huge umbrellas—Rome's *ombrelloni*—which ring the *piazza* in friendliness and simplicity. Tables are washed and set. The intelligence of hands, the dignity of human labor—the man who sweeps the streets might, with his earnest concentration, be harvesting a field. On the building across from mine, a frescoed Mary dressed in blue floats on fat pink clouds; this is the building that houses a *salumeria*, where I buy bread and prosciutto. A crooked man with a ponytail moves off in the direction of the senate, carrying an elegant pigskin case. Exactly at seven, plump hands open shutters as a convention of birds—looking as if they've been propelled, like practice tennis balls, from an insane machine—crisscrosses the sky; swallows and pigeons make idiot burping and screeching noises. Vespas, which look and sound more like agitated household appliances than motor vehicles, enter the *piazza*. With ritual indistinguishable from optimism, the city readies itself for another day. If this is the twilight of the civilized world, Rome—dignified, exuberant, prudent, judicious, operatic, pragmatic—can be counted upon to hold out, with brio against the barbarians.

Barbara Grizzuti Harrison is the author of one novel, Foreign Bodies, *as well as the nonfiction titles:* Unlearning the Lie: Sexism in School; Vision of Glory: A History and a Memory of Jehovah's Witnesses; Off Center; *and* Italian Days. *Her work has appeared in* The New York Times, Harper's, GQ, Traveler, *and* Vanity Fair. *She has lived in Libya, India, and Guatemala, and now lives in Manhattan, on the East River.*

＊

It is not listed in the telephone directory, and you can't find it on any city map, but the antiques market in Piazza Fontanella Borghese has long been an open secret among certain Romans and visitors. The name sounds familiar, yet this place is nowhere near the Villa Borghese Gardens or the Borghese Galleries, which are on the list of every conscientious tourist in Rome.

This particular market is tucked away in an old *piazza* in the heart of the city. But it is not hard to find. Start from the Spanish Steps, turn onto the Via dei Condotti until it meets Corso Umberto (the long street stretching all the way from Piazza del Popolo to the Vittorio Emanuele monument). Crossing the Corso and continuing in the same direction, you'll wind up in Via della Fontanella di Borghese, which opens into the Largo della Fontanella di Borghese—and then the actual site of the market, the Piazza Fontanella Borghese. Towering in the background is

Palazzo Borghese, still the home of the Borghese family, which has been prominent in Rome's history and artistic heritage since the 16th century.

Here, in this cozy corner, about 24 stalls make up the *mercatino*, as everybody calls it. This is the prestigious place for acquiring rare prints, books, maps, coins and other antiques.

The only people who know the market's official name are the clerks at Rome's municipal licensing bureau. For all the casualness of the setup, the mandatory license to operate a stall can be obtained only after careful screening of the candidate's social and financial status, and the standards are very high. Gone are the days when anyone with a pushcart and some old prints could open business anywhere he pleased.

—Vera Giannini, "Rare Finds in Rome," *Travel & Leisure*

THOMAS BELMONTE

* * *

In the Shadow of Vesuvius

Naples sears the mind of a visitor.

I ARRIVED IN NAPLES ON A COLD, WET, ABYSMALLY GRAY DAY OF
early April. I was frightened and apprehensive. I didn't speak more
than a few sentences of Italian, and I was geographically lost. As I
followed the crowds from the railroad station up what seemed to
be the main boulevard, looking for a hotel, I stole glances into the
side streets. The boulevard was modern and bustling, lined with
drab turn-of-the-century office and residential buildings. But the
side streets, the narrow, winding *vicoli*, appeared shadowy and broken, far older in architecture and somehow removed from the activity of the main street.

I soon stopped at an inexpensive hotel, grayer than the day itself but near what seemed to be a large working-class zone. I
checked in, and after a few minutes of rest in the dull room, I ventured into the old quarter for my first confrontation with the
world I had come to study and know.

The darkening streets echoed with the wailing of car horns and
phonographs and babies. They were hung with strings of lights and
had been built to human, not mechanical, proportions. The small
Italian cars were slowed down, pinned and trapped between groups
of people, blocked by other cars, or otherwise frustrated in their

movement. But there was a rush of humanity, teeming inward and outward from the buildings, flowing through the streets, collecting and pausing in the open spaces that were markets.

Girls walked by me, swaying and chattering, arm in arm, and pairs of young men strutted past close behind them. They also walked arm in arm. Boys shouted and darted in and out of doorways, while mothers hurried about everywhere, clutching at the hands and elbows of their offspring, who in turn held on to their straying younger siblings, in haphazard chainlike formations. And in the midst of this whirl of noise and voices and streaming, rain-muted colors, a boy on a motorbike zoomed up and down, savoring the joy of speed and caring as little for the lives of others as for his own.

The adobe-colored buildings leaned about me like low ravines. They were all festooned with laundry. Some had small, arched entranceways and deep-set windows. Others were more regal in aspect, with great iron-filigreed portals. In all of the edifices there were the same ground-floor cavelike dwellings, the famous *bassi*. In one of these little homes, which seemed cozy and warm to me, at least five small children were bouncing up and down on the large matrimonial bed, like little clowns on a trampoline.

As I walked I unconsciously stopped and looked at the scenes that drew my attention. People stared back and probably realized I was a foreigner by my clothes. The looks of the old women frightened me. They were the sentinels of that world, on guard for intruders. They sat about in the street on chairs and stools, and peered from doorways. Their faces were hard and embittered and drawn toward the mouth. They looked me over, up and down, as if to ask why I was there and why I would not go away. The faces of the young women were becoming like those of the old. Like the old, many were dressed in black, while by contrast their men were clad in the brightest of colors, stretched tight around the frame.

Stalls were everywhere, selling dry goods and cigarettes, bread, cheese, oil, wine, olives, and vegetables—all of it spilling out onto the cobblestones. The air was faintly scented with the odor of scallions. The colors were riotous. The fish displays impressed me as neat abstractions of black and white and silver. There were rows of white squid and bushels of sleek eels, and stacks of a long flat fish, like cut pieces of silver ribbon. I remember the delicate feet of the clams, the color of pure coral, waving back and forth in their large wooden buckets.

In the days that followed, I wandered through many of the poorer districts of Naples. I made forays into the forbidding labyrinth of dark lanes near the port, as old as Boccacio's *Decameron* whose tales they inspired. I explored the brighter section called Sanità, which looked as though it were hewn from a hillside of volcanic rock, then bleached by the sun and the rains of five centuries, so that now it gleamed like a crumbling honey-colored hive in the sun. I was approached with pistols for sale in the sinister market section of Forcella, which sells everything that the species is capable of smuggling. Finally there was the zone of my first exploration, the old Spanish quarter, which at night was dominated by the prostitutes, gathered near their fires, and the geisha-like faces of the transvestites.

In those early days I was apprehending only the surfaces of things, but there is much to be learned from surfaces. From the whole torrent of impressions a hidden figure seemed to be emerging (and receding as fast), a formal if loose arrangement of select qualities and contradictions. In the donning of a sweater, or the sipping of a *caffè,* there was always the same fine, brisk grace of movement, the same high sense of style. Etiquettes in all domains of behavior were elaborate and subtle, but people were comfortable with their bodies in Naples in ways that would scandalize an American.

What could be more typical of Naples than the occasional lavender veil of wisteria, softening some centuries-old façade? But even the most drab concrete apartment houses, stained with a wash of fading yellow paint and patched with the jagged blue fiberglass of their broken terraces—even these bunkerlike structures were rendered aesthetically unique by the arrangement of cement and metal and plastic, and the dozen or so flowerpots enlivening every balcony. Everywhere there seemed to be the same valley-like topography to the street scenes in the overflow of humanity and stall-produce, whether the walls were made out of homogenized orange fire-brick or gracious, crumbling, pink terra-cotta. Houses and pastry alike were decorated with the same colors, because life in Naples is an event to be celebrated, because existence is a movable, continuing feast.

I came to know the city better in the faces of its people, in their bearing, and in the flow of their speech. Faces were unmasked to me in Naples, fragile or tough, young, or else old, smooth or rough, with no room for middle or blurring categories. Returning to me always were the looks of the old women, hunched and suspecting, with their black steeled eyes glistening with hostility and warning. The sore of poverty was upon Naples, and the marks of age. Broken things littered all the streets of the old quarters, broken doors and furniture, broken walls, broken bicycles and toys. Everywhere I looked, bent, twisted old people moved painfully up the narrow, climbing lanes. Some moved in slow, throbbing, rhythms, and some with light, comically distorted motions. Some moved with bowed somber dignity, and some moved with the birdlike grace of children.

The language of the poor was expressed in shout and song as much as in ordinary talk, and seemed different from the conversational flow I was picking up in restaurants and bars. In effect there are two languages in Naples; and Italian, for the lower classes—if it is spoken at all—takes a low second place to the Neapolitan dialect. One day I went to the rocks by the port to get some sun. All around me there were groups of boys, of all ages, scattered in pairs and clusters. They were stretched out over the rough scorched rocks or diving into the cold blue water, shouting and calling to one another in the elusive, and to me, totally secret language of the dialect. If Italian, as I was learning it, seemed studied and clear and, in its crystalline grace, evocative of feminine beauty, Neapolitan struck me as primitive and flowing and masculine. In Neapolitan the voice is thick and husky and low. It makes women sound mannish. It streams outward, rough and fast, a veritable rapids of speech. Playing within it is a music, a faraway, languorous water music. In even the simplest cry and certainly the commonest, the oft-repeated *"Guagliu', vien' à ccà"* (Boy, come here), there is a complex orchestration of jubilation and longing and grief. For the call begins with an impulsive glad outburst of sound. It falls midway into a plea. It fades and dies in a low grieving moan. I realized intuitively that day, as I was to learn later, how the dialect as an exotic language enhances the fact of community, closing off outsiders. At the same time, it reaffirms, in its exuberant, rising crescendos, the imperative of sociality, while brooding, in its wearied, almost agonized descents, on the inevitable dilemmas of individual isolation.

The poor boys of Naples are the living symbols of its history and the carriers of its traditions, much as altar boys intermediate the flow of grace from deity to worshipper. In the elegant park by the sea, the Villa Comunale, they arrange themselves in circles on the sun-beaten green to

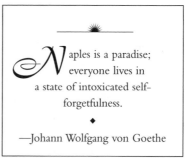

Naples is a paradise; everyone lives in a state of intoxicated self-forgetfulness.

—Johann Wolfgang von Goethe

play soccer or cards. They jump wantonly into the fountains; they strip naked, comparing and experimenting, heads tossing, their feet dancing as if on hot coals. In the luxuriant late-afternoon haze, a balloon-man floats by like an image from a dream. Wealthy women stroll, serene-faced, with their maids and baby-carriages, like Parisian matrons in a painting by Seurat. All are oblivious to the boys. It is part of divine order that all should be as they are, and it is left to the boys to protect the integrity of the scene. So to my foreigner's intrusive glance, one young fellow, wet and shivering, looked up at me and laughed and shook his penis furiously, imploring me to come close for a better look—his companions around him doubling over the jets of water, hopping with glee!

The pulsation of life impressed itself upon me in Naples as it has nowhere else, and not only in the teeming, romantic quarters. I recall walking, a few days after arrival, through the blighted periphery of the city—a confusion of gas stations and junkyards, warehouses and new and old apartment buildings. I came upon a large vacant lot, dusty and barren, circumscribed and enclosed as if it were a prison yard by a disintegrating wall of broken tenements. I noticed some children playing in a corner, when suddenly, appearing as if out of nowhere, a small carnival was in process of setting itself up, a clatter of poles and bells. And no sooner was one ride up, a small, circling ramshackle swing, than it was rushed into operation before any of the others could be assembled. As the children clambered on, their mothers gathered around, laughing and cheering for this diminutive spectacle, in one suddenly animate corner in that barren desert of a place, with the whitish sky above, and the strewn tires and the dust, and the crushed and shattered fragments of glass, like salt, below.

The spirit of place in Naples is a living force. It is resolute and passionate, but it is also unconscious, and insensate to the prod of awareness and reason. As such it can enrage, or it becomes hypnotic. The movement in Naples—the traffic jams, the pushy, shoving crowds, the absence of lines forming for anything, the endless barrage of shouts falling like arrows on the ears, the simultaneous clash of a million destinations and petty opposed intentions—combine into a devastating assault on the senses. Or else the entire scene retreats, slowing and setting finally into a brilliantly colored frieze. One could pass a lifetime just watching the show and contemplating; and pass away into one's own contemplations.

The tendency of the soul in Naples is toward forgetfulness, to let consciousness fall into abandon, into the simpler mode of unexamined living. But perhaps it was only the yearning of my inner self, removed from the pressures of past and future. How often I wanted to lose myself in Naples, in the endless procession of light tones passing, in the sunsets of rose gold with their light pressed from roses; the city at dusk, set like a fading ivory reliquary, beneath Vesuvius on the sea.

Thomas Belmonte is the author of The Broken Fountain, *from which this piece was excerpted.*

✳

I remember also the dialect of the city of Naples, which is Italian chewed to shreds in the mouth of a hungry man. It varies even within the city. The fishermen in the bay talk differently from the rich in the Vomero. Every six blocks in the squashed-together city there's a new dialect. But the dialect is Naples and Naples is the dialect. It's as raw as tenement living, as mercurial as a thief to your face, as tender as the flesh on the breast. Sometimes in one sentence it's all three...When they say something, the Neapolitans scream and moan and stab and hug and vituperate. All at once. And O God, their gestures! The hand before the groin, the finger under the chin, the cluckings, the head-shakings. In each sentence they seem to recapitulate all the emotions that human beings know. They die and live and faint and desire and despair. I remember the dialect of Naples.

It was the most moving language I ever listened to. It came out of the fierce sun over the bleached and smelly roofs, the heavy night, childbirth, starvation, and death. I remember too the tongues that spoke Neapolitan to me: the humorous, the sly, the gentle, the anguished, the merciful, and the murderous. Those tongues that spoke it were like lizards warm in the sun, jiggling their tails because they were alive.

—John Horne Burns, *The Gallery* (1947)

DUNCAN FALLOWELL

⋆ ⁂ ⋆

Signor Bananas

Shopping in Florence can be stressful.

OVER BREAKFAST I DECIDE TO BUY A LEATHER BAG FROM A SHOP I know off the Piazza della Signoria but, on descending to the street, discover that a busy market has sprouted all around my car. This is a problem, not least because I have parked on the pitch of a fruit seller who is now standing in front of me loudly informing me of this fact. He's about forty, hair cut medium short all over in the way Italian men do if they don't want a hairstyle. I can't understand a word he's saying but am more concerned with a king-size bunch of bananas he's shaking in my face. I don't know about you but first thing in the morning is not my brilliant time—in fact I'm often not really rolling mentally until way after lunch—so that this situation is more than I can grasp. One thing is certain. If I become involved with moving the car now I'll never have time to buy my bag—and besides, my luggage is still up in the *pensione*— so I say "Impossible, impossible!" to whatever he's demanding and walk off. A big mistake. He comes running after me—the market folk stop what they're doing and look to see what will happen. I keep walking, trembling, trying to shake him off, trying to rise above it/him/them/Florence/the World. He is now in a terrible rage, pursuing me with roars, shaking his bananas, spittle at the corners of his mouth. We are this morning's spectacle, me walking white and silent, him following red and noisy. Clearly he'll follow me all the way to the bag shop and may even strike me down beforehand. My nerve breaks first. I turn about, look him in his bulging eyes and say "OK!" I walk back to the car, agree to move it, although the compress of marketeers seems to make this absurd. And at this point Bananas suddenly changes. Changes completely. He says I don't have to move the car *at all*. I'm bewildered. No, no it's fine, he says. How long do I need to go shopping, one hour, two hours? That's fine...Very weird. But I'm not going to argue with him again. Perhaps he simply wanted me to acknowledge my turpitude. B-i-z-a-r-r-e...

I set out bagwards, distinctly paranoid, convinced that I've become a victim of a Florentine ruse, that the car will be stolen in my absence or tyres slashed at the very least. Bananas is bound to have dark friends. Walking along the Arno I become mesmerised by the bases of lamps which line it: shaggy squatting three-legged crotches. The central lamp-support pierces the crotch and embeds itself in the top of the riverside wall, so as one passes one is repeatedly presented with this representation of something hanging down between squatting shaggy thighs. As usual there is dog shit everywhere and scooters. Norman Douglas had a theory that the English walk along staring downwards in order to avoid dog shit on the pavement—this is true of me here. Pass a shop displaying antique sepia photographs. One particularly catches my eye—the Palazzo Bonagia in Palermo—a baroque staircase in a courtyard, several figures standing mutely on it in period dress. When I reach Palermo I shall find this intriguing place, so redolent of the south, and find out what was going on there—the photograph suggests many stories. Into the messy Piazza Della Signoria crammed with naked statues. Very healthy for Florentine children to grow up surrounded by these cyclopean pricks and bums and tits and balls (though Florenece is not a very sexy town).

In the leather shop, while the girl manipulates my credit card, I fondle the bag's wondrously soft and supple flanks. Oh gorgeous thing, you were worth it. But carrying the booty back across the river, I grow uneasy at the car problem ahead and decide to compose myself in the Boboli Gardens, a most enchanting resort behind the Pitti Palace. Decrepitude adds to the romance of it's endless adventurous pathways. To clip the very tall hedges round the *isolotto* today, the gardeners are using outsize step-ladders painted bright green. This enormous exaggeration in the size of a conventional item makes them appear to be the gardeners from *Alice in Wonderland*.

Struggling back through the crowded market, I discover the car where I left it, oppressed by shoppers on every side but unburglered, unslashed. Bananas comes around, almost joyous—he's kept an eye on it for me. But will it explode when I open the door? No. Is he after money? It seems not. It's all hugs and cheery slaps and, once I've rammed the luggage in the back, he assists me with waving arms to make the only possible maneuver which is to *back* out of this turmoil between piles of gaudy goods, past mamas with pushchairs—please God, let me not kill a baby, that really would be the end—shaving the obtrusive corners of stalls and those Latin bottoms and bellies. There are no more than two or three inches on either side of the car. While handling the wheel with the delicacy of one applying a scalpel to a brain, there breaks upon my concentration a broad Yorkshire accent. "Eee, you've got a job on your hands there, lad!" and he's gone. I'm sweating all over, tingling at the temples, wet in the small of my back.

But eventually the extraction is accomplished and the car rolls into a proper road with space in it. It's a narrow Florentine side street but it seems like Salsbury Plain to me. The relief...Ha, and now I feel *high*, feel that no matter what the Italian traffic flings at me, I shall survive. And I feel a deeper liberation too. Baptism by marketplace. I've interacted, broken through an inner resistance, a holding back from the life around me which always has to be overcome in a new place. Italy is beginning to exert its catalytic influence and from now on I'll know less and less. By the time Rome is behind us, I'll know nothing at all. One more thing. Bananas taught me a lesson in good manners. I was guilty of a coarse territorial infringement. There are few more offensive acts than depriving a man of his workplace. And he wanted me to recognize that. Once I had admitted I was wrong, he was happy. So feeling much less complacent and thoroughly improved, I set off for lunch at the Villa La Pietra.

Duncan Fallowell is the author of two novels, one biography, a collection of profiles titled Twentieth Century Characters, *and the libretto of the opera* Gormenghast. *He has also written two books on his travels,* One Hot Summer in St. Petersburg *and* To Noto or London to Sicily in a Ford, *from which this piece was excerpted.*

✳

Italians always have lived over the store. The *palazzi* of some of the grandest families have bricked-in arches at ground level, with remains of waisthigh stone counters where someone used to ladle out preserved briny fish from a vat to customers, or carve the stuffed pig, a job now performed in sleek open-sided trucks that ply the weekly market or sell from roadsides. I run my hand over these worn stone counters when I pass them. From odd windows at ground level, the *palazzo's* house wine was sold. First floors of some grand houses were warehouses. Today, my bank in Cortona is the bottom of the great Laparelli house, which rests on Etruscan stones. On the top floors, windows open to the night show antique chandeliers, big armfuls of light. Often the residents are leaning out, two, sometimes three to a window, watching one more day pass in the history of this piazza. The main shopping streets, lined with great houses, are everywhere converted on the ground floor to the businesses of hardware, dishes, food, and clothing. For many buildings, probably it always has been so.

—Frances Mayes, *Under the Tuscan Sun: At Home in Italy*

★ ✶ ★

Mediolanum

Milan is more than just
fashion and industry.

THE NEXT DAY MY FRIEND TOOK ME TO THE TOP OF [ONE OF]
Milan's…skyscrapers, a thin wedge of concrete that looked like the
work of architecturally minded termites, and from the roof we
looked into the dizzy depths of the streets below us, and outward
to the green Plain of Lombardy. In the densely inhabited portions,
which stretched for miles round the city, men were assembling
motor cars, making…radios and, by no means the least interesting,
arms and ammunition, a Milanese industry which extends back in
time to the spears and breastplates of the Legions and the armour
of mediaeval knights. Except in times of emergency and peril, I
suppose the sound of hammered metal has been heard in Milan
since the city was founded. How strange, as one looks down upon
such a spread of human energy, to reflect that men may be making aircraft or television sets today upon the same ground where
their forefathers of the Middle Ages mixed a little silver with the
metal of their hawk bells.

Mei thinkes these Milan bels do sound too full
And spoile the mounting of your hawke,

wrote Thomas Heywood, though the opposite view was held by

the sporting nun of St. Albans, Juliana Berners, who liked the two-toned silver bells of Milan and thought them best of all, and the most expensive.

What is there, I wondered, about some places which consecrates them to human industry even in the face of what would seem impossible disasters? Milan suffered forty-four sieges; it was vanquished thirty-eight times, and was razed to the ground twice. Yet time after time the inhabitants rebuilt their walls, their homes and their workshops.

Beyond the miles of streets and factories we saw the green plain with its rich alluvial soil, intersected with irrigation channels and with windbreaks of acacia and poplar. The descendants of mulberry trees planted centuries ago are still feeding the silk-worms, that ancient obsession of Lombardy, and fields of maize, wheat, barley, and rice stretched as far as I could see. To the north, looming in silhouette against the sky, I saw the Alps from whose passes the barbarians poured centuries ago to burgle the pleasant Roman world.

My companion was interested only in new suburbs and town planning, and after a time we began to bore each other since we were concerned with two different Milans—and both of them invisible! His Milan had not yet been born, and my Milan had vanished centuries ago.

As far as I know, the history of Mediolanum, or Roman Milan, has never been adequately written; and what a story it is. When the Emperors deserted Rome for military reasons about A.D. 300, they made Milan their capital, and for almost a century, while the imperial palaces stood deserted on the Palatine Hill in Rome, Milan was the most important city of the Roman west. Its provincial air vanished as architects built new and splendid buildings, as merchants flocked in from east and west, and as the luxury trades followed the court. The poet Ausonius, tutor to one of the princes, who lived in the "Golden House," as the palace was called, has described the city as he saw it, glittering behind its walls with palaces and long marble colonnades surmounted with statues, where the citizens, as in Rome, could walk in shade during the summer and in shelter during the winter. He described a whole quarter of the city devoted to bathing, known as the Baths of Hercules, after the Emperor Maximianus. The coins which poured from the Imperial Mint were stamped with the letters MD or MED—Mediolanum. They often turn up at London coin auctions, the only visible relics, apart from a line of marble columns, of the vanished capital of the later Western Empire.

As I looked from a skyscraper upon the busy city, it was not possible to trace a Roman pattern in its streets, for no plan of the old city exists, but, I thought, in a similar crowded scene the last Emperors of the West had held court, and led their armies across the Alps to put down the barbarian raids. Milan was the scene in 313 A.D. of one of the most important events in the history of Western man. The victorious Emperor, Constantine the Great, issued from the "Golden House" the famous Edict of Milan, which granted freedom of worship to Christians and emptied the prisons and the mines of Christ's limping champions. During the first Christian council that soon followed, many of the attending bishops appeared on crutches, some maimed in the torture chamber and others scarred with the branding-iron. Such were the men who drew up the Nicene Creed. It is said that Constantine saluted one by kissing his empty eye-socket, surely one of the most extraordinary acts recorded of a Roman Emperor. If the story is true, possibly Constantine was not, as some scholars have believed, an entirely cynical convert.

One remembers, too, that Milan was the scene of the final battle between Christianity and paganism. Somewhere in the city, on a site now carrying maybe some massive erection of steel and concrete where the typewriters rattle, St. Ambrose, Bishop of Milan, wrote those famous letters to Rome which led to the expulsion of the golden Victory of Tarentum from the Senate House. Perhaps it was in the church which stood where the cathedral is now standing that St. Augustine was baptized by St. Ambrose. Somewhere else, where the domes and campanili of churches may be seen above the clustered roofs, St. Ambrose spoke the funeral orations over the bodies of four Emperors. Always, in Milan, one comes back to St. Ambrose. Even members of the local Communist Party like to refer to themselves as "Ambrosiani," and you cannot read newspaper printed in the diocese without coming across a reference to Milan as "the Ambrosian City." So much has happened since Ambrose was bishop of the city nearly seventeen centuries ago, so many sieges, burnings, and two complete obliterations, yet the corporate memory of Milan flies over the great gap of time to that Roman lawyer-churchman on every conceivable occasion. He is Milan's Romulus, Remus, and wolf all in one, and Milan's image of him is one of the oldest loyalties in Europe.

My friend came over and nudged me, feeling no doubt that I was not paying attention. He swept his arm across the horizon, indicating the site of new marshalling yards, new factories, new suburbs. He seemed to me like the spirit of Milan: that restless, acquisitive spirit which has led this great city through so many adventures to the busy present day. We returned to the lifts, and were transported silently to earth.

During one of my early-morning walks I came unexpectedly upon the Ambrosian Basilica. Glancing through a gate across an austere paved atrium, I saw an old church which stands many centuries below the modern street level. It reminded me of early churches in Rome such as St. Clemente or St. Celilia, both of which have retained similar paved courtyards. The basilica of St. Ambrose, with its air of Roman gravity, its silence and peace, and, above all, its antiquity, was a contrast to the lively morning bustle in the streets near by, where trams and buses were rumbling along, bearing to work the first wave of clerks and typists.

Crossing the atrium, I entered a dark Lombardic church, cold as an ice-box. As I stood shivering, I noticed a glimmer of light under the high altar. I walked towards it and, descending a flight of steps entered a crypt where a number of old women dressed in black were waiting for early Mass to begin. They looked like a secret society or a gathering of primitive Christians. The verger hurried down with a bunch of keys. He unlocked the altar-piece in four places, and with four different keys, and this was then revealed as four painted steel panels which he cranked down into slots or grooves. As he did so, he revealed the object they had concealed and protected. As this came into view, the old women fell upon their knees and crossed themselves, for they were in the presence of one of the world's most awesome survivals.

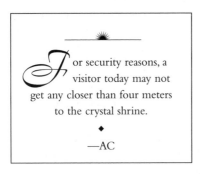

or security reasons, a visitor today may not get any closer than four meters to the crystal shrine.

♦

—AC

All I could see at first was a sheet of plate-glass, but when the verger switched on the lights a gruesome and extraordinary sight sprang into view. Three clothed skeletons were lying side by side upon a bed, or bier, within a crystal shrine, the central skeleton resting upon a higher level than those on its right and left. This was my first sight of the bones of St. Ambrose, whose remains have been preserved in the basilica since his death in Mediolanum in 397 A.D. An antique mitre rested upon the saint's skull, upon the finger-bones were red episcopal gloves, upon the skeleton feet were golden slippers, and in the crook of the arm-bones lay a crozier. The skeletons on each side are those of the martyrs, St. Gervasius and St. Protasius, of whom little is known except that they were Roman soldiers said to have died for their faith long before the time even of St. Ambrose. Ambrose, who was a law unto himself, exhumed these martyrs and placed their bones in his basilica at a time when the Latin Church forbade the removal of saintly bones. This was, therefore, the first translation of relics into a Western Church, for the custom did not become general until after the desecration of the Catacombs many centuries later.

Immediately the Mass was over, the verger cranked up the steel shutters and no one could have imagined what lay on the other side. The bones of the great Roman bishop are rightly too sacred to be one of the sights of Milan, and I was interested, in the days that followed, to find out, when talking to visitors, how few who had been to the basilica were aware that the relics of St. Ambrose are preserved there.

Naturally, one asks oneself what is the history of such an amazing relic? Are the bones authentic? How do we know that the skeleton is really that of St. Ambrose?

The saint died on the night of Good Friday in the year 397 A.D. On the following day his body lay in state in St. Maria Maggiore, the predecessor of Milan Cathedral. The next day, Easter Sunday, it was placed in a sarcophagus of porphyry and interred beneath the altar of his own Ambrosian Basilica, and, as he had requested, between the bones of St. Gervasius and St. Protasius. There it remained untouched for nearly 450 years, throughout all the barbarian invasions. In 835 A.D. the Golden Altar, which still exists in the church above, was put into position, and while making the foundations for this the three burials were found below. The bones of St. Ambrose, together with those of the two saints, were placed in the porphyry sarcophagus, and this was reburied beneath the new altar. There they remained untouched for 1,029 years, which brings us to the year 1864.

When restorations were being made to the church in that year, the sarcophagus, flanked by two empty *loculi*, was found and was seen to contain the three skeletons. As soon as the lid was removed a careful drawing was made, which can be seen in the Archives of the Basilica; it is also reproduced in *Il Nostro Sommo Padre*, by E. Bernasconi, which can be found in any Milan bookshop. This was a difficult time for the Church in Italy, and it was not until after the establishment of the Italian State in 1870 that a scientific examination of bones was made two years later. In 1873 Pius IX gave his authority to their authenticity, and during the examination an English visitor was present who described his impressions in a letter to Cardinal Newman. So far as I know, this letter has been printed only by Edward Hutton in *The Cities of Lombardy*.

The original is, so Mr. Hutton tells me, in the Birmingham Oratory, and the writer's name was Newman's friend, St. John.

"I was accidentally allowed to be present," wrote Mr. St. John, "at a private exposition of the relics of St. Ambrose and the Sts. Gervasius and Protasius. I have seen complete every bone in St. Ambrose' body. There were present a great many clergy, three *medici*, and Father Secchi, who was there, on account of his great knowledge of the Catacombs, to testify to the age etc., of the remains.... On a large table surrounded by ecclesiastics and medical men were three skeletons. The two were of immense size and very much alike, and bore the marks of a violent death; their age was determined to be about twenty-six years. When I entered the room Father Secchi was examining the marks of martyrdom on them. Their throats had been cut with great violence, and the neck vertebrae were injured on the inside. The *pomum Adami* had been broken, or was not there: I forget which. This bone was quite perfect in St. Ambrose; his body was wholly uninjured; the lower jaw (which was broken in one of the two martyrs) was wholly uninjured in him, beautifully formed, and every tooth, but one molar in the lower jaw, quite perfect and white and regular. His face had been long, thin, oval, with a high arched forehead. His bones were nearly white; those of the other two were very dark. His fingers long and very delicate; his bones were a marked contrast to those of the two martyrs."

The writer does not mention a peculiarity of the skull of St. Ambrose which puzzled the doctors. The right upper eye tooth was deeply set in such a way as to suggest a slight facial deformity. It was left to Achille Ratti, afterwards Pope Pius XI, to point out in 1897, when Assistant Librarian and Prefect of the Ambrosian Library in Milan, that the right eye of St. Ambrose was slightly lower than the other. In support of this theory, he drew attention to the earliest portrait of the saint, the fifth century mosaic in the Ambrosian Basilica, in which this deformity is unmistakable, but until then it had been considered a defect due to the deficiency of the artist. The mosaic may therefore be a true portrait which reflects the recollections of those who knew the saint. He is seen wearing a tunic and dalmatic, a typical Roman of the fourth century, dark-eyed and dark-haired, with an oval face and a close-cut beard covering his cheeks and chin.

I returned to the basilica morning after morning, the only man among all the old women, until the priest, if he noticed me at all, must have thought me the most devout character in Milan. The skeleton of St. Ambrose fascinated me. I never tired of watching the sides of the altar-piece crank down to reveal what I consider one of the most impressive sights in Europe.

H. V. Morton was born in 1892 and died in 1979 in Capetown, South Africa. He was the author of many wonderful travel books, including A Traveller in Italy, *from which this piece was excerpted.*

✳

A public relations genius could lure tourists to Milan simply by reeling off the names of tram and bus stops: Gioia, Passione, Magenta, Botticelli. The tourists who come to Milan stop here principally to see the cathedral and *The Last Supper—Il Cenacolo.* Leonardo da Vinci's masterpiece is to the left of a Renaissance church, Santa Maria della Grazie, in what used to be the Dominican friars' refectory—and very austere, not to say bleak, the refectory must have been. I went back several times and never found the church—which is said to have a lovely Baroque chapel—open; "abroad is always close," even its churches.

Il Cenacolo has been restored so many times; the building that houses it was bombed on August 16, 1943; protected by sandbags, the end wall on which *The Last Supper* is painted remained standing; the walls on which Leonardo painted in oils were always damp...How faded it is! By craning your neck, you can see the Son of God in prescient isolation, betrayed so that, according to solemn doctrine, we might live. Judas is more clearly present, in the dim fresco, than is Christ. The great work seems to be vaporizing before our eyes, its mortal music thinning. But to stand in its presence is unutterably moving. "Behold the hand that betrayeth me," Jesus said; Leonardo didn't use an arrangement of hands simply as a means to solve a technical problem. One is conscious of that hand, it is like a blow to the heart; it is also a glory; Judas's betrayal set in motion the wheels of salvation. And the photographs of the bombed refectory (the roof and one wall were destroyed) are a kind of counterpoint to Leonardo's work: They tell us that the Prince of Peace is betrayed daily.

—Barbara Grizzuti Harrison, *Italian Days*

MIRANDA MOWBRAY

✦ ✦ ✦

The Invisible *Trattoria*

Grills in the mist.

HAVE YOU EVER HEARD OF THE INVISIBLE *TRATTORIA*, A *TRATTORIA* in the middle of the Po Valley, but which from the road by which you arrive sardined together in the car you would swear that there was no *trattoria*, just a little shop, you enter and it's a shop and that's all, and you go on through a door at the back of the shop and into a little bare whitewashed room with ordinary tables and chairs, it can't be a *trattoria*, then you sit down and they bring you food of legend, food which you don't believe can exist, and at the end of uncountable dishes they bring you a bill which is impossible, it must come to more than that, but no really, and you leave along the road across the flat plain and from the rear window you see that there is no *trattoria*, there can't be, there's a little shop and that's all?

I'd heard stories like that at dinner parties in London when I was a schoolgirl, during the sticky pudding course and just before I was sent upstairs to read my book of Ancient Greek Legends under the blankets while the grownups stayed talking late into the night. I knew that the stories were just travellers' tall tales invented to make stay-at-homes jealous. But then I became a grownup myself, with Italian friends; and when I went to meet my friends in the Po valley, they took me to the invisible *trattoria*.

Wasn't there something about the Po in that book of legends? Yes. The standard version is that it was in the Aegean Sea that the beautiful boy Icarus drowned, when he fell from the sky. The version that I read claimed, eccentrically, that he fell into the river Po.

In the car on the way to the *trattoria* I was thinking about someone who used to sing with me. A lovely light voice. His death had shocked me into understanding that you must make friends, spend time with your friends, be with your friends, because our time together is limited, and what remains of us is in the hearts of our friends.

The flavours of the food of Emilia-Romagna are rich, intense, and very delicate. At the invisible *trattoria* the food seemed on the brink of nonexistence. There was Parma ham and shoulder of pork which were like eating the idea of these dishes separated from the corporeal part, *pancetta* which seemed liquid in my mouth, *cappellati* in broth and *tagliatelle* about to fly up out of the plate countergravity, *polenta* with a subtlety that was almost spiritual. And the *stracotto di asinello*, a dish which logically should weigh on the stomach like a rhinoceros, was rich and satisfying but light, light, a rhinoceros with wings.

I felt a pathos in the invisible *trattoria*. The feeling of eating those delicacies was too similar to that of seeing friends for too short a time. Everything seemed to lead to the same emotion, an intense pleasure which quickly evaporated. Like the rosy bubbles on the red wine. Like the tenuous, fragile moment when I put into my mouth the first *cappellato*. Like the mist over the river Po. Like the sunset and our dark silhouettes against a *polenta*-coloured sky. Like the touch of a hand to say good-bye. Like the *trattoria* that became invisible once more. Who knows when I may find it again.

Miranda Mowbray is a soprano mathematician. Her hair is red. She likes mango ice-cream, and lives in Bristol, England.

★

If soul immortal is, and winds its way
Into the body at the birth of man,
Why can we not remember something, then,
Of life-time spent before? why keep we not
Some footprints of the things we did of old?

—Lucretius, "On the Nature of Things"

PART TWO

SOME THINGS TO DO

TOM MUELLER

*　*　*

Underground Rome

"Downtown" means something different here.

BENEATH MODERN ROME IS A HIDDEN CITY, AS STILL AS ROME IS chaotic, as dark as Rome is luminous, with its own peculiar animals, powerful odors, frigid waters, and spectacular ancient remains. Explorers will find theaters, baths, stadia, imperial villas, apartment buildings, fire stations, and pagan temples—even an enormous sundial that used an Egyptian obelisk as a pointer. Millions of people come to Rome each year in search of antiquity, and walk unsuspectingly across these buried treasures during their tours of the celebrated surface ruins. Though structures like the Pantheon and the Coliseum are certainly impressive, they represent only a small fraction of the ancient city, and wind, rain, and air pollutants have not treated them kindly over the years. Wrapped in a thick protective blanket of earth, Rome's subterranean structures have endured the incessant chiseling of people and elements far better. With persistence and the occasional help of a guide, a visitor can explore this underground realm, to discover bright windows on Roman history and clues to the evolution of the modern city long vanished from the surface.

Ancient Rome slipped from sight gradually, in a 2,500-year process of natural silting and intentional burial that was already

well advanced in classical times. Roman architects frequently tore
the roofs from old buildings and filled their interiors with dirt, to
make solid foundations for new structures. They embedded earlier
buildings in tremendous landfills that raised the ground level of
the entire site by several yards. Sometimes they entombed whole
neighborhoods in this way. After the Great Fire of 64 A.D. devastated two-thirds of the city, Nero spread the debris over the wreck-
age of republican Rome and then reshaped the city to his liking.
Later, during Rome's long, bleak Middle Ages, nature continued
the interment. The population shrank to tiny pockets within the
broad ring of the imperial walls, abandoning the ancient city to
relentless erosion that wore away the uplands and redistributed
them over low-lying areas. Roman buildings that remained exposed contributed significantly to the landfill. Archaeologists have
estimated that the collapse of a one-story Roman house produced
detritus six feet deep over its entire plan. Considering that Rome
once boasted 40,000 apartment buildings, 1,800 palaces and numerous giant public buildings, of which almost nothing survives, it
is clear that the ancient city is buried under its own remains.

By 1850, when Montaigne visited Rome, the classical city was
all but invisible. He observed that when modern Romans dug into
the ground, they frequently struck the capitals of tall columns still
standing far below. "They do not seek any other foundations for
their houses than old ruined buildings or vaults, such as are seen at
the bottom of all the cellars." Impressed by the spectacle of the tri-
umphal arches of the Forum rising from deep in the earth, he
noted, "It is easy to see that many [ancient] streets are more than
thirty feet below those of today." Even now the burial process continues. Each year an inch of dust falls on Rome, composed of
leaves, pollution, sand from the nearby seacoast, and a stream of
powder from hundreds of ruins dissolving steadily in the wind. In
certain places we are more than ten yards farther from ancient
Rome than Montaigne was.

A good place to begin exploring Rome's layers is San
Clemente, a 12th-century basilica just east of the Coliseum.

Descend the staircase in the sacristy and you find yourself in a rectangular hall decorated with fading frescoes and greenish marbles, lit by sparse bulbs strung up by the excavators. This is the original, 4th-century San Clemente, one of Rome's first churches. It was condemned around 1100 A.D. and packed full of earth, Roman-style, as a platform for the present basilica. A narrow stair near the apse of this lower church leads down to the 1st-century structures upon which it, in turn, was built: a Roman apartment house and a small temple. The light is thinner here; cresses and fungi patch the dark brick and grow delicate halos on the walls behind the bare bulbs. Deeper still, on the fourth level, are several rooms from an enormous public building that was apparently destroyed in the Great Fire and then buried by Nero's architects. At about a dozen yards below ground the massive tufa blocks and herringbone brickwork are slick with humidity, and everywhere is the sound of water, flowing in original Roman pipes. No one has excavated below this level, but something is there, for the tufa walls run another twenty feet or so down into the earth. Something is buried beneath everything in Rome.

Most major landmarks, in fact, rest on construction that leads far back into the past. Tucked under Michelangelo's salmon-pink Senatorial Palace on the Capitoline Hill is a tidy little temple to Veiovis, a youthful Jove of the underworld, among the most ancient gods of the Roman pantheon. Beneath the sanctuary excavators have found traces of a still earlier shrine. A small passageway in the south exterior wall of St. Peters' Basilica leads into an eerily intact Roman necropolis that underlies the entire center aisle. The passage becomes the main street of a miniature city of the dead, fronted by ornate two-story mausoleums on which Christ and the Apostles stand alongside Apollo, Iris, Bacchus, and rampaging satyrs. This necropolis first came to light in the Renaissance, when the basilica was rebuilt: pontiffs and architects watched in horror as an endless stream of pagan relics issued from the floor of Catholicism's most sacred church.

In the cellar of the massive, four-square Palazzo della Cancelleria, in the heart of Rome, is a stretch of the Euripus, an ornamental canal that traversed this area, once a garden district. Now far below ground, it still brims with water, clear and un-earthly blue. Writing from exile, a homesick Ovid fondly recalled the Euripus flowing between elegant lawns and porticoes. Ancient graffiti still visible beside the canal express less-elevated sentiments. "Scummy Ready-for-Anything gives it to her lovers all the time," an anonymous Roman penned in careful letters. "Crap well," another wrote just beside, either in response or as a general exhortation to passers-by.

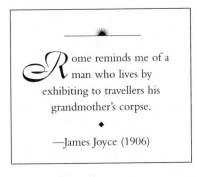

*R*ome reminds me of a man who lives by exhibiting to travellers his grandmother's corpse.

◆

—James Joyce (1906)

Striking subterranea underlie the most ordinary scenes. A trap-door in the courtyard of a bustling apartment complex on Via Taranto, not far from San Giovanni in Laterno, opens upon two perfect Roman graves, festooned with fresco grapevines and pomegranates, bewailed by red and blue tragic masks, guarded by mosaic goddesses. The non-descript *palazzo* at Via della VII Coorte 9, in the Trastevere district across the river, sits atop a complete Roman fire station, with its broad internal courtyard and central fountain, sleeping quarters, latrine, and shrine to the divinity who protected firemen. The busy train tracks on the eastern border of Porta Maggiore conceal a mysterious hall known as the Underground Basilica, apparently the temple of a 1st-century neo-Pythagorean cult. Handsome mosaic floors, three aisles, and semi-circular apse give it the look of a church, but stucco friezes on the walls show Orpheus leading Eurydice back from Hades, Heracles rescuing Hesione from the sea monster, and other scenes of mythological deliverance.

The grandest of all Roman subterranea lies beneath the shabby gardens on the eastern slopes of the Esquiline Hill, where home-less immigrants sleep and children play roughneck soccer against the startlingly big backdrop of the Coliseum. An entrance of crumbling brickwork leads down into the Golden House, a vast, megalomaniacal residence that Nero built atop ruins from the Great Fire; his successors, after damning Nero's memory, covered it with the Coliseum and other public buildings. An entire wing of the villa is buried here—a labyrinth of corridors, vaulted chambers, and domed halls immersed in total darkness. Here and there a flashlight will illumine sections of the original Roman decoration: landscapes alive with mythological beasts and odd anthropomorphic figures. These frescoes attracted the greatest artists of the Renaissance, who clambered down with torches to sketch the drawings, hold merry picnics of apples, prosciutto, and wine, and scratch their names unselfconsciously into the plaster (many famous autographs, including Domenico Ghirlandaio, Martin van Heemskerck, and Filippino Lippi, are still visible). They emerged from these underground rooms—"grottoes," as they called them—to decorate Rome in a new, "grotesque" style.

Exploring Rome's subterranea, one learns certain rules of thumb. Low-lying areas like Trastevere, which millennia of floods have paved in heavy layers of silt, are rich in sites. Even better are zones that have been continuously inhabited since classical times (the Campo Marzio, for example, with the Pantheon at its center), where subterranea

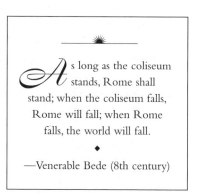

As long as the coliseum stands, Rome shall stand; when the coliseum falls, Rome will fall; when Rome falls, the world will fall.

♦

—Venerable Bede (8th century)

have escaped the violence of deep modern foundations. For much the same reason churches make excellent hunting. In many crypts and side chapels are shadowy locked doorways that the sacristan can often be persuaded to open, for a modest contribution. They lead down to Roman baths, taverns, prisons, military barracks, brothels, and other remains. Pagan temples are especially common, perhaps because Christian builders wanted to occupy and eradicate the sacred places of competing religions. Beneath the polished marble floors of San Clemente, Santa Prisca, Santo Stefano Rotondo, and several other churches are shrines to Mithras, an Iranian god of truth and salvation who was one of Jesus's main rivals during the later empire. These snug, low-roofed halls are flanked by benches where the worshippers reclined, with a niche at the far end for the cult statue: a heroic young Mithras in a flowing cape, plunging his sword into the neck of an enormous bull. By the warm light of torches all-male congregations once worshipped Mithras here in strange rites of water and blood, vaguely suggested in graffiti still visible beneath Santa Prisca: "Sweet are the livers of the birds, but worry reigns." "And you redeemed us by shedding the eternal blood."

For some Romans the hidden city beneath their feet has become an obsession. The photographer Carlo Pavia, lean and intense, has for the past twenty years rappelled down into ancient mines and apartment houses, scuba-dived in underground halls filled with icy groundwater, and pulled on hip waders and a gas mask and slogged back into the Cloaca Maxima, an ancient sewer that winds its way beneath much of Rome. He describes unearthly scenes: colonies of fat albino worms; rats as big as lapdogs; African and Arabian plants flourishing in the rooms beneath the Coliseum, grown from seeds fallen from the coats of exotic animals imported by the Romans for their entertainments. Packets of *saltericchi*, a kind of jumping spider, rove the deepest, most humid recesses. "At the first sign of light they panic and start hopping around," Pavia explains. "I have to move carefully, shooing them ahead of me with my lamp." Pavia even founded a magazine, *Forma Urbis*, that each month illustrates selected sites with his outstanding photographs.

Other subterraneophiles are less athletic but equally obsessed. Emanuele Gatti is a round, jovial retiree who has devoted much of his life to underground Rome. As a government archaeologist he oversaw more than thirty years' worth of construction projects in the historic center, and he has fleshed out his experiences with painstaking archival research to produce a detailed map of ancient remains—a kind of x-ray that lays a faint modern city over the sharp, clear bones of its subterranea. He runs his hand over the sea of symbols and annotations that is his magnum opus, eagerly indicating points of contact between the two worlds. "See here how the façade of the Parliament building rests directly on the façade of Alexander's Baths? Ancient walls still support modern buildings like this throughout the city. They are still 'alive,' you might say."

A few years ago Bartolomeo Mazzotta, then a graduate student in archaeology, assembled a handful of fellow experts to form Itinera, one of several tour services that specialize in underground Rome. These services provide the best way to explore many subterranea, presenting a detailed introduction to the history and archaeology of the sites and supplying government permits that are difficult for individuals to arrange. For a modest fee you join a group of ten to twenty on a visit that lasts about an hour. Though the commentary is normally in Italian, most guides can field questions in English as well. Veteran visitors bring a flashlight, wear sturdy shoes that will give good traction on wet ground, and drape a sweater or shawl over their shoulders, as subterranea are often chilly even in the summer.

Most of the tour services schedule their visits months in advance and have a devoted following, so it is a good idea to book by telephone at least two weeks ahead. The best ones, such as Itinera, are run by trained archaeologists with years of experience below ground. Other good choices include Genti e Paesi ad Città Nascosta, which generally take a more historical or art-historical approach. All these will arrange custom tours of multiple sites for groups. A complete listing of scheduled visits appears each week in *Romac'è*, a booklet available at newsstands in Rome and on the World Wide Web. Beyond specific tours he leads, an expert like Mazzotta is a gold mine of information about the best parts of underground Rome to visit, which sites are closed for renovation, and which can be seen without a permit. Mazzotta explains that most tour participants are Romans, who are increasingly eager to explore the lower city. He says, "*Roma sotterranea* is becoming a real cult."

In fact it is a very old cult, though some of its most ardent believers prefer to remain anonymous. Houses and workshops in the older neighborhoods of Rome frequently perch atop ancient remains, which here and there jab stone fingers up through the surface, just as Montaigne witnessed four centuries ago: massive granite columns sprouting from basement floors, Roman brick archways ridging foundation walls. The inhabitants, often elderly Romans whose families have lived in the same buildings for generations, may guard their secret subterranea carefully, fearing eviction by government authorities if word gets out. Gain their trust, however, and they will show off their underground treasures with great pride. They tell of other subterranea—deep tunnels that traverse the city, vast and mysterious sanctuaries and palaces, a realm of oral tradition somewhere between science and legend. These elderly Romans are acutely aware of the lower city beneath their surface lives. Rome, they say, is haunted by its subterranea.

Tom Mueller is a novelist and travel writer who has spent the last decade living in and writing about the Mediterranean world and, in particular, his favorite country on Earth: Italy.

★

The attachment of the Roman troops to their standards was inspired by the united influence of religion and of honour. The golden eagle, which glittered in the front of the legion, was the object of their fondest devotion; nor was it esteemed less impious than it was ignominious, to abandon that sacred ensign in the hour of danger. These motives, which derived their strength from the imagination, were enforced by fears and hopes of a more substantial kind. Regular pay, occasional donatives, and a stated recompense, after the appointed term of service, alleviated the hardships of the military life, whilst, on the other hand, it was impossible for cowardice or disobedience to escape the severest punishment. The centurions were authorized to chastise with blows, the generals had a right to punish with death; and it was an inflexible maxim of Roman discipline, that a good soldier should dread his officers far more than enemy. From such laudable arts did the valour of the Imperial troops receive a degree of firmness and docility, unattainable by the impetuous and irregular passions of barbarians.

—Edward Gibbon, *The Decline & Fall of the Roman Empire, Volume I*

SUSAN SPANO

✦ ✦ ✦

Living Briefly Like a Roman

What better therapy could there be?

I WASHED MY CURTAINS AND SCRUBBED MY BATHTUB BEFORE leaving for Rome in September. Someone was going to occupy my Greenwich Village apartment while I was away. I'd never met her, but was already exceedingly fond of her because she had a place in Rome where I was going to stay.

About six months earlier I had listed my apartment in a home-exchange catalogue called "The Invented City," and had then more or less forgotten about it—until the offers started rolling in on my fax machine. There was the house with a "luxury bathroom and courtyard garden beneath an elevated sun deck" in Sydney, and the one-bedroom apartment with "all amenities" in Los Angeles. But then I got a fax in English from a doctor named Laura who lived in Rome. It said: "I have a little, very typical apartment in the most characteristical quarter of Rome: Trastevere. This quarter is very ancient and finds its roots at the end of the Roman Empire. Besides, Trastevere is the very preferred place of musicians, painters, artists coming from every part of the world, almost like Greenwich Village in New York."

It was an apartment swap made in heaven. So I faxed Laura back, specifying when I could come to Rome, and learned that the dates were fine with her. But I didn't know what to do after that—clearly, there were details to work out, like the payment of telephone bills, and it might be wise to exchange references, I thought. But the doctor didn't pick up on this when I suggested it, so I let it drop because I didn't want to offend her by sounding distrustful. Instead, she faxed me saying I could get the keys to her apartment from the super, Mr. Bruno. She also gave me the phone number of her brother, Ugo, in Rome, who would help if I had any problems.

The whole business was like a slightly out-of-sync tango, conducted solely by fax—for the sake of clarity, or so I thought; my Italian is extremely limited and though I could understand the doctor's written English perfectly well, I lacked confidence in our ability to make detailed plans by phone. Still, I'd send a fax raising a certain question and get one back providing a clear answer to something I hadn't asked.

So I called Glenn London, director of "The Invented City," for advice. What about arranging a meeting with my exchange partner, I asked. On the day I was scheduled to leave I could show her my apartment, turn over my keys, learn more about her place in Trastevere, and then head to the airport. Mr. London said he'd done that once when exchanging his place for an apartment in Paris. It had worked out fine, except that when he'd arrived, the key didn't open the lock. Half crazed, he'd broken in, only to find that it was the wrong apartment.

Undaunted, I set up a meeting with Laura for September 19 at my apartment at 2 p.m. "If this doesn't work for you," I wrote, "let me know." I heard nothing more, and hoped silence meant assent. Romans are relaxed people, I decided, and tried to be relaxed, too. However, it didn't help when I finally discovered that the address on Laura's faxes wasn't in Trastevere at all, but near Termini Station. Perhaps that was her office? Anyway, I'd find out everything I needed to know when I met her.

On September 19 at 2 p.m. I had my bags packed and a nonrefundable ticket for a 6:30 flight to Rome in my pocket—but no Laura. At 3 p.m., still no Laura; I took two Ibuprofen. At 4 p.m.,

I went berserk. Where was she? I called brother Ugo to ask. With great cheer, he said Laura had had some last-minute problems at work and hadn't been able to make it to New York, but the apartment was there for me; he even gave me the address. So, wondering where Laura was going to stay if I took her place, and occasionally fantasizing scenarios that had me in the clutches of drug traffickers or worse, I flew off to Rome.

When I arrived at Leonardo da Vinci Airport I caught a train that stopped at Trastevere Station. According to my map, the station was about a half-mile south of my destination, Via Natale del Grande in the heart of Trastevere; so I flagged down a taxi. The friendly driver charged me more than I expected but I was too keyed up to raise a flap.

The Via Natale del Grande, I found, runs between the district's major artery (noisy, traffic-clogged Viale Trastevere) and the Piazza San Cosimato, the scene of a bounteous

*T*he minute you take your seat in a taxi the problem of appropriate interaction with the driver arises. The taxi driver is someone who spends all day driving in city traffic (an activity that provokes either heart attack or delirium), in constant conflict with other human drivers. Consequently, he is nervous and hates every anthromorphic creature. This attitude leads members of the radical chic to say that all taxi drivers are fascists. Not true. The taxi driver has no interest in ideological problems: he hates trade union demonstrations, not for their political orientation, but rather because they block traffic. He would hate a parade of Daughters of the Duce just as much. All he wants is a strong government that will send all private car owners to the gallows and establish a reasonable, but strict curfew— between 6 a.m. and midnight, say. He is a misogynist, but only as regards women who move about. If they stay home and cook pasta, he can tolerate them.

◆

—Umberto Eco, *How to Travel with a Salmon and Other Essays* outdoor market. Next to the big wooden door of Laura's apartment building was a compelling cheese store, and across the street a wine merchant and *pasticceria*. But I reined in my urge to grocery shop, and rang Mr. Bruno, who was clearly expecting me. Up we went in a small, old-fashioned cage elevator to the apartment on the fourth floor. At the door, he gave me the key, then wished me *buona sera*.

The apartment had two big rooms painted white, with framed art posters on the walls, a small kitchen with a stove, refrigerator, and dinette set, and a bathroom with a shower. It was clean, but sparsely furnished. There was a sofa bed, a futon chair and another futon on the floor that could have served as a single bed, a long plywood table, bookcase, and small desk holding a television set with a VCR—but no telephone.

It looked as if the place had been vacated several months earlier, leading me to suspect that Laura actually lived somewhere else (which was later confirmed). Best of all, there were two tall, shuttered windows overlooking the courtyard, painted the color of a ripe cantaloupe; often I sat beside the window in the kitchen, filling my glass from a bottle of 1984 Orvieto Classico and listening to the sound of voices wafting up from below.

Laura had left a welcome note, which included the number of her cellular phone. So I found a phone booth in the Piazza San Cosimato (which I visited so often that the flower merchant in the stall next door came to know me), and called her. She seemed genuinely pleased to hear from me, but was extremely busy with work. We made plans to get together (which unfortunately fell through—twice); she also explained that it was hard for her to arrange her vacations in advance, which made apartment-swapping difficult. I didn't want to press her, but when I mentioned that I'd probably be away from New York for a month in the winter, and that she could use my place, she said she'd try to make a trip then.

For the first few days of my two-week stay (during which the weather remained invariably perfect), I roamed around Trastevere—which occupies a scallop of land on the west bank of the Tiber River, bulging toward the Palatine and Aventine Hills—

in a daze, feeling vaguely guilty. The swap, which at this point was actually an apartment giveaway, seemed too good to be true. What had I done to deserve it?

But I got over it, and simply started living in Trastevere, walking the narrow, winding streets, strung with pennants of drying laundry, and imbibing the intense atmosphere of the place. It was composed mostly of classic Roman apartment houses, with stuccoed walls, wood beams, and sloping tiled roofs, but there were the ruins of a Roman fire station just off the Piazza del Dragon, Renaissance *palazzos* on the Via della Lungara leading north toward St. Peter's, and fortified medieval villas with towers and mullioned windows overlooking the Tiber. In Trastevere, as in the rest of Rome, the architectural remnants of age upon historical age seem to collapse into one another.

However, Trastevere distinguishes itself from the rest of the city because it could very well be a small, self-contained Italian town nowhere near Rome—particularly if you don't venture out of it. And what need, when every barbershop and dentist's office offers something to look at? In the Piazza San Cosimato market, zucchini blossoms worthy of a vase waited for the frying pan, and I bought perfect plump tomatoes, sweet pears, and a cantaloupe. The Pasticceria Sachetti on the *piazza* became my breakfast haunt, where every morning I stood at the counter savoring a caffè latte and a fresh *cornetto*. Afterward, it was on to the Regina Margherita Hospital, just steps to the south, where I found the little 10th-century church of San Cosimoto and a 12th-century cloister surrounded by broken bits of antiquity like the capitals of columns—now resting places for recuperating patients in pajamas; or to the church of San Francesco a Ripa to see Bernini's statue of Beata Lodovica Albertoni in Ecstasy, her garments a miracle in flowing stone; or to the sloping Piazza in Piscinula, hoping—ever in vain—to find the door open at the church of San Benedotto, where St. Benedict is said to have occupied a cell beneath one of the smallest, sweetest campaniles in Rome.

In the *Blue Guide to Rome* (which rarely left my hand), such lovely places merited only brief comment compared with the pages devoted to major sights, like the Forum and Vatican City. But wandering around Trastevere never felt aimless, because the neighborhood had its own notable places to see—above all the church of Santa Maria in Trastevere, with its beautiful 12th- to 13th-century mosaic façade glittering above a *piazza* that serves as the district's soccer field and social center, and Santa Cecilia in Trastevere, built atop the house of St. Cecilia, the patron saint of music who was martyred in 230 A.D.

Just down the street from Santa Cecilia, I found the Borghese Gallery at San Michele, housing spillover artworks from the famous collection in the Museo and Galleria Borghese, including Titian's unnerving *Sacred and Profane Love*, and Raphael's *Portrait of a Woman with a Unicorn*. And on a bright, breezy Sunday morning, I explored the popular but junky flea market at the Trastevere foot of the Ponte Sublico. At the northwest side of the district, the *ribald putti* in the *loggia* of the 16th-century Villa Farnesino (admission free) clearly exhorts visitors to leave their senses of modesty at the door, and the Janiculum Hill above it offers an airy place to jog, city-wide vistas, and Bramante's celebrated "Tempietto"—a small but perfectly proportioned Renaissance edifice in the courtyard of the church of San Pietro in Montorio.

Of course, I did eventually stick my nose outside Trastevere, finding Rome's historic center a fifteen-minute walk over the Ponte Sisto, and the Termini train station (where I bought a ticket for an excursion to Tuscany) also just fifteen minutes away, via the No. 170 bus.

Amazingly, though, thanks to my still-mysterious benefactor, Laura, I rarely worried about my expenses, because I had no hotel bill to pay. I simply did whatever I pleased—be it taking in a movie, shown in English on Monday nights at the Alcazar Theatre down the street from the apartment, buying a small black handbag at the closet-sized leather shop where it was made or splurging at a restaurant near Santa Maria in Trastevere called La Tana de Noantri: small bottles of Egeria mineral water and Valpolicella, mixed antipasti, osso bucco and a dish of radicchio sautéed with anchovies I will long remember.

At night little colonies of tables appeared on sidewalks outside restaurants, beckoning and boasting, as the novelist Elizabeth Bowen put it, "a diversity to choose from, and if the diversity is almost the same as yesterday's at a similar restaurant, what matter?" The long and the short of it is, I never had a bad meal in Trastevere. I'd give especially high marks to the chicken *saltimbocca alla romana* at pleasant little Da Carlone on Via della Luce and the pizzas from Ivo's on Via San Francesco a Ripa, where I particularly liked to place to-go orders, because it allowed me to stand by the big marble slab where the pizza chef worked.

Most of all, though, I will remember sitting on the steps of the fountain in the Piazza Santa Maria in Travestere, flipping the pages of Henryk Sienkiewicz's florid, deeply sentimental *Quo Vadis*. In the novel, Rome burned while Nero fiddled; meanwhile back in the *piazza*, sunset bathed the umbrella pines on the Janiculum Hill in garish pink.

Needless to say, when the time came it pained me to vacate Laura's apartment in Trastevere, I spent a morning sweeping, cleaning, and doing laundry, to leave the place in good order. And I bought Laura a bottle of fine

> *T*here is nothing like the smell of a *trattoria* in Rome. Italian restaurants elsewhere have as much relation to a Roman *trattoria* as pornography has to great sex.
>
> In Rome when the doors to a *trattoria* are opened, in one grand sniff the meal is revealed in the small mosaics of its parts, similar to the way an overture gives you a musical sample of what is to come. Prosciutto, salami, garlic, onions, oregano, wine, coffee, bread, olive oil, fresh white linen, vinegar, vigorous noise and convivial clatter, stone, dampness, marble, and almonds chorale into libidinousness which is stopped, (but no one realizes it) by the formality of the place and the starch and snap of the waiters.
>
> ◆
>
> —George Vincent Wright, *Cuisine Sauvage*

French Champagne as a thank-you gift. Though if you ask me, what she really deserves is a vacation in New York.

Susan Spano, a Lowell Thomas award winner, writes destination travel stories for both The New York Times *and the* Los Angeles Times. *In addition, she now has a regular Sunday travel column,* Her World, *which appears in the* Los Angeles Times.

✳

A man asked her why she was going to Rome. To ask my husband for a divorce, she thought; to tell my mother the truth. "Because of all the cities of the world I love Rome best," she said, which was true. The man—a Milanesi—said: "Rome is a sewer. A pestilence. Even the Romans hate their city. You see it written all over—SPQR: *Sono porchi questi Romani*—'They are pigs, these Romans.' A city for animals. Have a fig." How she loved Italians, so unruly.

—Barbara Grizzuti Harrison, *The Astonishing World: Essays*

GEORGIA I. HESSE

* * *

Cinque Terre

Here's a place to lose yourself,
but not your footing.

ONCE UPON A TIME THERE WERE FIVE LANDS, AND YOU COULDN'T get there from here. They were named, from north to south, Monterosso, Vernazza, Corniglia, Manarola, and Riomaggiore. They perched like afterthoughts above Italy's wild Ligurian coast and were called, collectively, the Cinque Terre. They had been around forever but we had heard of them only last Thursday.

Ken, Dariel, and I lunched outdoors at Taverna del Marinaio by the harbor in Portofino, our chairs creaking companionably on the cobbles as we consumed a certain amount of *spaghetti alle vongole* and toasted the golden day with the red wine of the house. The afternoon stretched out like a lazy dog.

As the sun sank, it seemed time to move south, in search of some place small and cozy to sleep. Somehow, we found ourselves at the menacing, black mouth of a tunnel, stuck at a red light. We waited, cool with contentment, as the minutes clicked by and cars stacked up behind us.

Then it was our turn. The light greened and we plunged into the tortuous tunnel that takes you to Moneglia and, if you survive, to the Cinque Terre.

Narrow, black, rough-walled as a mine, our burrow bore

123

through the very bowels of the earth. Faster, faster, deeper, deeper, we careened around inky blind curves, pursued by mad Italians: we were Alice, falling down the rabbit hole, and we giggled like children in a fun house.

We exited from Middle Earth in Moneglia, where the Locanda Maggiore hotel graciously accepted us despite its closed for the season sign.

Next day, in more sober but still antic style, we motored the few kilometers to Monterosso and settled, with sighs, into the 43-room Porto Roca overhanging the sea. On the horizon, green mountains climbed away toward Genoa.

In Monterosso, the medieval Aurora Tower stands on an outcrop called Cappuccini and divides the new town from the old. Small, sheltered, and shut-off Monterosso may be, but flyers everywhere announced the concert of a choir and orchestra from Lerici, bragged of a symphony from London.

We lunched on delicacies from the sea at Pensione R. Moretto and learned to like the local wine, *Sciacchetra*. (A handful of years later, my mother would dub it Scratchy Terra, which well defines its earthy essence.)

What one is expected to do in the Cinque Terre is to take the little train (one Prince Albert might have designed to carry guests from London out to the Crystal Palace) from the village of Monterosso (the first "land") to Riomaggiore (the fifth "land") and then to walk the walk back to Manarola (the fourth "land"). What some fools do is different.

Departing Monterosso at 9:01 one sparkling morning, we arrived in Riomaggiore at 9:14, having coasted through Vernazza in four minutes, Corniglia in five more, and Manarola in another three. The train cuts through the cliffs like (as Ken, the artist, put it) an arrow shot through a pleated skirt.

The ancient houses of Riomaggiore stand on each other's shoulders in a narrow valley sliced by streams. There are houses in pink, houses in gray, houses in homely indiscriminate shades, all fronted with green shutters battened against the brilliance of the sea-reflected sun.

We inspected the local church; we bought fresh, still-warm grapes by the bunch from a woman with relatives in the Bronx; we stepped out along the panoramic parade that leads to Manarola, the *Via dell'Amore*. So much beauty is dangerous; you want to wing off into the view as you do so easily in dreams.

So far, so smooth: a mere amble, we agreed it was, as we reached Manarola. Too bad it is too early to stop for lunch at Aristide with its seductive seafood smells. But we have our *Sciacchetra,* our *pane* and *formaggio* and a local sausage, so let's carry on to Corniglia.

My notebook gives out after Manarola. I have no record of the surfeit of steps that climb from the sea toward the *piazza* in Corniglia, no hint of the hot-dust path we plodded steeply up and always up, no note of the nagging weight of cameras or of our collapse in the blessed shade of an olive grove from which we gazed back at the wicked way we had come.

As we swilled the *Sciacchetra*, all the dogs in the village below burst into barks, quieted only when Ken broke into manic operatic voice. It would never go at La Scala, but it certainly silenced Cinque Terre.

Then I heard Byron's ghost speak: "There is a pleasure in the trackless woods/There is a rapture on the lonely shore." I forgot—for a moment—my feet. "Open my heart and you shall see/Graven inside of it—Italy."

When you have trudged so far, there is no way back, no way out. You are committed. Our track (I think now we were on the wrong one) had left the sea and wound up, around, up to a minuscule settlement not on our map. The rest of the day is a blur, a haze, a plod: we felt as stubborn and uncaring and mindless as mules. Somewhere en route, I became a medieval European, laboring leagues from walled town to walled town only to arrive after sunset to find the gates locked.

In the woods above Vernazza, the second "land," Dariel dropped into the autumn leaves. "Ken," she almost sobbed, "go on. And tell the children I've always loved them."

While Ken debated, I scurried into the village and into a bar and when the two wearies staggered from the shadows I (with the help of a bemused barman) had a table, three chairs, and three huge beers waiting in the middle of the street.

Twilight flickered on. The will said mush, you huskies. But the feet failed. Darkness approached and so did a train. We boarded it.

Back on our terrace at Porto Roca, we drank everything at hand, displayed our wounds to each other, and sighed significantly, heroes escaped from the wars. No one can know the trouble we'd seen: glory, hallelujah.

Once upon a time, I walked from the fifth to the second land. Once upon another time, I will make it to the first.

Georgia Hesse was the founding travel editor for the San Francisco Examiner *and spent twenty years in that position. She has traveled to 181 countries, authoring guidebooks on France and North America. She was awarded the French Order of Merit and recently graced the cover of the travel misadventure book,* I Should Have Stayed Home: The Worst Trips of Great Writers. *She lives in San Francisco.*

★

We dined our last evening under the yellow-striped awning of a trattoria nestled amid the pedestrian by-ways of Monterosso. It was one of those meals you wish would never end: the food, the star-bright evening, the company, all perfect. Afterward, we strolled toward the village's largest *piazza* which was ringed with chairs that faced a stage. Overflowing with instruments, amplifiers and speakers, it appeared that tonight's entertainment was to be a rock concert.

Just as the first bolt of lightning stung the sky, followed almost instantly by thunder, the young, long-haired musicians struck their first note. Jamie's jaw dropped. If Lawrence Welk and the polka had been Italian, this is what his orchestra might have played.

"Let's go."

"Just a minute; people are starting to dance."

And dance they did: chiseled Adonis's and bronzed beauties; fathers and mothers, children and grandmothers; grandmothers and grandmothers. They whirled and spun, their feet as one in intricate steps, arms entwined, they danced until the sky opened and drenched us all with raindrops the size of gnocchi.

Everyone scattered. We ran with many others under the raised concrete train trestle. Lightning flashed. Thunder barreled down the canyons. Wind raised goose-bumps on our wet flesh. Rainwater washed around our ankles on its way to the sea. Lovers kissed and clung. Small children climbed their parents and hung there like stacked cherubs. Grandmothers danced in place.

"Listen," I said.

Sweet swells of magnificent high-pitched twittering swept around us. It sounded as if we were swaying in the treetops with an excited flock of red-winged blackbirds. It was the Italians, still having fun. And we were glad to be there.

—Cameron Curtis McKinley, "Of Passages and the Cinque Terre"

WILLIAM G. SCHELLER

⋆ ⋆ ⋆

The Working World of Venice

For some, it's a living.

THIS AFTERNOON VENICE SMELLS LIKE LAUNDRY. NOT LIKE noisome summer canals or damp plaster in a tilting *palazzo*; not like fish sizzling in a *trattoria* or sea mist and doom. I am in a working-class neighborhood known as Santa Elena, and Venice smells like the garlands of laundry strung across the street.

Of all the world's cities, Venice most enjoys—or suffers—the cachet of being a place where fantasy looms larger than reality, where work runs a poor second to play. This is partly Venice's own fault. During the days of her 18th century decline, she worked hard at cultivating the playground image. The image stuck and the tourists kept coming.

Venice also answers for her sheer gorgeousness: in a world where aesthetics and economy are driven by the cold Calvinist north, any place this delightful to the eye must have been built to be a fey little theme park. Venice's great landmarks—St. Mark's Basilica and its *piazza*, the Grand Canal with its *palazzi* and quayside cafés, the palace of the doges and the Bridge of Sighs—stand in the mind's eye as the stuff of romance and the backdrops to a holiday.

The truth is that no city ever worked so diligently to such serious purpose, ever stroke so mightily after the almighty ducat...or did so much to set up shop for the rest of Western civilization in the bargain. If Venice is impossibly beautiful, it is because its builders saw no reason why beauty and work should be incompatible. The senators, artisans, and merchants of Venice had no trouble inventing commercial banking, while at the same time wringing a few extra decades of poetry from the vocabulary of late Gothic architecture.

But still the laundry had to be done, as it was being done this day in the secluded far eastern corner of the city, where I stood beneath this festoon of fresh linen. I had spent the past few days exploring outward from the Venetian epicenter of St. Mark's, making it my business to look beyond the Rialto Bridge, beyond the great paintings of the Accademia galleries, beyond the apricot-tinted sunsets behind the church of Sta. Maria della Salute.

Without ignoring gondola rides and Titian-filled churches, I wanted to see past the treasure gloss of Venice

*A*s I sit idly watching the crowds, a guide gathers his chickens and announces in English, then in French, that they are looking at St. Mark's basilica, and shortly he will take them to the Doge's Palace. I intercept a cry of help from man to woman, from husband to wife. I hear an American ask: "Say, honey, what are these Doges?" and the wonderful reply—"The kings of Venice!"

I smile to myself and remember the story, told by James Morris, of the Paddington householder, in London's "Little Venice" on the Regent Canal, who fixed the notice to his gate, "Beware of the Doge." What an inspired pun it is, for it could well have been the motto of Venice down the ages. Fear that the Doge might make himself king runs through Venetian history, and explains why that functionary had to accept restrictions on his personal freedom which are unique in the history of ambition.

◆

—H.V. Morton,
A Traveller in Italy

and to sense its everyday pulse. I wanted some glimpse of life in a
city that dates back 1,500 years, to the days when the first mainland refugee fled the barbarians' sack of Rome's Adriatic cities and
settled on the marshy, unpromising islands of the Venetian lagoon.

I got my glimpse, and then some. I found what I was looking
for on a narrow street, scant blocks from the fabulous Tintoretto
ceilings of the Scuola di San Rocco, in the neighborhood of San
Palo, where a metalsmith worked at his anvil in the back of a dusty
shop while his wife tended a brazier of coals. I sensed workaday
Venice as I looked through a shop window to watch an artisan
with a single strong needle craft a mattress from yard goods and
cotton batting.

I sensed it again on the soccer field at the naval academy, where
the heirs of one of the world's greatest maritime traditions butted
and booted their ball around. And I watched as two young civil
engineers set up their transit to survey for a new footbridge across
a canal on the island of Giudecca.

At another canal in another quarter, where workers had drained
the water away so they could shore up a Gothic foundation, I saw
brown mud where, on any other day, there would have been shimmering reflections.

"Do you ever find anything interesting when you drain a
canal?" I asked one of the workmen.

The man shrugged and gestured with his cigarette toward the
mud. There was his answer: bricks, last week's empty wine bottle,
a couple of broken flowerpots.

I was disappointed. One of my favorite Venetian stories con-
cerns the 18th-century magnifico who impressed his guests by
having his golden tableware tossed out the window after each
course of a banquet. Of course, he had servants down below, holding a net above the water. But it's fun to imagine that a fork or two
might have missed the net.

I went to that most modern and prosaic of institutions, the supermarket. Two or three exist even in Venice. In one, I discovered
the just-home-from-work-gotta-throw-dinner-together versions
of all the Venetian classics around which two-hour restaurant meals

are built. Here was *pasta e fagioli*, the rich local soup of macaroni and beans, dried and bagged by Buitoni. A frozen, shrink-wrapped assemblage of squid and shellfish was called *"misto per risotto."*

There was also a display of cat food large enough to fill the shelves of a giant American supermarket, its presence a reminder that Venice is a city of independent cats fed by everyone as a sort of community project. They aren't strays; they know exactly where they are. They aren't homeless; Venice is their home. They are the heirs of the comfortable kitty beneath the banquet table in Veronese's "Feast in the House of Levi," on exhibit in the Accademia, and none of them ever get run over by cars.

But streets that are safe for cats are losing their appeal for people who would dearly love to hop into their Alfa Romeos and drive to work. The maître d' at the rooftop restaurant of the Hotel Danieli lives in Padua, and it takes him two hours to get home. As I finished my grappa on a slow night, he had nothing but praise for proposals to ease travel in and out of the city.

"Someone wanted to build a new bridge into Venice, from the Lido di Iesolo in the north," he said, "and a metro line—a subway under the Grand Canal from the train station to the Rialto and St. Mark's. But the ecologists always say no. No one wants anything to be built in Venice."

The upshot, according to the maître d', is that not only do many Venetians move to the mainland and commute to jobs in Venice; some stay in the city and commute to the mainland to work.

So, Venice makes it hard to live in Venice. Yet someone is buying the frozen risotto mix: someone ordered the handmade mattress; someone is hanging out the laundry. Someone employs the pressman wearing the traditional square cap made out of a newspaper page, whom I saw walking into a bar for lunch. And someone, other than a tourist, buys produce from the little fruit and vegetable barges that tip up along the sidewalks.

Someone, with a Mac or a PC tucked behind Renaissance walls, must have been happy to see the printout banner in the window of a computer store that heralded: "Finally Venice has a connection with the Internet." La Serenissima, the Most Serene Republic, is on the information supercanal.

Of course, there are Venetian yuppies. There are so many Venetians walking around with cellular phones that if one asked another, "What news on the Rialto?" the answer would undoubtedly be, "*Un momento*—just let me check."

Suits are everywhere in Venice—even the old pensioner, his dogelike profile turned toward the winter sun as he naps in the public gardens, is turned out better than an American banker. But you can always tell when there's mercantile purpose in a Venetian's stride.

What is in short supply, sadly, is a new generation of Venetians. Of Venice's population of some 75,000 souls—down from nearly 150,000 about 50 years ago—fewer than 4,000 are children.

One afternoon I turned off the Fondamenta della Croce, between Palladio's church of the Redentore and the eastern tip of the island of Giudecca.

Before continuing on to the vaporetto stop at Le Zitelle for the short ride to the island and church of San Giorgio Maggiore, I ducked into the narrow lanes of the housing project that lies between two of Venice's most exclusive institutions—the "Garden of Eden," a walled private enclave planted by an Englishman with the paradisiacal surname, and the plush Cipriani Hotel.

The pathway I followed led to a grassy courtyard, surrounded by two-story apartment blocks that could have stood anywhere between Minsk and Minneapolis. I felt like an intruder in someone's yard. There was no one around except for a woman on a second-floor balcony; I tossed her a clothespin she had dropped.

But not long after I turned my back on the courtyard, I felt something small and hard hit the back of my neck. I heard giggling and turned. Half a dozen urchins, like the funny little snot-nose kids in Fellini's *Amarcord*, were ducking under a portico.

The game began. Every time I turned my back, another pebble would hit me; when I spun around, they'd jabber and point at each other as if to say, "Not me, it was him." Only 4,000 kids in Venice, and I had to run into this bunch.

They followed me out the alley before losing interest. Once I got inside the church of San Giorgio Maggiore, though, I didn't feel so bad: There was Tintoretto's "Martyrdom of St. Stephen," showing the saint being pelted to death with stones.

Among the grown-up pursuits of Venice, perhaps none strike as familiar a chord with the outside world as those having to do with the lagoon city's signature craft, the gondola. By no means are the gondoliers themselves anything less than authentic—the redoubtable Mario, who took me from the Grand Canal quay called the Riva degli Schiavoni and back via a labyrinthine route I could never hope to retrace, told me that his pedigree as a Venetian was untraceably long and that his father and grandmother had been gondoliers.

But the men who guide the long black boats are finally, in the front line of the tourism industry. The men who *build* gondolas are a step closer to the old pulse of Venice.

The small canalside yards where gondolas are constructed are called *squeri*, and there are four of them in operation in Venice today. Equipped with a map and some vague directions from the gondoliers who congregate in back of St. Mark's *piazza*, I finally found the *squero* of D. Manin on the Rio di San Trovaso.

The scene there was impossibly medieval. Wooden balconies, their railings crowded with geraniums, lined the two-story tile-roofed buildings around the little gondola yard. Two partly built gondolas lay half beneath a shed roof at the head of the sloping ways. One was overturned, its bottom being sanded and caulked with pitch. Even where I stood, across the canal, the pungent smell of pitch was in the air.

The *squero* I really wanted to visit was the one belonging to Tramontin and Sons, which Mario had told me made the best gondolas. He has a Tramontin, sixteen years old, and when it has run out its useful life in perhaps five years, he will replace it with another, at a cost of about $22,000.

Tramontin's establishment was in an even more remote part of the Dorsoduro neighborhood, at the intersection of two obscure canals. I was able to see the yard before I could figure out how to get to it; finally, I guessed that a gray steel door in a narrow alley was the only possible entrance. I rang a bell alongside the locked door, and in a moment I was buzzed in by Roberto Tramontin, whose great-grandfather Domenico had started the business.

A busy man, Roberto Tramontin or else a man of few words. I asked if I could come in and look around; he said yes. When I thanked him, he responded with a brief, *"Prego,"* the all-purpose Italian word that includes "you're welcome" among its meanings.

It was a privilege to be allowed so nonchalantly into one of the most rarefied manufacturing establishments on earth, and it was quite a surprise when Roberto soon disappeared and I was in the *squero* alone. It was like being left alone in an old small-town garage when the mechanic has gone out for a part, only this was a world of wood, not of metal.

There are eight different kinds of wood in a gondola—among them elm for the ribs, oak for the bottom, and walnut for the *forcola*, or oarlock. The seasoning stock was fragrant in racks beneath the rafters. A single gondola lay overturned, its bottom still only partly planked. Along one wall a long worktable held an array of hand tools that might have been laid down by men who had gone off to join the Fourth Crusade.

I was standing there staring at the tools and at an old photo of Domenico Tramontin, framed beneath two mock wooden *ferri* (the crested and serrated steel ornaments that grace gondolas' prows) when an old man walked into the shed. He went over to the partly constructed boat and began hand-sawing planking very slowly and with methodical sureness.

"Buon giorno," he said, and that was all. I let myself out by the steel door.

In a water city, the water is the place to look to see the day's work being done. Watching the traffic on the lagoon and on the larger canals is like watching the rest of the world with its wheels removed, sending up a wake. As I stood for a few minutes along the Fondamente Nuove, the broad quay on the north side of

Venice, I saw a speeding ambulance, a shipment of oranges, a veterinarian's boat (a cat emergency?), and a fire boat. A brown-and-white boat went by with "United Parcel Service" emblazoned on its side. Another boat was carrying a new dishwasher, and on the prow was the single word "Whirlpool." And—startling yet perfectly logical—a hearse boat chugged past with a shiny mahogany coffin on deck. San Michele, the cemetery island of Venice, was only a few hundred yards away; behind me, along the Fondamente Nuove and its little side streets, the marble workers were busy cutting and polishing headstones and tombs.

One afternoon I set out across the water, to a corner of the lagoon between Venice proper and the long barrier beach called the Lido, to visit a little-known religious and intellectual outpost. Here, in this city of churches and of the original Jewish ghetto— where Hasidim still keep a strict Sabbath in the streets where Shylock walked—one of the busiest retreats of the godly is on the little cypress-studded island of San Lazzaro degli Armeni, home of the mother house of the Armenian Catholic Mechitarist fathers.

The Mechitarists have been here since 1717. Within these walls Byron once studied classical Armenian, and today fifteen priests and as many seminarians edit and publish editions of old Armenian manuscripts (more than 4,000 books and documents, some dating back to the seventh century, fill the community's library), along with modern works on Armenian culture.

A genial, dry-witted priest explained it all to me and to a small group of tourists I had come over with—that is, after he finished explaining where Armenia was.

"It's in Armenia," he answered drolly, after disabusing a geographical naif of the notion that it was in Israel. Fluent in Italian, English, German, and both the classical and vernacular versions of his native Armenian, he made it seem the most natural thing in the world for a tiny religious order with roots in the Caucasus to publish books in 32 languages on an island in the Venetian lagoon. The connection has a lot to do with the old saying that "the enemy of my enemy is my friend"; traditionally, Venetians and Armenians alike shared, along with a common Christianity, an antipathy toward the Turks.

To Turks and other enemies of the old Republic of Venice, one of the most feared sights on the high seas was a banner bearing the image of a lion holding a bound gospel—the lion of St. Mark, Venice's age-old symbol.

The lion is emblazoned all over the city, but as I rode the vaporetto back from the Mechitarists' island, I saw it at its most impressive: set in bronze on the superstructure of a giant freighter, the *Fenicia*, making its way down the Giudecca Canal. Painted on the stern was the ship's port of registry, Venezia. Here was a vivid link with the lagoon city's storied maritime past.

For centuries—almost since those first late-Roman refugees began to gather on this marshy little archipelago—Venice had understood that its destiny lay upon the water and its wealth lay in moving goods, at a considerable profit, from where they were made to where they were wanted. The *Fenicia*, no doubt, was delivering something other than spices and silks, and Venice is no longer master-merchant to the world. But that ship carried tradition and pride, and in its figurative wake all the commerce of the West had arisen.

On my last day in Venice I went out into the countryside without ever leaving the city limits. The island of San Erasmo is less than a half-hour's *vaporetto* ride from the busy quay of Fondamente Nuove, but it might as well be a hundred miles away. The morning sounds I heard there were not the bells and bustle of St. Mark's but the trill of songbirds, the crowing of a rooster, and the chugging of a tractor in a distant field. Another surprise, after a week during which I had seen nothing mounted on wheels other than baby strollers and handcarts, was that the people of San Erasmo had bicycles, motor scooters, and cars. Like a train station in an American suburb, the vaporetto landing was surrounded by vehicles left for the day by commuters.

San Erasmo is not merely a bedroom island. Venice's vegetables have to be grown somewhere, and that somewhere may as well be nearby. San Erasmo is all farms and vineyards with a small village attached.

I walked down the narrow lane from the landing, past fields of salad greens, past the straight rows of pruned vines waiting for the warm spring sun to bring them into leaf. The soil was dark and rich. Houses were few and far apart, and people scarcer still.

Here and there someone was hoeing weeds; several times I was passed by women on bicycles, all of whom wished me good morning after looking a bit surprised that any outsider other than the mailman (who had been on my boat) would bother setting foot on San Erasmo. With their black bicycles and sturdy woolen coats, the women seemed like phantoms from Europe's early postwar days as they cycled along the flat, tilled fields.

My hike around the island took two hours, and it was only at the end of that time that I came to the town center that served these farmers and their commuting kin. There was little more than a nursery school named after Pope John XXIII (the onetime patriarch of Venice), a small food market, and a new church with a Romanesque font inside for holy water.

Almost a millennium ago, when that font was freshly carved, the landholders of San Erasmo were no doubt busy at the same fields and vineyards through which I had just passed. And some of them, the young and more adventurous, probably crossed the lagoon, like today's vaporetto commuters, to pitch in at the task of making Venice work.

William G. Scheller wrote this story for Islands *magazine.*

✳

This is a city of petty thieves. In the eighteenth century pick-pockets who took their haul to the city guards were allowed to keep a percentage of its value: a traveller who inquired the purpose of this iniquitous system was told that it "encouraged an ingenious, intelligent, sagacious activity among the people." When Titian was dying of the plague in 1576, robbers entered his house and pillaged it while he was still on his death-bed, some say before his very eyes. In the fifteenth century a house-breaker even succeeded in boring a hole into the Treasury of the Basilica, and getting away with an immense booty (he was hanged, at his own wry request, with a golden noose). Venetian burglars are sometimes equally impudent today. They are skilled at climbing through the windows of canalside houses, stealing a handbag or a necklace, and drifting away in a silent boat, so that the big hotels have watchmen on the canals, the private houses are heavily shuttered, and the summer newspapers are full of burgled Finns, disillusioned Americans and spluttering Englishmen. "What can you expect," say the Venetians cheerfully, "if they *will* sleep with their windows open?

—Jan Morris, *The World of Venice*

FRED L. GARDAPHE

∗ * ∗

Feast in Puglia

In primitive feasts and games,
a visitor touches his origins.

WHEN I FIRST TRAVELED TO CASTELLANA GROTTE IN PUGLIA, I
believed I was going back to the place my grandparents had left
more than fifty years earlier. My expectations had been fed by
years of stories about what it was like before they had come to
America, and I believed that this trip was going to take me back
in time. But when I arrived Italy was no less modern than
Chicago. I was disappointed when I saw the skies over Castellana
filled with television antennas and the streets stuffed with cars.
This was not the place I had in mind from all the stories my grandparents used to tell me.

While I was there, I met a cousin who was a photojournalist.
Renato had a strong distaste for contemporary Italy and a longing
for the old days. One day he came up to me and said, "How would
you like to go back fifty years, to see what Italy was like when your
grandparents were children?" I thought he was crazy, but as he explained, he was going to do a three-day photo shoot of a *festa* that
was hundreds of years old.

During the Feast of the Madonna Nera, or Black Madonna, the
peasants put down their plows and for three days forget about their
daily worries and frustrations. Thousands travel from all over these

mountains to come to a cave in Pollino where many, many years ago the Madonna had appeared to a shepherd. It is told that she spoke to him from the darkness and that is why they call her La Madonna Nera. But others say it is called the Festival of the Black Madonna because years ago, the South of Italy was invaded by pirates from Arabia, who raped women and pillaged the land. Many of those Arabians settled there, and so many of the Southerners have black blood. When the Christians came to convert these isolated patches of mountain people, they found dark painted idols. When they tried to replace the black idols with figures of Christ the people rioted. So, they had to let them worship the Mother of Christ, whom they allowed to be painted black.

"You will see thousands offering prayers, money, even strands of their hair to receive the grace of the Madonna to cure ailments, to have newborn children blessed, to have their lives improved," said my cousin Renato as he drove. "They spend the days praying at the small chapel and performing many contests. At night they camp in makeshift tents, cook, eat, and dance. On the morning of the last day, after a solemn Mass, they make a procession through the mountains. But you know this festival is more than a religious event. People say that this festival is the remnant of an ancient peasant culture, a life that archeologists are only beginning to piece together from diggings they are doing farther south. This is the first time I will photograph it. The last two years I came without my camera, just to be a part of it, to get to know the people so that when I bring my camera they will not treat me like a stranger. That is what is important, to become one of them before you try to depict them." We were heading up…. It's up in the hills of Puglia, near a town called Pollino.

To get to Pollino you have to take dusty stone roads that wind through deserted foothills. The road split through hills studded with sheep and white-shirted shepherds who waved until they disappeared. Tiny stone-walled towns crowned the hill tops. These towns are centuries old, built from the limestone that was taken out of the land in the valley to make it tillable. They were built atop the hills to protect the inhabitants from the pirate raids that plagued the coasts of eastern Italy until the 19th century. The buildings are clustered together with walls meters thick. In the summer they shade each other from the fierce sun and the stinging scirocco and keep the insides consistently cool.

My cousin and I stopped along the way to pick wild almonds, figs, and oranges. The back of the truck was becoming a mobile cupboard. Renato pulled off the main road and headed up a steep path. We began moving vertically, trees seemed to be bowing toward us as the window filled alternately with sky and the crest of the hill. The wheels spun, gripped the dry dirt between the stones, moved ahead, spun on a clump of grass, caught some broken rock and moved further up the hill. When we reached the top, Renato yanked the hand brake, turned off the car and said, "This is as far as we can go by car."

When the road stopped we walked into the forest, carrying packs and his equipment. The grey light faded and the sun outlined the mountains in a reddish purple light. We descended from the grey light into a dark forest.

"Renato, are you sure you know where you're going?" I asked.

He laughed. "I think I know where we are, though I have never

> *T*he strangest sight in all Puglia...[is] the octagonal Castel del Monte, which Frederick II built in the 1240s. This is the most striking of a series of buildings associated with Frederick, the Swabian Emperor whose achievements were such that he was called Stupor Mundi, or "Wonder of the World." His huge-turreted castles and Romanesque cathedrals with wondrous sculpted doorways and fantastical column capitals, all in bone-white local stone, dot a series of nearby coastal towns.
>
> ◆
>
> —Corby Kummer, "The Pull of Puglia," *The Atlantic Monthly*

been through these woods at night without one of my Pollinese friends. If I am right, it's just through this forest and over that crest. We'll be there in no more than twenty minutes."

Three tiny forests, two hilltops and one hour later there was still no festival in sight. Renato swore and muttered to himself then motioned for me to stop. We sat down on a rock. Renato pulled out a bottle of wine, took a swig and handed it to me.

"We've got to be close," Renato sighed.

"It all looks the same to me," I said. "I think we are just walking in circles."

A wolf howled in the distance.

"Shish!" whispered Renato. "Listen."

I stopped and heard nothing. "What do you mean? There's nothing but the wind and perhaps a couple of hungry wolves."

"No, no, listen."

I stood still, cupping my ear with my hand. I heard the faint crackle of what I thought was twigs breaking.

"Smell! Inhale deeply. It's roasted sheep!"

I sniffed at the air. "I just smell these woods and…"

"Fires! Don't you smell them? Can't you hear the fires?"

"No!"

"Listen!"

I brought my hand to my ear. "I hear a bird."

"That's no bird. That's a *zampone*!"

I concentrated and thought I heard a tooting. "What is *zampone*?"

"It is a bagpipe made from a sheep's stomach. Come walk quietly and we'll follow the smell and the sounds."

As I followed him I began to hear the faint whistle of the bagpipe interspersed with voices coming from up ahead. I looked up and saw the dark fir tree branches glimmering in a shadowy yellow light.

"Aha!" yelled Renato. "Just over that ridge!"

As we neared the ridgetop an eerie *baahing* ripped the silence. It crept through me and I shivered. It was a sound I had never heard before. It slowed my pace.

"What is that sound?" I asked in a whisper.

"It's the sheep. They know they're going to die."

When we reached the top of the ridge, we stopped and looked out over a plateau. Thick clouds of fragrant smoke filled the flat land that stretched out below us. I saw an entire forest was afire. My eyes teared as a wind blew the smoke up into our faces. Through the clear patches I could see pink-skinned sheep skewered by poles turning on wooden spits, roasting over the flames. Thousands of people were singing and dancing around the campfires. I felt I had stumbled upon some prehistoric site and was still standing on the ridgetop as Renato slid down. I hesitated and allowed him to move ahead of me. I felt as though I was a scout in a Western film, viewing the Indians in a trance-like curiosity that blended wonder with fear into a paralysis. I was hypnotized by long knives flashing in the burning light, slashing the throats of the sheep.

"Frederico. Come. I want to find my friends. Come down," yelled Renato.

I followed slowly. As I neared the fires I could hear the dripping fat sizzle as it flowed onto red hot logs. We made our way through crowds of people who were rushing from one site to the next, goatskins of wine, large rounds of bread and baskets of fruit and vegetables dangling from hands that were not waving into the air, brushing smoke out of eyes. I felt a warm splash of liquid spray across the back of my shirt. I turned quickly to scowl at a tiny old man (knife in one hand, the other holding the head of a sheep) who hunched his shoulders and tilted his head to one side in apology. I reached my hand to my back and touched my shirt. Bringing the finger to my face I flinched at the spot of blood that stained it.

Down among the people the noise was deafening. Accordions were squeezing out-of-tune notes into the air, joined by the shepherds' goatskin bagpipes. People were shouting as though they had not seen others in years and were singing songs, not one of them the same as the next. Tambourines were slapping into shadowed palms raised over heads that flashed in and out of the red and yellow fire lights. Renato called my name many times before I could hear it through the clamor. I followed him to a group of young Italians who were seated around a large fire.

That night we slept around a fire listening to Renato tell stories of his travels. I never spoke a word; I just listened to all the sounds and stared at a sky full of stars until I fell asleep. Early the next morning, I woke to see people stooped around campfires, stirring large pots that cooked over the smoldering charcoal, drinking from ceramic cups. Farther off a group of women had gathered at the mouth of the cave and were beginning to sing to the Madonna. It was a mournful, moaning harmony, which reminded me of playing the keys of an electric organ before it had been completely warmed up.

I followed Renato through the crowd, stopping to drink coffee and eat roasted bread and cheese that was handed to me by smiling women as my cousin charmed the subjects of his photographs. We made our way to the cave, where thousands of people were singing. The oldest women knelt, semi-encircling the mouth of the cave; behind them were rows and rows of middle-aged women, with their youngest children at their sides and behind all these women were the men, sitting, standing and playing with their knives and axes. A group of these men had straddled a tree that had just been felled. They all chopped at the branches, which younger boys carried off to throw onto a large pile of garbage that had been gathered that morning.

"What are they doing?" I asked as we neared the men.

"You will see! They are getting ready for the games."

I spent the morning wandering around with my cousin. The people who had seemed so menacing by night all seemed to be so friendly in the daylight. By noon the crowds had moved from the cave to the center of the plateau, where the games would be held. Renato took the opportunity to photograph the cave.

Carved into the hillside, the tiny cave was filled with thousands of candles. At the foot of the statue were piles of food and sweets wrapped in colored paper. Renato knelt down to photograph the statue. An old woman entered the cave and screamed. Her voice echoed across the plateau and hundreds stopped and turned toward the cave. The old woman tugged at the camera that I had slung across my shoulder. I tugged it away from her and Renato stepped between us, his hands on the woman's shoulders, speaking forcefully yet calmly, explaining that he meant no harm and was only intending to use the photograph to show the people of Italy the wonderful way the Madonna was honored in Pollino. People hurried toward the cave, some fearing that the statue of the Madonna was being stolen or worse, destroyed. Renato was soon surrounded by the people, who after listening to him suddenly moved in front of the statue, where they turned and posed for a photograph. When he was done, Renato thanked the people and led them out of the cave toward the field where the games were beginning.

The huge tree that had been felled was now planted into the ground, poking almost thirty feet into the cloudless sky. Atop it sat a straw basket filled with cheese and fruit and other prizes. The long, barkless pole had been greased with sheep's fat and was surrounded by men who were taking runs trying to climb it. The younger men were encircled by older men, who themselves were encircled by young women and finally the older women. Everyone cheered on those who tried to climb. One man, clothed in rolled up pants and a vest over his muscular, shirtless torso made it within a hand's

*P*uglia's agricultural puissance, long based on wheat, survives in olives: the region produces far more olive oil than any other in Italy, much of which is blended and bottled by producers in Tuscany. Light industry has brought both prosperity and pollution to the ports of Bari and Brindisi—places tourists know, if they know them at all, as stopovers on the way to ferries bound for Greece, and cities I usually avoid.

◆

—Corby Kummer, "The Pull of Puglia," *The Atlantic Monthly*

reach of the basket before he lost his balance and slid down into the crowd. He jumped up and wanted to try again, but had to take

his place behind the others waiting their turn. The man who finally made it was in his fifties and shimmied up with the ease of a
monkey. As he reached for the basket, the entire crowd cheered in
one voice. He slid down the pole with one arm wrapped loosely
and the other waving the basket out over his head. He hit the
ground and immediately bowed, tipping his cap to the people.

"That man could have been your grandfather sixty years ago,"
said Renato. "Come, soon the procession will start."

Ever since I was a child I had been to the *festa* of Our Lady of
Mt. Carmel. Each year, since 1894, the Italians of my home town
would parade through the streets carrying the Madonna on the
Sunday closest to July 16, the Madonna's feast day. So I was pretty
sure I would be familiar with what would happen at Pollino. But
as we followed the statue through the hills, on dirt paths, the procession seemed less like a parade and more like a march of
refugees. And for me, that day gave me a sense of what it must be
like to be an alien in a new country. My cousin took off, shooting
photos like a wild man. And while I stayed near his friends, I felt I
was alone. My Italian might have been good enough to get by in
the city, but out here, where dialects reigned, there were few with
whom I could easily speak. My communication was reduced to
nods, smiles and gestures. While this made me uncomfortable, I did
have a sense of having been here before. I felt that, in a funny way,
I actually belonged here, as though I had become my grandfather
and had returned home.

*Fred L. Gardaphe is Professor of Italian American Studies at SUNY-Stony
Brook. He is Associate Editor of* Fra Noi, *editor of the SUNY Press Series
in Italian American Studies, and co-editor of* Voices in Italian Americana,
a literary journal and cultural review. His books include Italian Signs,
American Streets, *and* Dagoes Read: Tradition and the Italian
American Writer.

⋆

The old women of Bari near the sea sit in the small shadows of open
doors. Their faces are beautifully darkened in the sunlight. Their hair is
gray enough. They have seen the wars. They have known the young

Germans blundering and falling out of the sky like poisoned moths. The young in Bari today swagger and smirk as though no one had ever lived before, as though no one had ever died. Forever titivating their lank hair in the Adriatic breeze, voluptuously caressing their own armpits, they love to be told they are the lost youth, unemployed and betrayed by The System. Their motorcycles whinny insanely along the dark streets, and they are interested in women only to frighten them. They are too mindless to be skillful thieves. But the old women of Bari in their open doors know that young men will find something else to do, and I walk in this city as frightened as an old sea woman startled by moths.

—James Wright, *The Shape of Light*

PATRICIA HAMPL

* ✳ *

Walking to Assisi

The mysticism of St. Francis lingers on.

WE LEFT SPELLO EARLY, BEFORE SUNRISE. BREAKFAST WAS CHEESE
tucked into hard rolls, which we ate as we walked. We had a long
hike ahead of us, all the way up Monte Subasio and down into
Assisi. Diana wanted us to get the lion's share done before the heat
of the day.

Departing was always difficult. Every morning I had the same
regretful sensation: why are we leaving, this place is perfect, let's
stay. I was sure I would never again be able to find any of these little towns we had reached by walking through fields and forests, off
any clear path much of the time, occasionally sharing our way with
a meditative cow, but often only with bright poppies. In the distance, each hill town seemed to slip down from the top of its peak
in a drift of medieval stone like snow caught in pink sunlight cap-
ping a mountain.

As we left each town, it seemed to resorb into the mist of the
region, and return to its medieval existence, lost in golden haze as
if in prayer. Absurd, of course: we were always near the *autostrada*
where the maniacs careened around hairpin turns, taunting one
another, tailgating within a millimeter. Still, it seemed that the
roads we traveled were strangely careless. Walking can do that: put

one foot in front of the other, day after day, moving across a land-scape away from the main thoroughfare, and it doesn't feel like travel; it feels like history. The centuries peel away. The woman in the kerchief who ran out of her house on a dusty road, rushing up to us with two bottles of her homemade wine: she wasn't being friendly in a modern way, she wasn't trying to *connect*. She handed over the black-green bottles to Diana, smiled from a face the color and corrugated texture of the road we stood on, and then ran back into her small, low house guarded by great spears of cypress, and we never saw her again. She met our thirst, not our personalities. The gesture was a million years old, far beyond courtesy, rooted in ancient communion.

It felt better than friendship, this anonymous acknowledgment of human need. We sat in the shade of a plane tree by the side of the road, passed the bottle around, swigging, not wiping the rim, handing it to the next person. Strange, how we fell silent. Even pert Louise put her head back, closed her bright eyes, and drank it in.

Walking allowed such timeless moments, making us slow-moving parts of the landscape we passed through. Maybe the world isn't, at its daily heart, as modern as we tend to think. As we walked, it kept reverting to an ancient, abiding self. We stopped to watch a man working on a small building: the house he was making for his wife and new baby. He pointed to the red roof tiles. They were curved and fit together in a series of ripples. The shape, he said, was from Roman times: masons took the still-wet clay, cut it in squares, and then shaped it over their own thighs, making the curved form, which then dried in the sun. "Like me," the man said, grinning, putting one of the tiles on his leg, where it fit, "Roman."

I could sit forever, I thought, on the terrace of the Spello hotel, letting one hazy day slough off into the next, the statue of Venus flowing in the dark, Alma worrying her worries by my side, Cecil galumphing in with his tray of drinks. I would be content to watch Lloyd and Louise raising their eyebrows meaningfully to each other when I say something egregiously American, and then Will diving into his Petrarch off by himself in a shadow. The days spent walking in this streaming terrain, where light and land ach June the village of Spello, just around the hill from Assisi, celebrates its annual *infiorate*, or dried flower festival. Here is what happens: the night before the *infiorate* the men and women of the town, having divided into groups, begin tracing chalk outlines (planned months in advance) on the pavement of the *piazza* and surrounding streets. Meanwhile children and old widows in black sit on the sidelines in wooden chairs, separating by color fried and fresh petals: *fiori del melograno* (pomegranate flowers), *garofolini* (sweet william), *ginestrella* (greenweed), *tagete* (marigold), cedar of Lebanon, rose, *fiordaliso* (cornflower). Boxes and boxes of color, deep golds like curry powder, royal blues, hot pepper reds, that as dusk approaches the Spellini begin, very carefully, to scatter inside the traced outlines. (The color scheme, like everything else, has been long foretold.) Until dawn, Spello is an enormous coloring book, in which nature provides the crayons.

◆

—David Leavitt and Mark Mitchell, *Italian Pleasures*

refused to divide themselves into separate categories, made even our rough human edges smooth, made us one thing. Analysis had turned to relish, and my notebook bulged with wildflowers and blank pages, which seemed to say it all. The more we walked, the lazier I became.

But the point was to achieve Assisi. We had caught a glimpse of it the day before, perched like an ink cap on a pointed hill. It looked as if we could just march a straight line across a field of red poppies and we'd be there. Once at the base of its hill, however, we would have to shimmy up an almost sheer face to get to the town. That's what it looked like; in fact, it was farther away than it appeared.

"Take a good look," Diana said. "You won't see it again until we're in it." For our route lay by Spello, over and then sharply down Subasio, the mountain where St. Francis first roamed when he began his nomad life.

Now, this last morning of the hike, though we were

walking toward it, we could no longer see Assisi. "Take it on faith," Diana said. "Just keep moving."

It was an unusually quiet walk, maybe because we'd started so early. Everyone was sleepy, happy to be left alone. By ten o'clock, the sun was high enough to make trouble, and we were silent just from the effort of climbing. Ian saluted gamely with his walking stick as I passed by; he was leaning against a tree, taking a break, too winded to speak. Lollie, the oldest of the women, was ahead of everyone else, her wiry body and steady pace keeping her out front. But she didn't stop for the flowers today. We were stripped of everything but left, right, left, right.

Even Lloyd had finally fallen silent from the effort. He had started the day by saying loudly as we set off from Spello that he, for one, did not consider cheese with one of last night's buns *breakfast*.

Louise said in her stage whisper that this sort of thing would never happen with the Ramblers, another group to which she and Lloyd gave their hiking business. The Ramblers had always proved to be entirely satisfactory. She wished she could say as much for Diana's firm.

On the other hand, she said, you're contending with Italy, aren't you? And that means Italians. The Ramblers stuck to England—and mind you, plenty to see right there.

Each of us reached the summit alone. We had to give in to our own pace, panting and wheezing along as best we could. I stopped once, disheartened because I had counted on a certain turn leading to a flat stretch, and instead the path had turned even more steeply up. I threw myself flat on the ground and thought I couldn't/wouldn't/mustn't go a step farther. They must have carts to haul people out of here, I thought. I didn't care, I had no pride. Even Cecil, passing by, didn't tease me, but just dragged on, his hand still gripping the invisible rope which I had fatally let go.

Eventually, I got up and without any will for it, started again: left, right, left, right. I admired my dumb paws as if from a great distance, as they kept making the effort my mind had long ago stopped demanding. My legs felt springy with exhaustion.

Then, just as I'd heard runners claim, I got a sudden burst of buoyancy. It came from nowhere, and it had nothing to do with me. It was not just energy but a kind of intelligence bounding through me. It wasn't left, right, left, right. There was something serial about it, the left and right giving over to a higher good, moving in an orbit of rhythm I hadn't known existed. I was carried forward by this rhythm. It was a command. I obeyed.

By the time this sensation ended, I wasn't far from the top. The heaven of that rhythm departed without my being aware of exactly when it left. I made it finally, panting, dizzy, the blood pounding in my temples.

St. Francis was there at the summit.

In the wind. The gusts almost knocked me down; it seemed pointless to try to speak, because of the loud whacks the wind laid across my ears.

It's not true that a place hallowed by an extraordinary life becomes a husk, that after so many years the meat had been scooped out and fed to the beast of tourism so that nothing is left. Francis was on top of Subasio, the first time he's turned up in all my walking of his steep province.

The place itself was bare, a desert at a great height, just a tough salad of green here and there, no paper-thin wildflowers. It was all view—that was the purpose of the place, I sensed. A world without airplanes, when this peak gave the dizzying biblical thrill: to achieve a high place, to see the world at your feet, to encompass it all with your eye. And like Jesus with his tempting devil, like Francis at the threshold not only of the Renaissance but of the modern mercantile moment, to refuse possession. To forgo ownership and become all attention at this commanding height. To become awe.

A long hermitage, looking like a stable, and empty, sat at one quadrant of the summit. It didn't appear to be a ruin, but it was hard to believe that anyone lived there. Diana said religious pilgrims sometimes used it a few days at a time. Several American monks, their nylon windbreaker hoods pulled over their heads like cowls, sat here and there, backs straight against the wall, silent, meditating. Some of them had assumed the lotus position. One was simply leaning against the wall of the building, looking out, still as stone. The wind slapped his jacket, jeering.

Out of nowhere a boy on a motorcycle flashed by, the hyena yelp of the engine cutting the air. None of the monks looked up. Where had he come from? Where did any of us come from? From the future this place was trying to hold at a distance. The lad yelled to his buddies, and reared up on the back wheel of the bike, poised there for an instant, and then let the front wheel down in a thump and was off again down the mountain, engine squealing.

The hike down was even worse. It seemed steeper than the way up, and more treacherous, because the path was covered with small white stones, rough as gravel, which made a shifting surface. It was hard to place your foot and expect it to stay put. The stones became little skates.

Louise said they should have indicated this degree of difficulty in the firm's bro-

*T*he daylight of next morning brought together a great gathering of pilgrims to participate in the Feast day of Assisi's patron saint. Each town and region was represented by colorful banners as music and dancers gave way to speeches by dignitaries in the square before the great basilica of St. Francis. The most remarkable and effective crowd control tool I've ever witnessed was the use of long whips wielded by folk-costumed youths. The snap of the whips was like pistol shots and caused the crowd to part obediently without a word from these youthful parade marshals.

We planned to leave Assisi that evening. As we were under a time constraint we chose to visit only the hermitage on Monte Subasio a couple of miles outside the walls. Francis was wont to withdraw in retreat to this quiet place tucked into the mountain. The presence of many white doves in this particular spot struck us a witness to the lasting presence of a spirit that drew them as surely as it had drawn us.

◆

—Francis O'Reilly, "Gool's Excellent Adventure"

chure. Ian said a walking stick was the ticket. And Lollie, still in the lead, picked her way sagely, sure as a deer and never slipping.

I skidded down a section of the path, astonished that I kept on my feet. Sometimes I grabbed the frail sticks of underbrush to keep from losing my grip. There was no precipice, but the fear of falling was intense. We weren't taking the road, but a path, just a passage tramped by animals over the centuries. It was so sheer you felt that once you fell you would keep rolling until your broken body landed God knows where.

Sometime about three in the afternoon, things got easier. The awful white stones gave way to earth, and the twisted roots of trees corded over the path. We came to a fountain in a shadowy park-like setting and threw ourselves on the benches around the water which gushed and burbled in the broken light of the place.

Soon after, we hit a paved road. I was exhausted, gritty from falling, my hair tangled from the Subasio wind. I walked stupidly along, passing under a stone arch which was part of a wall I hadn't noticed, lost in the overgrowth.

On the other side of the wall, Lloyd stood lounging. I hardly noticed him and just kept moving. "Don't you realize where you are?" he asked. "This is it, girl. You're in Assisi."

Patricia Hampl is a writer whose work has appeared in The New Yorker, Antaeus, *and* Best American Short Stories. *She is the author of two collections of poems, a prose meditation, and* Virgin Time, *from which this story was excerpted. Ms. Hampl is the recipient of awards and fellowships from the NEA, the Guggenheim Foundation, the Bush Foundation, and has recently received a MacArthur grant. She teaches at the University of Minnesota.*

★

In all the towns and villages of Europe people became aware of poor men in grey who were speaking urgently and movingly of God, and the friars even invaded the Moslem East. At that moment, the year 1219, St. Francis himself stepped into secular history in the most extraordinary way: he arrived in Egypt to convert the Sultan, al-Malik al-Kamil, when the Crusaders were besieging Damietta. Of all the situations in which we are able to visualize St. Francis—tramping the roads of Umbria, preaching to the birds, tending hares and fish, praying on La Verna—surely this is the most fantastic, as the siege engines battered the Moslem walls and the Greek fire came hissing down to the screams and curses of the armies. "He had come to the East," writes Steven Runciman, "believing, as many other good and unwise persons before and after him have believed, that a peace-mission can bring about peace." Nevertheless, incredible to relate, he received permission to see the Sultan and was sent to the enemy lines under a flag of truce. After a moment of suspicion, it was "soon decided that anyone so simple, so gentle, and so dirty must be mad," and he was treated "with the respect due to a man who had been touched by God."

There was a story that the Sultan had placed a carpet decorated with crosses in front of his divan. "If he treads on the cross I will accuse him of insulting his God," he said; "if he refuses to walk on it, I will accuse him of insulting me." As St. Francis walked straight on the carpet, the Sultan taunted him, and St. Francis replied: "You should know that our Lord died between two thieves. We Christians have the true cross; the crosses of the thieves we have left to you; and these I am not ashamed to tread upon."

The Sultan was charmed with the Saint's simplicity and sincerity, and, after listening to him with the respect and courtesy which all cultured Moslems give to a holy man, sent him safely back to the crusading army; and so ended one of the most remarkable encounters in history.

—H. V. Morton, *A Traveller in Italy*

JEANNE CONTE

⋆ ⋆ ⋆

On Climbing the Dome of St. Peter's

This is one climb not to pass up.

ON LOOKING BACK, IT WAS ACTUALLY AN AFTERTHOUGHT, TO climb the inner maze of Michelangelo's Dome on the top of St. Peter's Basilica. Like wide-eyed children, we couldn't satiate our curiosity—couldn't see enough of the wonders that surrounded us. Everywhere was such beauty, such loveliness, so when we found ourselves near a ticket-taker to what promised to be even more, we eagerly purchased passes to the top, not realizing quite what lay ahead.

Having gone as high as the elevator would take us, without hesitation and in high anticipation, we entered the labyrinth of circular ascending steps that wind through the inner parts of the Dome.

Our first thoughts were of being at one with this master's masterpiece. How marvelous the design to actually be allowed to wind within, ever upward over the tomb of St. Peter. They seemed a bit close, and steep, the steps. But hey, we were there and this memory we could share with our children's children. What a sight it would be to see Rome from the top!

I thought of taking a couple of steps at a time, but the stairway was crowded. There were people before and behind us so we matched their pace and it was not long before I realized that the climb wasn't as easy as I had first thought. I was becoming short of breath and I nudged my partner to wait-up a moment, but the man behind me would have none of that.

"Move on!" he ordered, and I did—but a trifle slower.

Soon after, I was panting. I exercise regularly, so it had to be the extraordinary stress of the steepness of the steps. And it was becoming warmer. There were no windows—no air conditioning— and the closeness of the many bodies increased the heat. I slowed a bit and inquired of my partner who seemed oblivious to these problems. So with sweaty brow and panting breath I struggled on, and on.

I began to notice it was not only my own sweat I was smelling, not only my own body's heat I felt. And then, almost imperceptibly, the stairwell narrowed, closing in, and I wanted to stretch my arms and reach out and breath deeply, but I could not.

Claustrophobia set in with ferocity and grew with each step. The walls were closing in on me and I wanted to scream. I stopped, breathing hard, murmuring (then bellowing) that I *had* to go back—I couldn't go on—but the man behind me, with increasingly open impatience, ordered me on:

"Impossible! No one can return! There is no room! Hurry up! When we get to the top we will *push* you off!"

That last phrase I heard reiterated frequently as I dragged myself ever upward—ever onward—and the stairs became in their closeness a rising coffin encasing my body. The man *was* right. It was impossible to return once one entered this 16th-century maze.

"You can do it," my partner urged. "Close your eyes and think of yourself on a mountain."

Too hot; too stifling. With closed eyes I became dizzy. Vertigo—a new adversary. And there were the words of the man behind me.

An eternal nightmare? I sought some sign of light—it must be

near—the top. My eyes searched ahead constantly, but mine was a
never-ending journey; I was sure of it. With each step the claustrophobia increased. With every inch the breath came shorter. A
rising terror gripped me, and then, quite suddenly—we were
there! An *explosion* of light—a great, grand gush of fresh air and the
world opened!

An indescribable relief, and I thought of how a baby is
born—shoved through the narrow, stifling claustrophobic canal
into the world and there is this great howling cry; I understood
for the first time what it actually *feels* like to come new into
the world.

There we were on top of St. Peter's looking down on Rome
below where visions of thirty centuries unfolded before us. Like
welcoming arms I saw the colonnades of St. Peter's extend themselves, then open and narrow as if in embrace. In the center rose
an ancient Egyptian obelisk, brought from Heliopolis to Rome by
Caligula in the 1st century A.D. What secrets of times past did that
obelisk hold?

Beyond this I saw the Tiber River curving through Rome and
wondered at the story of Romulus and Remus, twin babies left
adrift on those waters, hidden in a basket by their mother in the
way of Moses. Could a she-wolf possibly have nursed them? Did
Romulus really mark Rome's first boundaries with a plow in 753
B.C.? What was the life of the Etruscan Kings who ruled here before the Romans overthrew them in 509 B.C.?

Rome stretched before me, the birthplace of law as we know
it, where long before the Common Era, criminals were tried by
juries, and lawyers were appointed to defend them. Senators and
consuls were elected by the people in the first republic of
Rome.

Passing along on the ancient streets below were parades called
Triumphs where Roman generals carted shackled slaves and carts
full of treasure after their victories, too numerous to count. I imagined cheering crowds, felt the agony of those enslaved, wincing at
jeers jabbing their souls. I could almost hear the swelling roars and

smell the garlic-breath of spectators at the Coliseum who watched in jaded callousness, grueling, gruesome Death.

Caesar was stabbed not far from there, his friends and foes fearing for his loyalties because of Cleopatra. Here Augustus "...found Rome brick and left it marble." From here an empire ruled the known world from England to Egypt and Arabia, from North Africa and the Middle East to the Caspian Sea.

Below us, in Caligula's Circus beside the high obelisk, the mad Nero martyred Christians; the ground ran red with their blood. Gladiators killed and were killed. Rome fell to successive raids, war and bitter struggle.

But a sweet softness came—a delicate beauty in the building stone-by-stone of cathedrals and other grand churches filled with art directed toward a love above power, a kindness greater than gold yet described in gold and precious art for all to see, bathing the centuries with a gentler light. And I was standing on this.

While gazing down, I imagined wave after wave of invaders sacking and struggling. The Risorgimento came, bringing Rome again to power. Then world wars. But the beauty continued....

And we were there, in the high place of Michelangelo's Lantern on top of his Dome overlooking the Eternal City. It was a God's-eye view.

Descending from that point nearest Heaven was easier than the rise, but it was to the world below. What could one expect?

Jeanne Conte is a writer and photographer whose work has been published in numerous publications in several countries and is listed in Who's Who of American Art. *She is an avid world traveler, and is married with a family of both adoptive and naturally-born-to-her children. She lives in Ohio.*

＊

One woman said that there was a lot wrong with the way Catholics practiced the religion, but that their paintings and the sculpture told the truth. "They knew how a mother feels when her child is in pain and she can't do nothing about it," she observed. Their pastor said, "If I had somebody like that Michelango to paint my church, a man that inspired, we couldn't stay in there. We would need a bigger place. They would feel the truth vibrating through that paint. Yes, sir, when you stand in that Vatican, you can't help but feel the glory behind everything."

—Stanley Crouch, *Notes of a Hanging Judge: Essays and Reviews*
1979–1983

FRANCES MAYES

✦ ✦ ✦

Etruscan Sunlight

Long before the Romans…

THE IDEAL APPROACH TO MY NEW HOMETOWN OF CORTONA IS first to see the Etruscan tombs down in the flatland below the town. There are tombs from 800 to 200 B.C. near the train station in Camucia and on the road to Foiano, where the custodian never likes the tip. Maybe he's in a bad mood because he spends eerie nights. His small farmhouse, with a bean patch and yard-roaming chickens, coexists with this *tomba* that would appear strangely primordial in the moonlight. A little uphill, a rusted yellow sign is all that points to the so-called tomb of Pythagoras. I pull over and walk along a stream until I reach a short lane, cypress lined, leading to the tomb. There's a gate but it doesn't look as if anyone ever bothers to close it. So there it is, just sitting on a round stone platform. Niches for the upright sarcophagi look like the shrine at the bottom of my driveway. The ceiling is partially gone but enough of the curve is left that I can see the dome shape. I'm standing inside a structure someone put together at least two thousand years ago. One massive stone over the door is a perfect half moon.

The mysterious Etruscans! My knowledge of them, until I started to come to Italy, was limited to the fact that they preceded the Romans and that their language was indecipherable. Since they

built with wood, little remained. I was almost all wrong. Not much
of their written language has been found, but much has been
translated by now, thanks to the crucial find of some strips of linen
shroud from an Egyptian mummy that travelled to Zagreb as a
curio and were preserved later in the museum there. How the
Etruscan linen, inscribed with text in ink made from soot or coal,
became the wrapping for a young girl is still unknown. Possibly
Etruscans migrated to Egypt after they were conquered by Rome
around the 1st century B.C. and the girl was actually Etruscan. Or
perhaps the linen was simply a convenient remnant, torn into strips
by embalmers who used whatever was at hand. The mummy carried enough Etruscan text to provide several key roots, although
the language still isn't totally translated. It's too bad what they left
written in stone is gravestone information and government fact. A
friend told me that last year a local *geometra* discovered a bronze
tablet covered with Etruscan writing. He kicked it up in the dirt
of a farmhouse where he was overseeing a renovation and took it
home. The police heard about this and called on him that night;
presumably, it is in the hands of archaeologists.

Of the local Etruscan culture, an astonishing amount continues
to be unearthed. Beside one of the local tombs, a seven-step stairway of stone flanked with reclining lions intertwined with human
parts—probably a nightmare vision of the underworld—was discovered in 1990. Nearby Chiusi, like Cortona one of the original
twelve cities of Etruria, only recently found its town walls. Both
Cortona and Chiusi have extensive collections of Etruscan artifacts
found both by archeological digs and by farmers turning up
bronze figures in their furrows. In Chiusi, the museum custodian
will take you out to see some of the dozens of tombs found in that
area. The Romans considered Etruscans warlike (the Romans
weren't?), so they come down to us with that rap on them, but the
tombs, enormous clay horses, bronze figures, and household objects reveal them to be a majestic, inventive, humorous people.
Certainly, they must have been strong. Everywhere they've left remains of walls and tombs constructed of stupendous stone.

In the land around Cortona, tombs that have been found are

called *meloni* locally, for the curved shape of the ceilings. To stand under one of these for a few moments is all you need to absorb the sense of time that prepares you for Cortona.

Leaving the tombs, I start uphill, gently at first, then in a series of switchbacks, I begin to climb, glimpsing through the windshield terraced olives, the crenelated tower of Il Palazzone, where Luca Signorelli fell off scaffolding and died a few months later, a broken watchtower and tawny farmhouses. A soft palate: the mellow stone, olive trees flickering moss green to platinum; even the sky may be veiled by thin mist from the lake nearby. In July, small mown wheat fields bordering

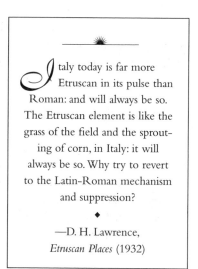

*I*taly today is far more Etruscan in its pulse than Roman: and will always be so. The Etruscan element is like the grass of the field and the sprouting of corn, in Italy: it will always be so. Why try to revert to the Latin-Roman mechanism and suppression?

◆

—D. H. Lawrence,
Etruscan Places (1932)

the olives turn the color of lion's fur. I glimpse Cortona, noble in profile as Nefertiti. At first I'm below the great Renaissance church of Santa Maria del Calcinaio, then, for a 280-degree loop of the road, level with its solid volumes, then above, looking down on the silvery dome and the Latin cross shape of the whole. The shoe tanners built this church, after the common occurrence of the appearance of the Virgin's face on their tannery wall. She is Saint Mary of the Lime Pits because they used lime in tanning leather and the church is erected on their quarry grounds. Odd how often sacred ground remains sacred: the church rests on Etruscan remains, possibly of a temple or burial ground.

A quick look back—I see how far I have climbed. The wide-open Val di Chiana spreads a fan of green below me. On clear days I can spot Monte San Savino, Sinalunga, and Montepulciano in the distance. They could have sent smoke signals; big *festa* tonight, come on over. Soon I've reached the high town walls, and to get one more brush with the Etruscans, drive all the way to the last gate, Porta Colonia, where the big boggling Etruscan stones support the base, with medieval and later additions built on top.

Whizzing past, I love the fast glimpses into the gates. In town, they sell old postcards of these views and they look exactly the same as now: the gate, the narrow street sloping up, the *palazzi* on either side. When I enter the town, the immediate sense is that I am *inside* the gates—a secure feeling if hoards of Ghibellines, Guelfs, or whoever the current enemy are spotted in the distance waving their lances, or even if I've only managed to survive the *autostrada* without getting my car mirror "kissed" by a demon passing in a car half the size of mine.

If I come by car, I walk in on Via Dardano, a name from deep in time. Dardano, believed to have been born here, was the legendary founder of Troy. Right away on the left, I pass a four-table *trattoria*, open only at midday. No menu, the usual choices. I love their thinly pounded grilled steak served on a bed of arugula. And love to watch the two women at the wood-fired stove in the kitchen. Somehow they never appear to be sweltering.

I'm fascinated by the perfect doors of the dead on this street. Traditionally, they're considered to be exits for the plague dead—bad juju for them to go out the door the living use. If this is so, the custom must have come from some superstition much older than Christianity, which was firmly the religious preference of that time. Some suggest that the raised, narrow doors were used in times of strife when the *portone*, the main door, was barricaded. I've wondered if they were not simply doors used when stepping out of a carriage or off a horse and right into the house in bad weather—rather than stepping down into the wet, probably filthy, street—or even in good weather to protect a long silk skirt. George Dennis, 19th-century archaeologist, described Cortona as "squalid in the extreme." That the doors are rather coffin shaped, however, lends a certain visual reinforcement to the door of the dead theory.

The *centro* consists of two irregular *piazzas*, joined by a short street. No town planner would design it this way but it is charming. A 14th-century town hall with 24 broad stone steps dominates the Piazza della Repubblica. The steps serve as ringside seats at night when everyone is out having *gelato*—a fine place to take in the evening spectacle below. From here, you can see a loggia on the level above across the *piazza*, where the fish market used to be. Now it's terrace seating for a restaurant and another perch for viewing. All around are harmonious buildings, punctuated by streets coming up from three gates. The life in the street buzzes, thrives. The miracle of no cars—how amazingly that restores human importance. I first feel the scale of the architecture, then see that the low buildings are completely geared to the body. The main street, officially named Via Nazionale but known locally as Rugapiana, the flat street, is only for walking (except for a delivery period in the morning) and the rest of the town is inhospitable to drivers, too narrow, too hilly. A street connects to a higher or lower one by a walkway, a *vicolo*. Even the names of the *vicoli* make me want to turn into each one and explore: Vicolo della Notte, night, Vicolo dell'Aurora, dawn, and Vicolo della Scala, a long rise of shallow steps.

In these stony old Tuscan towns, I get no sense of stepping back in time that I've had in Yugoslavia, Mexico, or Peru. Tuscans are of this time; they simply have had the good instinct to bring the past along with them. If our culture says burn your bridges behind you—and it does—theirs says cross and recross. A 14th-century plague victim, perhaps once hauled out of one of the doors of the dead, could find her house and might even find it intact. Present and past just coexist, like it or not. The old Medici ball insignia in the *piazza* until last year had a ceramic hammer and sickle of the Communist party right beside it.

I walk through the short connecting leg of street to Piazza Signorelli, named for one of Cortona's hometown boys. Slightly larger, this *piazza* swarms on Saturday, market day, year round. It hosts an antique fair on the third Sunday in summer months. Two bars' outdoor tables extend into the *piazza*. I always notice the rather forlorn-looking Florentine lion slowly eroding on a column. No matter how late I go into town, people are gathered there; one last coffee before the strike of midnight.

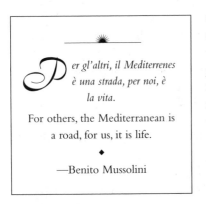

Per gl'altri, il Mediterrenes è una strada, per noi, è la vita.

For others, the Mediterranean is a road, for us, it is life.

◆

—Benito Mussolini

Here, too, the *comune* sometimes sponsors concerts at night. Everyone is out anyway, but on these nights the *piazza* fills up with people from the nearby *frazioni* and farms and country villas. In this town of dozens of Catholic churches, a black gospel choir from America is singing tonight. Of course, this is no spontaneous Baptist group from a Southern church but a highly produced, professional choir from Chicago, complete with red and blue floodlights and cassettes for sale for twenty-thousand lire. They belt out "Amazing Grace" and "Mary Don't You Weep." The acoustics are weird and the sound warps around the 11th- and 12th-century buildings surrounding this *piazza*, where jousts and flag throwers have performed regularly, and where on certain feast days, the bishops hold aloft the relics of saints, priests swing braziers of burning myrrh, and we walk through town on flower petals scattered by children. The sound engineer gets the microphones adjusted and the lead singer begins to pull the crowd to him. "Repeat after me," he says in English, and the crowd responds. "Praise the Lord. Thank you, Jesus." The English and American forces liberated Cortona in 1944. Until tonight, this many foreigners may never have gathered here since, certainly not this many black ones. The choir is big. The University of Georgia's students form the art program in Cortona are all out for a little down-home nostalgia. They, a smattering of tourists, and almost all the Cortonese are crushed into Piazza Signorelli. "Oh, Happy Day," the black singers belt out, pulling an Italian girl on stage to sing with them. She has a mighty voice that easily matches any of theirs, and her small body seems all song. What are they thinking, this ancient race of Cortonese? Are they remembering the tanks rolling in, oh, happy, happy day, the soldiers throwing oranges to the children? Are they thinking, Mass in the duomo was never like this? Or are they simply swaying with the crude American Jesus, letting themselves be carried on his shoulders by the music?

The *piazza*'s focus is the tall Palazzo Casali, now the Etruscan Academy Museum. The most famous piece inside is a 4th-century B.C. bronze candelabrum of intricate design. It's remarkably wild. A center bowl fed oil to sixteen lamps around the rim. Between them, in bold relief, are animals, horned Dionysus, dolphins, naked crouching men in *erectus*, winged sirens. One Etruscan word, *tinscvil*, appears between two of the lamps. According to *The Search for the Etruscans* by James Wellard, *Tin* was the Etruscan Zeus and the inscription translates "Hail to Tin." The candelabrum was found in a ditch near Cortona in 1840. In the museum, it is hung with a mirror above so you can get a good look. I once heard an English woman say, "Well, it is interesting, I suppose, but I wouldn't buy it at a jumble sale." In glass cases, you see chalices, vases, bottles, a wonderful bronze pig, a two-headed man, many lead soldier-sized bronze figures from the 6th and 7th centuries B.C., including some in *tipo schematico*, an elongated style that reminds the contemporary viewer of Giacometti. Besides the Etruscan collection, this small museum has a surprising display of Egyptian mummies and artifacts. So many museums have excellent Egyptian exhibits; I wonder sometimes if anything from ancient Egypt ever was lost. I always visit several paintings I like. One, a portrait of the thoughtful Polimnia wearing a blue dress and a laurel crown, was long thought to be Roman, from the 1st century A.D. She's the muse of sacred poetry and looks quite pensive with the responsibility. Now she's believed to be an excellent 17th-century copy. The museum has not changed the more impressive date.

Appealing family crests emblazoned with carved swans, pears, and fanciful animals cover the side of the Palazzo Casali. The short street below leads to the Duomo and the Museo Diocesano, formerly the Chiesa del Gesù, which I sometimes pop into. Upstairs, the treasure is the Fra Angelico *Annunciation*, with a fabulous neon orange-haired angel. The Latin that comes out of the angel's mouth heads toward the Virgin: her reply comes back to him upside down. This is one of Fra Angelico's great paintings. He worked in Cortona for ten years and this triptych and a faded, painted lunette over the door of San Domenico are all that remains from his years here.

Just to the right of Palazzo Casali is Teatro Signorelli, the new building in town, 1854, but built in a quasi-Renaissance style with arched portico, perfect to shade the vegetable sellers from sun or rain. Inside is an opera house straight out of a Márquez novel: oval, tiered, little boxes and seats upholstered in red, with a small stage on which I once witnessed a ballet troupe from Russia thump around for two hours. It serves now as the movie theater in winter. Midway through the movie, the reel winds down. Intermission. Everyone gets up for coffee and fifteen minutes of talk. It's hard, when you really love to talk, to shut up for an entire two hours. In summer, the movies are shown *sotto le stelle*, under the stars, in the town park. Orange plastic chairs are set up in a stone amphitheater, kind of like the drive-in with no cars.

Off both of these *piazzas,* streets radiate. This way to the medieval houses, that to the 13th-century fountain, there to the tiny *piazzas*, up to the venerable convents and small churches. I walk along all of these streets. I never have not seen something new. Today, a *vicolo* named Polveroso, dusty, though why it should be more or less dusty than others was impossible to see.

If you're in great shape, you'll still huff a little on a walk to the upper part of town. Even in the mad-dog sun right after lunch, it's worth it. I pass the medieval hospital, with its long portico, saying a little prayer that I never have to have my appendix out in there. At meal times, women dash in carrying covered dishes and trays. If you're hospitalized, it's simply expected that your family will bring meals. Next is the interminably closed church of Saint Francis. At the side the ghost of a former cloister arcs along the wall. Up, up, streets utterly clean, lined with well-kept houses. If there are four feet of ground, someone has planted tomatoes on a bamboo tepee, a patch of lettuces. In pots, the neighborhood hands-down favorite, besides geraniums, is hydrangeas, which grow to bush size and always seem to be pink. Often, women are sitting outside, along the street on chairs, shelling beans, mending, talking with the woman next door. Once, as I approached, I saw a crone of a woman, long black dress, black scarf, hunched in a little cane chair. It could have been 1700. When I got closer, I saw she was talking on a cellular phone. At Via Berrettini, 33, a plaque proclaims it to be the birthplace of Pietro Berrettini; I finally figured out that's Pietro de Cortona. A couple of shady *piazzas* are surrounded by townhouse-style old houses, with pretty little gardens in front. If I lived here, I'd like that one, with the marble table under the arbor of Virginia creeper, the starched white curtain at the window. A woman with an elaborate swirl of hair shakes out a cloth. She is laying plates for lunch. Her rich *ragù* smells like an open invitation, and I look longingly at her green checked tablecloth and the capped bottle of farm wine she plunks down in the center of the table.

The church of San Cristoforo, almost at the top, is my favorite in town. It's ancient, ancient, begun around 1192 on Etruscan foundations. Outside, I peer into a small chapel with a fresco of the Annunciation. The angel, just landed, has chalky aqua sleeves and skirts still billowing from flight. The door to the church is always open. Actually, it's always half open, just ajar, so that I pause and consider before I go in. Basically a Romanesque plan, inside the organ balcony of curlicued painted wood is a touching country interpretation of Baroque. A faded fresco, singularly flat in perspective, shows Christ crucified. Under each wound, a suspended angel holds out a cup to catch his falling blood. They're homey, these neighborhood churches. I like the jars (six today) of droopy garden flowers on the altar, the stacks of Catholic magazines under another fresco of the Annunciation. This Mary has thrown up her hands at the angel's news. She has a you've-got-to-be-kidding look on her face. The back of the church is dark. I hear a soft honking snore. In the privacy of the last pew, a man is having a nap.

Behind San Cristoforo is one of the staggering valley views, cut into diagonally by a slice of fortress wall, amazingly high. What has held them up all these centuries? The Medici castle perches at the top of the hill, and this part of its extensive walls angles sharply down. I walk up the road to the Montanina gate, the high entrance to town. Etruscan, too; isn't this place ancient? I often walk this way into town. My house is on the other side of the hill and from there the road into this top layer of Cortona remains level. I like to go through the upper town without having to climb. One pleasure of my walk is Santa Maria Nuova. Like Santa Maria del Calcinaio, this church is situated on a broad terrace below the town. From the Montanina road, I'm looking down at its fine-boned shape, rhythmic curves, and graceful dome, a deeply glazed aquamarine and bronze in the sun. Though Calcinaio is more famous, having been designed by Francesco di Giorgio Martini, Santa Maria Nuova pleases my eye more. Its lines counter a sense of weight. The church looks as though it alighted there and easily could fly, given the proper miracle, to another position.

Turning back from the gate toward town, I walk to the other treasure of a church, San Niccolò. It's newer, mid-15th century. Like San Cristoforo's, the decorations are amateurish and charming. The serious piece of art is a Signorelli double-sided painting, a deposition on one side and the Madonna and baby on the other. Meant to be borne on a standard in a procession, it now can be reversed by the custodian. On a hot day, this is a good rest. The eye is entertained; the feet can cool on the stone floor. On the way out, almost hidden, I spot a small Christ by Gino Severini, another Cortona boy. As a signer of the Futurist manifesto and an adherent to the slogan "Kill the moonlight," Severini doesn't readily associate in my mind with religious art. The Futurists were down on the past, embraced velocity, machines, industry. Around town, in restaurants and bars, I've seen posters of Severini's paintings, all color, swirl, energy. Then, over a table in Bar Sport, I notice that the modern Madonna nursing a baby is his. The woman, unlike any Madonna I've seen, has breasts the size of cantaloupes. Usually a Madonna's breasts look disassociated from the body; often they're as round as a tennis ball. The Severini original in the Etruscan museum just escapes being lugubrious by being tedious. A separate room devoted to Severini is filled with an interesting hodgepodge of his work. Nothing major, unfortunately, but a taste of the styles he ran through: Braque-like collages with the gears, pipes, speedometers the Futurists loved, a portrait of woman rather in the style of Sargent, art school-quality drawings, and the more well-known Cubist abstractions. A couple of glass cases hold his publications and a few letters from Braque and Apollinaire. None of this work shows the verve and ambition he was capable of. Of course, all the Futurists have suffered from their early enthusiasm for Fascism; baby went out with the bathwater. They've suffered more from the tendency we have had, until recently, to look to France for the news about art. Many astounding paintings from the Futurists are unknown. For whatever reasons, Severini, in his later years, returned to his roots for subjects. I think there's a microbe in Italian painters' bloodstreams that infects them with the compulsion to paint Jesus and Mary.

As I leave San Niccolò, walking down, I pass several almost windowless convents (they must have large courtyards), one of which is still cloistered. If I had lace needing repair, I could place it on a Catherine wheel, where it is spun in to a nun to mend. Two of the convents have chapels, strangely modernized. On down the hill, I encounter Severini again in a mosaic at San Marco; if I climb this street, I'm on a Crucifixion trail he designed. A series of stone-enshrined mosaics traces Christ's progress toward the Crucifixion and then the Deposition. At the end of that walk (on a hot day I feel I've carried a cross), I'm at Santa Margherita, a large church and convent. Inside, Margherita herself is encased in glass. She has shrunk. Her feet are creepy. Most likely, a praying woman will be kneeling in front of her. Margherita was one of the fasting saints who had to be coaxed to take at least a spoon of oil every day. She shouted of her early sins in the streets. She would be neurotic, anorectic toady; back then they understood her desire to suffer like Christ. Even Dante, it is believed, came to her in 1289 and discussed his "pusillanimity." Margherita is so venerated locally that when mothers call their children in the park, hers is the name most often heard. A plaque beside the Bernada gate (now closed) proclaims that through it she first entered the city in 1272.

The major street off the Piazza della Repubblica leads to the park. The Rugapiana is lined with cafés and small shops. The proprietors often are sitting in chairs outside or grabbing an espresso nearby. From the *rosticceria*, tempting smells of roasting chicken, duck, and rabbit drift into the street. They do a fast business in lasagne at lunch and all day in *panzarotti*, which means rolled bread but loses something in the translation. It's rolled around a variety of stuffings, such as mushrooms or ham and cheese. Sausage and mozzarella is one of the best. Past the circular Piazza Garibaldi—almost every Italian town has one—you come to the proof, if you have not intuited it before, that this is one of the most civilized towns on the globe. A shady park extends for a kilometer along the parterre. Cortonese use it daily. A park has a timeless quality. Clothing, flowers, the sizes of trees change; otherwise it easily could be a hundred years ago. Around the cool splash of the fountain of upside-down nymphs riding dolphins, young parents watch their children play. The benches are full of neighbors talking. Often a father balances a tiny child on a two-wheeler and watches her wobble off with a mixture of fear and exhilaration on his face. It's a peaceful spot to read the paper. A dog can get a long evening walk. Off to the right, there's the valley and the curved end of Lake Trasimeno.

The park ends at the *strada bianca* lined with cypresses commemorating the World War I dead. After waking along that dusty road toward home for about a kilometer, I look up and see, at the end of the Medici walls, the section of Etruscan wall known as Bramasole. My house takes its name from the wall. Facing south like the temple at Marzabotto near Bologna, the wall may have been part of a sun temple. Some local people have told us the name comes from the short days in winter we have on this side of the hill. Who knows how old the name, indicating a yearning for the sun, might be? All summer the sun strikes the Etruscan wall directly at dawn. It wakes me up, too. Behind the pleasure and fresh beauty of sunrise, I detect an old and primitive response: the day has come again, no dark god swallowed it during the night. A sun temple seems the most logical kind anyone ever would build. Perhaps the name does go back twenty-six or so centuries to the ancient purpose of this site. I can see the Etruscans chanting orisons to the first rays over the Apennines, then slathering themselves with olive oil and lying out all morning under the big old Mediterranean sun.

Henry James records walking this road in his *The Art of Travel*. He "strolled forth under the scorching sun and made the outer circuit of the wall. There I found tremendous uncemented blocks; they glared and twinkled in the powerful light, and I had to put on a blue eye-glass in order to throw into its proper perspective the vague Etruscan past..." A blue eye-glass? The 19th-century equivalent of sunglasses? I can see Henry peering up from the white road, nodding wisely to himself, dusting off his uppers, then, no doubt, heading back to his hotel to write his requisite number of pages for the day. I take the same stroll and attempt the same mysterious act, to throw the powerful light of the long, long past into the light of the morning.

Frances Mayes has written for The New York Times, House Beautiful, *and* Food and Wine. *She is also a widely published poet and food and travel writer. Ms. Mayes divides her time between Cortona, Italy and San Francisco, where she teaches creative writing at San Francisco State University.*

✳

It must have been the Tuscan hills on a September morning that inspired Dante's *Paradiso*: the pure and boundless light; the planted hillsides, with their rows of vines and silver olive trees, looking as if they had been painted; the valleys, with their fields of sunflowers, the walled towns in a blue haze cresting the hills. To see all this from the hilltop farmhouse that some friends and I rented for a few weeks is to know what Dante meant when he said that he had found, at last, all the leaves of the universe bound into one volume.

—Jason Epstein, "This Side of Paradiso," *The New Yorker*

★ ★ ★

A *Trulli* Rich Woman

Welcome to the strangeness of the boot.

AFTER THE LIMPID HARBORS AND LUSH GREEN TERRACES OF eastern Sicily, Apulia, the heel of the boot, came as a jolt. The coastline was disastrously industrialized, the inland landscape austere and fouled. Bari, itself, had a menacing feel—factory buildings blank and sealed, scrawled with sinister graffiti, their windows like broken teeth; brooding stevadores fresh off cargo ships from Bengazi prowling the bars looking for a good time; the women hidden away, perhaps sewing pictures of dead lovers into their hems, moving their lips in silent rosary.

Even the restaurants in fish-famous Barium, as Horace called it, failed to please—the incessant chirp of cellular phones into which receivers modish customers chatted between courses; the streets peopled with pinstriped businessmen who walked briskly adjusting their Ray-Bans with one hand, carrying their pull-out car radios in the other; the bold drivers who inched into intersections like matadors faking out a bull. Depressed by the inhospitable atmosphere, I drove out of town in search of some welcoming corner to counteract the indifference of the urban scene.

Alberobello, the village of the *trulli*, lay midway between the Adriatic and the Ionian Seas. The mystery of the place intrigued me. No one seemed to know the origin of the *trulli*, the white-washed domed dwellings decorated with symbols and glyphs that hinted of black magic. I had read that they were constructed by Byzantine monks: I had also read that they were constructed as tombs like those in Mycenae and Syria. But there seemed to be no theory as to why these huts with their domed roofs of overlapping slates were peculiar only to this region of Apulia.

The village looked magical when glimpsed from afar. As I drove toward it, the heat lay in shimmering layers. I parked in the shade and trudged up a steep hill. There wasn't a soul in sight and there was a strange absence of sound. Between the heat and the silence, I felt wrapped in batting.

Feeling as other-worldly as if I'd stepped into the pages of a fairy tale, I tiptoed through lanes that twined like vines around the mysterious dwellings, past silent doorways hung with beaded curtains, expecting at any minute to see an olive-eyed Hansel and Gretel skipping down the cobblestones hand-in-hand.

As I passed an open doorway, I was startled by a squawk coming from somewhere inside one of the *trullo*. The sound tore the silence like a gunshot. I stopped, trying to figure out where it came from and who—or what—made it. Was it a parrot?

Not a breath of air stirred. I took a few cautious steps and peered around a corner just as a gnarled hand pushed aside a beaded curtain and a crone in a black headscarf, swathed from head to toe in black, squinted from the doorway, cocking her head, the better to see me. Her body was curled like a question mark.

"*Veni ca, veni ca. Non ha paura,*" she croaked, sensing my reluctance.

Eager to see the inside of the odd structures, my curiosity got the better of my fear and I ducked through the low doorway into a tiny living room no more than eight feet in diameter. It was furnished with a battered chest of drawers and a balding velvet loveseat that sprouted a garden of horsehair from its numerous worn spots. Yet another conical structure, attached like a honeycomb to the first, contained a night table and a single bed whose dough-colored spread bore traces of debris at the foot, fragments of dried leaves and crumbs of mud as if someone had rested on the coverlet with their shoes on.

"*Cucina*," she cawed, gesturing to a three-by-two-foot kitchen carved out of the living room, in which stood a slender icebox leaking murky fluid. On the ledge of the tiny window high above the floor stood three posthumously-watered plants trailing brittle tendrils, the vessels dribbling down the mud walls and pooling on the floor in a fetid puddle that merged with the overflow from the icebox.

She crooked her finger, bent as a twig, and I followed her outside to a parched, postage stamp–sized backyard, trampled and unpleasant. Nettles clawed at my ankles. There was a beehive oven set amidst the overgrown weeds. I half expected the woman to invite me to bend over and inspect its interior so she could shove me in.

Gnats swarmed at the edge of my vision and fleas nipped my shins. I restrained myself from slapping at them so as not to hurt her feelings. I nodded and smiled and tried to convey how enchanted I was. When I had exclaimed long enough, she led me back into the house, following closely.

"*Dormi?*" I thought she said. It was hard for me to understand her, not only because of her Apulian dialect, but also because she had no teeth to hold her nose and chin apart. Not to mention that I hadn't much Italian. I shook my head, not understanding.

She led me inside and gestured up at a messily painted lime-green loft that was jerry-built over the living room. The smell of fresh enamel bit at my nostrils, and I knew if I touched the moist-looking paint blisters that pimpled the surface of the wood, they'd deflate into concave craters.

"*Dormire?*" she asked, folding her hands and laying her cheek on them. She pointed at the opening cut into the wooden platform, in which rested a ladder. I climbed a few rungs and peered into a windowless conical space about three feet high. I could make out a rust-stained mattress and the whine of mosquitos.

"*Molto interesante*," I said.

It was suffocating in the *trullo*. A net of flies flew in layers at

eye level, darting and retreating in the conical room that smelled
of rancid olive oil and melon rinds and the sweet decay of the
old woman.

The conicalness was starting to get to me. Everything was conical—all the houses, and all of the rooms in all of the houses, the
beehive oven, the old woman's hump. I imagined waking at three
a.m. to the drone of mosquitos dive-bombing my face, trapped in
a conical cell above the conical living room under a ceiling too
low to even sit up in, nothing to read—in fact no light to read
by—no water with which to down a Valium, no partner to whom
to complain, swatting at gnats and longing for morning.

And what if I had to use the bathroom? Had there even been
one? Maybe she did her business among the nettles in the wee
hours. Maybe we would encounter one another under the light
of the moon, squatting in the briarpatch next to the conical oven,
trying to keep our balance as we chatted about our children,
mine scattered across the face of the U.S. with children of their
own.

"*Dormire,*" she said again, pointing to the loft.

Be charitable, I told myself. This could be you, alone at ninety.
But my only impulse was to escape.

"*Grazie tanto,*" I said, "*ma ho stato in un hotel.*"

I was annoyed with myself for spurning the hospitality of a
lonely old woman isolated in this little pocket of the world, eking
out her existence. I envisioned the drabness of her days, lying on
the coverlet with her shoes on, staring up at the dome of the ceiling. No TV, no books, no diversion, starved for the company of
others, especially foreigners who might feed her dreams.

Was I so spoiled that I could not bring myself to give up comfort for one night? Did I need to insulate myself in a hotel? Why
did I travel anyway, if not to try on other people's lives? I
agonized over my American expectations of comfort and enti-
tlement as I stood with her in the doorway, ready to leave. The
old woman nodded and heaved a shuddering sigh, adding to my
guilt. I wanted to give her some token of my gratitude for letting
me into her home, but I was worried that a gift of money might

offend her. I rummaged in my purse and found a dog-eared snap-shot of me taken in Pisa and I offered it to her as a reminder of our brief encounter.

"No, no," she said, shaking her head vehemently and pushing it away as if she wanted the real article, not a reproduction.

I could think of no other way to express my gratitude and so I handed her 10,000 lira, a token. "*Grazie mille, Signora,*" I said. "For more flowers." I pointed at the three dead plants.

She smiled up at me brightly. "*Tedeschi? Francia?*"

"*Stati Uniti,*" I said.

She beamed as if I had given the right answer. "*Ah-h-h. Stati Uniti. Un momento,*" she said.

"I don't understand."

"*Un recordo, un souvenir,*" she cawed, pulling from her pocket an ancient coinpurse. "*Dolar!*"

I fumbled in my pocket and found I had no dollar bills, only a twenty.

"Sorry," I said, "*Non ho dolar....*"

She smiled. Her gnarled fingers struggled to open the swollen coinpurse which burst spontaneously from sheer bulk, spilling its contents onto the dirt floor.

"OK," she said and snatched the twenty from my hand. Scrambling to gather up the rest of the deutchmarks, pounds, francs and yen, she stuffed them back into her coinpurse.

Then, grinning and nodding, she practically shoved me out the door.

Kelly Simon is the recipient of a Lowell Thomas award for her travel writing. Her work has appeared in The Quarterly, Ellery Queen, NPR, The Washington Post, Grand Tour, Ploughshares *and* Travelers' Tales: Food. *She is also the author of a Thai cookbook. She lives in San Francisco with her pests.*

★

An Italian research institute, the Eurispes, put out a book called *The Italy That Cheats.* While Italians have become accustomed to seeing their dirty laundry washed in public, the book, by Bruno Taraletto, came as a surprise to many because it did not deal with political corruption, terrorism, the Mafia, drugs or any of the crimes that have made regular headlines in Italy. Rather, the study exposed the petty crimes of the average citizens.

In 80 chapters, the book, published in Italian by Koinè Edizioni, addresses the different ways in which some Italians cheat, including absenteeism, impersonating invalids, contraband, tax evasion (a long chapter), false advertising and various swindles.

The book at times cannot hide a smidgeon of subdued pride in the artful ways of the average Italian citizen, noting that they betray a "typical Mediterranean creativity, in short, the famous art of getting by." The book also condemns the hypocrisy of people who are quick to criticize corrupt politicians and equally quick to forgive their own shortcomings. In the long run, the book says, just a handful of people have cheated on a large scale, while millions of average citizens cheat the state in one way or another.

—Elisabetta Polovedo, "How Do I Bilk Thee?" *The New York Times*

THERESA M. MAGGIO

✦ ✦ ✦

Ancient Islands

Odysseus sailed these seas.

FROM MY HOME ON FAVIGNANA, AN ISLAND OFF THE NORTHWEST coast of Sicily, I could see the sun rise over Erice, Aphrodite's home atop the Sicilian headland, and I could see it set in red-orange splendor behind Santa Caterina, an 11th-century castle straight out of my Tarot deck. Across the water, at night, the flickering lights of Marsala and Trapani snaked along the Sicilian coast. And when a fishing boat churned through the strait in the moonlight, its foamy white wake sparkled with phosphorescent plankton.

Favignana, Levanzo, and Marettimo, the mountainous Egadi Islands, are three beautiful sisters rising from the intense blue waters of the Tyrrhenian Sea. They form a single municipality, with about 200 people living year-round on Levanzo's 1,200 acres, nearly a thousand on Marettimo's seven and a half square miles, and about 3,000 on the butterfly-shaped Favignana, five and a half miles from wing to wing.

Last spring I spent two months on Favignana to study the workings of the *tonnara*, an ancient communal method of capturing giant bluefin tuna during their spring migration from the west coast of Africa. The 63 fishermen of the Favignana *tonnara* still recite the ritual prayers, sing the traditional work songs, and submit to the almost feudal authority of their chief, the *rais* (from the Arabic for prince). It is the last traditional *tonnara* in Sicily, where just 40 years ago there were 25. (At Bonagia, near Trapani, the only other remaining Sicilian *tonnara*, the men no longer sing the work songs.)

Favignana, named for *favonio*, a wind more commonly known as the *sirocco*, is the largest and most developed of the three islands. It is one of those seductive places that lure city dwellers into quitting their desk jobs. Some people go there to die, the town librarian told me, and I know why: it's almost heaven.

Favignana's eastern wing is full of eerily beautiful limestone quarries and sunken gardens. In spring, poppies and buttercups swathe its field in color. Hidden coves and white sandy beaches dot its coast.

Some students of *The Odyssey* say that Favignana was the home of Circe, the enchantress who turned Odysseus' men into swine and held them captive for a year. Others say it was here that the nymph Calypso rescued the shipwrecked Odysseus, then kept him for seven years in her love cave. ("It was indeed a spot where even an immortal visitor must pause to gaze in wonder and delight," Homer wrote.)

The island has many striking visual connections to history. About a mile and a half before entering port, vessels arriving in late spring must skirt red and yellow floats that mark and support a rectangu-

There are 32 islands off the coasts of Italy, ranging in size from Sicily and Sardinia—the largest in the Mediterranean—to little specks in the sea, where convicts get government-paid holidays for life. Some islands, Capri-fashion, have blossomed (or withered, depending on your point of view) into full-blown resorts, where you can count more signs in English and German than in Italian. Others, such as Ponza, Pantelleria and the Egadi Islands, are among Italy's best-kept secrets.

◆

—Dana Facaros and Michael Paul, *Italian Islands*

lar tuna trap made of netting. Bigger than two football fields, the trap originated 1,200 years ago with the North African Arabs who settled these islands. Above the port towers Santa Caterina, the island's 1,000-foot-high central massif topped by a castle, also called Santa Caterina. It was built by the Normans, who took Sicily—and Favignana's *tonnara*—from the Arabs nine centuries ago. Built on the remains of an Arab lookout tower, the fortress is now an unmanned military radar station, officially off limits to the public but visited by many just the same.

The Romans began their empire in these waters in 241 B.C., when they sank at least 50 Carthaginian ships to win the naval battle that ended the First Punic War. Archeologists who found marijuana aboard a Carthaginian wreck think it may have been issued for the crew the way British sailors once got their tot of rum.

Relics of antiquity abound. A farmer whose fields is in the island's archeological zone at Punta San Nicola plows up Roman coins and mosaic marble tiles, chunks of amphorae and Phoenician glass every year.

Facing the sea, the Palazzo Florio, once the spring residence of Ignazio Florio, a 19th-century Sicilian entrepreneur, gives the port its elegance. The villa, which now belongs to the town, looks across the jade-green bay to the buildings of the *tonnara*. Florio bought the extremely lucrative tuna works, once the property of Sicilian kings, in 1874 and devoted himself to making it the "Queen of the *Tonnara*." He hired Palermo's best architect, Giuseppe Damiani de Almeyda, to design the new buildings. The interiors of the boathouse, the net storage building and the cannery are vaulted, soaring places whose repeated Norman-Arab arches evoke Palermo's Palatine Chapel and the Cathedral of Monreale.

It's a short walk from the port to the green dome of the Chiesa Madre, the island's largest church, and the *piazza* in front of it. The church was set slightly askew to give the cannons at nearby Fort San Giacomo a clear shot to the sea. The medieval fort, built on a 1,000-year-old Arab foundation, now serves as a jail that houses some prisoners in unheated caves.

Visitors can get information and a free road map at the Pro

Loco office on the square. Across the street, the Bar Due Colonne, social headquarters for vacationers and locals alike, serves complimentary *bruschetta* with drinks at cocktail hour. Cristine Torre, the *caffè's* co-owner, keeps a cork board covered with postcards and pictures of tourists who have fallen in love with the island and who now write, homesick for the piazza and its camaraderie.

Favignana has hotels, inns, bungalows, and campgrounds, but I rented a house by contacting one of the residents on a list provided by the Pro Loco. It was the last house on the eastern tip of the island, at Bue Marino, and it came with a bike, all I needed to get around. At nightfall I'd pedal home through the warmed, swirled scents of pine, oleander, and jasmine. I'd climb into bed and the soothing hypnotic beam of a lighthouse would sweep over me.

My house was of thick limestone blocks, an isolated whitewashed cube against the cobalt sea. Two starkly beautiful exhausted limestone pits stretched out from the foundation like moats. The quarry walls rose sheer and square, washed in pink and peach, crosshatched with cutters' marks. Wild capers grew from the cracks, their flower an orchidy white trumpet blowing a spray of silky, violet stamen.

Until shipping costs priced it out of the market, Favignana's dense stone, prized by builders, was a chief export. Now people plant orange and lemon trees in small disused quarries for protection against the dry, salt-bearing wind. In summer you see clotheslines strung across the deep, cool pits where some islanders set up housekeeping to escape the heat.

It's easy to island-hop to Egadi. Ferries and the faster hydrofoils crisscross between the islands several times a day. I have often taken a day trip to Levanzo, a two-street town, population 200, just five minutes away by hydrofoil. Levanzo's sea wall of jumbo cement blocks jutting into the port's cerulean blue waters echoes the village's blue-shuttered white cube houses.

Levanzo's smallness and utter quiet have an immediate sedative effect, but those with only a few hours to spend should go see the engravings and 10,000-year-old cave paintings in the Grotta del Genovese, the oldest cave paintings in Italy. The stylized figures of dancing men and the limbless torsos of violin-shaped women show prehistoric man just beginning to use symbols. The silhouettes of a dog, bulls, an ass, dolphins, and a precisely drawn tuna mark it as a ceremonial cave where prehistoric men once asked their gods for luck in the hunt.

The religious tradition continues. In mid-May, when the *rais* calls for the first *mattanza*, the first of several rounds of killing trapped tuna, fishermen ring a bell, take off their hats and shout the name Jesus three times. The news spreads through town like wildfire. At dawn the next day the well-drilled team of fishermen provides free passage to anyone who wants to see this strange event. It is not for the faint of heart.

The rectangular, submerged trap is an elaborate structure that takes about three weeks to set up every year. It is divided into several "chambers," or holding pens. The fishermen chase the tuna into the last pen, the Chamber of Death, the only room with a floor, and form a square of boats above it, a process that may take four hours. Hand over hand, they pull up the net sack to the rhythm of a haunting, dirgelike chant, the first of three songs they sing this day. A few dorsal fins slice through unnatural swells, then, in a sudden wall of sound, the sea boils with hundreds of terrified bluefin.

Their wild thrashing whips this small square of sea into a white froth tinged pink with their blood. An average bluefin tuna here weighs about 220 pounds, but some of the giants reach nearly three-quarters of a ton. A prize specimen destined for a Tokyo sushi bar can command $30,000.

Eight men to a fish, they pierce the blue marble flesh of the struggling behemoths with barbed gaffs and labor to hoist them aboard, to the amazement and astonished applause of onlookers. In these days of pollution and overfishing with purse seine nets, 1,000 tuna is considered a good year's catch for the *tonnara*, quite a drop from the record 14,000 taken in 1848, and even from a more recent record of 3,983 taken in 1975. The entire catch, except for the smallest fish, is shipped to Japan.

Gioacchino Cataldo, 54, a gentle giant of a fisherman, once asked me what Americans think of the *mattanza*. "Those I tell about it think it's barbaric," I said.

"You tell them this is what's barbaric: to *raise* a calf and feed him and make him believe you're his friend, then to butcher him and eat him," he said. "I don't know the tuna. He comes to me, and I kill him."

Far from what the islanders see as the frantic pace of Favignana, half an hour by hydrofoil, is Marettimo, the wildest, most verdant and most remote of the three sisters. Here even the air seems suffused in blue. The ancient Greeks called the island Heira, or Sacred. Marettimo is known among divers as one of the Mediterranean's last underwater Edens, but the islanders love their 2,263-tall Monte Falcone, as much as the blue deep around it.

Visitors can board boats at either of Marettimo's two small ports to tour the island's solemn marine grottoes, to be dropped off at a sandy beach or rocky cove (Cala Bianca will knock your eyes out) and retrieved later, or to snorkel or scuba dive. The regional government has made a marine reserve of the waters off the western side of the island where divers will find sunlighted grottoes, clouds of colorful fish and remnants of the Punic War, such as vases and stone anchors.

Except for the whitewashed village, most of the island is a

mountainous nature preserve open to the public. The forest service has cleared, marked, and maintains footpaths to the island's points of interest: a Bourbon castle, Roman houses (probably built in the 1st century), the lighthouse of Punta Libecciò, and a tiny, domed, 12th-century Norman church. Wild rosemary and scrub oak scent the trails. Early morning walkers may see wild boar or a herd of mountain goats, both introduced species.

On my last visit, Filippo Lipari, a friend who works for the forest service, took me to the top of Marettimo's second-highest peak, Punta Campana, 2,067 feet. In silence we watched the clouds below us float over a rippling blue infinity. There was no horizon; sky and sea fused in the milky blue distance. A great orange oil tanker passed and sounded its ship's horn in heartbreaking wails.

The captain or the crew must be from Marettimo, Filippo explained. "They can't stop so they salute the town this way as they pass on their way around the world." These mournful, lonesome blasts bore all their sad longing for their birthplace, their sacred island.

Theresa M. Maggio is working on a book about the tonnara, *the tuna trap which takes place off Favignama in Italy.*

⋆

Nets mended and boats caulked, the crew begins its work in April when the long, low wooden boats are brought down to the water's edge and the fishermen fold in the huge nets with care so that they will feed out smoothly and quickly. When they are being addressed by the Arabic title of *rais*, the crew works to the rhythm of a chant which at the end of each net becomes a prayer to the Virgin that the net may be filled with a good catch.

The *tonnara* proper is an enormous rectangle formed by huge cords that are floated by corks and stretched taut by forged iron anchors eight feet tall. Nets drop down vertically from the cords to the sea bottom to form a long corridor, the shore end of which is open to admit the fish. More nets, placed crosswise along the length of this corridor, can be raised or lowered to create a series of chambers through which the *tonnaroti* force the fish toward the closed end of the corridor, known as the "death chamber."

Once this elaborate mechanism is set up, the long wait begins (it was not rare in the past for the statues of the *tonnara's* patron saint to get a dunking if the fish were slow in coming). When at last the lookouts announce the arrival of a school of tuna, the boats drive the fish into the mouth of the trap and then gather round the "death chamber." The *rais* waits till the nets are full to order the closing of the doors, and then the *tonnara ti* begin the slow pulling in on the ropes, leaning and heaving to the beat of the *cialoma*. Each verse of this ancient chant begins and ends with the cry "*Aimola! Aimola!*" which some say derives from "*Allah! Che muoia!*—Allah! May it die!"

—Mary Taylor Simeti, *On Persephone's Island: A Sicilian Journal*

JAMES GARDNER

⋆ ⋆ ⋆

The Hall of Maps

All of Italy awaits you here.

IF YOU'VE BEEN TO MICHELANGELO'S SISTINE CHAPEL AND
Raphael's Stanze, both in the Vatican, you have also seen the
Galleria delle Carte Geografiche, or Gallery of Maps. But if you're
like most tourists, you will have experienced all 400 feet of this
gallery as a bluish-green blur separating you from the epic High
Renaissance frescoes of those masters. Few tour guides stop with
their groups in the Gallery of Maps, which is probably the most
impressive undertaking in the history of cartography, not to mention one of the most charming, and most neglected, examples of
16th-century Italian painting. In execution, aptness of detail, and
overall graphic sense, the maps, also frescoes, are among the crowning beauties of the Vatican.

The ornate vaulted gallery has on either wall sixteen maps of
Italy and its regions, each about ten feet square, along with eight
smaller maps. For all the minute accuracy of their scholarship and
their precise measurements, they are, in fact, fantasies.

Most maps are abstractions. When you open the average atlas,
you do not imagine that you are looking down at the earth from
a great height; you are merely inspecting a flat surface with useful
information. The Vatican maps, however, live up to—and perhaps

even inspired—Ruskin's fantasy in *The Stones of Venice*: "Let us, for a moment, try to raise ourselves even above (the flight of birds), and imagine the Mediterranean lying beneath us like an irregular lake, and all its ancient promontories sleeping in the sun."

Egnazio Danti, who executed the maps in 1580-81, was moved by the same impulse. He has enabled viewers to float over the lush green seagirt expanse of the Italian peninsula on a flawless spring day as though they were in a 16th-century blimp. The maps present a view of Italy that none of Danti's contemporaries could have seen, since even the tops of the

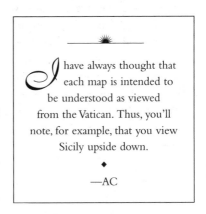

I have always thought that each map is intended to be understood as viewed from the Vatican. Thus, you'll note, for example, that you view Sicily upside down.

♦

—AC

Alps and Apennines do not offer so perfect a prospect.

Danti had a few misconceptions about air travel. For example, he didn't realize that from a great height details are lost and landscape becomes pure pattern; his perspective could be that of a hot air balloon or the Space Shuttle. Some of his Italian towns consist of a few houses and a church, together with the town's name written neatly at the side.

Danti also added a wealth of mythological material, often painted with great gusto. In the first map, an overview of the Italian peninsula, Italia herself is seen wearing a miter and sporting a pink parasol, while all around her fruit-bearing *putti* float like hummingbirds. Another map, an arching view of the Ligurian coast, reveals the Tyrrhenian Sea filled with ancient sailing ships and the bearded Neptune pulled along by sea horses and flanked by Nereids.

Danti, who was born in Perugia in 1536 and taught mathematics in Bologna, was surely one of the more intriguing figures in late-16th-century Italy. Though known primarily as an astronomer and mathematician, he came from a distinguished artistic family (his brother was the Mannerist sculptor Vicenzo Danti). Because of his role in formulating the Gregorian calendar in the early 1580s and his translations of Euclid and Galen from the Greek, he would have earned a prominent place in Western intellectual history even if he had never created the Vatican maps.

Before receiving the commission for them from Pope Gregory XIII, he had a kind of dress rehearsal in the Guardaroba of the Palazzo Vecchio in Florence, where he painted a series of world maps. But these are somewhat stiff in comparison with the Vatican frescoes, which were completed within two years.

The Galleria delle Carte occupies a peculiar place in the history of landscape painting. As a distinct genre, the landscape did not really exist in Western art before the 17th century; it was merely an adjunct to the figural subject, a condiment to the main course. The artistry of Danti and his assistants ranks with that of other 16th-century landscapists like Giulio Romano and Niccolo dell'Abate, except that what for them was a background or a frame for some biblical or mythological drama became with Danti, for the first time, the artistic goal. His painterly maps are suggestive of Italy's fertile countryside. Whether depicting the sunbaked rockiness of Calabria, the tortuous windings of the Alps, or the unfurrowed smoothness of the Paduan plains, Danti and his assistants awakened the spirit of the landscape. They seemed able, as has been said of Velazquez, to paint the air itself.

The maps also present views of scores of Italian cities as they looked in the 16th century, preserved on the Vatican walls as though in amber. Here is Rome before the great reforms of Urban VIII. St. Peter's already has the noble dome of Michelangelo, but only a void where later the curving arms of Bernini's porticoes would extend. Though Milan has yet to burst out of its medieval fortifications, Florence already has Vasari's Mannerist Uffizi, site of the later art museum, and Turin's square grid is well under way.

Venice, of course, is always Venice, the pink and pearl city coiling around its Grand Canal. But behind the archipelago on which the city is built is the terra firma of the mainland, a pristine bucolic setting with no trace of the modern causeway and the smokestacks of Mestre and Marghera.

Today it seems obvious why Danti lavished so much attention on Italy. But to the people of the 16th century it wouldn't have been obvious at all. The state of Italy, which did not become a political reality until the second half of the 19th century, was not even an aspiration of the men and women who lived during the *cinquecento*. They would have described themselves as Venetian, Roman, or Neapolitan, never as Italian. But Danti saw beyond this campanilismo, or parochialism. He anticipated the Risorgimento of three centuries later by creating the Galleria delle Carte Geografiche, an elaborate paean to what the Italians still call *Il Bel Paese,* the Beautiful Land.

James Gardner is the editor of The New York Review of Art.

✷

One begins to realise how old the real Italy is, how man-gripped and how withered. England is far more wild and savage and lonely, in her country parts. Here since endless centuries man has tamed the impossible mountain side to terraces, he has quarried the rock, he has fed his sheep among the thin woods, he has cut his boughs and burnt his charcoal. he has been half domesticated even among the wildest fastnesses. This is what is so attractive about the remote places, the Abruzzi, for example. Life is so primitive, so pagan, so strangely heathen and half-savage. And yet it is human life. And the wildest country is half humanised, half brought under. It is all conscious. Wherever one is in Italy, either one is conscious of the present, or of the mediaeval influences, or of the far, mysterious gods of the early Mediterranean. Wherever one is, the place has its conscious genus. Man has lived there and brought forth his consciousness there and in some way brought that place to consciousness, given it its expression, and, really, finished it. The expression may be Proserpine, or Pan, or even the strange "shrouded gods" of the Etruscans of the Sikels, none the less it is an expression. The land has been humanised, through and through: and we in our own tissued consciousness bear the results of this humanisation. So that for us to go to Italy and to *penetrate* into Italy is like a most fascinating act of self-

discovery—back, back down the old ways of time. Strange and wonderful chords awake in us, and vibrate again after many hundreds of years
of complete forgetfulness.

—D. H. Lawrence, *Sea and Sardinia* (1921)

ELIZABETH ROPER MARCUS

⋆ * ⋆

Sibling Rivalry, Italian Style

*Human nature continues its rough slouch
towards civilization.*

THE HISTORY OF ITALY IS A GORY TALE OF NON-STOP INTERNECINE fighting. If the country were a cartoon, we'd see the top of the boot trying to amputate the toe, the left side trying to scorch and burn the right, the grommet trying to strangle the lace. To walk the otherwise charming old streets is to tread on centuries of dried blood, fratricidal blood. Shards of the victims' bones crunch under our feet. Travelers tend not to focus on this aspect of the country. Their attention is drawn to other Italian traditions—artistic glory, religious passion, sybaritic pleasure. But then other tourists don't travel with my two warring teenagers.

When we left for Italy last spring, our two children were at a stage where they could barely tolerate proximity to us or to one another. For years our daughter had been lording it over her younger brother, not infrequently making her point with a savage squeeze. Now our son was surpassing her in height and strength. This was a tremendous moment, one he had been anticipating for the better part of a decade, the way a prisoner dreams of his release. The shift of power had, however, not yet been put to the final test. Zoe (16) and Jared (15) were still at the sparring stage but it was clear that it would not take much to bring on the final showdown. Meanwhile, wherever I looked, in Italy past and present, I was greeted with reflections of our family's fractious passions.

What looks at first like one unified country, is, in fact, two loosely connected cultures: the prosperous, industrial North and the depressed, backward South. In fact, the two subdivisions of the country have had distinctly different histories since their fortunes diverged at the end of the first millennium. The North saw the development of powerful, striving city-states while the South continued to be dominated and pillaged by a succession of foreign invaders, with banditry the local form of control, precursor to today's all-powerful Mafia.

Perhaps their continued hostility should not be surprising. Unified Italy is only 125 years old, barely out of its adolescence as nations go. But the main irritant is not Garibaldi's scarcely contested annexation of the South, but simple economic disparity. While the country as a whole has become one of the leading industrial nations of Europe—with, incidentally, the most successful businesses largely family-owned and run—the average income in Southern Italy is barely half and unemployment almost double that of the North. Despite the fact that billions of dollars in the form of new roads, utilities, and industries have been poured into the South, prosperity has not resulted. North and South Italy are like the two branches—one prosperous, one not—of a large, divisive family. The rich cousins view their poor relations, for whom no hand-out or helping hand is ever enough, as having earned their apparent bad luck through laziness and lack of initiative. The disadvantaged cousins, for their part, resent their well-off and smug relatives to whom, they feel, dumb good luck has brought an unearned birthright of wealth and opportunity.

With hostilities fueled by the almost farcical excesses of Italy's governmental bureaucracy, it's a wonder the union holds. Most of the country's police officers, postal workers, and teachers, in civil service jobs disdained by Northerners, are recruited from the South and awarded their positions via political patronage. Civil employment is a tenured track, notorious for absenteeism and inefficiency with the rare employee working the full 36 hour week. In part to justify the bloated administrative apparatus, red tape is endemic. Hours are required to get through the series of lines necessary to register a child for kindergarten. Southerners, moreover, take jobs in the North in order to get a foothold in the system, only to begin immediately pressuring for a transfer home. The result is busy Northern railroad stations chronically under-staffed and sleepy, Southern outposts with more ticket agents than daily trains. With as much as one-fifth of the Italian work force drawing a salary from the taxpayer and providing abysmal civil ser-vices, it is a common Northern viewpoint that their hard-earned tax money is stolen and squandered by their Southern compatri-ots. Paul Hofmann, the former chief of *The New York Times* Rome bureau, reports that in the early 1980s when Mount Etna, the Sicilian volcano, was going through a period of eruptions, highway graffiti appeared on the overpasses near Venice: "*Forza Etna!*" "Go Etna! Go!"

In the North/South competition for *our* family's tourist dollars, the South lost; our itinerary took us due north from Rome. With some difficulty we squeezed ourselves into the "medium-sized" car we'd ordered from the States. The luggage fit, but the newly attenuated limbs of our teenaged son and daughter just barely. They fought for the opportunity of sitting behind me since I could pull my seat up and generate a few precious extra inches. Both kids had come prepared with portable CD players and ear phones, and they quickly retired to the envelope of privacy pro-vided by the deafening music. But, in the physical confinement of the small car, our own personal Etna lay only temporarily dor-mant. When fatigue or boredom reached an invisible threshold, my stashes of snacks were all that stood between an apparently pleasant family excursion and fratricide.

In fact, minimizing cramping legs and crabby temperaments was the main organizing principle of our entire itinerary. I was as much a military strategist on a peace-keeping mission as I was a tour guide. We were on our way to Venice, taking three days to go less than 300 miles. On the first leg of our journey, we would be visiting fortified towns around Siena, but not Siena itself, since we would be returning there at the end of our trip for five days of horse-back riding. Pisa was on the itinerary because of its high-profile landmark, familiar to our children from pizza box tops. Verona made the list because *Romeo and Juliet* is in the 9th grade curriculum. Florence was out: too much great art. For years our children loudly and jointly expressed their aversion to high culture. "No museums!" they shouted, the way pre-vegetarian generations had taken a stand against spinach. Perhaps I should have been grateful for this one area of agreement between them.

In the car, when the kids tuned out, I read aloud to my husband about the towns we were passing or about to visit. After the fall of Rome in 410 A.D., the history sounded like centuries of anarchy interspersed with periodic invasions. I had particular difficulty keeping track of the long-term quarrel between the Church and the Empire which, for most of the Middle Ages, divided Northern Italy into two teams: the Guelphs who supported the Pope in Rome and the Ghibellines who championed the Emperor. Orvieto, 60 miles from Rome, was Guelph but Arezzo, only 40 miles further north was Ghibelline until forcibly annexed to Florence, where matters got really

San Gimignano is, of course, famous for its slab-sided towers, which when they are seen from a distance resemble the towers of lower Manhattan. These stone towers were probably erected by feuding groups of Guelphs and Ghibellines—the former owing allegiance to the Popes, in Rome, and the latter to the Holy Roman Emperors, on the far side of the Alps. Their quarrel was complex and has puzzled generations of historians, but perhaps it is not entirely unlike the disputes today between advocates of a strong central government and those Italians who prefer regional autonomy.

◆

—Jason Epstein, "This Side of Paradiso," *The New Yorker*

complicated. In Florence there were citizens of both persuasions. Initially the Guelphs succeeded in driving out the Ghibellines who then joined with Florentine enemies, notably the Sienese, and seized power in turn. Six years later the Guelphs retook the city and created a republic that was itself undermined by an internal division into two contingents: Black Guelphs, loyal to the Pope and White Guelphs, opposed to the Pope. At this point our guide books gave up and did not attempt to explain the difference between an anti-Pope White Guelph and a pro-Emperor Ghibelline. As far as I was concerned, Mercutio had it exactly right: "A plague 'o both your houses." Reading on, I learned that, in Florence at least, his curse was actually fulfilled in 1348 when the Black Death killed off more than half the population.

Although the plague did succeed in dampening the fighting, it could not completely neutralize the intercity hostilities. They live on today. The Sienese and the Florentines both hate the Southerners, but they are also passionate about their loathing for one another. Autumn mushroom hunting in the forests near Siena has become a favorite Florentine outing but the Sienese have strong territorial feelings about their porcini. As a result, in the past few years, angry locals who identified Florentine invaders by the license plates on their parked cars slashed so many tires that the system of numbering plates had to be changed. Where else but in Italy would a feud dating from the Middle Ages find its modern flowering in a mushroom war?

We followed the Guelph-Ghibelline wars to Verona, the setting for the "canker'd hate" of the Capulets and the Montagues, whom the Veronese, pushing the historic basis of the story, claim were members of the two medieval political camps. Ever since the era of the European grand tour, the town has marketed itself as the site of Shakespeare's play and particularly touted the supposed palace of the Capulets with Juliet's famous balcony. Although we were traveling during off-season and Verona, like the rest of Northern Italy, was not particularly crowded with visitors, the inner courtyard of Juliet's house was standing room only. Five guides, in five different languages, instructed their unruly groups on the significance of the location. We could tell from their position—on bended knee, one arm upstretched—when each guide got to the famous couplet, "What light through yonder window breaks..." It was a babble of warring recitations, as, stressing their lungs to the utmost, the guides tried in vain to outshout one another.

Happily Verona had much more to offer, in particular, marvelous Roman ruins and Renaissance streets. Occasionally these were superimposed, one on top of another, as in the oval Piazza delle Erbe which occupies the footprint of the old forum without erasing its ghostly presence. Fortifying ourselves with *gelati*, we pushed on to the high point of our visit, literally and figuratively, the first-century Roman amphitheater. These days it is the site of a famous summer opera festival, but the original gruesome spectacles for which the building was constructed sprang unsolicited to mind. I tried to call up Lucia di Lammermoor, but my brain seemed stuck on the Roman sports channel: mortal combat between two gladiators, two wild beasts, or a beast and a man.

The Roman Arena is the first thing you see when you enter Verona. It's only slightly smaller than the Coliseum in Rome, but its setting within a large, open piazza makes it even more striking.

The Piazza Bra is the perfect place to take a stroll, bask in the sun, or sip an espresso while you admire this impressive structure.

And on summer nights the Verona Arena hosts one of the most prestigious summer opera programs in Europe.

◆

—William Petrocelli, "The Chorus That Ate Verona"

Although it was less than an hour from Verona to Venice, having spent most of the day touring, we arrived on our last legs, primed for temperamental fireworks. The drama of the floating city stunned us into an uncharacteristic silence. The surprise of having to drag our suitcases onto a *vaporetto*, the aquatic, Venetian equivalent of a public bus, short-circuited incendiary tempers. Even hauling our belongings, after disembarking, over bridges and around sharp little corners only to miss our hotel—three times— seemed more ludicrous than exasperating.

For a while I thought that Venice itself, like Cinderella's fairy godmother with her stardust-trailing magic wand, had anointed us and returned us to an earlier time when, at least as I like to re- member it, family life was less contentious. The irresistible charm of the city, whose architecture suggests nothing so much as a sugar candy fantasy in stone, seemed to inspire an unreal sweetness in our children. Setting out from our hotel in the morning was like stepping through the looking-glass. In Venice no path is straight, or even flat, as streets abruptly swell up into charming bridges and the image of every streetscape bordering a canal is repeated, upside- down, in a watery reflection. The peculiar realities of a pedestrian life in a floating world, the absence of cars and traffic, were odd enough to appeal to hard-to-please teenagers.

Our children, normally slightly nervous in foreign cities, felt safe among the promenading throngs and enjoyed walking around by themselves, exhilarated by the delectable foretaste of real inde- pendence. Rushing off to a concert one night after dinner, my husband and I anxiously left them to find their way home by *vaporetto*. This was a perfect opportunity for a little internecine nas- tiness: our fast-sprinting daughter could try to "lose" our son with the prospect of giving him a good scare. Instead, we arrived at the hotel later that evening to find them companionably supine in their familiarly messy room watching CNN and munching giant gummy worms, which they had bought, pooling their *lire*, in a burst of friendly good cheer. We backed out of the doorway on figurative tiptoe, afraid of breaking the spell.

In our three days in Venice, in fact, we had only one breakdown of social order. But, by all definitions, it was the worst ever. Paradoxically it occurred during a side-trip we took expressly for the children's entertainment to Murano, one of the small islands in the Venetian Lagoon famous for their production of crafts.

Murano, itself made up of smaller islands linked by bridges, is the location of the famous glass works which were moved there in the 13th century to protect the city from the dangers of smelting furnaces. No churches or museums—just artisans forming glass into everything from tiny giraffes to enormous chandeliers. A child-friendly tourist site. I suppose in hindsight I should have realized that our children had outgrown tiny giraffes. Five minutes of watching a bit of molten glass repeatedly worked into the same shape and they were ready to leave. But as it had taken us over an hour to get there, my husband and I were inclined to see if the island didn't have something more to offer.

We pushed on against the kids' objections when I turned around to discover the two of them down on the sidewalk, Jared on top of Zoe, wrestling in the street, their faces contorted like gargoyles. I was horrified but afraid to step in. Two people brawling in public was bad; three could only be worse. They were inches from the edge of the quay and I could barely restrain myself from shrieking a warning, a sure way to get at least one pushed into the canal. "Do something," I pleaded with my husband, and cravenly rushed around the next corner where I waited, listening for the splash which never came. Having gotten to the brink of murderous rage, they pulled themselves back. When they rounded the corner the two were still smoldering, but they were dry and in one piece. With no restaurants or food shops on Murano, we beat a speedy retreat.

Later I asked for an explanation of what had happened but symmetrical glowers were as far as I got. I couldn't let go of the incident. What made my daughter so angry at my son? "I don't know… Everything!" What made my son so crazed—specifically? "I don't know.… Her face, her mouth, the way she chews!" The existence of the other was more than either could bare. They seemed to be gasping for breath, choked by invisible forces from which they were struggling to free themselves.

I was mortified that my children should be pulled down by such primitive animosity, but it turns out that they were following in an old Venetian tradition, the *battagliole,* or the mock battles of the bridges. This phenomenon of late Renaissance Venice was a ritualized warring of workers and artisans for the honor of dominating certain bridges in the city. The battles were fought by two factions, the Castellani and the Nicolotti, descendants of the original two groups that migrated to Venice, one from the mainland and the other from the islands around the lagoon. As early as 800 A.D. there were stick battles between the two antagonistic groups. More formalized *battagliole* began almost as soon as the city's wooden bridges were rebuilt in stone around 1500, and continued for two hundred years. The competitions, initially fought with pointed wooden poles, were later restricted to unarmed shoving and punching. The largest battles were prearranged and were proceeded by days of preparations, but fights could also be set off spontaneously by the slightest provocation. In either case, squads of pugilists, fighting under a *capo*, followed a series of unwritten rules.

Basically the *battagliole* were turf battles. Except for a few parts of the city too public for either side to claim, such as The Rialto or San Marco, the city was divided in two. Certain bridges became the natural focus of the tensions and the locus of the mass fistfights because they stood on factional boundaries and were large and strong enough to support the armies

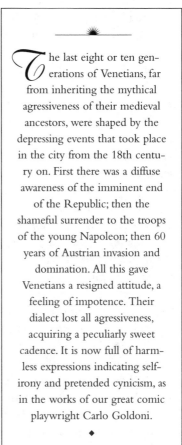

The last eight or ten generations of Venetians, far from inheriting the mythical agressiveness of their medieval ancestors, were shaped by the depressing events that took place in the city from the 18th century on. First there was a diffuse awareness of the imminent end of the Republic; then the shameful surrender to the troops of the young Napoleon; then 60 years of Austrian invasion and domination. All this gave Venetians a resigned attitude, a feeling of impotence. Their dialect lost all agressiveness, acquiring a peculiarly sweet cadence. It is now full of harmless expressions indicating self-irony and pretended cynicism, as in the works of our great comic playwright Carlo Goldoni.

♦

—Paolo Lanapoppi, "Valentines to Venice," *Travel & Leisure* of fighters and crowds of onlookers. They were perfect stages for these public performances since they elevated the fighters and kept the audience at a safe distance. The battles sometimes involved as many as 1000 combatants and another 30,000 spectators, who cheered the fighting from the street, from boats, and from windows and rooftops. Although they were as much a form of festive competition as they were factional struggles, the fighting often resembled chaotic rioting and many participants died or suffered serious maiming and injury. Henry III of France, watching a melee of some 600 armed artisans in 1574, declared the event "too small to be a war and too cruel to be a game."

Why these battles remained popular in spite of their real dangers is a question posed even by contemporaries. To some onlookers it appeared insane. Normally rational artisans with families and livelihoods could go berserk, excited by the crowds and factional passions, the quest for glory, the wish to assert their individualism and independence. Venetians of the time explained the depth of passion by a farfetched reference to a mythic event of two hundred years earlier involving the brutal murder of a bishop over a question of taxation. But whatever the source of the hostility, as any parent of fighting children knows, deconstructing animosity by searching for its origin is futile. Feuding siblings, like the Hatfields and McCoys, invariably trace their anger back to a prehistory of original injury.

However they began, the antagonisms of the Castellani and Nicolotti were reinforced by economic and status competition between deep sea fishermen and eel fishers, between sailors and ship builders, and between various artisan groups who declared allegiance to one team or the other. Was this another reincarnation of the Guelphs and the Ghibellines? Robert Davis, in his 1994 study of the bridge battles, rejects the connection. According to him, "there is little to imply that the two factions ever stood for any position beyond simple opposition to one another."

Eventually, however, the phenomenon did come to an end. The last full-scale *battagliole* took place in 1705. While the battle deteriorated into a near riot, a fire broke out in a nearby convent, and, with no one free to fight the fire, the church was gutted. Perhaps such excesses convinced the majority of Venetians that the bridge battles had gone too far. Or perhaps it was the state's loss of patience with such a disruptive activity, or the decline in prestige and financial support that resulted when the elite's interest shifted to the more refined pleasures of the Enlightenment. For the next hundred years, the factional energy of the *battagliole* was diverted to acrobatic contests involving the construction of human pyramids composed of seven or eight layers of men, 40 feet high. The regatta, rowing competitions which had been popular for centuries, were the final repositories for Venetian competitive passions and continue today, although now largely for the benefit of tourists.

Davis mourns the demise of the Venetian rivalries. "The factionalism that gave life and identity to an entire populace—the great antagonisms that brought Castellani and Nicolotti to the bridges by the tens of thousands—has dissipated for good, along with the Venetian people and their once remarkable culture." Although, with my current preoccupation, it is hard for me to share Davis's sense of regret, I am intrigued by his premise that the vitality of Venetian culture and its historic rivalries are linked. Perhaps by extention it is generally true that Italy's vivid, passionate way of life is inextricably connected to its intense factionalism.

Although sibling warfare is on the wane in our house, my preoccupation with this theme remains as strong as ever. The national division into two competing factions seems ubiquitous. The whole world seems fractured by murderous sibling animosities: White and Black America, the Northern Irish Protestants and Catholics, the Israelis and the Palestinians, the Tutsis and the Hutus, the Serbs and Croats, the Chechens and Russians, the Sunnis and the Shiites. Two brothers who can only picture themselves as sitting face to face on a common see-saw, the rising fortunes of one necessarily at the other's expense. Two groups who have more in common with one another than with any other group in the world never-theless defining themselves as polar opposites. Their differences, seen through the distorted lens of resentment and jealousy, appear to them greater than their common ground.

With only one language, race, religion and culture, Italy's wide-spread factionalism is particularly curious. Perhaps it is related to the intensity of the Italian family, the source of exceptionally suc-cessful enterprises and personal achievement when all goes well, but of powerful feuds between or even within them, when some-thing goes awry. In Italy, however, where daily life has been refined to a fine art, fractious passions are for the most part transformed with characteristic elegance and refinement. The Northerners and Southerners, the Sienese and Florentines, the *contradaioli* of the Tower and Goose despise one another. And yet today the Italians essentially manage their rivalries without resort to violence. In many cases they relish them. They have moved from armed battle to ritualized fist-fights to horse racing: from war to sport. They have progressed from hating one another to loving to hate one an-other, a subtle but significant distinction. Cultural alchemists, the Italians transform even devisive rivalry into extravagant celebra-tions of human passion.

Elizabeth Roper Marcus used to work as an architect. Now she travels to experience all the places she's never seen and writes to figure out where it is she's been. She lives in Boston.

★

It is a remarkable fact that the land of grand opera lacks a world-class symphony orchestra. Italy has produced great conductors from Toscanini to Giulini, Abbado, and Muti, great sopranos and tenors, but there is rarely excellence in ensemble work on the Italian stage or in the orchestra pit. Players in an Italian musical body—always referred to as the "professors of the orchestra"—dislike being subordinate to the conductor as much as local soldiers detest having to obey their sergeant or lieutenant; exhaust-ing rehearsals until a score is rendered flawlessly by all instrumentalists the way the maestro wants are as incompatible with the Italian temperament as is close-order drill in the courtyard of the barracks compound. An Italian musician wants to be Paganini, not second fiddle.

Fellini depicted the breakdown of cooperation in a musical ensemble in his film *Orchestra Rehearsal*, using it as a sardonic metaphor for the anarchistic tendencies in Italian society: players ignore the conductor, quarrel with one another, do their own thing (one couple is making love in a corner); they are intent on anything but preparation for a concert. The result is bedlam.

—Paul Hofmann, *That Fine Italian Hand*

BOB SHACOCHIS

✦ ✦ ✦

The Sands of Thyme

*Sardinia sets the scene for
a culinary hurricane.*

FEBRUARY 22, ROME. "JUST BELIEVE IN ME," I SAID TO MISS F. WITH all appropriate emphasis, since February, in the lives of sun worshippers, is the month of desperately consummated beach fantasies. When I must coax faith from her, she understands, obviously better than I do, that the limits of her endurance are about to be well-tested.

I had proposed that we arrive in a notoriously severe foreign land and, without benefit of plates, utensils, grill or fuel, proceed to create a romantic, elegantly composed meal, which we would consume on an uncivilized strand, under a canopy of unrelenting springtime. A barbarian seaside feast in "unconquered Sardinia," as D.H. Lawrence described the second-largest island in the Mediterranean. *Banditi*, wolves and wild boars still haunt its volcanic peaks. There are wild horses on the austere plateaus. (The Italians filmed their spaghetti Westerns here.) Hawks and eagles own the air. It seemed to me to be a place where Miss F. and I could unwind after a winter of genteel academic oppression in Rome, but she was regarding me with disheartening ambivalence—in her eyes, I was pushing my luck.

"You would think," I said, "considering my culinary vigor in the out-of-doors and the countless times you have gorged yourself like Catherine of Aragon around my humble fires, that an encore in the land of the Sardinians might be something you could say you were looking forward to."

"I might say that," said Miss F., warily watching me slip a garlic bulb into my shaving kit, "if you weren't so goddamned resolute about your cookouts. Now that it's in your head to do it, you're going to do it, no matter what, even if it means you have to defy nature."

She unkindly reminded me of the very last time we had dined on the beach, the time I had been forced to hunker under the lowered tailgate of our pickup, tending the brazier and its sad coals as the rain poured down.

For better or for worse, I was not inclined to be discouraged by this fracture in Miss F.'s confidence—she had supped well at my hands, lounging voluptuously, humming with contentment, on the beaches of the world. Nor am I readily daunted by the variability of the weather, though I do, in fact, harbor a deep appreciation for its relevancy. I would take what the gods bestowed and behave accordingly.

"You?" snorted Miss F. "Ha! Never."

Sardinia. Bright sun, balmy temperature. Disheveled as refugees from a night on the ferry, we picked up our rental car and began a ninety-mile jaunt down the infamously rugged eastern coast. The guidebook warned that it wasn't always easy to find your way to the sea by car—"erratic signposting." Within an hour, we were lost in the middle of an uninhabited nowhere, setting the tone for the week ahead. The coast was inaccessible without a parachute. Miss F.'s fear of heights was stirred by our slow weaving through the surrealistic peaks and gorges of the Sopramonte, the vertical vistas just off the road, thousands of feet down to tortured valleys spotted with Byzantine churches, decayed castles, vineyards centered with odd cones of stone built by Bronze Age people. Past noon, we found a seaside village, embedded like an amber jewel in the harsh coast. A wearying search for an open shop. Finally, bread, Sardi cheese and potent Cannonau wine for lunch on the water. I entered my gathering mode and bought a tiny box of plastic forks, a roll of extra-wide heavy-duty aluminum foil, a jar of capers, two tomatoes and a glowing head of *finocchio* (fennel). Miss F. worried that I might not have energy left for a cookout when we landed that evening.

Our itinerary shifted us back up into the untamed mountains to witness bizarre pre-Lenten village festivals with origins unknown but ancient, as overtly pagan as are animal sacrifices. We were served an equally weird meal—sliced pig's head marinated in sweet vinegar, a round steak of jackass and, most incredible to me, a raw artichoke. Miss F. happy with her discovery of *culingionis*— Sardi ravioli resembling pirogi. Weather: perfectly lovely.

The next day, a morning's drive up the southwestern coast, headed for Oristano's medievalish carnival celebrations. Breeze fresh, sky a bit overcast; seas began to show a scattered lace of whitecaps. A weak cold front seemed to be passing through. Beaches perfect, but we were com-

---

> By about 6000 B.C. the Sardinians, probably the same people who had been painting caves in paleolithic Liguria and Provence, had arrived over a land bridge from Corsica.
>
> By 1500 B.C. they were building odd massive towers of granite or trachite, most often conical and about 40 feet in diameter and about 50 to 65 feet high, that are still the most frequently encountered man-made feature of the entire Sardinian landscape—hills, dales, coast and hinterland. They are called *nuraghi*, and embody—both in popular imagination and on cork souvenirs—the strong and independent spirit that has always characterized Sardinia. It has never considered itself Italian, and the *nuraghi* are there to prove it.
>
> ◆
>
> —Maureen B. Fant, "In Sardinia, Sea, Ancient Stones..." *The New York Times*

pelled to move on. I assured Miss F. that the slight moodiness of
the weather would play itself out by the morrow.

That night, we listened to the wind ripping the zinc sheeting
off the roofs of the buildings behind our hotel.

Onward, up the western coast: the 20th century is only a dim
rumor here, according to our guidebook. Miss F. displayed a bit of
anxiety about this as the gusts battered our Peugeot back and forth
across the road north. We stopped at a wind-ravaged beach. Miss F.
refused to leave the car. "Don't worry," I told her. "It'll blow itself
out by dark." To keep my spirits up, I stopped at a market when
we left and bought an onion and a lemon.

The first day of March. Approaching the Costa Paradiso. The
tomatoes were ripening. I scoured the city of Alghero for an open
fish market, but the boats had not put out to sea in three days.
Headed north to round the tip of the island for the coves of the
leeward side. Miss F. overly concerned that I will "make" her eat
on the beach today. She unnecessarily sought a guarantee that I was
on "her side." Found an open *pescheria* and liberated a pound of
shrimp and two plump calamari, expecting fortuitous conditions
in the afternoon. Incredibly, wind velocity increased throughout
the day. Much debris whizzed through the air.

At Castelsardo we admitted we were weather-beaten and
checked into a hotel. The proprietor agreed to store my provisions
in his refrigerator.

It is our last day in Sardinia; we woke once more to the hellish
wolf-pack howl of the wind. Tempest unabated, but by midday
sunlight speared through the clouds and I felt we would soon be
in a position to outmaneuver the worst of it. I spied an open
pescheria and hit the brakes.

Miss F. gave me a wild-eyed look. "For God's sake," she begged
"expel those thoughts from your mind."

"Just want to run in here and see what they have," I said, hoping for some fresh red mullet. The fishmonger ranted about the
malo vento—the bad wind. I bought a kilo of wonderful razor
clams, found a *panificio* and bought bread. Saw a butcher shop and

was inspired to buy a rope of fresh Sardi sausage, just the thing for grilling up later, a midnight snack on the ferry. Miss F. decided she had nothing more to say to me but braced herself for a wretched afternoon of outdoor fun.

Some hours later, I finally managed to plant her behind the windbreak of an elephantine boulder. Though she had to wear a heavy jacket, she could stretch unmolested in a sudden wealth of sunshine and gaze out into the turbulent channel of the Maddalena archipelago and the island of Corsica, with mountains crowned by the brightest blue air.

"Are you hungry, sweetheart?" I asked gently. Hurricane-force winds wear you down in five seconds—the poor girl had grown weak the past few days. I was pleased to hear she was starving.

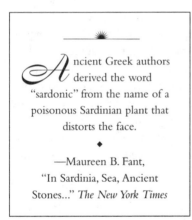

ncient Greek authors derived the word "sardonic" from the name of a poisonous Sardinian plant that distorts the face.

◆

—Maureen B. Fant, "In Sardinia, Sea, Ancient Stones..." *The New York Times*

"Feeling relaxed now?" I asked, cueing her for words of appreciation. She told me to uncork the wine, a bottle of the dry white for which Alghero is famous; she had a long slug of it. I trudged off to collect driftwood, scattering a herd of cows on the beach. Back at the base of the boulder, I scooped a hole in the sand and concentrated on the architecture of campfires. Miss F. sucked the bottle of wine, sighed, meditated on her millionaire's view, found it satisfactory and lay back in the sand, taking a P.D. James novel from her pocket. The wind still cast little puffs and squirts into our hideaway, but we were doing okay, doing all right. I reached for the roll of foil.

Aluminum foil is the secret to cooking a full-course meal on the beach. Prepare whatever you want, however you want it—fish, seafood, pasta, sauces, vegetables, ragouts—double wrap it in foil loosely to prevent scorching (except with corn on the cob and baked potatoes, which should be wrapped tightly), and toss it on the coals. I made up four packets, four little bombs of gastronomic pleasure—sliced fennel and tomatoes; shrimp, seasoned with fresh rosemary and doused with *bianco di Alghero*; razor clams with chopped garlic, minced onion and lemon juice; calamari stuffed with chopped olives, sweet red peppers and capers, painted with tomato sauce and olive oil.

I lit the fire, tended it reverently. The wind teased, flexed, slapped flames at me, singeing the hair off my forearms. Nothing to worry about...why worry? "Is the wind shifting?" wondered Miss F. "It is, isn't it?" I spread the packets across the coals. Miss F. roused herself, impaled a piece of sausage on a stick and began to roast it. The foil packets must be rolled every few minutes so the food inside cooks evenly. I flipped them over and learned a valuable lesson about beach cookouts in Italy: Italian aluminum foil ignites. Disappears. I snatched the bundles from the fires and swaddled them in more foil, until they were as big as soccer balls. Finesse is the *sine qua non* of cookouts—don't dare leave home to conquer Sardinia without it. Somehow, everything worked out, and a half hour later we were sprawled in the sand, well-fed and immensely relieved.

"Not bad, eh?" I ventured.

"Not bad," Miss F. conceded. "You outdid yourself with the calamari, but don't gloat."

The fire crackled, making magic. The ghost of our Irish setter, Tyrone, romped along the water's edge, bringing us a melancholic glimpse of all the happiness we had shared, on all the beaches of our life together. Then a rogue cuff of wind showered us with confetti of dried seaweed. The sun disappeared behind a lengthening train of clouds. No gloating from me. We packed up and got the hell away.

Bob Shacochis counts among his honors and awards a James Michener Award, an American Book Award, and Playboy's *Best New Fiction Award. He is the author of* The Next New World *and* Domesticity: A Gastronomic Interpretation of Love.

✶

When God made the world, says a Sardinian legend, He gathered up all the leftover bits of dirt, hurled them down and stamped His foot on them. Thus He created Sardinia. The story is evidently multicultural, since the Greeks called Sardinia "Ichnoussa," meaning footprint. This was both descriptive—according to what passed then for cartography, and because it was a stappingstone in the sea—and prophetic. Stepped on for millennia, Sardinia is still underrated. Italians generally think of only one thing in connection with Sardinia: summer vacation. And most non-Italians think of only two, bandits and the glamorous resort area called the Costa Smeralda, one undesirable, the other expensive. But the first is not a problem and the second is not the only destination on Sardinia.

The island has all the requisites of paradise: ancient mysteries, a spectacular coastline, rugged mountains, great beaches with clean water, birds and animals, fragrant herbs, full-bodied red wines and refreshing light whites, suckling pig, *bottarga* (the pressed and dried roe of gray mullet), lobster, few people (and those few quite discreet), archeology galore, human-scale museums and plenty of folklore. It is also conveniently situated in the geographic center of the Mediterranean, less than an hour's flight from Rome.

—Maureen B. Fant, "In Sardinia, Sea, Ancient Stones..."
The New York Times

PART THREE

GOING YOUR OWN WAY

✦ ✦ ✦

What's in a Name?

A traveler shakes the dirt
from his roots.

I'M HAVING SECOND THOUGHTS NOW WHILE ON THE TRAIN RIDE from Milan to Genoa. I've spent the last 24 hours traveling from San Francisco to Italy by car, plane, bus, and now train. As I near my final destination, it is just beginning to occur to me that maybe this isn't such a great idea after all.

For years I vaguely knew that the Sturla side of my family had immigrated from Genoa and settled in San Francisco sometime during the Gold Rush. Now, on the train, as I approach the cradle of my family, I do so with a certain degree of dread. The myth of Sturla is soon to be supplanted by the reality. And the reality, at least according to *Let's Go: Italy,* is not pretty. "If Calabria is the toe of Italy and Rome is the knee, then Genoa is just about the crotch…an entanglement of dispiriting shop-filled streets…heavily rebuilt after World War II bombings, the city's commercial center doesn't merit a visit…. The historical district is riddled with drugs and prostitution…it's an extremely bad place to get lost. Don't wander the streets at night."

Rebuilt after World War II bombings? Are there no cobblestone alleyways winding mazelike through medieval neighborhoods? No third-story apartment windows for jolly Sturlas to lean out of as they welcome me back to the homeland?

But wait a minute. What's the point of focusing on the architecture? I'm not traveling as a sightseeing tourist. I'm here on a mission. And my mission is to meet distant cousins and to discover how much we have in common even though our family trees split generations ago. I'm here for my people. What does *Let's Go: Italy* say about the people of Genoa? "The Genovesi are... known as the Scots of Italy for their reputed cheapness."

I hail a taxi after disembarking into Italy's "crotch" region. I ask the driver to take me to Sturla—strange feeling. To my ear it sounds like I'm asking him to take me to myself. After a few minutes, we drive over a small rise in the road. Behind us lie the port and commercial center of Genoa, but in front of us lies a slice of the Italian Riviera. To the right is the Mediterranean. The water is dark blue and glistening in the afternoon sun. The beaches are not sandy but rocky with millions of black-gray rocks the size of small fists. Along the road are a row of shops. Behind them is an arid mountain range similar to

> *S*traggling improbably across a series of hills hard by the busy Tyrrhenian Sea, Genoa is a city that sends out conflicting signals—and justifies them both.
>
> It's a bit old-fashioned, to be sure, as the name of its oldest daily newspaper—*Secolo XIX* (19th Century)—suggests. But it's haughty, too, as its nickname in Italian—*La Superba*—implies.
>
> It's earthy in equal measure. Superb.... The city produces a distinctive flavor all its own.
>
> This city produced seven Popes, two Nobel Prize winners, invented banking, denim, and yes, the Genoa jib. "There may be a prettier woman in Europe, but I doubt it," observed Mark Twain, innocently abroad in 1869.
>
> ◆
>
> —William D. Montalbano, "Summer Previews, Double Exposure," *Los Angeles Times*

the Santa Ynez range near Santa Barbara. Scattered across the mountains are pastel-colored Italian colonial villas. I smile. This is it.

I dump by bags off at a sweltering, un-airconditioned hotel and hit the town with my pocket camera. The first street sign I encounter reads. "Via Sturla." I can't stand it. I walk across the road to take a picture of the street sign, which is actually a street plaque. A slab of chiseled marble set into the side of a building. I'm trying to frame the picture when I notice a knot of three taxi drivers staring at me. I turn and smile at them. One of them begins speaking to me in Italian, gesturing at the road sign and then the beach. I get the feeling he's saying, "What are you doing taking a picture of this wall? Why don't you take a picture of the beach or something?" Now's the chance to use all of that Italian I learned on the flight over and find out if this guy is a relative.

"*Mi chiamo Sturla.*" My name is Sturla. The driver winces. I think that the first thought to cross his mind is that I'm definitely not Italian. The second thought is what the hell language is this guy speaking? "Sturla? Sturla?" He asks. "Aww you mean STOOR!lah. STOOR!lah."

What? Is this how I should say my name? STOOR!lah instead of Stir-lah? I flirt with the idea of permanently changing the pronunciation of my last name. I would go back to California and insist my friends call me Vince STOOR!lah. "STOOR!lah," I would yell correcting them, "STOOR!lah." For proper inflection, I could even lean into their faces while screaming the first syllable.

"No. No. No." My new buddy, still speaking Italian, calls me back from my daydream. "You are not Sturla. This is Sturla." He points at the ground. "This is the Sturla Quarter." He waves his right arm around. Thank goodness Italians speak with their hands. I can halfway follow this guy. I have some Dutch friends back home who usually talk to me with their arms folded, using the same expression to describe the birth of their fourth child or the purchase of a loaf of bread. I have an Italian friend, however, who, with graceful hand and arm gestures, can talk about painting his house and make it sound so exciting that I can't wait to do it when

I get home. "You are not Sturla," my new *compaesano* gestures at me. "This is the Sturla Quarter. Your name is?"

"STOOR!lah." I yell, leaning into his face.

He shakes his head and looks at his two friends. They shrug their shoulders, defeated. They don't say anything, but I can tell what they're thinking. It's written all over their faces. It's the Italian equivalent of "What a bonehead."

"Wait," I say. "One minute." I reach into my black travel satchel. My "adventure bag" as my wife derisively refers to it. I pull out my passport and show it to my friend. "STOOR!lah. *Mi chiamo Vince STOOR!lah.*"

He looks at my passport and brightens up. "STOOR!lah, from California." They look at my passport and laugh. "Boy, what a co-incidence."

Coincidence?

Now who's the bonehead? "No. No. My family came from STOOR!lah."

"Your family is from Genoa? From here?"

"Yes."

"How about that? Hey guys, he's a Genovesi from America. That's great. That's great. I'll take your picture in front of the Via Sturla sign." I pose in front of the sign, but one of the other drivers has a better idea. "No, not here. Let's take his picture in front of the Piazza Sturla sign."

I really don't understand too much of what they're saying, but I do get this. Loud and clear. Piazza Sturla! There's a Piazza Sturla! "*Dov'e il Piazza STOOR!lah?*"

"Here! Here!" They say. They lead me across a small side street and point to a marble plaque. Sure enough: Piazza Sturla. One problem though, where's the *piazza*? I've only traveled about twenty feet from the Via Sturla sign to the Piazza Sturla sign, and I don't see a whole lot of difference. Except behind me, where three roads converge, is a triangle of concrete decorated not with a fountain or an obelisk, or a statue of one of my heroic ancestors, but with road signs.

What they call a *piazza* in Sturla, we call a traffic island in California.

No problem. I'll take it. My old *compaesanos* place me in front of the marble plaque and take a picture of a stupidly grinning me. After a little inquiry, I find out that none of my buddies are Sturlas. Odd. Nice guys, but I'm here to meet Sturlas. So with a future 24x36 inch fireplace photo now safely in my camera, I head off down the road in search of my primary goal: other Sturlas. Distant relatives left behind by my ancestors 140 years ago.

I stroll along the road that skirts the coast. I can't believe it. I'm in Sturla. The one spot in the one country that I can feel perfectly at home even though I've never been here before. Many of the businesses are named after a Sturla. Cartolibreria Sturla, Sturla Gomme, and Carrozzeria Sturla.

I duck into Sturla Gomme, which is a tiny Michelin tire shop. If you know Italian, then this would make sense because *gomme* is the plural for tire in that language. I don't know Italian. I only think I do. I think Sturla Gomme is a hyphenated last name. That somewhere down the line a Sturla married a Gomme. I ask a man working in the shop if he is Sturla Gomme. He furrows his brow for a moment and then in Italian says yes *this* is Sturla Gomme. Thank goodness. At last a Sturla, well a semi-Sturla, anyway. I show him my passport and wait for my welcome home hug. He shrugs and hands me back my passport. "Are you a Sturla?" I ask again. "No. No. My shop is called Sturla Gomme."

"Where are the Sturlas?" I ask.

"Sturlas? There are no Sturlas. This area is called the Sturla Quarter. It is the name of the district. It is the name of my shop. It is not the name of a person."

WHAT? No Sturlas? Hey, buddy, you need to quit recapping tires and get out a little more often. No Sturlas in Sturla? "*Grazie signor.*" I thank the man and head off down the street. Clearly, I'm wasting my time with this shut-in.

On the beach side of the road, I come across Sportiva Sturla, which is a combination private beach and swimming club. I walk inside and approach a handful of chatting employees. They're all wearing Sportiva Sturla t-shirts. Oh my. The ultimate souvenir. I go through my tortured, learn-Italian-in-a-day explanation as to who I am. And once again I'm met with confused looks. In much the same way I might look at a tourist on the corner of Market and Van Ness who tells me in broken English that his name is San Francisco. But after the ritual passing of the passport, all is made clear and the staff of Sportiva Sturla welcomes me back to the fold. With my connection firmly established, the big moment has finally arrived: a face-to-face encounter with an honest to goodness Italian Sturla. "Can I speak to Mr. Sturla?"

Uh oh. I'm getting that look again.

"Who?"

"Sturla...*Signor* Sturla." The staff of Sportiva Sturla exchange confused looks.

"But you are Sturla. You are *Signor* Sturla," a barmaid tells me.

"No. Not me. *Signor* Sturla. *Signor* Sturla. The owner of Sportiva Sturla." Mind you, this is a rough translation. The conversation is actually taking place in Italian and advancing at a far slower pace.

"But there is no *Signor* Sturla. Sportiva Sturla is named after Sturla Quarto, not Sturla the person."

Hmmmmm. I'm finally beginning to see a pattern here.

> *A*lmost always when non-English-speaking Italians met in the course of a day's activities discover your Italian is not fluent, they (unlike Parisians) exhibit no contempt and happily hear you out as you mangle their beautiful language. But when they speak in return, they give no quarter; faster and faster they go. Is this the Italian equivalent of Americans speaking louder and slower to foreign-speaking people, as if to idiot children? Is it a form of homage to your intelligence? What it probably means is that it is utterly incomprehensible to them that anyone cannot understand their language.
>
> ◆
>
> —Barbara Grizzuti Harrison,
> *Italian Days*

"Well, where are the Sturlas?" Again the look.

"There are no Sturlas, *signor.*"

"You mean there are no Sturlas in Sturla?"

"Yes."

"Are you sure?"

"I've lived here for many years. You're the first Sturla I've met." The rest of the staff nods in agreement.

Oh man.

I guess they all left years ago. Where did they go? Did they all migrate to the United States?

I can't believe this.

I head back to my hotel for a bad night's sleep. I get up at dawn and go for a run up Via Sturla. The road winds through the hills. The Mediterranean is at my back. Well this is pretty neat. It's safe to bet that my great-great-great-great-great-great-grand-daddies made their way up and down this very same road. Afterward, I stop at a café and have a cappuccino and *focaccia.* Just like home. Well what the hell. For today, at least, there's a Sturla back in Sturla. And all these carpetbaggers who moved in when my ancestors moved out seem to be enjoying that almost as much as I am.

For the next couple of days I stroll around the neighborhood assaulting locals with my rough Italian. They put up with it good-naturedly. If not accepting me as a distant relative at least as a de facto native son. Even though this is my first trip to Italy, I now declare myself an Italian American. Don't believe me? Go check out my *piazza.* Those other half-dozen nationalities in my background are no longer an issue. I'm no longer a generic American. I now have an ethnic identity. Why have I always loved pesto, cappuccino, and the sea? Because I'm a Genovesi—an Italian! Now to that list I add an appreciation of opera, Frank Sinatra, and World Cup soccer. I can't help it. It's in my blood.

A few weeks after my trip to Italy, my wife and I receive a call from some friends of ours who have just returned from a trip to Scandinavia. "You won't believe this," they tell me. "There are so many Sturlas in Iceland, and they go back centuries."

My first inclination is to hang up and dismiss this as some sort of crank call. But upon further investigation I find that, indeed, the Sturlas can be traced back in Iceland for at least a thousand years. I also discover that Sturla is probably not an Italian name, but more likely a German one. My way-back ancestors were probably marauding members of some warlike Teutonic tribe that plundered their way into Northern Italy about a millennium-and-a-half ago, while the black sheep of the family made their way north and east toward Iceland.

Oooooooohhhhh. So I was not so much born with a demitasse in my hand as a war club. But that shall remain a family secret. Just between you and me, right?

Vince Sturla plans on chucking his career as a journalist and run for mayor of Sturla, Italy. His pasta-loving wife and kids support his political ambitions.

★

On a rather humid and warm Sunday morning a group of Toledo, Ohio, public school teachers and I were traveling by bus on the *autostrada* between Florence and Rome. After enjoying Florence's Renaissance sites we were eager to visit the Eternal City. In transit through, I believe, Viterbo Province, we stopped at a service area. Immediately behind the service area were two outdoor restrooms. As I was in the process of using one, a man with a straw broom entered and proceeded to sweep the floor an inch or two from where I was standing. He then began to sweep my pant leg, all the while shouting in Italian at me and pointing to the restroom entrance. Not familiar with the Italian language, I quickly excused myself and exited the restroom. What had I done to cause this person's ire? Talking later with Italian friends in Rome, I learned that workers in that particular *autostrada's* service area had gone on strike that Sunday morning for an hour or two to protest government wage proposals. Apparently, the occurrence of the strike meant that one had to put one's bodily functions on hold as well. Since then I have traveled to Italy on numerous occasions and I am pleased to report that the insolence of this restroom incident has never reoccurred.

—Malcolm B. Campbell, "Reminiscence of Italian Travel"

CATHERINE THORPE

⋆ ⋆ ⋆

Adventures in Leather

...are not always what they seem.

I ONCE HAD AN ITALIAN SUITOR. HE WAS VERY TALL, DARK, and handsome, and he offered me discounted leather goods. I refused him.

I was a lass of sixteen, newly arrived in Florence with a group of fellow students from my high school and several hapless chaperones, who'd given up on enforcement back in Rome and now happily spent their evenings drinking in outdoor cafes. We were on one of those "educational" trips with a title, something like "The Glories of the Ancient World: Roman and Byzantine Art and History"—ostensibly an academic endeavor which in reality was primarily a celebration of the availability of alcohol to minors (and, lately, to chaperones) in several European locales.

Despite these straightened circumstances, I was enthralled with Florence. In the birthplace of the Renaissance—when, arguably, Europe awakened from childhood into a more earthy and humanistic age—I wandered the streets in the kind of trance occasioned by a surfeit of stimuli. The tawny buildings luminous with afternoon sun, the Duomo's bright facade glimpsed unexpectedly from a crook in the cobbled street, the *piazzas* inviting indolence with their lounging statuary: all served to encourage an ecstatic reverie.

Perhaps more importantly for the adolescent mindset, I had been primed for this experience long in advance. My mother had given me E.M. Forster's *A Room With A View* for Christmas, and I had devoured it as our holiday feast cooked; in the intervening months, I'd seen the film three or four times, obtained a copy of Baedeker's guide to Florence, and ensured that the soundtrack would swoon in my head at the appropriate moments.

> "*P*oor girl? I fail to understand the point of that remark. I think myself a very fortunate girl, I assure you. I'm thoroughly happy, and having a splendid time."
>
> ♦
>
> —Lucy Honeychurch, in
> *A Room with a View,*
> by E. M. Forster

All my fervent hopes were rewarded upon our arrival at the hotel, when I was assigned to a room with shuttered windows that, when flung open, revealed a splendid view of the Arno and the Ponte Vecchio. My roommate and I ecstatically agreed to keep the windows open all night, which we did—despite a spectacular thunderstorm. It was, I believed, a propitious start: Florence would certainly be the setting for a reckless—and suitably picturesque—Romantic Adventure.

My prospects, however, seemed dim. At school I was known as a solitary and bookish type—traits which hardly appealed to my male companions on this trip, who were more interested in testing every variety of Italian beer than visiting Dante's birthplace. In the evenings I found myself sipping potent red concoctions purchased by an empathetic chaperone and sighing in frustration as I gazed at my classmates, invariably in a raucous group a few tables away.

By my third day in Florence, I knew drastic measures were necessary. We had the afternoon free, and I declined to view the Pitti Palace in favor of accompanying a larger group of my classmates—including the four or five boys I had a crush on—on a shopping trip. We went to an excessively well-heeled school, and had been instructed that Florence was for buying leather; so we girls perused purses and belts while the boys posed in motorcycle jackets in shop after shop in the touristy quarter between the Arno and the Duomo.

The third or fourth such store was larger, with several rooms showcasing a wide array of goods. We fanned out and, as usual, I eventually found myself trailing behind one group of girls and then alone, this time with a double-decker rack full of black leather skirts of varying lengths.

I was bending over the lower rack, admiring this or that item and breathing deeply of the opulent leather smell, wondering if perhaps a daring purchase would endear me to my classmates, when he approached: a young Florentine merchant garbed in a fashionable olive-colored suit.

"Are you looking for something special? Let me find you something." His accent gave the query a plaintive tone. "What are you looking for? A skirt? You like a mini-skirt?"

There was certainly no harm in trying something on. "Sure, a skirt," I said.

"Here." He handed me a rather small specimen. "You go try it and come show."

When I appeared out of the dressing room, fidgeting awkwardly, he clasped his hands in delight. "Fantastic! Come! See!" He took me to the full-length mirror. "You look great. Fantastic!"

The skirt covered barely enough thigh, and I was fairly sure I didn't want it—I still wasn't seriously shopping anyway, I told myself. Still, I stayed in front of the mirror, contemplating the rather-non-bookish person staring back at me: recognizable, but different. This skirt was not suitable for a romantic picnic.

The salesman hovered, now holding a sumptuous matching jacket. When I protested, he begged, "Please! Just try it. It will be great!"

I was intrigued, and slipped it on. Now the image in the mirror was pure vamp—with the jacket's padded shoulders and cinched waist, the silhouette suggested outright danger; were my legs really that long?

"Fabulous!" he cried, a proud Pygmalion. "Look!"

I couldn't help a blush of agreement. I was enjoying this diversion, so when he returned with a co-worker and a pair of stiletto heels, I slipped into them almost eagerly. Several of my classmates appeared momentarily at the doorway and watched with marginal interest before slipping away.

"Gorgeous!" he cried. He beamed at me reverently. "Truly a goddess! Tell me, how old are you?"

"Sixteen."

"Sixteen! *Una bambina!*"

His associate chortled something in Italian, and a short conversation between them ensued.

"Do you have a boyfriend?"

When I shook my head, the salesman was indignant, almost distraught: "No boyfriend?! You should have fifty thousand boyfriends! A million boyfriends!"

I tore my attention from the foreign image in the mirror; my classmates had disappeared. Had they "ditched" me and moved on to the next shop? I forgot my game of dress-up. It was time to go. With a lingering farewell gaze at my short-lived persona, I pivoted on my wobbly heels and headed for the dressing room.

"Wait! Don't you like it?" asked the salesman.

"Yes.... I—I'm just not sure," I said.

"For you, I make a special deal. I give you the jacket and the skirt for—"

"No," I said. "I...don't have any money with me."

He kept pace with me as I moved again toward the changing room, and slung an arm around my shoulders in a gesture of complicity. "How much you want to pay? Whatever you want, you should have it. I shouldn't make special deals, but for you, anything. Anything you want."

I stepped away from him at the dressing room door. "Nothing for now. I'll think about it," I lied. I was almost annoyed at his persistent sales pitch. Couldn't he see I was in a hurry? "Maybe I'll come back tomorrow."

He took my arm again quickly and turned me toward him. In my stiletto heels, I couldn't avoid looking into his dark eyes, which exuded an admittedly delicious, soulful vulnerability.

"Let's forget it," he said. "I'll take you dancing. Let's go dancing. I'll take you out. You are so beautiful."

I panicked. "Can't," I blurted, stumbling back a step and grabbing his arm to keep from falling. "I'm with a group from school. We have chaperones. We're all going to dinner tonight."

"I will meet you later. After dinner. Please! Leave your group. I will show you around town. You could bring your friends. We could all go together."

"No—I just can't!" I ducked into the dressing room with adrenaline agility, leaving him behind. The leather skimmed off quickly despite my shaking hands. This wasn't supposed to be happening, everything was completely loused up. I had lost the group, and with it my chances for a proper Romantic Adventure. E.M. Forster hadn't prepared me for a waylaying Florentine merchant.

Securely swathed once again in my blouse and long flowing skirt, I emerged from behind the curtain to find my suitor leaning against the wall in the hallway just outside the main dressing room door. He held his head in his hands in a gesture of anguish, and when he saw me he begged, "Please! You are so beautiful! Like Venus!"

I gave him a venomous glance, and was about to elbow past him when he leaned forward and gave me a quick kiss on the cheek before I could move away.

"Please! You drive me crazy!" he pleaded. "Please!" he cried, as I wound swiftly out of the store. "Come back! Come back tomorrow! I will wait for you! You come find me! I love you!"

Much to my relief, I found my faithless classmates three stores down the street. It was time to rejoin our chaperones for dinner. At the restaurant I recounted my predicament, my shock, my escape. No one showed much interest. The other girls affected disdain.

The formerly empathetic chaperone was pitiless. "That's what you get for going leather shopping," he said.

It wasn't until days later that I wondered whether the incident had, in fact, been an Adventure. But the thought of the salesman was painfully embarrassing—definitely not, I was certain, a sensation associated with romance. I tried to forget about it and gamely continued my hopeless crushes.

As time passed, though, I began to remember the situation with more tolerance. I never managed to consider what might have happened if we'd actually met; the idea of sneaking out of the hotel, perhaps by the window, into the moonlit city was enough. In retrospect, my suitor became rather attractive. After all, he likened me to Venus. He didn't assail me in the dressing room, or spy on me as I disrobed. He didn't care whether I was popular or liked partying. He had been handsome. He had given me beautiful Italian compliments and a refreshing new perspective of myself. I thought a lot about that kiss.

In subsequent years, even a feminist disinclination to being objectified couldn't dislodge the pleasure associated with the memory. I later returned to Italy hoping for another chance at Adventure, but never received an offer so courteous or poetic as that of the Florentine merchant's.

And, of course, never again was I offered such a bargain: $350 for a leather skirt and jacket. What had I been thinking?

Catherine Thorpe is a journalist, flamenco dancer, and student of vice. She lives in Northern California with her husband, Edwin Richards, and owns one leather skirt.

★

Travel, as Paul Fussell advises, should jolt one into reverie about the human condition. Travel's false twin, *touring* (or insulated, prepackaged, overscheduled sightseeing), leaves one unruffled and not a jot wiser. If we remain unprovoked by travel, we might as well stay home and agree with Emerson that all travel is a fool's paradise, since the unregenerate tourist merely carries "ruins to ruins." But real travel, with its fortuitous dislocations and unforseen thrills, is not necessarily salutary; roused, our buried self may find itself confronted by desperate thoughts.

—Robert Chianese, "Gypsies, Ik and the Human Condition,"
The Humanist

MATTHEW SPENDER

✦ ✦ ✦

Seravezza

A sculptor goes in search
of Michelangelo's "tag."

I READ SOMEWHERE THAT MICHELANGELO TALKED OF CARVING A
whole mountain into a sculpture, up behind Carrara. It's one of
those stories I think about from time to time, as if I were mentally
touching a horseshoe for luck.

"It should still be possible to see where he worked, I think,"
Vittoria told me years ago, outside the Biblioteca Nazionale in
Florence. "Michelangelo opened one of the mines up behind
Pietrasanta; it is in Vasari. I do not know which quarry, and perhaps
it is only a legend. But it would be nice to find out, no?"

She was combing her hair as she spoke, and her feet were
pointed in opposite directions like a dancer at the barre. The day
was warm, and I liked these preparations, tidying up her hair for
the benefit of ancient manuscripts. I still retain a clear image of the
occasion. She was fresh to research, pleased with herself for having
come this far already.

"It would be easy to recognize, because he carved his initial—
the letter M, no?—high up on the wall. It must be a famous, a
well-known thing in Pietrasanta, don't you think?"

I thought about this for a moment. Sometimes Vittoria's sense
of irony was too subliminal for me.

"Do you really see Michelangelo carving his initials on a wall?"

"But of course!" she said, hitching up her bag to march off. "At Sounion Lord Byron carved his name on a column when he visited it. So Michelangelo would have done the same. Surely?"

She left before I could think of an answer. I could see from the way she walked up the steps, zebraed by sunlight, that she was very pleased with herself, for having had the last word.

Pietrasanta is a small town underneath the mountains of marble above Pisa and Lucca. A paradise for sculptors, with a greater concentration of those who carve and those who cast bronze than anywhere else in the world. These days this local population of master craftsmen is heavily salted with young foreigners there to learn the trade, or old masters having their polystyrene mock-ups turned into stone. All meet convivially in the local bar to catch up on recent gossip, and pass the word for new jobs or places to stay.

I had been there a number of times without ever having followed up the questions of the quarry of Michelangelo. From time to time, generally late at night, we would talk about the hole in the side of the mountain, and the young apprentices would passionately repeat the rumour that an unfinished statue by Michelangelo was still up there. The locals when pressed were skeptical. No quarry, no square inch of any quarry, could remain unexplored after all these years. There are no secrets, they said.

Then one evening in the *piazza* with an American sculptor called Caio, I found myself talking about the abandoned mine in the hills. He thought the whole thing absurd, but ran his fingers through his extraordinary black hair and looked behind him into the bar to see if any of the old stonecutters might be there.

He took me by the shoulder and pushed me in. There at the back, among the card-players and under the flickering TV set, a hard old man stood at the bar among his mates, shouting about this and that. Caio with difficulty extracted him, introduced us, and talked about this trace memory of Vittoria's, the letter M, high on the wall of marble in a disused quarry.

Romano nodded, unsurprised. If it existed, he said cautiously it would be on Monte Altissimo behind Seravezza the next town along as you skirt the Apuan Alps. He had worked in all the quarries in Seravezza since the age of twelve, he said. I was thrilled to meet him, amazed at his good health, full of admiration for his extraordinary experience. Behind him on the TV among the bottles young girls dressed as butterflies began to disrobe. He accepted a glass of something, put his elbows on the bar and waited for more questions.

Once he spoke, his reply was thorough and precise. "Michelangelo was working in Carrara, but he did not get on well with Carraresi. Then the pope ordered him to go to the new mines at Seravezza, because they had found a vein of very fine marble at a place called La Tacca Bianca."

"What does that mean?" I asked, groping for a pencil.

"*Una tacca* is where you hit it with a chisel. *Tac!*" He mimed a blow. "They called it this because the very first time a workman hit the rock to test it, a piece of pure white stone came out. Anyway, although it was remote and difficult, Michelangelo worked the mine and took from it the marble he used for the big *Pietà* in Rome. The one at-

> *M*ichelangelo loved the very quarries of Carrara, those strange grey peaks which even at midday convey into any scene from which they are visible something of the solemnity and stillness of evening, sometimes wandering among them month after month, till at last their pale ashen colours seem to have passed into his painting; and on the crown of the head of the *David* there still remains a morsel of uncut stone, as if by one touch to maintain its connexion with the place from which is was hewn.
>
> ♦
>
> —Walter Pater,
> *The Renaissance* (1873)

tacked by a mad German with a hammer. Also the big *Moses*. And the columns for San Lorenzo which he never built, the stone of which was stolen in Rome."

Caio asked about a road. Wasn't there some road which Michelangelo...? "Oh yes," I said excitedly, "the road was in Vasari too, come to think of it."

"The road he made to get the stone down from the mountain ran from Riomagno to Malbacco behind Seravezza, near the school, and is called today the Via Michelangelo Buonarotti," said Romano solemnly. "Above the bridge it becomes Via Monte Altissimo, and I do not think that Michelangelo built it. He brought down the stones to the head of the road on a *lizza dura*, which is a kind of heavy sledge made from the trunks of two large trees tied together. They came down the river bed. Here and there he had to make short cuts at the side of the river, but most of these do not exist any more."

A man in a tuxedo on the television congratulated a young lady on being more or less naked, and offered her a silk kimono.

"It must have been here on Monte Altissimo that Michelangelo worked," said Romano, puffing his cigarette, "because when they came to make a film about him, they shot it here at Seravezza and not at Carrara. The one with Tsarles Hess."

"Charlton Heston?"

"*Esatto*: in the part of Moses."

"You mean in the part of Michelangelo," said Caio. "He did Moses too, but that was another film."

"That I do not know, but the film was made here. I remember because they made me show them all the mines."

A far-away look came into the eyes of this marvellous old man, and he started talking about the mines. My envelope was not large enough to write them all down. Monte Bardiglio, both the quarry on the coast and the one up at the chapel. Monte Altissimo, where Michelangelo truly was. He even showed the film troupe the mine at Cervaioli where the arabesque marble comes from, which is six miles on the other side and has nothing whatever to do with Michelangelo. "They saw them all," said Romano, "and they never stooped to examine a single stone!"

The television kept up its stylized amateur striptease with the sound turned down. Romano thought for a moment, then became both passionate and secretive. Fragmented extensions of bare legs and arms like vertical smiles glowed in each of the bottles among which the TV stood.

"They say that once, many years ago, a shepherd found a block of lapis lazuli up there. He told no one, but took a small piece to the Medici, hoping for a reward. He died before he could say where he found it, and though they sent down all sorts of experts from Florence, they never discovered the source. Nor has anyone since. So there is still a treasure somewhere up there in the mountains..."

At Seravezza the houses went up the side of the hill, and two rivers met by a square of leafy sycamores in the French style. A humpback bridge crossed over one river, where bored young men on bikes tried to decide which side was the right place to be. Caio made me drive through them, against the one-way system, pursued by a tired *"Ao!"* and a raised arm of rejection.

On the other side we hesitated, asked the way in a pretty *piazzetta*, and then drove north, joining a road on the left of the branching valley.

This new short piece of road was Michelangelo's, leading to the quarry he revived. The road ran parallel to an empty river bed and the landscape on either side soon became steeper. We went through a little hamlet and crossed over to the eastern bank. Between us and the stream were small factories, where waste fragments were cut into tiles that were stacked between the bus-stops and the telephone poles.

The bed of the stream was dry, filled with white boulders tumbled into spheres by the torrential winter floods. Caio said that there were pools down there, cold but clean, and in summer the sculptors of Pietrasanta often came up here to swim.

Up above us the peaks were fringed with trees against the sky, with a heavy crimping of greenery beneath. There would not be much light in winter, but now the sun was up there somewhere, discouraging the wispy condensation from becoming cloud.

"It's a mountains' mountain," said Caio semi-seriously. "As you have a painters' painter, or a poets' poet."

In the flank of the extraordinarily steep peak which we were approaching there appeared a black hole near the top. The quarry of Michelangelo. The road became narrower and Caio made me sound the horn at every corner. By the side of the road a cheerful woman held up her hand as her husband winched down a stout log recently cut. The woods were blackened just above. It had been a bad summer for fires, and there were cauterized areas all along the coast.

The asphalt came to an end. We took a sharp turn to the right, up the steep shale slopes of a dirt track, the vegetation changing, cluttered with ferns. There was no sign of marble that I could see. The road had been made ready for the winter with gulleys and ramparts dug and thrown up transversely every fifty yards, to catch the run-off in the rainy month of November.

Passing through an untended part of the wood we came to a gully with a ledge on which stood a heavily boarded house. We stopped. The shutters rejected our friendly approach. A Chinese sculptor lived there last year, Caio said. He went to the edge of a balcony set over the chasm and hollered across the valley. Silence, waiting for an echo. To me the place seemed haunted. I said we should go on.

Not far off we came to a green plateau, upon which a grey-haired young man was setting a simple fork beside a knife upon a blue wooden table by a rock. Born bachelor, battered Citroën, mongrel dog. Caio vaguely recognized him. They performed the cowboy greeting of artists, hands poised above imaginary pistols, showing their teeth.

He told us his name was France. His number-plate was Austrian and his bumper had a sticker for the Salzburg festival. He had a little tent and a table, chair and bottle of wine. He also had an altar at the edge, three splayed sticks tied together at the top, with a rope that dangled down between them, ending in a perforated stone. Just to tell the time he told me, seeing my dubious look.

Behind us, where the road forked, was a gaudy shrine to the Madonna, bright blue frame and fresh flowers. The procession had come up two days before, said France. Nearby on an abandoned shack I saw a sticker saying "VIRGIN MARY PRAY THOSE WHO WORK IN THE QUARRIES." Crude black letters of supplication or command.

Caio and France chatted about Manhattan.

The abandoned masons' shack was neat and clean, with plates, cutlery, wooden boards, evidently imported recently by France. The ancient lavatory was newly polished, a handmade throne of wood.

One branch of the road went straight on, the other curved to the right, over the hill. A fresh rock-spill of gigantic proportions blocked the straight branch. I could see the truncated path on the other side of the gully, covered with fresh grass of extraordinary bright green. That, I took it, was Michelangelo's route down from the rock face, from the quarry to where the sledge made of trees waited in the bed of the river.

"They stole my stones," said France smiling as we got back in the car. "I collected them last year and now they are gone. Maybe they tipped them back into the valley."

I told him that Michelangelo had suffered from plundering too.

"Ah well," he said cheerfully. "To be in his company…"

He said that the worst was over. We drove onwards, leaving the trees behind. The world became still steeper, more remote.

Monk's pepper grew in the shade of deep places in the road where the sun shone rarely. Crags and spills threatened the sides of the car and there were overhangs across the road at the hairpin bends. The sun gave way before the cloud, which accumulated gradually between us and the mine. The hole became a black mouth squarely inserted into the misty scree of the Monte Altissimo.

By and by a truck filled with quarry workers passed us, going down. No one stopped to ask our business, or give us a smile and a wave.

Further up the hill we found the modern quarry, a segment of the mountainside mathematically amputated. A crystal negative of perfect right angles surrounded by blocks of several tons, each the size of a small car. The hole was huge; plastic tape warned strangers not to fall in. There was no one about. One could look down at a huge cross-section of the marble bed, see the wavy striations of grey among the white just as it had been deposited by the tide on the sea floor, the angle of the lines now a sharp diagonal, formed when the mountain was forced upwards. A long fault of sand and shale ran like a line drawn in charcoal through the middle. "*Dino, ti amo*" was sprayed in black upon the beautiful marble face in front of the car, and then cancelled in red: "*Silvia, stronza, mi hai tradito.*"

The road's ending. But across the quarry it seemed that a disused path continued up the hill behind an orderly stack of boulders....

The clouds were within grasping distance now, forming momentarily and vanishing again some hundred yards vertically above....

Behind a penultimate curve we came across a small landslide, with shelves of rock shuffled like a pack of cards. Below the path the hard scree fell away at an angle of forty-five degrees, right down to the cliff beyond which, on his domestic ledge, stood France, just visible by his tent. A good place from which to let down rock gently towards the river bed; a bad place for an intrepid traveller to fall.

At this point Caio began to tell me how he loathed heights, how once on Machu Picchu he had been marooned by his mother and with his eyes tight shut for twenty minutes and so on. I looked at him standing there, motionless on a slab of rock, huge shoulders, bronzed, with the chest of a man who daily carved a life-sized marble mastodon out in the yard before breakfast. It took me a moment to realize he was being serious. Actually he said, "I do have this, ah, thing about heights."

I held my hand out across to him and told him not to look down. Thus the heroes managed to get by the rockfall without leaving their battered corpses in the dell. Caio tried not to shake as he stepped down again on to dry land.

The last hundred yards were handsome, like the avenue to a castle, not a road to a hole in a mountain.

Debris of rusted railway-lines at the entrance. Wooden struts engraved with filigree tendrils of moss growing like fur within the soft summer rings of each year's growth, the air of a serious

concern abandoned many years before. A winch hut containing
roots of iron where an engine had been. From the window feelers
of wire trailed over the edge into the valley. A rotten soapbox, a
green spittoon (so it seemed) and the haunches of a motor bike
with springs grinning through the saddle. All durable debris, you
might say. No matches, cigarette butts or other jetsam of the day-
to-day.

The quarry now rose above us like the mouth of a petrified
whale. It was hard to look at it. Indeed we did not dare go in, but
walked sideways along the disused road sniggering and joking, past
a lean-to of corrugated iron, until unexpectedly we found a lateral
shaft in the mountain which somehow seemed less daunting.

On the left as we went into the tunnel the sheer wall was buffed
to a hard sheen like the interior of a cathedral rubbed by the
sleeves of pilgrims. The floor was soft with powdered emery and
marble dust. Our footsteps were muffled.

We came to the quarry inside the mountain. On our immediate right a strange ladder descended from above. It was irregularly
fixed to the wall with a diagonal row of holes drilled into the
marble. From time to time a shelf of wood hung free on a web of
old wires which curled and bent, feathery with the accumulation
of rust.

We were approaching, via the transept, a cathedral cut from the
core of the mountain, the cuttings themselves having been re-
assembled into real cathedrals outside in the air, emulating the void
from which they had been taken. A quarry that was in part a
cathedral, in part a drowned ship, slanting as the floor followed the
imperfect division of some natural layer of sediment.

From the roof down to about a third of its height from the top
the quarry had been cut by hand. If the M of Michelangelo were
anywhere, it would be up there. Below that the stone was cut by
wire right to the ground. The layer cut by hand and the layers
below it cut by wire were like relics from two different dynasties.

I took out my glasses. A bad time to discover I had stepped on
them the night before. With a bright left eye and a lame right I
searched for the initial M somewhere on the roof, but saw only

ladders made of cutting wire and old wood suspended from impossible perches. Looking upwards into the air was to look downward under the sea. The decaying ladders on the roof moved like seaweed in a current on the ocean floor.

Caio allowed me to shush the adventurer in him for a moment while we listened to the noises that this place might make. First there was nothing but the roar of the tide in the inner ear. Then I could hear the gentle noise of droplets falling from a great height on to sand or stone fragile and faint but with a rhythm that was regular. Now and again there was a louder clap, as some wayward element struck a rock or abandoned drum of oil, a flailing ladder or dislodged stone. A remote rivulet pattered.

The colours of the walls were beautiful, with a patina laid down by time and air. There were steaks of oxides of red and green, of iron and copper, where minerals had bled through a thin fissure. As in a cathedral, the light took on a quality different from any source which could be observed, as if light itself carried the colour. Pale green dominated the empty space.

Caio pointed out a huge natural fault on the farther wall, running vertically through the stone. We traced it to our side: we were sitting within it. Some lateral crack caused by the upturned landmass, it flickered like an artery in the striated substance of the marble.

We thought about the men working there and became restless. To decide which nests halfway up a sheer wall had held some foreman directing the machines, to work out how they ran the cutting wires, how they fed the drills from hole to hole, how they set down dry boards across the sumps and trickles in the floor, was to awaken the spirit of those who had abandoned the place.

At the end of the tunnel from which we had come the light of day seemed suddenly bright and fresh. After we came out we stood for a while at the edge of the canyon and looked down on the mountains, the populated plain beyond, and the Ligurian Sea above Viareggio upon whose beach the drowned Shelley had been cremated. Cloud was descending from the right, from Genoa. The setting sun could not dissolve it.

The white torrent shone immediately below us; then I remembered the river bed contained not water but marble. And France with his red car beside it, his tent the size of a plum.

"Zilarating," said Caio, "that's the word I've been groping for. Just zilarating."

Craning over the edge he began to whistle. I had never heard anything like it. He added an extraordinary series of trills, grace notes, baroque ornamentation, enough to turn a nightingale green.

I listened dumbfounded. He stopped, put his head on one side as if listening for a reply and said slyly, "It gets me credit at the bank."

From below came the cheerful double toot of the bus taking a corner. It seemed to be time to go.

A moon smudged by thin cloud rose above the lower quarry as we drove down. When we passed France he was carving a boulder, against the background of a whole gulley of boulders.

"I don't quite understand," said Caio a mile or two from this side of Pietrasanta, "what this marble business has to do with Michelangelo. If you want to write about Michelangelo, you don't have to even mention Monte Altissimo, do you? I mean you aren't going to suggest that his images depended on the quarry the marble happened to come from, are you?"

Dusk and an approaching storm coincided as we reached the valley floor, and the world became suddenly much darker. On the outskirts of Fabriano we passed parked cars with number-plates in black on white, Rosenheim and Starnberg, Munich and Berlin. Their owners were crammed into a pizzeria a little further on.

"The answer," I said at length, "comes from a dream. It's a bit difficult to explain, as it sounds so feeble. Anyway, I dreamed I was looking at a whole exhibition of Michelangelo's sculpture (some of the pieces never made by him, but imagined in the dream), and I suddenly became aware how much their quality depended upon shadow, on holes, empty bits, discarded soft blackness. The dream moved to the quarry he worked in, and it struck me as being the place of ultimate shadow, in my dream, the place where they all came from…"

We drove on down through the outskirts of Pietrasanta, groping through to a quiet restaurant on the other side, with wind

bending the trees all about
us. Large leaves of sycamores
browned by the summer
flapped across the road, and
water began to pour from the
heavens as if from a tap, just
as we parked the car.

Summer is the busiest
time for restaurants along the
coast, and finding a place to
eat was a tangled episode,
well laundered by the heavens. So it was luck that we
ran into a friend called
Gianni sitting at an empty
table and with an unexpected
desire to hear all about the
day up the mountainside. It was hard to shout down the babel of
languages, but the other customers looked like people who
worked with the locals masters, rather than tourists.

As an infant,
Michelangelo was
cared for by a wet nurse whose
family were stonecutters. He
grew up loving, above all, to
carve marble statues. He called it
"stone fever" and said, "Nothing
was right with me unless I had a
chisel in my hand."

♦

—Wenda Brewster O'Reilly,
Ph.D., *The Renaissance Art Game*

Gianni was a retired journalist and, as it happened, had spent
some time on the subject of Michelangelo and Pietrasanta, just to
keep the old brain working, he said. His version went like this:

"Michelangelo was working in Carrara in the Fantiscritti
mine. He was happy to be there because Count Alberigo di
Malaspina gave him a percentage back from the pope's account
for the stone he was buying. Michelangelo *sapeva i fatti suoi*, knew
how to take care of himself, so *in parole povere*, to cut it short, he
took a bribe.

"The mine at Seravezza had been worked in Roman times, but
was now almost disused. The citizens of Seravezza decided that the
best thing they could do to get it re-opened would be to *give* it to
the Medici, for free. After all, even if they did not charge for the
stone, they would still be employed as quarrymen up there, no?"

Caio leaned over and helped himself to the wine.

"So they met in the *piazza* of Seravezza and shouted with one voice, '*Palle, palle!*'—which means 'Balls, balls!'—the Medici coat of arms being, as you know, a lot of balls on a shield."

Gianni shouted out *"palle"* quite loudly.

"Pope Leo X was a Medici, no? He immediately ordered Michelangelo to leave Carrara and go to Seravezza and work the new Medici mines. Perhaps he knew that Michelangelo was getting a bribe from Malaspina, and perhaps he didn't. Maybe they earned their money like Arabs in those days, taking from buyer and seller—not that we've changed all that much. Anyway, Michelangelo did everything he could not to go. He said the marble of Seravezza was bad, full of veins of quartz, the road did not exist. Anything! His letters are full of complaints which the historians take very seriously, but you don't have to believe him."

"Yes," I said, "but he did have to spend time making a road up there, didn't he? That's a bit of a waste of effort for a genius like Michelangelo, don't you think?"

"That is true," said Gianni, "but he didn't exactly make them personally, did he? Any more than Mussolini, who gave Italy all those roads, ever went out there with a pick in his hands."

We all thought that very funny.

"If you look carefully at Michelangelo's road, you'll see it is really quite a short stretch, right at the end. After which, incidentally, he turned and went straight to the sea—which in a sense was the foundation of Forte dei Marmi. If he could see it now!"

"Right," said Caio, "I've always seen the Sistine Chapel as Muscle Beach."

"The medieval road from Seravezza went along the old Roman Via Valentina, and ended up on the sea at a place called Malamocca, which is just above Viareggio in fact. The new road was much better...I would not be surprised if it was not easier to get the rock from Seravezza to the sea, along his Nuova Strada di Marina, than from Carrara. Mind you, the place was a swamp full of mosquitoes and malaria in Michelangelo's day, as they only drained it in the seventeenth century..."

Gianni was evidently prepared to give a rapid run-down on every inch of the countryside.

"And which sculptures were carved from Seravezza marble?"

"They say that the *Moses*...I personally don't think that matters so much, do you? What is for certain is that he worked hard here getting down the columns for San Lorenzo, columns which are all lost, or almost all."

By now we had drunk all Gianni's wine, and Caio shouted for more. Something you can only do if you know the owner. Down he came, a man with black-rimmed glasses and a stoop, who asked Caio to whistle before he gave him the menu.

"A fine man," said Caio playing for time, "he is also my bank manager...I told you, didn't I?"

Each had the other by the arm, pushing and pulling for the wine list. I got up and went to the open door, and as I walked Caio relented and performed. He warbled and trilled under the clatter of the rain, while people stopped eating and turned towards him.

I could hear the storm come in from the sea in waves, crossing the building from one side to the other, drum-rolling the corrugated roof of the kitchen. The passing headlights flickered on asphalt and chrome amid a general staccato of wetness. The cars moved slowly, like animals fighting through undergrowth. Laughter, clapping for Caio behind me. The parallel lines of sycamore, pollarded three or four years back, whipped their thin branches rapidly all down the road. The gutter was already full, though the deeper channel for a stream on the other side was empty.

The rest of the street turned black.

Sculptor Matthew Spender left his home in England for what was to be a brief visit in Tuscany. He and his wife now call Tuscany home. His book, Within Tuscany, *is a memoir weaving history, anecdote, and observation. This story, as well as "Satyric" in Part Four, were excerpted from this book.*

★

Countless numbers [of minute organisms] die over the years and leave microscopic fragments of themselves sparkling downwards to the sea floor.

Large bodies of water move over the same area in the same way for millennia and the sea acts as a sieve, precipitating the material into coherent strata. The silt, the mush of bones, the limestone paste, sink to the bottom to form a thick layer of aspiring rock.

Nothing seems more uniform than these millions of square miles of seabed covered with the same promising stuff, below countless tons of water whose weight will eventually create stone. Yet chance punctuates it constantly. Plumes of undersea mineral-bearing spouts shoot up from deep volcanic fissures. Shelves of crust hitch and grind against each other, sift and split. The continental plates never stay still. Mountains are created from folds of stone, generating immense extremes of heat and pressure. *"Il peso non dorme,"* they say in the quarries: "Weight never sleeps."

—Matthew Spender, *Within Tuscany*

$\star\ ^{\star}\ \star$

Night Swimmer

And so donning sandals immortal…

I SQUINTED AT THE FERRY AND TRAIN SCHEDULE BY THE MOON-light cast through the gap in the shutters and the window casing (hotel electricity had gone off promptly at 11:30 p.m.): I would be able to catch the 8:15 ferry to Messina, and then the 9:04 train to Barcelona, the departure point for the islands of Lipari. These islands, still only a brief image from a guidebook, were fast expanding into nothing less than the saving graces by which I would be returned to the blessed arc of the kind of final trip in Italy I so desperately wanted to have as a signature, in my memory, of the time I had lived there.

I made it to the main island, the island of Lipari, in the early morning aboard an *aliscafo*. I found the hostel and had breakfast—yogurt and toast—looking out over the sea from the dining room of the converted castle. There I met Mark and Antony, who were traveling together. Mark was from New Jersey and Antony, an Iraqi, was from London. We decided to go together to the island of Vulcano, named after the lame blacksmith of the gods, Vulcano (Hephaestus in Greek). It was there, deep in his volcano in the sea, that he was said to labor, working the bellows of his fiery furnace. He was married to Aphrodite, Goddess of Love, who was not shy about sharing her gift—with others. The volcanic eruptions in the area, naturally, were said to be his doing—his own way of blowing off accumulated jealousy. At the time of our visit, Vulcano (the island) was not so active (perhaps Aphrodite had learned about commitment) and was best known for its therapeutic mud baths and sulfur springs.

When we arrived, we quickly avoided the crowds of large pink Germans becoming large mud people and clambered up the crater shell. On the way, we came upon many sulfurous, reeking cracks. The heat of their activity, combined with the August midday sun, made it hotter than Hades and forced us down into the cool water. After a while we explored the nearby sulfur and thermal springs, and even took a dip in the therapeutic mud. Then we caught the boat back.

Back on Lipari, we split up: Mark and Antony went to the hostel, and I bought a mask and snorkel and took a bus to Spiaggia Bianca. It was a beautiful time to be there, towards the end of the afternoon, and I swam with pumice floating around my ears and with obsidian visible at my feet. The sand, true to its name, was the whitest of

*A*ctually, the Aeolians have been welcoming wanderers since ancient times. Homer put the islands in the *Odyssey*, making them the home of Aeolus, god of the winds. (From my vantage point, amid whitecaps, it was obvious why.) When Ulysses showed up on Aeolus's doorstep, the god graciously sent him off with a bag of winds—tightly sealed so they could not blow the ship off a homeward course. Of course, curiosity got the better of the crew, who opened the gift— loosing the winds' full fury. Blown back to the Aeolians, Ulysses and company were fated to wander on.

Thousands of years later the winds were still blowing, and the waves were still tossing little boats on the sea. But unlike Ulysses, I was in no hurry to go home.

◆

—Joan Tapper,
"Aeolian Odyssey," *Islands*

whites. When the sun started to drop I reluctantly got up and went back to the road where I caught a ride back with "Joe," a local fisherman, who had a niece just married and living in New Brunswick.

At the hostel, Mark and Antony were having dinner with a Spanish girl and two French girls whom they'd met. We all ended up getting a little drunk together on red wine. I told them of my afternoon swim at Spiaggia Bianca in such effusive terms that we all decided to go for a midnight dip.

We walked down to the port area and then out along the rocks of a promontory to an isolated spot. I took off my shorts and shirt and slipped in. The moon had just started to rise. There were no lights from behind us on the island, so the stars were bright. Ahead the sea beckoned, dark. From the surface you could see clear to the bottom, fifteen feet down. Everything was clear, though wrapped in the mystery of moonlight: rocks, starfish, algae—even fish— were all reflected upwards through the water by the pull of moon's soft light.

I was out in the water ahead of the others, trying to appear as if I weren't looking back intently at the girls undressing (they had wisely let us boys go first).

Which is why I didn't see it at first. Instead the girls, who were just getting ready to go in off the rocks, started calling out to me and pointing excitedly. My heart contracted. I immediately imagined a horrific sea monster rising up behind me.

As I jerked around I heard Mark yell, "Holy shit, Kevin! You're glowing!"

It was true. As I splashed around to confront the jaws of a giant squid I noticed a shower of sparks shoot off my shoulders. There were thousands of light particles shimmering around me. I stopped in wonder at the display. The shimmer slowly vanished. I splashed again. Again the water glowed preternaturally, gleaming effervescence in the cresting storm of air bubbles around me.

"This is unbelievable!" I heard Antony exclaim.

I turned to see him sweeping big arcs of light in the water with his arms. He held up his right hand: water glowed in his palm. One of the French girls leapt in and crystals of greenish-white light splashed into the air above where she'd gone under, and shone downwards, too, along with the outline of her body, as if she'd been dropped into a test-tube of gleaming Pepsi.

"What *is* this stuff!?" Anthony shouted.

I vaguely remembered reading something about phosphorous in the water and the light of the moon. I thought of Cyrano de Bergerac and his many schemes to arrive on the moon.

"It's bioluminescent plankton," Mark said. "When you agitate it, it releases light. Because it's night, it looks like a sparkler display. It's seasonal. We just happened to be here at the right time."

I turned and swam further out into the dark. Before me was an endless expanse of dark sea. I swam the breast-stroke out into the unknown and gradually grew acutely aware of my body, suspended and nude over a watery galaxy, trailing stardust over the black mass of water. I felt blessed, like I was that Greek lover who swam from Lemnos to Sestos every night in order to see his love. Or better still, like Byron, who had swum those straits just to see what it was like.

But I quickly became afraid. I realized I was exposed to an enormous dark nether world, spread-eagled, my vulnerable side open—genitals, belly, chest and throat. I felt the enormous solitude of creation. I felt the depth of the water and the energy with which it was suffused. All was dark, and getting darker, except for the soft explosions of phosphorous light around my body, spreading out in the currents of salt water. I was the first man, swimming out of aqueous creation, the sparks of life brushing off an emerging vital body and lighting the dark way forward.

After a long time out in the sea, I made my way back to the promontory and then up onto the beach. With my clothes in my hands, I set out to get dry. The others, already back in their clothes, were chatting on wooden chairs. I ran by them at a great clip, still naked and still possessed by the mania I had absorbed in the water. I felt as if I had swallowed light, and it was glowing in my center. I ran along the beach towards a sheltered cove around the bend, my feet crunching the sand, legs lifting and pumping, my skin breathing the air as I rushed through it. I was a Greek warrior, a god. Fleet-footed Achilles, with no famous armor but my birthday suit, which was fast dissolving, melting away due to its contact with the air. I felt again what I had known suspended in the water not fifteen minutes before: that I had become elemental, honed to a moving body of elements gathered loosely by skin but absolutely permeable to the world at large.

In fact, it seems my body had turned into a single-cell organism, a natural ion pump, circling particles of energy into me, through me, and back out of me, effortlessly. A pure transfer: no friction, no loss, no waste. At first I felt anxious, as if I had been swallowed into a dynamic pattern with no boundaries, but at the same time, reassurance began to grow in me and I became even more powerful. I felt the sparks fly off my heels into the sand, as if I were wearing iron sandals, or iron chariot wheels. I was charged, and the beach was a charged track—I was skimming over it fast, no friction and no energy consumed. I turned and ran back by the others on the wooden chairs, continuing to sprint back and forth before them, running faster each time. I was not getting tired (or very dry, either). The last time by I continued past them and on towards the bend and then into the unknown.

Snorting fire and tossing my hair into the wind I rounded the bend of the cove fully prepared to meet a monster or a god. This is where it would be. I was sure. Alone, loitering off the beaten path and away from human eyes. It would have pulled its visitor to it, for a singular purpose, for a one-on-one encounter. I didn't know what I would do if I met it. I thought that I would be afraid, but, actually, I was simply ready—and curious. I stopped. I looked around. No gods or demons here. I could make out nothing in the dim light and vague shadows. Just my hushed breathing. I looked at the cliffs. There were fissures and crevices and plants. But I could make out no recognizable forms. I thought they would appear as they had been described in the myths. They could be there—I just didn't know if I was able to see them.

But I was closer. Standing naked in the presence of the place, I had come closer, still glowing from the brush with stardust. I couldn't see their forms yet. But I felt their presence. The spirits there. It was their shine coming. Like a soft light out of the night.

Kevin Di Pirro spent a year in Florence trying to augur the flight of the blackbirds around Giotto's Campanile and attempting to find surviving Etruscans throughout Italy. He has written two nationally produced plays, Through Shite to Shannon *and* Mobl'd Queen's Good, *and is currently working on a third, inspired by Book 16 of* The Odyssey, *about family relations in an auto salvage yard under the Bay Bridge. He teaches in the Writing Program at the University of San Francisco.*

✳

Lipari is the largest island, about fifteen square miles, and the town of Lipari is the administrative capital of the archipelago. Eight minutes on the hydrofoil ride from Vulcano and I was enjoying my second coffee of the morning in a shady café on the Marina Corta, below the 16th-century castle and cathedral perched on their basaltic eyrie high above the harbor. The town is by far the largest community of the islands, whose total resident population barely exceeds twenty thousand. Possibly because of the wealth of black volcanic glass obsidian, and their proximity to the shipping lanes of the Straits of Messina, the islands have experienced a vigorous history. Remnants have been found of prehistoric settlements dating back to the 16th century B.C., although the first formal colonization took place around the year 588 B.C. by a small Greek clique, who went on to build a powerful fleet as a defense against Etruscan pirates and, in turn, took to piracy themselves. In later years the islands were dominated by the Carthaginians and the Romans, whose alum mining on Vulcano brought considerable prosperity to the populace. In 1340, the kings of Naples took possession until 1544, when Lipari itself was ransacked by the ferocious pirate Ariadeno Barbarossa, who captured, transported, and sold the entire population of the island as slaves. Eventually the town was rebuilt, and the island, repopulated by Charles V, has remained linked with Sicily and the Kingdom of Naples since that time.

—David Yeadon, *Backroad Journeys of Southern Europe*

✳

Body and Soul

*Jazz and the Renaissance have more
in common than you might think.*

DURING THE DAY, ROME HAS THE FEELING OF ROT AND REVELA-
tion one experiences when in the private domain of a handsome
old woman, where sweat, sex, cologne, rouge, yellowed notes and
papers, bottled remedies with indecipherable labels, crumbling
flowers, photographs that seem to have been taken in a brownish
gray mist, clothes stained with experience but never worn any-
more, and the smells of countless meals have formed a heavy collective presence in the air. Its ruins are like the sagging and corded
throatline of a beauty once too sensuous to be believed and now
too soulful to be perfectly understood. Of course, nothing we
worry about is old in the halls where the laws of nature were written, but in our human effort, with everything over so fast, a city
like Rome seems very, very old.

On the last morning there, I decided to beat the summer sun
to the punch. All of the notes, timbres, rhythms, and harmonies of
the festival called Umbria Jazz, the feelings of awe and mystery,
blood sacrifice and integrity that resonate from the cathedrals and
museums of Perugia, Assisi, and Florence were moving from my
memory to my spirit, and it was fully an hour and a half before
dawn. The forthcoming heat of the day was presaged by the qual-

ity of subtly repressed steam given to the morning air by the slight humidity. Two stars shone in apparent sympathy with the slow and gooey low notes of a brood of pigeons clustered somewhere up on the roof of our hotel, and outside in the street men were loading a white newspaper truck. From the distance of perhaps 70 feet, they seemed to be singing as they spoke in the sleep-laden, grumbling, dictatorial—even celebratory—Italian that makes so much of vowels that the most mundane order or response can sound like kindling for an aria. I thought again of how the flares and loops of Italian speech remind me of the sound and feeling of jazz, where the sensual weight, inflection, and rhythm of notes count for so much.

Within an hour I was on the street, intent on an early morning walk. After seven or eight blocks I turned, and nearly a mile away stood the Coliseum. As I walked toward it, part of the pleasure was watching the structure grow even larger and more distinctive as I grew closer. There had been a light rain sometime in the night and the wetness gave the Roman oval an evaporating sheen that seemed to fuse past and present, since the droplets that fell from one place or another made it appear freshly excavated and washed down. But mostly the Coliseum looked like a huge crown of chopped and perforated stone. Its circumference and height were less breathtaking than hypnotic, giving off an imagined hum of history much like that of a movie projector as my mind computed the emotion accumulated through a montage of associations, from Hollywood to the history book: decadents and gladiators, religious fanatics and lions. Of course, the greatest gladiator of our age came from Kentucky and attempted to immortalize his Olympic victory in 1960 with some pool hall doggerel—"How Cassius Took Rome"—at a press conference held on the newly painted red-white-and-blue steps of his home in Louisville, where his father broke out with a patriotic song in his best Russ Columbo imitation.

In the winter of 1982 I had been invited to Umbria Jazz by Alberto Alberti, an alternately melancholy and exuberant ex-

soccer player who books the bands. He described Perugia as a
charming medieval town in the hills, and guaranteed me that I
would love it and the music and the people. I thought he might be
right, but I also figured that there would be much more to write
about than fine jazz playing, since I could do that in New York.
That section of the world, stretching from the Greco-Roman era
to the Renaissance, had inspired in me a repository of images:
Poseidon hanging out down Africa way, enjoying fast women of
river hips who baptized him nightly; the tugs of literal war between the Greeks and the Carthaginians for control of Sicily;
Hannibal; the genetic footprints of boots in the boudoir that left
an olive complexion and a twisted wooliness to the hair of certain
Italians; and the Renaissance paintings in which the solemn black
king is right there in the manger at the beginning of Christianity.
No doubt about it: I would go. ...

We arrived in Rome and took a bus to Perugia, the headquarters of Umbria Jazz, traveling north on roads that passed between hills that supported both simple tiled houses and, now and
again, castles embodying the will to security and civilization that
resulted in armaments as well as the quarrying and dragging of
the stone up that terrain. From those heights, the citizenry
fought for sovereignty from invaders and rival provinces or, much
later, against the control of the church. Perugia, whose history
stretches back to the Etruscan age, is at the pinnacle of an especially steep group of hills, now partially surrounded by walls that
provided the Romans with models of unscalable protection.
Because of its very long past, Perugia, like all of Italy, is so steeped
in a complex range of human time that it pulls together the superficial incongruity of the historical periods that create its atmosphere—the ancient walls, the misty and green and faded-or-
ange landscapes already familiar from Renaissance paintings, the
churches, the town squares, the sloping stone streets, the small
cars designed to get through them, the motorcycles, the buses
whose wide turns barely miss the walls and pedestrians, the opera
house, the sidewalk cafes in which the culture of the city slowly

sizzles, and the clothes that look a season or two ahead in elegance and verve of style.

Later, on the train to Florence: Out that window, where Italians are presently sunbathing, had come Hannibal, fighting at Lake Trasimene in 217 B.C., utilizing the beginnings of tank warfare, his Negro mahouts on elephants, the pachyderms girded for battle, their voluminous bellowing in the Alpine air behind them, their tusks and tonnage ready for the Roman legions that would be whipped to their knees and crushed. The survivors of slain Flaminius's decimated army fled throughout Etruria and Umbria, some hiding within the walls of Perugia, Perugia that was to send doomed volunteers to the terrifying Roman defeat at Cannae, where Empire seemed at end, and Perugia that was to furnish wood and grain for Scipio's fleet, helping to bang the gong on the big Punic dream of victory within the bastion of the boot, since Hannibal—great, wily, eloquent, and treacherous Hannibal—after seventeen years of fighting, would return to an invaded Carthage, sue for peace, be refused by a bitter Scipio, and face his multitongued army's destruction at Zama, elephants and all.

> *M*any of us are not aware of just how close Hannibal came to conquering Rome. Hannibal looted and plundered the Roman countryside at will, defeating or holding at bay many of Rome's best generals. He is considered by some historians to be one of the greatest leaders and military strategists of all time.
>
> ◆
>
> —Sean O'Reilly,
> "Hannibal at War"

Umbria Jazz wasn't like any other festival I had attended because it included jazz clinics, films, and concerts for audiences that sometimes had better ears than I expect even in New York. Those ears were also evident in the Italian tenor players I heard in the clinic, many of whom startled me with more soulful sounds than the canned Coltrane you hear so often in New York. Somewhere down the steep stone streets and around this corner and that, passing through the cool shadows of buildings that date back to the Middle Ages, the classes were held in an edifice that bore the inscription "Charlie Parker School of Jazz" an insignia that bespoke a conquest much different than the Roman seal of "Augusta Perugia."...

In the warm afternoon light of the courtyard of the Hotel La Rosetta, over meals served under big umbrellas by waiters in white coats, Italy, as unfamiliar and foreign as it was, recalled the best in the American South. But in the streets, people seemed to float or sit in a meditative silence, or fashion their own angles on an effortless aristocracy shaped equally of confidence, curiosity, and sympathy, all of which could explode into lucid laughter or the metallic chatter of argument. The disdain for excessive activity during the hottest part of the day meant that Perugia's streets were nearly empty from one in the afternoon until four, when the shops opened up and the people filled the outdoor cafes, drinking mineral water or coffee or beer or wine, often mulling over ice cream, then strolling or stretching. I was convinced of the parallels when I found out that what we call hanging out is known there as *dolce far niente*—sweet time for nothing. As Albert Murray was to say when I asked him about Italy later, "Long before there were Southerners in the USA, there were Southerners in Italy, and it also meant a certain climate, a certain hospitality, a certain musicality in the language, and sometimes even a certain kind of violence and tendency to vendetta. In the more learned circles, the European vision of the Southerner is much like that of anyone who understands our South: the feeling created is that of an easeful relationship to culture and a spontaneity that says, deep down— the point of learning how to cook all this food and talk this way and wear these fine clothes is to have a good goddam time, man!"

In that atmosphere, usually in the courtyard or the hotel's bar, the moody and attractive George Coleman, who has the demeanor of a powerful Memphis deacon, would move from mournful aloofness to earthly humor, from impassive sullenness to buoyancy, carrying his ex-fullback bulk in a relaxed march, his arms swinging almost straight up and down, his long elegant fingers ever ready to throttle from the tenor saxophone virtuoso passages that manifested the loneliness of many years of discipline. In residence at Il Panino with the wonderful Ronnie Mathews Trio, Coleman was to play every night as he always does, giving everything he had, working mightily for his money and not backing up until he'd forced roars and loud applause from the audience. He is clearly one of the lords of his instrument, but, above all, he is a house-rocker.

Rocking a house is not the same as rocking a tent, and that is what was expected of the players the first few nights. The procession of events began at lunch, after which many of the musicians, observers, and listeners would go to see Chertok's films in Teatro Pavone, the opera house with painted ceilings, gold-leaf railings, five tiers of boxes, and an atmosphere reminiscent of the finest American movie palaces. The splendidly photogenic faces and forms of artists like Louis Armstong and Duke Ellington, Lester Young and Charlie Parker, Jo Jones and Thelonious Monk, recalled Kenneth Clarke's description of the men in a Masaccio: "They have the air of contained vitality and confidence that one often sees in the founding fathers of a civilization."...

Italy is a land of many masters, and it would have been provincial not to take advantage of what was available on walks or at the National Gallery of Umbria right there in Perugia, or at the Cathedral of St. Francis in Assisi, less than an hour away by bus. On a morning when I had decided to explore the city or travel someplace near, I would be out on foot, feeling the uneven stone of many of the streets as the people seeped from their homes and the sounds of footfalls, rustling clothes, and voices replaced the silence. As I made my way to the Assisi bus past the farmers wheeling their produce into Perugia, I saw a Gypsy boy with a concertina and a frazzled cat on a chain. For some reason, he reminded me less of a kid imitating an Italian organ grinder than of the street preachers of my youth who used to stand at the bus stops, chanting the promises of damnation for most and salvation for the rest each time one of the big yellow and green vehicles would stop and release passengers.

After taking a bus down from Perugia into a valley, then through flat lands backdropped by low hills, where little farms were pressed together as closely as possible, going on through small towns with their second-story windows covered by wooden shutters that kept out the day's early heat, ascending again on roads that rolled and weaved until arriving in Assisi, only to see the Cathedral of St. Francis at the higher part of the city, I experienced the calm such places must have provided for their congregations as soon as I entered the huge church, felt its easy coolness, and began to concentrate on the craft and the emotional radiation of its painted walls. And though there are still those who think that the Negro, like Caliban or the gigantic Moor in Bernini's *Fountain of the Four Rivers* in Rome, should recoil in bitterness, disgust, and alienation at the abundance of those works that document a star-bumping plateau of Western Civilization, I felt that the painted walls were as familiar in feeling and function as the religious and secular music I had heard as a child in church and at home. People are exalted by a great religious painting hung in a gallery in much the same way they are by a superb recording of Mahalia Jackson.

Whether in biblical tales or annals of the suffering of the saints, perhaps the most important religious vision projected through the Italian plastic arts is its sense of moral responsibility. It can cost your life, or tear your heart, but it can also separate you from savages. They understood the costs in blood and also, as one sees in Donatello's *The Sacrifice of Isaac* in Florence, the costs in overwhelming anguish. Oh, yes, I had encountered that sense of life in those Negro churches, where the deacons stood before us, big men humming and singing in their soaked white shirts and dark suits, where the choir would enter from the rear in their swishing robes and so fill the room with mighty song that the roof seemed in danger of loosening and blowing away, where the tales and dreams of the Bible became almost three-dimensional as the worshipers rose to an impersonal oneness with what they expressed, preaching or crying or singing of the rumblings and the ruthlessness—and the *rightness!*—in the bosom of this old world.

Just as biblical lore had provided a comprehensive range of human situations for the painter, the sculptor, and the architect, Christianity had proven a perfect conduit for the movement from the vital though superstition-ridden world of Africa into the accumulated complexity of theme and ethics inherent in the biblical stories, an accumulated complexity that stood them well in the society of successive riddles that is America. Not only did the body reinterpret Old Testament beliefs born in rebellion against the Roman Empire speak to the slaves, but they sometimes fought to give voice themselves, reenacting the sedition of their forebears in Rome. I recalled how I had been told in Texas that, since old evil master didn't want his chattel property practicing religion, the slaves would wet down the walls of the cabins at night and gather many buckets and bowls and basins of water to also absorb the sound so that they could preach and pray in secret, separating themselves from the savages who owned the big house and the beasts of the fields.

Somebody was playing the violin, waking me in the small hours of the morning. I was in the center of Rome listening to "Danny Boy!" Whoever it was put heart and soul into it and it seemed to me that the heart and soul of Ireland was there, too: the longing of those far from home and yet joy also, joy in the risen Christ for it was Easter Sunday morning.

At breakfast I inquired of my fellow guests, but no one had heard anything, not even my sister who was in the next room. Mystified, I just caught the faintest smile on the face of an Irish Franciscan priest.

◆

—Anne Hillam, "Far From the Back of the Mill"

In much the same way the Italian painters made their religious figures look Italian rather than Middle Eastern or even Negroid in features, facial expression, and dress as they personalized the lessons of Alexandria and Constantinople, the Negro slaves modified the stiff hymns to fit sensibilities that demanded richer conceptions of melody, percussion, and call-and-response. By adding an African-American dimension to religious material that remained Protestant, they made music that would provide an essential model for secular Negro musicians in the same way the mastery of perspective is essential to secular Renaissance painting. And eventually the sermons of the most imaginative ministers evolved into a poetry that functioned as an oral equivalent of Dante, who brought to the vernacular literature of Italian Christianity what Homer had to the mythology of Greece....

When I considered how the development of African-American music telescoped the evolution of Italian art, I had no difficulty seeing slavery and segregation as American versions of the Dark Ages, or recognizing how the soaring self-assertion and mocking false faces of the parades and social clubs of New Orleans provided the local musicians with a Renaissance sense of carnival. After all, Berenson says, "The moment people stopped looking fixedly toward heaven, their eyes fell upon earth, and they began to see much on its surface that was pleasant. Their own faces and figures must have struck them as surprisedly interesting.... The more people were imbued with the new spirit, the more they loved pageants. The pageant was an outlet for many of the dominant passions of the time...above all (the) love of feeling...alive." Given the attempts to depersonalize human beings on the plantation, or reduce them to the simplicity of animals, it is understandable that a belief in the dignity of the Negro and the joyous importance of the individual resulted in what is probably the century's most radical assault on Western musical convention. Jazzmen supplied a new perspective on time, a sense of how freedom and discipline could coexist within the demands of ensemble improvisation, where the moment was bulldogged, tied, and given shape. As with the Italian artists of the Renaissance, their art was collective and focused by a common body of themes, but for jazzmen, the human imagination in motion was the measure of all things....

It was the next night and the last night of tunes in the tent, and Dizzy Gillespie looked less handsome than angry. He had been loudly booed after kicking off his performance with two dull would-be funk numbers. I was told later, "In Italy, we feel if a musician is great, he should be great. In America, it may be necessary for Miles Davis or Sonny Rollins to play rock and roll—or perhaps it is less painful to act young than wise. Here we feel sad or angry when a great man will abandon wisdom for ignorance. The more polite would say innocence. Why should they travel this far to put on a silly mask?"

The booing was to the good: Gillespie, who had been sulking on the piano bench, rose and roared forth with a succession of improvisations of such savage invention it must have been somewhat difficult to be Jon Faddis standing there next to him, knowing the only thing you could add that night was higher notes. The old master feinted, ducked, and worked out phenomenal accents that italicized the abstractions within his long phrases, proving that when angered, a sore-headed bear will rise to beat the band. Trombonist Curtis Fuller was exquisite and guitarist Ed Cherry worked some pulsive variations on the voicings of McCoy Tyner. Everyone left that evening aware that they had witnessed a master in matchless form.

You cannot have a Renaissance without a Giotto. He stripped away what Clark calls the "decorative jumble" of images that made the medieval school both highly stylized and emblematic, offering in its place the weight and the sacrifice, the disappointment and the exaltation of human beings concurring and conflicting. In a sense, he discovered the individual in the pageant and, sometimes with the aid of bas-relief halos, pushed the force and substance of experience right at us, settling for neither mush nor surrender. Berenson points out that all of his lines are functional, that they are defined by movement, that he charged trivial objects with a power that not only transformed them but ignited the consciousness of the viewer.

In his own way, Louis Armstrong did the same. He discovered that his powers of imagination could stand alone, with the clarinet and the trombone of the conventional New Orleans band silenced, no longer needed to express the intricate and subtle musicality provided by the multilinear antiphonal style. His monumental ideas swelled a fresh world above his accompanying improvisers....

Unlike Giotto, Armstrong had immediate impact. He became a hero of epic proportions to fellow musicians. One remembers first hearing him sound like an archangel from a riverboat, another touching him just as he was going on stage and feeling an electric shock. Yet another recalls him taking the measure of a challenge at a cornet supper in Harlem and standing the listeners on their chairs, tables, and plates as he played notes that were like hot, silver solder splashing across the roof that supports the heavens. In his sexually and daredevil displacements of his abstractions, Armstrong is more in spirit with Picasso, but his position in an African-American Renaissance is unarguable. He delivered a virtuosity fresh from the frontier of his imagination, giving the trumpet an expressive power it never had. Armstrong brought a purer sound to the instrument's upper register, playing high notes that were functional rather than decorative, and his strings of eighth notes lifted the horn from a vocal, shouting riff style to a standard-bearer of melody interwoven with virtuoso rhythms. And it is clear that in the spirit of Giotto, Armstrong ignited the consciousness of his listeners by charging often uninteresting songs with artistic power, spontaneously transforming them through both an editing and embellishing process. When you hear Armstrong at his finest, he is like the Negro acrobat in the Roman sculpture, calmly balanced on the head of the crocodile of the moment. Berenson says that what a major artist does is show that human beings can cope with the complexities of life— and who could deny that in the face of Armstrong's greatest improvisations?

The final night of Umbria Jazz in Perugia, before the festival's actual conclusion in the mountain town of Narni, took place at Piazza IV. A bandstand had been set up next to the Great Fountain, which dates from 1275, and in front of the Cathedral of St. Lawrence, where a bronze statue of Julius III sat facing the back of the stage and the eyes of the assembled masses. In a way, the feeling of festival that had been building all week was now swelling in the streets with the people. There were African students in small clusters, Americans who were there studying Italian, Europeans on vacation, but, most of all, Italians, from the very young to the older women with calf muscles built from walking the inclines of the stone streets. There were no costumes and no streamers, yet the air felt full of colors and thick with the moisture of dance....

A very hot stage was set for the Umbria Jazz All-Stars.

It was late when the All-Stars took the stand, bringing with them the lore of many a dancehall, night club, jam session, and party rich with fine women, handsome men, whiskey, whist, coon can, dominoes, and the smells of downhome food steaming the pots.... On song after song, with the rhythm section simmering and steaming under them, the veterans tore away everything that stood in the path of celebration, creating a pulsation that could be answered only with dance. And dance they did engender, especially with the inevitable encore—"Flying Home"— lifting the crowd with the bells of their horns to a massive articulation of unsentimental happiness. As green Julius III gave his blessing and the medieval Great Fountain bubbled over a democratic series of reliefs spanning local politicians, Christianity, astrology, history, education, Roman origins, and the most popular fables of Aesop, I heard the sound of American democracy become an international phenomenon and thought that if Hannibal had these kinds of troops, he would have easily taken the Roman Empire. With a song.

Stanley Crouch is a jazz critic and staff writer at The Village Voice. *His work has also appeared in* The New Republic, Esquire, *and* The New York Times. *He is a recipient of a MacArthur grant. This story was excerpted from his book,* Notes of a Hanging Judge: Essays and Reviews 1979-1983.

★

For some reason known possibly to God in His more responsive moments of attentiveness, one of the softest passages of the Verdi's Requiem was joined from the rear end of the [Verona] Arena by an extremely coarse whistle of the sort that New York delicatessen managers make when they catch small children in the act of snitching candy placed by an oversight near the entrance to the store. I do pray our cousins from Jersey go elsewhere for their vacations.

The musicians paid no attention whatever, and softly though they sang, their music rose above his cacophony, as Verdi himself, a human artist whose soul had the shape and sound of something greatly made, was present among us at once in time and beyond time, almost beyond sound, at the same moment and in the same space on one of the earth's loveliest places, both diminutive and vast, very like the city of Verona itself.

Very, very like.

—James Wright, *The Shape of Light*

✦ ✦ ✦

Big Butts and Walnuts

It's all in the eye of the beholder.

WE'RE WALKING DOWN THE STREET AND I'M TALKING WITH Molly, remembering Italy. The photograph that she took of the cat sleeping next to an old broom inside the Colosseum, the view from the top of St. Peter's, the dopey picture we took in Pisa. That time in Florence. "With the ice cream," I say, "the, uh, ...*gelato*."

She smiles and gives a little sniff of a laugh. "Sure," she says, "you were so put out. My big scoop and your tiny one. My basketball and your—what did you call it?—your walnut."

"Yeah. That's right," I say. "A walnut."

It had been a hot day, and we had walked up to a *gelato* cart in Florence, just a few blocks from the Uffizi. *Due gelati*, I said, holding up two fingers to the young man beneath the umbrella who ignored me to stare at her, stare at the long russet-colored hair, the face out of Botticelli, a wide smile on his dark, youthful face. He assembled a gigantic mound on a cone, then shaved off the overflow at the edges and handed it to her. When she took it and smiled back and said *grazie*, the boy touched his fingertips to his mouth and said *bella, bella* and shook his head in affected wonder and pulled his heavy lips back over even white teeth. I coughed to get the boy's attention, then held up two fingers once more and pointed at myself, and finally, reluctantly, he shoved a tiny sphere of pale orange into a cone and thrust it at me, never taking his eyes off Molly, off the summertime that is still printed on her lightly-freckled nose.

We both laugh and keep walking. Now she gets into it. "Then there was that train ride. Remember? The one from Florence to Venice," she says. "Oh, I'm *sure* you remember that." She looks sideways at me, moves her hair behind her ear and lifts one corner of her mouth—the right corner as always—in that little mocking, sexy half-smile.

"Oh God, yes." I clasp my hands in front of me. "All I thought was 'Am I glad we're almost at the station.'"

What I remember most, remember *immediately*, is not Venice or the train, but the July heat. It had been insufferably hot in the second-class car, although it was nearly empty, and both of us sat there exhausted, wet. I still recall every detail: the worn, brown velvet-like fabric on the seats, the rolling, green Tuscan country-side, the stale-sweet smells of perspiration and that heavy tobacco that Europeans smoke. The way the motion of the train moved Molly's hips toward me, then away as she sat facing me across the narrow slot between the seats.

After two hours of alternately dozing and looking out the win-dow, I said something—more jokingly than seriously, I thought then—about her butt getting bigger what with all the pasta and *gelato* we had been eating. She said nothing. Just stared at me for a few seconds. Then stood up and walked to the back of the car, stopping in the narrow passageway to rest her hands on the railing and look out the window. I shrugged and picked up the guidebook lying on the seat next to me and thumbed through it to the pages that described the Grand Canal.

When, twenty minutes later, I hoisted our packs and walked back to join her, the message having just come over the loud-speaker that Venezia was coming up, I found her backed up to the window of the narrow aisle between our car and the next. A man faced her. He was tall and solidly-built, with thick, black hair and dark eyes. His face was close to Molly's. He was smiling, looking hard into her eyes and saying something in broken English about a capuccino in St. Mark's Square. Lemony sunshine, music. The two of them. She smiled and looked down, shaking her head. Sorry, she murmured, can't. My husband, she said, using her favorite ruse, and nodded toward me as I approached, one backpack in my hand, the other casually hooked over a shoulder. The man had slowly turned and looked me up and down, making not even a token effort to disguise his contempt.

You, he said, looking back at her and then again, in melodramatic disbelief and holding an open hand toward me—*you* are married to...to

> The constant love we share and wear so near,
> our fun and games and
> talking lip to lip,
> the closely strained embrace
> of our amorous bodies,
> the gentle little bites on
> tender mouths,
> the wanton pressure of
> tiptilted breasts—
> ah, all these pleasures which
> you shared with me
> are broken, wasted, ruined
> now for ever.
>
> ◆
>
> —Plautus, "Pseudolus (64)"

this? I carved a smile, though not a particularly happy rendering. Then the train stopped and the man, with a final scornful sneer punctuated by an elevated chin, stepped off the train and walked away, shaking his head and throwing up his hands.

Molly reached for her backpack and fixed me with an expressionless stare. Then she tossed me that smile, that cute, coy, nasty little thing of hers. *Big butt, huh*, she said and stepped off the train.

Doug Rennie is a Portland, Oregon writer whose essays and short stories have appeared in American Way, Chicago Tribune Magazine, The Quarterly, Berkeley Fiction Review, *among others. He also writes a monthly travel column, "On the Road," for* Runner's World *magazine.*

Italian men are still fascinated by women; whereas in England men expect women to turn them on, Italians expect to be firmly discouraged. Courtship still goes on, and every kind of psychic energy is put to the task, while at more mundane levels flirtation (as distinct from sexual harassment) is still possible. Just the other day, as I fidgeted in the queue of people lining up to reinsure their cars, my face pinched and cross and my hair a mess, the counter clerk looked up and said, exactly as if he simply couldn't help it, "*Madonna, che occhi che hai!*" (Holy mother, what eyes you have!) and looked back at the form he was writing out. The blood rushed to my face and I felt the puckers ironing out. I don't know if he meant it or if it was simply an act of gallantry, but it was done with simplicity and charm and it worked a little magic.

—Germaine Greer, "Celebrating Italy," *Vogue*

DONALD GECEWICZ

⋆ ⋆ ⋆

Indirections to Rome

Feeling renewed at 40 by ancient Rome.

NOT LONG AGO I REACHED MY FORTIETH BIRTHDAY, WHICH IS considered a rite of passage. I did not want to pass the day in Chicago, the city where I was born and still live, so I went to Rome. Why Rome? As Federico Fellini says in *I, Fellini* (a book of interviews with Charlotte Chandler), "Rome became my home as soon as I saw it. I was born that moment. That was my *real* birthday. If I remembered the date, it is the one I would celebrate." So I went to Rome. Rome is the model for all other cities, so why not return to the source for my minor passage? Besides, I already was aware that Rome knew something about birthdays.

A few years before, I had been in Rome on the city's own birthday, 21 April, a curiously exact date (for a city). The Romans decorate the buildings on the Campidoglio with candles. After dark, flames flicker in the bowl-like candles on the steps and balustrades. The Capitoline Museums on either side of the *piazza* designed by Michelangelo are more enchanting than usual, a study in his strong sense of composition and muscular geometry, shimmering and scumbled in a sure sign of the powers of the moon, candlelight, and the effects that heighten Romans' delight in the atmosphere of their city.

That year, Rome was celebrating its 2,741st birthday by the traditional reckoning *ab urbe condita*, its founding, although in fact Rome is much older. The countryside around Rome has been inhabited for thousands of years. In the Alban Hills, some of the towns that may have founded Rome are even older and just as venerable.

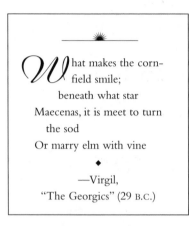

What makes the corn-
field smile;
beneath what star
Maecenas, it is meet to turn
the sod
Or marry elm with vine

◆

—Virgil,
"The Georgics" (29 B.C.)

To celebrate Rome's birthday, my traveling companions and I went to an Abruzzese restaurant just off the Piazza Navona. We started with stuffed squash blossoms and followed with two kinds of *risotto*. One *risotto* was a springlike green, and the other was tinted saffron by still more squash blossoms that had been chopped in small pieces and cooked with the rice. To a group of Americans unused to the Italian delight in eating flowers, the squash blossoms were a wonderful treat (accustomed as we were to the American lack of interest in fritters of elderberry blossoms or *granita di gelsomino* [jasmine ice] or capers or artichokes—which are flowers, after all.) Almost all Italian food is flowerlike, though, in being strongly scented and highly colored, even if you happen to be eating pale breadsticks or a *gelato di vaniglia*. After the two *risotti*, we ate *abbacchio* (roast lamb), a traditional specialty of Abruzzese restaurants in Rome and an ancient festival dish. Then we walked into the seemingly calm Roman night, which turned out to be filled with sweet Roman deceptions.

Fireworks were being shot from a boat in the Tiber. Red, gold, and white lights ribboned across the sky. Romans crowded staircases, landings, and balconies to get a better view of the sky streaked with pink and copper flowers. The orderly rows of candles lining the public buildings still flickered a pale yellow as people walked up and down the steps and pointed at the latest colorful explosion. Below the Campidoglio, the resurrected forums glimmered in weak light.

I have always found Romans to be well behaved in crowds. The city is poorly lit at night by American standards, a chiaroscuro painting rather than the brightness of Edward Hopper, but groups of Romans usually look unthreatening and gentle. Maybe Romans are good in groups because of the long glances that they give and expect in return, or because of the way they dance around each other in passing (although I sometimes have gotten a *gomitata*, an elbow in the side), or because they drink so little and remain humorous and lucid. I had a strong sense of being with the right kind of people in the right place, and even a hint of how Rome was created from three basic elements. The Tiber (that brings gods and fireworks) and the Isola Tiberina in the river made Rome a strategic crossing. The now ghostly forums were the lowlands where the Romans traded, played, and debated, and the hill I was standing on, the chief one of the famous seven, is a center of power and holiness.

So, a few years after celebrating Rome's birthday (and with those pleasant memories), I was drawn back to Rome to celebrate my own birthday. Why is Rome more alluring than any other city? When I think of Rome's eternal qualities, I think of its long civic tradition, of the eternal endeavor that an ancient city is, of the daily effort needed to maintain Rome for the Romans and still captivate the foreigners eternally arriving.

Rome is much too old to bother to distinguish between travelers and tourists, since the Romans know of every possible reason for a trip to Rome. The Romans have withstood Celtic and German invasions, Mussolini's March on Rome, Japanese tourists seeking to understand the resilience of the West, Junior Year Abroad, and politicians from the Lega Nord who now blame the city for corruption and *malgoverno* and want to strip it of its power. Rome sees milder invasions, too, of polite Dutch and Scandinavians in search of the sun and of Westerners seeking to understand our own civilization.

Rome also awaits pilgrims, even though pilgrimage is a duty

less commonly observed now. One of Rome's nicknames is still *Roma la Santa*, Holy Rome, and Rome's famous sanctity existed long before the arrival of Saints Peter and Paul. Palestrina, for example, a few miles from Rome, was the site of a temple of Fortune and an oracle that made up one of the major religious centers of antiquity. The mountain where the ruins sprawl still feels numinous and somewhat eerier than the Campidoglio, which is just as sacred. The air is heavy with the electricity of unemployed spirits (and still worth a trip).

But Rome surpassed the other Latin towns long ago, and it is a city of temples and churches crowded with the living and the dead. Many of the foreigners one sees are on pilgrimage. They have saved for years to travel to Rome from Brittany or Nebraska or Korea to see St. Peter's Basilica and catch a glimpse of the pope. They obediently follow guides through Michelangelo's Sistine Chapel and the Raphael Rooms, taking in the wonders produced by the Italians. They sit patiently in rows of buses outside the Vatican, and from there they may journey to Assisi, to honor St. Francis, who embodies the earthier, more compassionate, and more enduring kind of Catholicism. Even Italians take these tours. They make pilgrimages to Rome, mixing in with Catholics from other countries and the occasional bewildered Protestant.

Rome breaks down categories. At the same time, it sometimes seems that "Rome" is the only category that matters and that everything already has been written about Rome. In Rome, though, travelers become pilgrims, a long-established sensuality rules, and the city's beauty overwhelms.

Beauty, sanctity, and sensuality tend to conflict. So it is best to approach Rome by indirection and to be prepared to collapse distinctions. In Rome, atheists need to duck into churches and light candles. I recommend San Giovanni in Laterano (St. John Lateran), the cathedral of Rome. San Giovanni has a contemplative medieval feel and a better use of color and ornament than St. Peter's, which reeks of the Church Militant and overweening. In San Giovanni, the walls are colored with the old Italian palette of mauve, burnished gold, malachite, and aqua, and sculptured saints rush through the nave, looking very *sbrigativi*, as the Italians would say, or like barely clothed track-and-field stars to Americans. Believers, on the other hand, should be prepared to poke around the decrepit Galleria Chigi in Via del Corso in late afternoon, where for the past few years, tarot readers, wizards, and palmists have assembled, each disciple of the occult advertising discoveries and miracles. Inevitably, the Galleria Chigi will become a superfashionable mall, but the wizards will remain, hidden among the Italian silks that cling like Roman glances.

Rome is simply too enormous and too astounding to approach directly. Maybe that is why pilgrims traditionally came to the city slowly on foot. Now that many of us fly to Rome, one way of getting one's bearings is to take a long walk, possibly along the Tiber to see the river and the bridges, and definitely with a side trip into the elegant Via Giulia (especially on a quiet Sunday).

I took that walk on the Sunday that happened to be the day before my birthday. A friend of mine had decided to join me in Rome, so I picked Liz up at her hotel and we headed for a long stroll and conversation. When we reached the southeast end of the Via Giulia, we walked over to the synagogue in the Lungotevere Cenci in the ancient ghetto. The names of the members of the Jewish community who died after the infamous roundup on 16 October 1943 are carved on the wall facing the Tiber. Alexander Stille, in *Benevolence and Betrayal*, and Elsa Morante, in *History: A Novel*, movingly describe the hard facts of life in wartime Rome. Roberto Rossellini's *Open City* shows the devastation in working-class neighborhoods similar to the Ghetto.

We crossed the river into Trastevere (which was once Etruscan country) and walked toward the entrance to the Orto Botanico, the botanical garden, in the Largo Cristina di Svezia. Piazza Trilussa is worth lingering in along the way because it is tiny and picturesque, a specialty of Trastevere. The name of the *piazza* honors a poet, and there is a monument incised with one of Trilussa's poems in *Romanesco*, Rome's semiprivate form of Italian.

The botanical garden is well kept and, on most afternoons, is peopled mainly by women with children in strollers. We contin-

ued on the paths up the Gianicolo, stopping here and there to read
the labels on the trees and plants. Farther up the hill, we were able
to see more of the white-and-ocher-and-pale-gray city below us
and across the Tiber.

Rome has few skyscrapers and few grand plazas built on a scale
too large for human beings. The populace has not been stacked or
dispersed. This makes Rome's narrow, short streets even more
crowded with people and their noisy vehicles. Few other spots in
Rome, though, are as woodsy and serene as the botanical garden
in off-hours. It is a good place to contemplate Rome for a moment, because Rome and the Romans, in spite of their beauty and
sensuality, are not self-conscious or all that contemplative.

My birthday, 7 March, happens to fall on the same day as Anna
Magnani's. Suffice it to say that few actresses would dare to appear
in a film (by Pier Paolo Pasolini) called *Mamma Roma*. Few cities
have been portrayed as a combination of (1) devoted and tough
mother, (2) bemused fallen woman full of the sharp wit that
Romans love, and (3) proud vegetable seller in an open market in
Rome's stark and ugly suburbs. Magnani's appeal is hard to catego-
rize, but her energy and sweet power, like Rome's, are undeniable.

That night we were invited to a birthday dinner at the apartment of my friends Pat and Giangi. They live a few steps from the
Campo de' Fiori, on a narrow street in a neighborhood that was
"full of thieves," as Pat said, when they moved there twenty-five
years or so before. Now the quarter is elegant. Pat is from the
American Midwest originally, and Giangi grew up in Vicenza in
the Veneto.

After midnight, after a long Roman conversation about the
prolonged political crisis and weird Roman flirtations with right-
wing politicians—punctuated by few glasses of Tenuta di
Pomino—Liz and I left. Her hotel was near the Pantheon. I was
staying near the Piazza Navona.

We crossed the *piazza* in front of the Pantheon. I was in a
Rome-induced haze—birthdays, the Campo de' Fiori, Tenuta di
Pomino, that hint of mortality that lurks behind every celebration.
A man and woman hurried past. The couple was not happy, even

in that dramatic and historic place. The man was upset. He gestured toward me and said loudly, "And these fucking Italians, who don't even *like* us." We were in the middle of a quarrel between two American exchange students, or maybe they were just Americans whose honeymoon had hit a bump.

Liz and I stared. We were not surprised to hear English, because Giangi had spoken English all evening to accommodate his three Americans. His English was polite and had a Venetian accent. There was an odd *momentino* when neither Liz nor I had anything to say in English. The couple stalked off. I saw Liz to her hotel and returned to mine, where they had locked up but were still drowsily waiting for me.

Of course, the callow American was partly correct, even in his braying anger. I am partially of Italian descent, and I suppose, the inexorable pull of Italian genes and the inventiveness of Italian culture cannot be ignored. They show up even in the color of my skin. Each time I have been to Rome, I have approached the city indirectly. I have spent hours in the museum in the Villa Giulia studying the Etruscan mirrors and the luxurious sarcophagi decorated with smiling couples. (Who knows why those couples are smiling in death? Is it possible that even the Etruscans don't "like" us?) I have taken the subway to the Museum of Popular Arts and Traditions in EUR to admire the toys, jewelry, charms, puppets, spindles, and distaffs. I have walked to the Piazza Mincio off the Via del Po to admire Gino Coppedè's architectural designs in his eccentric style similar to Art Deco. (Look for the building decorated with a spider poised in its web.) It was an odd and fine gift to become a complete "fucking Italian," even for a few moments after midnight as my birthday was fading away in the mother-of-pearl shadows of the Pantheon.

A few days later, I left Rome for a brief tour—Bologna, Ferrara, Mantova, and Lucca—beautiful cities ignored by non-Italian tour operators. I returned to Rome from Lucca. Fellini once said, "No matter how many times I leave and return, every time I go back to Rome, it seems to me more wonderful than I remembered." Returning is a pleasure for a non-Italian, too.

I took a cab to the hotel. The Cesàri, in a tiny street just off the Via del Corso, is one of the oldest hotels in Rome. I was given a tiny single suite (a suite, of all things), consisting of a narrow sitting room, a small bedroom, and a large bathroom tiled in white. These rooms were up near the roof, and the door was narrow and low.

That weekend I took part in something resembling a protest. I have chanced on more than one Italian protest, and recommend them. Although Italians may seem confrontational, they are usually indirect, which is why they have their famous one-hour strikes. Because I was still celebrating hitting the age of 40, a little protest against the powers that be was appropriate.

For several years, the Italian environmental organization FAI has succeeded in opening a large number of historic and religious sites throughout the country for a single weekend a year. Many of the sites belong to the government, but the government does not have the money to open them to the public regularly. Italians are always skeptical when they hear claims that a ministry does not have the funds to open a frescoed church or an archeological dig to the public. So FAI has forced the issue by opening up these sites and providing volunteers to staff them for one or two days a year.

I consulted with my friend Pat and settled on two accessible sites in the center of Rome, a tapestry factory in a fashionable shopping street off the Via del Corso and the convent attached to the church of the Trinità dei Monti at the top of the Spanish Steps. Both would be open on Saturday afternoon. The tapestry factory has been in business for about four hundred years, which makes it new by Roman standards. The convent is still in use by nuns, and most of it is hardly ever open to the public.

Announcements listing the buildings and churches that would be open that weekend appear only in Italian newspapers. Most travelers in Italy do not speak much Italian, and mass tourism does not encourage learning languages. Over the years, though, as my Italian has improved, my experiences of Rome have become more intense. The city that is warm and cordial and sometimes mercenary to English-speakers has enveloped me as I have become better at speaking and reading Italian. Because Italian is not a true international language, most guidebooks play down the need to speak it. The authors usually resort to a few phrases (and often give incorrect pronunciations). But the life of the city goes on in Italian (and in Romanesco), and in the bookstores and newspaper stands. There is such a thing as too much indirection. Rome is a readable city if you happen to know Italian, which helps in getting the endless wordplay and jokes. If you rely exclusively on English as an "international language," you may have a pale "international" experience, since there is no such thing as world culture.

The environmental organization's challenge to the government meant that the tours of the monuments and churches were an internal, family discussion (in Italian only). Volunteers led the tours, even though Italians have tended to rely on the government to maintain the "national patrimony," the family inheritance that the cranky American had bestowed even on me. But Italians are also willing to stand in long lines to be ushered in small groups through a tapestry factory, for example, to show their interest in preserving their heritage. We signed guest books to note our presence. Fellini touched on this sense of personal responsibility for the city when he said, "Whenever I'm not in Rome, I worry about the city, afraid that something will happen to it while I am away—as if, by being there, I could protect it, save it."

As always, the Romans were good in crowds. The views of Rome from the steps of the convent overlooking the Spanish Steps were lovely and made the wait and the protest worthwhile. At the foot of the Spanish Steps are the opulent shopping streets filled with Italians brought up in rich postwar Italy, the economic marvel. Beyond is the city of churches, tobacconists, bookstores, *trattorie*, temples, theaters, and winebars on the quiet streets where a dignified life goes on—life colored by the knowledge that civilization requires constant, dogged effort and a willingness at times to die in droves, as in the Punic Wars or so recently at the Fosse Ardeatine.

When I left Rome a few mornings later, I got on the train for Fiumicino Città instead of Fiumicino Aeroporto and lost about fifteen minutes. I suppose that my mistake was an attempt not to leave, or at least to leave by indirection. Maybe it was just a turn back toward Rome by a preoccupied pilgrim. Turning 40 in Rome may mean that I somehow belong to the city. I can only hope so, because Rome is endlessly fascinating, too human and hard to leave.

For centuries—since Saturn retired to Latium to inaugurate his fortunate reign—Rome has drawn travelers. Rome's sanctity, beauty, and sensuality have been part of everyone's sentimental education, and a traveler there learns that these enduring qualities offer a slight hope of outwitting time and decay.

Donald Gecewicz is a writer and editor who lives in Chicago. His translations of Dario Bellezza, Emanuela Andreoni Fontecedro, Dante Maffia, Sandro Penna, Giovanni Raboni, and Gabriella Sobrino appeared in the Fall 1997 issue of International Poetry Review.

★

There's nothing more helpful for mortals than sensible disbelief.
                                                    —Euripides, "Helen"

JAN WARNER

* * *

Rocking the Gondola

What was that about a free ride?

ONE FINE EVENING, LONG BEFORE AIDS AND MARRIAGE AND middle age, I sat alone at a table in the Piazza San Marco sipping a Pernod. Is Pernod, I wonder, still served in a clear chilled glass, accompanied by a silver dish of ice? The stars were bright overhead and the moon smiled down as men from time to time took the chair opposite me, hoping for whatever it is that men hope for from lone women on cool summer nights. The orchestral music wafted over us. I heard that the Pope had been here the day before. Had he been sorry to miss me? Silly conversations of that sort lead nowhere in particular. I was calm, unruffled, unyielding.

Around 11 p.m. I began a solitary stroll back along the winding streets to my hotel near the Teatro de Fenice. Dame Fortune twisted the path so that the way seemed to go in various circles that never quite reached any intended destination. After a while I was approached by a young man with curly black hair who inquired in broken English if I desired a ride in his gondola.

"Oh," said I, "that would be far too expensive."

"Ah," said he, "for you there is no charge."

It would be a less than honest tale that pretended I had no inkling of what the charge would be; but adventure beckoned and

I followed. With wine to drink and bread and cheese to eat, we were well prepared. Soon, I was climbing awkwardly into my first and only gondola. We glided into the black water that shimmered with the bright reflection of the still smiling moon.

Exhausting our supply of sensible common language our giggles rippled out over the Grand Canal as we resorted to "Macaroni, rigatoni, spaghetti, ravioli." So young was I, I had not heard of tortellini yet, nor pesto.

I reclined back upon the cushions as he poled his true lady love smoothly along. The true lady love was, of course, not I—but the gondola itself. A gondola that had passed from his father to himself and in which he took great pride. Eventually he parked us in a darkly secret side canal and an interlude took place from which the great philosophical wisdom was derived: "When having a gondola moment, always take the upper position to avoid extreme discomfort." I know the import of this sentiment because someone whose name I had long forgotten told me that it was by this that he always remembered me.

The interlude complete, and back in the middle of the Grand Canal, I was given permission to become my own gondolier. Never overly graceful, I stood quite silently in awe of myself as I attempted to balance on the curved edge of my narrow transport. In my hands I held a very long and heavy pole.

It was a moment of great beauty and peace. Little me, amidst the glory and brilliance of Venice. The moon was winking at me now. I was winking back.

Far too soon, the moment that shines so bright in my memory ended. I relinquished the pole and stumbled back down into my seat.

Enrico, or perhaps it was Ernesto, poled his women to safe harbor. I clambered back up onto the harsh reality of safe pavement. The material with which he tenderly covered his gondola he called her pajamas. He lovingly tucked her in for the night and escorted me back to my hotel. Suddenly the way seemed rather direct and not at all confusing. I declined his kind offer to see him again the following evening. Some moments remain perfect only within themselves. I went alone up to my room, put on my own pajamas, and lay down between the clean crisp sheets to dream a satisfied dream.

Jan Warner is a vagabond by nature with a patient and loving husband who stays comfortably at home while she wanders around. In addition to solo travel, she and her daughter spend every Thanksgiving in a different part of the world. In past lives she was a psychotherapist and bookstore owner. She is now a fledgling writer living in Phoenix.

✳

I've read somewhere that the average length of a stay in Venice is eighteen days. Henry James said that after two weeks in Venice one becomes as restless as if one were on shipboard. I sometimes think that there are two ways to see Venice. One is to let it have its way with you for three days, time in which to glide up and down the Grand Canal, thereafter to make for the open sea; time to sail to the lovely island of Torcello, mother city of Venice, zigzagging through pales (exaggerated twigs) in the water, an experience which defeats the most stubborn unhappiness; and time also to sit for leisured hours in St. Mark's Square, which for good reason has been called Europe's greatest drawing room (a "*piazza* of pure stone and pure idea") and which not to take pleasure in is absurdly snobbish and pretentious. The other way to see Venice is to stay at least six months, to know intimately its watery streets and its painters, and, in long months, to allow the initial stunning impact of the water kingdom to be replaced by the more enlightened affection of understanding. The trouble with staying in Venice for a week or ten days is that the seductive city is likely to betray you; you may feel at first, as Goethe did, that you are lord of the Adriatic, but you may later feel that you are a denizen of dark alleys, lost in a sinister maze.

—Barbara Grizzuti Harrison, *Italian Days*

ADRIA BERNARDI

✦ ✶ ✦

The Errant Steps
of Wooden Shoes

The author practices the zen of indirection.

I MUST HAVE MOVED DIFFERENTLY THEN, BUT I CANNOT EXACTLY remember.

There is something about being slightly taller in these elevated shoes, taller but also level, this is part of it, and something else I cannot describe that has to do with a pushing against the sternum from inside, I cannot call it boldness, because I was quick to feel unease, and now that this new pair of wooden shoes is on my feet—I have not worn a pair in nearly two decades—something has been knocked loose and what I am trying to remember is what it felt like physically then. It has something to do with a heavy solidness to each step, it wasn't quite a stride, I have never had a stride, but rather an impulse forward, a push, a pressing outward, a *spinta*.

In Florence, in Italy, in the fall, I wandered. Not in the sense of a vagabond with a knapsack on my back, which is how I wanted to wander, vaguely, like a hippie, maybe to Greece in the winter, maybe to Morocco, maybe make my indefinite way to Indonesia. It was not this kind of wandering, but a kind of confined wandering. It was a wandering within the boundaries of academic study with a group of American college students. It was a polite, almost reverential wandering. There was no knapsack for me: We will not have you traipsing across Europe, young lady, like all those others with packs on their backs, loaded down like mules. So I arrived carrying American Tourister luggage of coral red vinyl, and I did not traipse or travel widely and without restriction. I was an earnest, diligent wanderer, even though, in keeping with those times, I wanted desperately to be a "free spirit." Again, I try to remember what this meant and am having trouble locating it, but it had something to do with roving and bounding, a way of being that may never have been within my grasp, although I torment myself still with the thought that it was there for the taking, and, had I just been able to step less fearfully, there would have been a lifetime of bold, indeterminate movement.

And, now, to go back to the shoes, the new-old shoes which I have put on again for the first time in many years, the wooden peasant shoes, the *zoccoli* which made my mother cringe, my grandfather shake his head, my grandmother indignantly sputter, seeing me wear shoes that were for walking behind the beasts, behind the sheep, behind the cows, shoes to be worn while carrying a herding-stick in the muddy fields, to return to the subject of these shoes as I approach age 40, I am elevated again, a bit taller, and there is an unexpected little tap-tap, tap, like the knuckle of an index finger against a wooden door, a knocking from inside the ribcage, and it is making me walk differently, stimulates some kind of movement from before, a bounding outward, albeit stiff, and what I recall now is that I wandered.

I should be able to remember the details of this wandering and as soon as I tell my brain to find them, the images should start to appear.

You turned right out of the door of the *pensione* and it was a short walk to the river.

If I was in my room during the day, I tiptoed around the woman who cleaned up, embarrassed that someone was my maid, a woman past retirement age, as if it were my grandmother who was my *serva*, changing the sheets on my bed.

The floor was cold on my bare feet in the morning. I wore a pair of brown flannel slippers.

The tiles of the bedroom floor were white and mottled.

Or were they grey?

The mail was left on a table in the dining room.

Or was it left on the buffet?

The owner of the *pensione* complained that the Americans were using up all the hot water taking long, hot showers.

Or was there no shower and only a tub?

I'm walking around now in memory, adrift in vagueness. *Vago*, which means both "wandering" and "vague." Wandering. Moving from point to point with imprecise direction. Vague. Indeterminate, imprecise, approximate. Unstable, errant. The word *vago* embodies all these possibilities.

A pair of earrings was to be a sign that I belonged.

Pierced earrings made of gold wires bent into concentric circles, and, in the center, a pale blue semi-precious stone. Each earring was fastened by snapping a stiff wire into a narrow groove where it was clutched. The earring was unremittingly attached, secured so that no brush of a collar, no untended flit, could knock it loose unbeknownst to the wearer. They were "old fashioned," immigrant earrings, a piece of ornamentation that stretched the earlobe longer, pulled the pierced hole into a long fleshy line.

A gift from my great-aunt, I would wear them and they would say: here is the proof, earrings that have travelled across the ocean and back again, proof that I am not a tourist, I am not here for Gucci and Ferragamo, no, I am a woman of serious intent. I have my hippie earrings, sure, dangling earrings made of beads of wood and glass, glittering with stars and moons, silver and turquoise, yeah, but what I am presenting myself wearing are earrings from another time.

So, one day in early September, I walked to a building on Via Fiume into the Scuola d'Italiano per Stranieri. It was on the left side of the street, a massive building. I walked up a long flight of stairs. At the top, a group of classmates was gathered around the instructor, who was handsome, with an unshaven face and un-kempt hair through which he wearily ran his hands. He wore an oversized sweater of mottled colors, broken-in, rumpled with wide-gauge stitching, blue jeans. He was a decade older than the rest of us, in his early 30s. He had the radical student look, I-am-a-man-of-the-Left-of-intellect-and-of-moral-integrity. He was the kind of man a girl like me would have liked to have had for a boyfriend, or less than a boyfriend, for a romance, a fling. He was laying out the situations, which museums would be visited when, which day trips would be taken where. Assisi, Rome, Venice. As he spoke, he looked from one to the other. His eyes darted past me. Then skittered back and settled on the earrings. There was a squint, a dry shallow swallow, a wince of distaste.

Before I had even started to wander, a stumble.

This same instructor later said, "They all expect to find the Italy they left in 1920. They think they'll find the poor, poor Italy they left behind. Misery. But we're not peasants any more. And it makes the Americans, the sons and daughters of the immigrants, so angry to see we've become modern without them, that we have cultur-ally surpassed them."

You can always pick out an American in the crowd. An Italian pointed this out.

How?

Just look at the shoes. Functional. No style whatsoever. Hideous.

The shoes, the *zoccoli*, were not delicate. But the shoes were part of the code and at that time even certain Italians were wearing them. The Italian weekly *L'Espresso* spells this out in an article about the clothing of youth in 1977.

Wealthy daddy's girls wore kilts and carried purses by Gucci.

Young men on the extreme Right chose the "gangster look," with fedoras, gold watches and pointy leather shoes.

A *freak-sinistrese*, Leftist freak, was psychedelically dressed, in jeans with mutely-colored patches, hot pink and orange, brightly colored over-the-knee boots, a top hat, anything that suggested whimsy.

On the Left, young men wore large knit, oversized sweaters and jeans. A hodgepodge of clothing, maybe a worn-out tweed jacket from a father's closet.

And the young women on the Left, here, this is what I am looking for, the young women who were feminists but not separatists, who participated in the demonstrations, wore sweaters with loose gauge, jeans, or skirts with tiny floral patterns, and on their feet, here it is, here is the part I am looking for, these young women wore *i sabots indispensibli.*

The indispensable clogs.

In Florence, I had to learn a different way of walking.

For example, when two pedestrians pass on the narrow sidewalk, who will be bumped off? Who will be splattered with mud? At first I yielded, a polite young woman from the Midwest, but after being pushed into the wall a few times, I started to hold my ground.

I had to learn how to cross a street. Trams rattled out from nowhere. In front of the train station, there were chains on all the corners. In order to cross one street, you had to cross four others. Only Americans leaped over the chains. Everyone else went to the appropriate corner to cross. Nobody jay-walked, not even, it seemed, the anarchists.

I went jogging along the bank of the Arno but I could not tolerate the scrutiny. The stares, the sneers. I was exerting. *Cittadini* do not exert, only peasants and laborers do. I was messy and sloppy and sweaty. And, oh, those hideous shoes.

> *Florence! One of the only places in Europe where I understood that underneath my revolt, a consent was lying dormant.*
>
> ◆
>
> —Albert Camus

In Florence, in order to learn how to walk through a museum, I made rules. I forbade myself from passing to the inner galleries until I had mastered the first ones. Madonna and Child with gold leaf background, stiff Byzantine forms. I scrutinized the shape of eyes. Wide, narrow, almond. I studied the shape of halos. I quizzed myself to place the painting in time. Is the Christ Child standing or sitting? Is he suckling at his mother's breast or grimly blessing the viewer? I tested myself. Cimabue? Correct. Duccio? Wrong. I tried to differentiate between the various schools, Florentine, Sienese, Pisan. I studied the figures sitting rigidly or kneeling solemnly in profile, Pietro Lorenzetti, Ambrogio Lorenzetti, Simone Martini, Bernardo Daddi, Taddeo Gaddi, Andrea Orcagna, taking my copious notes.

The *pensione* was near the cathedral, near the Strozzi palace, in a neighborhood with aristocratic door knockers, on the Via Tornabuoni. When my great aunt, who had given me the earrings, heard where I was staying, she said, *una signorina davvero.* A real rich young miss. She had worked in Florence as a maid, sent down from the Apennines to the house of *signori* at the age of thirteen. She raised one of her eyebrows and said, "My college was walking in back of the sheep, herding them with a stick. And my grammar school was the same."

I could not indulge myself, I had to make my money last, I could not be calling back home to daddy. I was responsible with my money, frugal. I did not have my clothing laundered, but washed it with a bar of clothing soap the size of a brick. I did not enter the small boutiques, but went to the super-store Standa for necessities like toothpaste. For a splurge, I would go to a fast-food place at the corner of via Fiume, where I would sit at the counter and order a bowl of polenta covered with *ragù,* sprinkle it with a little cheese. I ate all of my dinners in the dining room of the *pensione*, where the portions were minuscule, and fennel was served at every meal, in every imaginable way.

I was parsimonious, but the desire for beautiful objects seeped in, drifted in, and before I knew it, before September was over, I was window shopping as if I had done it all my life, deciding what

exactly it was I would buy, objects of subtle beauty. I knew that I
would never buy them, I would never spend that kind of money,
but I affirmed my good taste just the same. I noticed when a window display was changed, when a scarf I had been eyeing was removed. I commented to myself that this cloth was more beautiful
than that cloth, that this pair of shoes was better made than that
pair. I did this, even though, in my heart of hearts, I was a strident
opponent of consumerism.

I wore a pair of brand new leather gloves that I had purchased
at the open air market next to San Lorenzo. The gloves were only
a few hours old, they made my hands feel sophisticated.

I lingered inside an exclusive shop near the Piazza della
Signoria.

I was fingering the material, pure silk.

The shopkeeper peered down at me.

Signorina.

He wore half-glasses.

La prego non toccare le sciarpe.

Remove your gloves, he told me.

Oh. Yes. The gloves.

And I stumbled out of the shop.

One of the instructors, not the one who silently

When I returned to
Barga as a married
woman, I began to understand
the charm of what my mother
had called "civility" and everyone
else called *bella figura.* "Let's go
look at the windows," she would
say when I was little, expressing
her delight in the ornamentation
shop owners were wont to display. There was a sense of inherent design that she enjoyed. She
never tired of examining hand-
embroidered tablecloths and
finely-knit sweater suits. Like her,
I knew that *figura* had to do with
looking good. As a speaker of
Italian, I was always using phrases
connected with it. "Let's put the
flowers on the table where they
will really *fare figura,*" I would say
as we prepared the meal for
important guests. Or "Which
shoes make for a better *figura?*" as
we got ready to go out.

◆

—Gloria Nardini,
"A Trip to Barga"

remarked on the earrings, wanted to talk about American literature. Hemingway, Fitzgerald, Faulkner. Hemingway in his cultural context, Fitzgerald in his. The syntax of Faulkner. How
Faulkner drew on walls, making maps of Yoknapatawpha
County, the terrain of his imagined landscape. I was silenced,
ashamed that he knew so much about American literature and I
knew hardly anything.

In our studies that fall, we moved forward into the heart of the
Renaissance. Masaccio and Masolino. Masolino with his placid
classicism and distinct, exact, pristine, brushwork. Masaccio with
his bold, almost clumsy strokes and slashes. The dark severity of the
eyes. The way his work seems to wander.

We stood outside Santa Maria del Carmine, in drizzle, under
umbrellas and ponchos, circled around the professor. The door was
locked, we would return later, but in the meantime she gave us a
preview of the Brancacci chapel inside, twelve frescoes on three
walls, the cycle of St. Peter, Masolino, Masaccio, Filippino Lippi. *St.
Peter and The Tribute Money*, *St. Peter Healing with His Shadow*, *Adam
and Eve*. We could come back later, she said, the church door was
locked, but in the meantime, we were asked to consider this:

"The cycle demands to be read without regard to narrative or
chronological sequence. We are invited to make connections across
time, to consider ideas suggested by visual analogies and con-
straints, not only within a single scene itself, but also from one
scene to another adjacent, opposite, even diagonally across from it
on another wall."

In November, I went back up into the Apennines. It was foggy
and damp and it sleeted.

I saw what remained of the house of my grandfather's sister, the
interior totally destroyed by a fire which had occurred just a few
weeks earlier. I had seen the house intact in the summer. This
house had survived World War II, when the German army gar-
risoned it, used as part of their headquarters in this town in the
mountains that was on the line of demarcation during the last

phase of the war. The house had survived this period of violence, resistance, reprisals. My grandfather's sister had buried plates and soup tureens so they might not be destroyed. Now the walls were pot-ash and soot. The timbers in the ceiling were charred and wet. My great-aunt was stiff and wooden and hollow, her eyes sunken.

When I was ten, she showed me how to crochet as we sat in the small, square dining room. We sat in wooden chairs alongside the table. Clickity-clickity-click. *Hai visto?* No. Clickity-clickity-click. Do you see? No. I couldn't see it, it went too fast, and she had no more patience. So she taught me instead how to knit, and I learned on oversized lime-green plastic needles.

They would fix the house. The debris in the dining room would be cleared out. She would be sad for a while but then she would be better. She was in shock. They would put the house back together. The walls would be made new, the acrid smell would dissipate. Of course, they would rebuild, and then she would return to herself. I thought these things but did not say them. What did I know? A product of so much privilege.

How many times have I traveled to Italy?

I am sitting at a red light now in Chicago asking myself this. It seems I have made many, many, many journeys, I think about Italy so often. I talk to myself in Italian, admonish myself in Italian. The light is still red, I'm counting. The first time I was ten. Then again in high school. Then my junior year of college. In 1983 to the mountains. In 1988 to Sicily. In 1993 to Rome. Most recently to Turin, Venice, and the mountains. Seven. Seven trips. I had expected the count to come closer to twenty.

The *traghetto* pulls away from the dock at Lipari. It is morning. We are going to look at two other beautiful islands, Panarea and Salina. There is a crowd of young men, in their teens and twenties, waiting for another boat. They are going to work in the pumice mines, pumice which is used to make blue jeans look stone-washed, used to make new denim look old. The morning light falls across the dock, with hills of volcanic rock, chalk and scrub, the background behind the young men. They stand on the dock smoking cigarettes. One of them holds a boom box on his shoulder. Sound bounces against the rock, and the song that travels across the perfect still blue of the water, is Bruce Springsteen's "Downbound Train."

A bus stop in Rome on the via XX *settembre*, nine-thirty in the morning. A crowd begins to drift from its center. A man, who is perhaps seventy, swings a stick at three girls who are dressed in dirty skirts and sweaters. The eldest is ten. They have coffee-colored skin, have wild, uncombed hair, wear thin mesh shoes of pink plastic. The girls hold their arms above their heads to ward off the blows. They are wincing. The shop owner swings his stick at them, not cracking it over their heads, but arcing it sideways, whoosh, whoosh, to clear them out. He is swinging at their legs. He is telling them to get away, to stay away from his shop. His jaw is clenched, he is saying the word, *gittani*. The children walk away, looking back over their shoulder, on the verge of tears, glowering. The oldest one rubs the back of her calf. A block away the children straighten up, start laughing. The stick he wields is the length of a broom handle. Longer than a walking stick, more like a herding stick that used to hit the flanks of beasts.

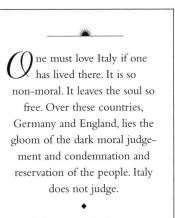

*O*ne must love Italy if one has lived there. It is so non-moral. It leaves the soul so free. Over these countries, Germany and England, lies the gloom of the dark moral judgement and condemnation and reservation of the people. Italy does not judge.

◆

—D.H. Lawrence, Letter to A.W. McLeod, April 26, 1913

At San Pellegrino in Alpe, a museum that documents the history of work in this part of the Apennines, a room recreates a shoemaker's shop, and hanging from a wooden shelf by shoe laces are pairs of rough-hewn shoes, *scarpe a zoccoli*. Leather shoes, laced and ankle-high, with unbending wooden soles.

My cousin says, "Probably, when your grandfathers left for America, they wore shoes like this."

And, probably, the first thing they did there, was to get rid of them.

The museum's catalogue says that the use of well-crafted shoes among the poorer classes was limited to the winter or during important festivals. It was more common to walk barefoot or wear *zoccoli*, the soles of which were made from light-weight, wood such as poplar or alder. The rigid sole, the catalogue says, protected the wearer from injury on paths that were uneven and irregular.

"And you're going again?"

"Tell me," says my grandmother who now rarely ventures outside her house, "what is it that you see in Italy? What's there? Why do you keep going back?"

I've dealt with it. I cried and cried. It's finished, now, it's done. This is what she implies. I sold my house in the mountains to rich people in the city who come up only in the summer. We put away our ambivalence, once it was done, it was done. No going back and forth. Now, you're going back another time?

Turin. This time I am pushing my two-year-old son in a stroller. I walk and walk along a broad boulevard with a tram line in the middle. It is a warm, glorious, October day. I look at the apartment building from across the Corso Re Umberto. I want to take a picture, but now that I am here, I cannot, I cannot take a picture of Primo Levi's house, it seems a violation. So all I do is point it out to my son, for whom it has no meaning, but I do it just the same, and consider an admonition:

> You who are safe
> In your warm houses,
> You who find, returning in the evening,
> Hot food and friendly faces:
> Consider if this is a man
> Who works in the mud

Who does not know peace
Who fights for a scrap of bread
Who dies because of a yes or no...
Meditate that this came about:
I commend these words to you.
Carve them in your hearts...
repeat them to your children,
Or may your house fall apart,
may illness impede you,
may your children turn their faces from you.

Before returning to the hotel, we stop at Piazza Solferino, and I let my son out to play with his toy cars and his five plastic horses. The pavement is dirty, dusty, but he needs to move around. He sits on the ground, then runs in wide circles. I collect the toys, but one of the little horses is accidentally left behind.

That evening, we are window shopping in Turin. It is five o'clock. My husband and I are bickering. What should our strategy be? Can he make it until seven o'clock, seven-thirty, eight? If we can find pizza by the slice. And as we debate prandial strategy, pushing the stroller, my son pulls his shoes off, tosses them over his shoulder. He has become expert at taking his shoes off. We put the shoes back on him once, twice, three times. We retrace steps to look for a little lost sock. We give in. He wears no shoes or socks. It is not cold, but cool. We walk along window shopping. We are in Turin in the fall and we are fortunate, we are out with everyone else taking our *passeggiata* before dinner.

I hear comments of people strolling arm in arm as they pass us, whispers. No shoes! No shoes? That child is wearing no shoes, they say.

It's not cold, I am tempted to say. It's cool, and he's not a china doll.

Mature women glare, give me *sguardi*, dirty looks. What kind of a mother is she? Teenage girls tisk-tisk. Grown men do double takes. Teenage boys, swivel heads, turn and stare, incredulous, at the baby's naked feet.

✦

My grandmother is correct. I keep going back there. Why I do not know.

The expectations are so elevated.

The potential for discomfort so great.

She has asked about this matter of traveling to a place where a word, *vago*, means "wandering," with all the possibility of stumbling and bumbling and being off balance, and the same word also means "vague"; it is Calvino who pointed this out in an essay named "Exactitude." And this same word, *vago*, which implies vagueness and movement, has another third meaning, a kind of pleasure and beauty that is not obvious or immediately apparent.

In Florence, on a narrow, crooked street, between the *pensione* and the Duomo, toward the river, there was a shop with fabric in the window. There were no mannequins and the cloth was draped into different shapes, bunched, folded and cascading. Inside, it was dark, and there was a narrow aisle, a wall on the left with dark wooden shelves that lined the wall from ceiling to floor. Bins, cubicles, one yard wide, two feet tall, were filled with bolts of cloth stacked one on top of the other, muted colors that receded. A ladder attached to casters above could be moved across the wall.

I asked to look please at the velvet. I wanted material for a skirt. Tiny floral patterns.

I pointed out a green cloth and she took it down for me. She unfurled it on a table.

Pineneedle, juniper, thyme.

The pattern was made with vines and blossoms and buds and petals of deep greens that receded into each other and gave the piece of cloth the illusion of near-solidity.

Yes? No? I could not decide. I told her I had to think about it.

Twenty years later, I see this green again in Venice. My husband is up ahead pushing our son in the stroller. I am lagging behind, looking around, wandering.

Across the threshold of a locked side door of the church of San Zanipolo, a woman lies flat on her back, on the single step, sprawled. Her head is on the left, her feet point toward the right. Her hands are thrown back over her head, her breasts point to the architrave. Her hair is shock-white and uncombed. Her left leg, alongside the closed door, is bent in a V, her foot flattened against the step. The other leg lies along the step. Her legs are swollen, and around her thick ankles, rolled-down stockings. An empty upright bottle stands next to her right pelvic bone. Her right foot is shoeless and a backless slipper lies on the pavement.

It is late afternoon in October. The light falls in a late afternoon slant, it brushes over her obliquely. The walls of the church are the color of dust. The pavement of the *campo* is amber. Her unbuttoned coat falls open; it is a subdued, muffled green, a color I cannot not place, a green with hushed dignity. I finger my camera. I cannot photograph this, a woman, asleep, drunk on the doorstep of San Zanipolo, but neither can I take my eyes off it, the balance, the symmetry, the union of form, the tall narrow rectangle of the door, her stretched-out body across it, the muted color of the palette. It was perfectly composed. It was inestimably beautiful. Again I had wandered into the trap, fallen for it, silenced by exquisite light, dumbstruck by a transparent, tinted veil that had been dropped lightly over misery.

In Venice, near the Arsenale, on a nondescript public walkway where a piece of corrugated tin was embedded into the top of a concrete wall, I photograph, instead, a place called Ramo del Zoccolo. Renaissance Venice gave the Western world a refined *zoccolo*, a Chopine, an elevated wooden shoe, made to allow a lady to walk without soiling her garment in mud. They were decorated with inlaid mother of pearl or embroidered cloth. These shoes were built on exceptionally tall stilts, some fifty centimeters or more, and because of the height of these shoes, ladies needed help to walk, personal assistants to prop them up or, at the very least, a wooden walking stick.

"*Siete tutti vagabondi.* You're all vagabonds."
We, she says, meaning the new generations.
My grandmother says this with a teasing tone, laughter, but there is criticism for all this wandering, and there are different words to say it. Giramondo. Globe-trotter. Zingaro. Gypsy. Girovago. Vagabond.
"*Ma perché,*" she asks, "*vai sempre in zonza*? Why are you always drifting around?"

In early winter, in Florence, the stiff wooden soles knocked against the pavement. I had shin splints from so much walking. I crossed the Ponte della Trinità. At the foot of the bridge, I turned right and walked along the river on Lungarno Guicciardini. I turned left, right, then left, and there it was again, Santa Maria del Carmine. I tried the door. It rumbled. Locked. Locked. And locked. I had already tried to enter several times. I was annoyed, desperate, irritated in an American way. Can it be so truly difficult to establish regular hours? I would leave without seeing the frescoes.
Wait. Do you want to go in? I'll let you in.
Yes. Great.
A caretaker said he would let me in.
I remember there being scaffolding against the left wall of the chapel, the ubiquitous, permanently temporary scaffolding. I remember having to peer through and around it to look at *The Tribute Money* and *The Raising of Theophilus,* maybe my memory is vague now, but, certainly, before entering the chapel, on the right side of the entryway, I saw up above, and I saw it unobstructed, Masolino's *Adam and Eve,* being tempted, still serene in the garden. I saw his distinct figures and their distinct features, a soothing moment, all calmness and grace.
And directly opposite it, on the entryway above and left, bouncing off against it, Masaccio's *Expulsion.* Adam, choking a

sob, turning away his face in shame, a darkened zone of indistinguishable features. Eve covering her right breast, her flattened forehead a glare of harsh light, her eyes furrows, indistinct features made by dark slashes, her mouth a dark ambiguous hollow that unleashes a wail.

Quick. Choose. Toward which one are you pushed, which one propels you forward? Masolino's tranquillity or Masaccio's anguish? This, the aesthetic question posed during the course of study.

I walked a wide circle, but it was not broad enough to take in a whole. I tried to enter into discourse. I was poised to hold up a banner but by the time I found one, the roughly shod youths who had unfurled it had vanished. I was peripheral, I passed through.

It was December, it was the end of that wandering.

Adria Bernardi is the author of Houses with Names: The Italian Immigrants of Highwood, Ilinois. *Her translations of the poetry of Italian screenwriter Tonino Guerra are forthcoming in a collection entitled,* Abandoned Places. *She was the recipient of the 1995 James Fellowship awarded by the Heekin Group Foundation.*

*

One hot afternoon during my time in Rome I went for a walk and found myself wandering into the entrance of an old monastery, and then I found myself sitting on a stone bench in a small inner courtyard. There was the coolness of green plants, and it was so quiet, with nothing but the sound of a fountain dripping water, and then I was stunned by a powerful feeling of having been in this place before, though I never had been in this particular courtyard before. And the idea came to me: to be a woman in an Italian family is to live in a courtyard. It is beautiful, safe, offers comfort and aesthetic pleasures and companionship; at the same time, the courtyard is confining, it keeps you away from the world and keeps the world away from you. I wrote an entire novel exploring these contradictions—the attractions of the courtyard and its deprivations. I could define the contradictions but I couldn't resolve them completely. When the novel was published, some part of my Italy sadness lingered.

—Anna Monardo, "Return to Italy"

HENRY ALFORD

* * *

Vacationing with Mom

Just say yes.

LIKE SO MUCH OF MY MOTHER'S LIFE, IT WAS BORN OF IMPULSE. Last Thanksgiving, when Mom heard that I was planning a ten-day trip to Italy, she dropped a bombshell: "You know, I have never been to Europe," she said. "Maybe I could come along."

I have to admit I was surprised and a bit discomfited by Mom's auto-invitation; when you think of getting away from it all, this "all" generally includes your mother. My concern was further heightened by the fact that I was planning the trip with my boyfriend, Jess, who, over the course of our four-year relationship, had not spent much quality time with Mom. I wondered how she—a voluble, 60-something bird-watching Republican—would handle the concept of traveling with her gay son and his companion. But then I remembered that, candor being chief among my mother's virtues, any unease she experienced would be instantly and audibly broadcast; indeed, when I had introduced her to Jess, she looked at us and remarked "You two look exactly alike! Ugh, the height of narcissism!" And so, with caution thrown to the wind, Jess and I agreed to have Mom along on our journey.

It turned out to be a wise decision. Mothers are ready, helpful traveling companions. They can fold maps. They elicit sympathy in the hearts of hotel clerks. They are eager to avail your rental car's windshield of their wetted hankie. And most importantly, vacationing with your mother affords you a golden opportunity to witness aspects of her personality hitherto unknown to you. It's like returning to the classics: You keep discovering something new.

MY MOTHER THE ART CRITIC: Given Mom's artistic leanings (she tried to buy wool in each town we stopped in so that she could knit something she called a "memory garment"), we were eager to show her Rome's cultural treasures. On this score, Mom was winningly game; while we gazed up at the glories of the Sistine Chapel, she explained that the sore neck she was getting from this activity was not a problem for her. "I'm a bird-watcher," she reminded us, "and warbler season is quite the same." However, some of Rome's treasures proved disappointing to her. She felt shortchanged, for example, by the lack of carnality she perceived in Bernini's sculpture of Pluto raping Proserpine. "That's not much of a rape," she said. "He ought to drop his loincloth and really get at it."

MY MOTHER THE LITERARY CRITIC: Unabashed by her highly tenuous grasp of Italian—oddly, the French word "*jamais*" figured large in her arsenal of phrases—Mom sometimes took it upon herself to fraternize with the natives. At the entrance to St. Peter's she fell into conversation with a Vatican security guard. "How is the book doing?" she asked, referring to His Holiness's then-new bestseller, *Crossing the Threshold of Hope.* "Is the Pope happy with sales?" I squirmed in embarrassment. The guard looked baffled and said, "We aren't that close with the Pope. He is...far." Putting her arm around me, Mom barreled on, "Oh, because this is my son. He's a writer, too, and I thought maybe the pope could talk to him." The blood drained from my face. But the guard came to my rescue: "No...it would not be possible."

MY MOTHER THE ADVENTURE TRAVELER: In Rome, we rented Vespa motor scooters. After Jess and I had spent the better part of a day negotiating the teeming masses and anarchy-plagued streets, we encouraged Mom to take the wheel herself at the Piazza del Popolo, one of Rome's busiest squares. Mom revved the engine cautiously and then set off, alerting pedestrians to her rapidly approaching presence by cautioning them, in English, "Careful! Careful!" Once she got on the road that encircles the *piazza*, she reasserted her essential theme of menace by driving against the traffic. Then, back in the pedestrian area, she nearly clipped two Asian boys.

A few days later, in Sicily, Mom, who had earlier on the trip expressed a desire to see a Sicilian "taken care of," seemed eager to demonstrate how unflappable she was in the potential presence of the Mafia. At the Palermo train station, I mentioned that the local police made me somewhat anxious, given their submachine guns. Mom weighed in, "And you just know they're all on the take." Later that day, in a café, Mom pointed at a squat, middle-aged man and whispered "C-A-P-O."

Traveling with my mother has revealed to me her essential fearlessness—a comforting thought to anyone who remembers the childhood disillusionment of discovering that one's parents are not omnipotent and omniscient. Our trip provided a sensation quite the opposite—the discovery that coiled beneath the placid exterior of Audubon guides and woolly raiments lurks a Maori warrior. But was this Maori warrior broadened and acculturated by her trip to the Continent? I'm not sure. Several days after we had returned to the States, I called her at her house in Massachusetts to see if the film from Jess's camera, which had somehow ended up in Mom's luggage, had been developed yet.

It hadn't. "There are going to be some mystery pictures, too," she told me, "because Jess had already taken some, remember?" I corrected her, explaining that we had started the trip with a new roll. "Oh, phew," she said, relieved. "Because I thought there might be some gay orgy scenes, and I wasn't sure if Bristol Pharmacy could handle that."

Henry Alford is the author of Municipal Bondage. *He lives in New York City.*

*

What Americans are apt to call anxiety attacks, Italians call gastritis. Gas is a frequent subject of conversation. As American sophisticates discuss sexual mores at a dinner party, Italians discuss the Romans—"who regarded the blood as juice of the fiber of which the flesh is composed"—located concupiscence in the liver, which they defined as "the blood factory."

If a German child in lederhosen gets wet in the park, he is rushed home by his Italian nanny so as not to get a draft on his *fegato*. The only children one sees in the park in March are the children of foreigners with their foreign mothers; cold winds are said to affect the liver adversely.

—Barbara Grizzuti Harrison, *Italian Days*

TREY ELLIS

* * *

The Visible Man

A black American's sojourn in Italy.

WHEN I ARRIVED IN FLORENCE IN 1981, I WAS SURE A BLACK FACE
in Italy would be no novelty. Yet during the six months of my
sophomore year abroad from Stanford, about the only time I saw
another black American was when I looked in the mirror. My per-
ceptions and loyalties shifted; I became closer to white American
students than I had been in the states. Every Stanford girl was
called *Biondina* (Blondie) even if her hair was dark brown. A Santa
Barbara surfer and I were now both minorities.

Yet as I slowly learned to express myself in Italian with fewer
appeals of *"Come si dice?"* ("How does one say?"), my allegiance
began to tilt from the Californians to the Italians. Other students
also itched to experience behind-the-scenes Tuscany, but somehow, it seemed easier for me. In my case, being a minority was
nothing new: I grew up in Irish- and Italian-American middle-
and working-class suburbs outside Ann Arbor and New Haven.
Hearing an Italian child shout *"Guarda, mamma, un nero"* ("Look,
ma, a black man") before the mother slapped the child's pointing
finger was cute compared with watching old ladies in Connecticut
cross the street to avoid sharing the sidewalk.

In fact, I soon metamorphosed from an ugly American into one of those insufferable school-year-abroad students who pretend to have been born Continental. I started to dress better and gesticulate with my hands. I almost wanted to take up smoking. In the mornings I'd peer over my bowl of *caffé latte* at the other students' soggy presweetened cereal as if I'd never dumped out whole boxes of the stuff just to get at the plastic snap-together spaceships. Back in my New Haven neighborhood I'd bridled aggressively against my own Yankee assimilation. But in Florence, speaking Italian, I was soon over-aspirating my c's, trying to mimic the Tuscan accent. I'd say *"Hoha-Hola hon la hannuccia horta"* ("Coca-Cola with a short straw") in a more flagrantly Florentine way than any descendant of Dante.

Physically, of course, I could never pass for an Italian. On the streets I was usually mistaken for an African drought refugee. Old women would stop and squeeze my arm. *"Sei uno dei nostri Eritrei?"* ("Are you one of our Eritreans?"), one once asked, soothed by seeing her weekly church contribution made flesh. Others, after discovering I was an *Americano nero,* assumed I was some kind of civil-rights celebrity. *"Ce l' ho un sogno!"* somebody once said to me—"I have a dream!"

Yet Italians accepted me more readily than any people I've ever known. They shared with me their Easter dinners, their beach houses, their grandparents. Every weekend a pack of us would hike 500-year-old cobblestone streets to visit little-known hillside monasteries or hunt the Chianti region for obscure grape festivals. I was an absolutely equal member of a wonderful group of Italian friends who—except for me—had known each other since high school.

Then at year's end I had to leave. On the plane home I thought about why Italy had embraced me so effortlessly. Sicily is just 90 miles from North Africa and, thanks to Moorish incursions as far north as Naples, I was fooled daily in the streets, waving to Sicilians I mistook for high-yellow Alabamans. Northern Europeans see themselves as pure, while all Mediterraneans to them are hot-blooded Afro-Europeans. They're right. As for this

Afro-American, finding myself among people who liked to sit outside with friends and lyrically argue and seduce and brag, I felt as comfortable in a *piazza* as on my grandparents' front stoop.

Back at school, I didn't realize how uncomfortable I sometimes felt in the States until I remembered how at home I'd felt in Italy. So after graduation and months of rejection as a TV comedy writer in New York, I knew it was time to get back on the plane.

When you arrive in a new country and know that you're only staying a few months, you can afford to fiddle with your identity. But returning to Florence this time and not knowing when or if I'd ever go home, I began to act less Italian. Despite my Italian friends' jokes, I resumed eating eggs in the mornings and drinking cappuccino at night. No longer insecure about the language, my ridiculous Tuscan mellowed to standard Italian. I realized that as a foreigner, my entire mystique was my black Americanness.

I brought two duffel bags, twenty pages of my unfinished novel and savings for two months. The savings stretched to 3 1/2 months until finally Italian stereotypes about blacks landed me a job. I walked into a store called Sarallo Sport to buy a windbreaker, and the owner asked me if I'd ever seen a black skier. He'd just seen one of us in a documentary about Aspen and was fascinated. Black skiers *are* indeed rare, but I told him I happened to be one of them. He offered me a part-time job selling ski equipment. I knew he just wanted a walking marketing gimmick, but my stomach decided *va bene*.

That inspired me to see what other stereotypes I could exploit. After constantly being asked loony questions about black tanning and hair care. I figured I deserved at least one perk. So after work one evening I stopped by the Silhouette Club, Florence's toniest gym. I sort of hinted to the manager that I was a world-famous athlete and personal trainer. "*Come* Carl Lewis," I told him. He let me go to the gym for free until a spot opened up for a weight trainer. I knew he felt that having a black American work out in his Italian gym was a gold star of approval—like Chinese people eating in a Chinese restaurant.

Soon my days found a routine: until noon I'd fill page after page of the same three-ring notebook I'd been using for schoolwork since the eighth grade. My novel, *Platitudes*, was inching forward at twelve pages a week.

Lunch was pasta or risotto and frozen fish sticks, then I'd floor my Ciao moped to the other side of town and my jobs. I'd tell people to lift harder at the Silhouette Club (*"Piú forte! Ancora, pigro!"* "Harder! One more, lazy!") until four, then cross the street and sell skis at Sarallo Sport (*"I bastoncini non devono arrivare fino all'ascella."* "Your ski poles don't have to reach your underarms.") until seven. That left me an hour to inhale dinner and speed through crazy Italian rush-hour traffic to the Scuola Leonardo Da Vinci. There, two other Americans and I taught English to Italians. My work day would end around 10:30.

At Easter, my friends Vanni, Francesca, Rainer, Vanna, Laura and I rented a former Winter Olympics bunkhouse just outside Cortina d'Ampezzo for a week. As I carved an intermediate trail on packed powder, the Italians were as shocked at seeing a black skier as my boss had been back in Florence. They yelled down at me from the chair lift, *"Nero! Nero!"* I tried to escape celebrity, skiing the back side of Cortina where the German-speaking Alto-Adigiani live. Springing through a beautiful field of moguls, I heard screams from overhead, *"Schwartz! Schwartz!"*

Enough, I stopped and took in the crown of white mountains that surrounded me without end, aggressive in their beauty. My head ballooned with one thought: I was the only person with skin this brown, hair this curly, for as far as the eye could see. There, in the most wide-open place I'd ever been, claustrophobia overcame me.

On the way back to Florence an old song came on the radio, and my friends sang along, floating back on their sweet memories of high school. I prided myself in knowing contemporary Italian pop better than all my friends, yet no matter how long I stayed, I'd never share their childhood recollections. And they'd never dream of *Lost in Space*.

I knew then I would visit Italy for the rest of my life, but that I'd never emigrate. I couldn't imagine myself in ten years, a stranger in every land. I needed to move on, but I wasn't ready to go home.

A visiting childhood friend lugged the 353 pages of my novel's rough draft back to the States in a waterproof cocoon of trash bags and tape. The reward to myself for finally completing it would be a great trek. But after Florence I wasn't about to hostel-hop through Europe like every other American post-grad traveler. No, my Grand Tour would be of Africa. I'd try to hitchhike through Greece to Egypt, down to Kenya, across Uganda and Zaire to Nigeria, then north through the Sahara to Tunisia and, finally, back to Florence. In Africa I hoped to find high adventure and to discover just how far I hadn't come from my family's first home.

I landed in Cairo where an Egyptian my age put his forearm next to mine and said "Look my brother, we are the exact same color." He then ushered me to a slimy hotel costing fifteen times my allotted budget. After that night, however, Africans treated me as a heroic civil-rights freedom fighter. They wouldn't let me spend my money. I couldn't eat all the food they offered. I couldn't carry all the gifts they gave.

Floating down the Zaire (also known as the Congo) one night, in the middle of a continent three times larger than the United States, I looked out at the wide black expanse of river, the low and dark silhouette of zillions of trees and the white fireworks of far-away tropical lightning, and I thought, for the first time in my life, for as far as I could see, I was a majority.

It was only then that I knew I was ready to come back home to America. For a while.

Trey Ellis is a novelist and screenwriter who lives in Santa Monica, California. His novel, Right Here, Right Now, *will be published by Simon & Schuster.*

★

For me, the lure of Italy has always been my family. I've had friends who've become addicted to Italy by way of the art, the fashion, the men, the movie stars, the bike paths, the back roads of history. It's different for everyone, but no matter what the pull Italy has on you, I believe that for all of us it translates into that moment Willa Cather captures succinctly in *My Antonia*: "That is happiness; to be dissolved into something complete and great." In Italy I felt I belonged.

—Anna Monardo, "Return to Italy"

DAVID ROBINSON

⋆ ⋆ ⋆

Lunch at Pensione Suisse

Food was not the only thing
on the menu.

AT PENSIONE SUISSE, WE ALWAYS MAKE SURE WE WAKE UP IN
time for lunch. As I swing open the heavy shutters, the hot
Neapolitan sun, already high in the sky, floods the bare room with
its brilliance. I quickly wash in the corner sink and join the others
at the table. Mama Mia (she is all of ours while we are in her *pensione*) is in the kitchen. The sound of her voice and the smell of
her food entwine and drift in to where we are seated expectantly
at a large oval table. I have never eaten food so good, but the true
bounty of this table is in the people seated around it. I am dining
as I do every day with the other guests of the establishment, two
or three of the women who have no customers at lunchtime, one
of the six Chinese tailors taking a break from measuring American
sailors, Erica, the Swiss girl put up there by her industrialist
boyfriend, and Senor Bea, an airline official bored by ordinary hotels. We are served by the maid, Bianca, and waiter, Antonio, better known as Antionetta, vamping as he serves. I am here with two
American friends. This is my first trip to Europe.

Except when Mama Mia enters the room, we Americans tend
to focus on the women seated at the table with us. No wonder.
Across from me is Marisa, a back-alley bombshell with light flaxen

hair. She has a wonderful body, full and fleshy, which even in repose radiates sensuality. I watch her lips and observe the lingering traces of red she leaves when she eats an apple or smokes a cigarette. I can distinguish hers among all the other butts in the overflowing tray. I don't know her story; why anyone is here is pointless to ask. But even when Marisa is lounging at the table in a simple house dress, I see her as a sophisticated lady. She could be a star for me in any environment. She has a baby girl, around 18 months old, blonde and adorable, who looks just like Marisa must have. There is no father; the father would be a guess, maybe not even a memory. It's not clear what happens to the baby when she entertains, and I never get up the nerve to find out.

Next to me is the Sicilian without a name, just Number Two (her room). There is nothing subtle or sophisticated about Number Two. Everything about her is black, her hair, her dresses, her moods, a perpetual storm cloud. Another great body pushing out at every seam, she leaves an imprint of flesh behind as other women leave a scent. Anna Magnagni in *The Rose Tattoo* pales by comparison. I could play her Burt Lancaster. Provocative, hot, passionate in even the smallest gesture, Number Two flaunts her sexuality and dares you to do something about it. At the table she leers and cracks jokes in dialect which I don't understand but the meaning of which is unmistakable. One day after lunch, I accept her dare and knock on her door. She yanks open the door, looks me up and down, laughs a loud "Ha!" and slams it shut. She doesn't do charity. Soon everyone in the *pensione* knows; there are no secrets here. Some of the other girls, hearing about this episode and seeing a chance, offer themselves, but burned once, I decline another humiliation.

Sonia is the plainest of the lot and therefore the easiest to be with. In comparison to Marisa and Number Two, she appears uncomplicated, even dull. She has only an average body which she doesn't bother to flaunt. Sonia seems happy with life's simple pleasures like the picnics we take together in the countryside. She is memorable for defending Mussolini and his terror with the simple logic that only those who deserved to die died and all who died deserved to. She doesn't allow complicated matters to trouble her. Thus, I find it hard to reconcile the stories I hear about Sonia with Sonia herself.

It must be Senor Bea, the only one at Pensione Suisse with any sense of history, who tells us that Sonia "in her youth" had "made a fortune" in Argentina. In her youth? She's still in her twenties. "Doing what?" I ask naively which produces much guffawing around the table. In silence then, I wonder about the dimensions of this reputed fortune, how much could it have been, what might have happened to it. Sonia herself never speaks of Argentina.

Stories about Sonia emerge in her absence. We learn Sonia has a boyfriend—in fact she has two boyfriends—and that her life is not so placid after all, because one boyfriend loves her, she loves the other and the first is jealous enough to come spying. It's hard to imagine jealousy in the context of Pensione Suisse—what does the jealous lover think is going on here anyhow?—and Sonia in particular doesn't seem to inspire jealousy. But Carlo, from a well-to-do family and desperately in love, lavishes money on Sonia which she in turn bestows on the man she truly desires, Attilio. Thus Sonia continues to make and spend her fortune.

Eva is the oldest, fat and gap-toothed, but she has landed a U.S. soldier who she swears to my obvious incredulity wants to marry her. A northerner and in Naples only after years of working the small towns where supposedly she was regarded as something of a star, she is now definitely teetering over the hill, rescued just in time by the American. He comes by almost every evening. The two of them sit side by side on two chairs in the darkened hall outside her room for hours holding hands and saying nothing. He speaks no Italian, she no English. It seems to me the language of love must have its limitations. After a certain amount of hand holding, they adjourn to the bedroom to cap the evening, and later he leaves. She gets up to join us for lunch. This routine leaves Eva lots of free time during the afternoon to play cards, talk or whatever. She is not above having other men or making a pass at me when we are in the same room, although I take care to make sure we are never alone. She reaches for me across the large bed where Sonia and a group of us are playing cards, but I have the image of being chased by a cow across a field, and I scramble free.

I do not escape the clutches of the harridans who wait below on the street, nor do I particularly want to. I have been conditioned by living for weeks in the Pensione Suisse; sex is in the food, in the Neapolitan air. It permeates every part of one's being. After a while, I feel that I will burst open at any moment. That this desire has nothing to do with love shocks me at first.

My one attempt with Number Two aside, I am still shy and keep my new family off limits. The women working the street all know me and surround me every time I step out the door. Naples is renowned for the earthiness of its street walkers who blanket the city. The ones outside Pensione Suisse have been pushed back to this poor neighborhood where their clientele is mostly local, the husband out for a cigarette or the passing worker. After several glasses of wine one night I figure why not and take one of the old women upstairs. I put the weightless ten lire coin in the jerky elevator, and

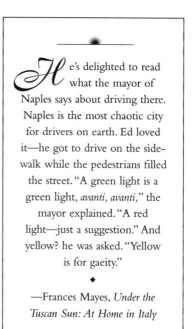

*H*e's delighted to read what the mayor of Naples says about driving there. Naples is the most chaotic city for drivers on earth. Ed loved it—he got to drive on the sidewalk while the pedestrians filled the street. "A green light is a green light, *avanti, avanti,*" the mayor explained. "A red light—just a suggestion." And yellow? he was asked. "Yellow is for gaiety."

◆

—Frances Mayes, *Under the Tuscan Sun: At Home in Italy*

we slip past the somnolent doorman into my bed. The morning after on the street below, she ribaldly shouts her triumph at me for all the rest of the women to applaud, and I don't mind. It even gets easier. But one night the doorman, Peppino, wakes and spreads the word in the *pensione*.

Peppino is happy to be of use, delighted suddenly to have a new story to tell. He too has somehow landed at Pensione Suisse, old and spent. Unlike the rest, he revels in the past, with repetitious tales of Ethiopia where he claims to have been an important Fascist official during the Italian occupation. With his discovery of my exploits, we are linked, and he begins to treat me like a new friend. After several nights, the old woman, my lover, takes to reaching into my pockets on the street, grabbing loose change or whatever else she can put her hands on, and still I don't care. Upstairs, life goes on too.

It is called Pensione Suisse because Mama Mia's husband is Swiss. One look at the two of them gives you the whole picture, but the image that comes to mind also makes you blink. He is a fraction of her size and could be a heroic mountaineer scaling the heights of Mount Mama, but while the scale is apt, the personality is not. He is too wizened and submissive. Pensione Suisse is his Blue Angel, Mama Mia his Marlena. One can guess how the two met. It is his money that bought the *pensione,* but it is his and Swiss in name only. Mama Mia runs the place and everything in it and endows all with her vast, embracing Neaploitan personality. When visible at all, Senor Suisse—no one calls him anything else—sits hunched at the front desk talking to Peppino or doing the accounts. He never eats lunch with us.

Mama Mia herself was in the same business she now oversees when she was young and so too her daughter, Lela, who often comes to visit with her small son and scrawny husband. Lela has exquisite white skin set off by jet black hair and the fluffy pale sweaters she favors. Soft and plump, she, like Mama Mia must have been, is a beauty. It's not clear whether she is still working or has retired fully to family life, but Lela would fit right in at Pensione Suisse, and I have no trouble picturing her joining us at lunch or in other activities, no trouble at all.

The back windows look out on the popular quarters, rabbit warrens of old apartments crammed with the poor of Naples. There is a street market below, and food for lunch is hoisted up each day in a basket lowered from the kitchen window. We eat incredibly well. We always have fresh fruits and vegetables, and good meats too. Anything but fresh pasta would be a scandal. It is Mama

Mia who does all the marketing and the cooking and supervises the staff. Leaning out the window, she shouts down her orders and her imprecations lest any vender try to overcharge her or give her less than their highest quality at their lowest price. All the negotiations of the bazaar are conducted by shouting back and forth. Even six stories below, her presence is felt. When she leans out the kitchen window, we are on the safe side of a blast furnace.

The kitchen is the center of Mama Mia's domain, and everyone comes there if they need to talk to her. The business of the *pensione* is conducted in the kitchen, and her desk is the chopping block behind which she stands while preparing the food for lunch. I have never seen her sitting down. Emotional and volatile, she is an Etna of a woman given to frequent eruptions. She can be scathing, and her denunciations are accompanied by a full panoply of Italian gesture. To be next to her when she is working with a knife in her hand is to risk evisceration over even a minor point of dispute. Like the others, we are wise enough to stand respectfully clear.

We are often joined at the table by other guests in the *pensione*. Pasquale is the youngest of the six Chinese tailors living there. (He was born in Portuguese Goa, hence the unusual name). He has fallen rapturously in love with Marisa's baby girl—if not with Marisa herself. Pasquale adores playing with the baby and gives Marisa money, a lot of money it is rumored around the table, for the baby as well as for herself. Marisa has conquered with her baby, as well as with her body, but in Naples, any survival is okay. There never could be a debate here about ends justifying the means. Life is unblinkingly amoral. The other Chinese keep to themselves and pass up Mama Mia's food for their own which they cook on hot plates in their back rooms. They go out every day to the U.S. ships to sell made-to-order suits and do a booming business. It's not clear what they think of Marisa or of Pasquale's entanglement.

Erica, the Swiss, has been stashed here by her industrialist boyfriend to keep her handy but out of sight of his family. She doesn't seem to mind the arrangement. Tall, blonde and very good looking, she seems a cut above the rest, but she is just as dependent on the desires of a man as are the others, and any class distinctions fade in the face of this common reality. She has a friendly disposition and accompanies Sonia and us on our picnics. Her boyfriend, Rudi, a Swiss-Italian, calls for her in the evenings. No friend of the working class, he runs a large family-owned tomato processing plant and has nothing good to say about the hundreds of southern Italian workers he employs. He likes to tell us of their scandalous transgressions and how many he has "had to" fire. No one in this working class *pensione* challenges his views, not because he is a man, although that is appreciated, not because he is rich, although that too is appreciated, but simply because that is who he is and what he thinks. Pensione Suisse is all-accepting and can afford no moralists or crusaders.

Each of the women at Pensione Suisse seems to have found herself some sort of male benefactor: Marisa, Erica, Sonia, Eva, Mama Mia, Lela, all except the outrageously independent Number Two. These women know men inside out and seem to have a very clear-headed attitude toward them and their usefulness. Neither cynical nor romantic, they are above all else, practical; only Sonia seems to lose her head in love. These women seek men not for romance but for security, in whatever form and for whatever duration it may occur.

Senor Bea has the appearance of a gentleman, refined, reserved and elegant. He is the only other man included at lunch, and he eats with us only when he can get off work. He says he prefers the atmosphere of Pensione Suisse to other hotels (as do we) for its vitality. Although he is a senior executive at the airport, he seems totally at ease in the world of Pensione Suisse. From Senor Bea, we get an education of another sort. He is well-read and speaks fluent English, and after lunch, we linger over coffee in long discussions with him about literature, history, politics and philosophy. He says he is a socialist—the only one I've ever met.

He also knows the gossip about those around the table and is not above slipping us delicious morsels from time to time. He and Bianca act as the court jesters and between them provide such oral history of the realm as exists. Apart from their stories, it's not always clear how we come to know all we know about our companions at Pensione Suisse. We observe and listen, we pick up clues in the swirl of conversation and constant bantering, but there are seldom explicit recountings and almost never anything said about the past. The women here do not sit around the table talking to one another of previous experiences. We Americans are never asked about our lives in the U.S. or about our parents or hometowns or what we do. There are no childhood reminiscences offered us either, no tales of family, work or past exploits. We understand not to ask. Even if everyone here has a past, no one has a history. Life begins afresh each day.

Sometimes the *pensione* takes in temporary boarders, and then they too join us for lunch. Innocents can get quite a shock. One day, an American couple, Kansas tourists, come to table with no idea of what they are getting into, but Number Two makes sure they are properly indoctrinated. The only common language she needs is a banana. The husband shows some signs of interest—he'd have to be brain dead not to—but the wife hustles him out of there fast. I don't think they even finish their soup.

Unexpectedly one day I run into another friend from college who had just docked in Naples aboard a U.S. navy ship. I invite him back to lunch at the *pensione*, and after several months at sea, he has no trouble appreciating the bounty of the table. After indulging in what is for us a typical four course meal, he expresses interest in some further indulgence and Marisa, understanding the situation, is willing. With Eva's intervention, the five of us set about haggling, negotiating the issue of how much for what until finally an accommodation is reached. It takes all of us half an hour around the table to arrange what left to the two of them would have taken a couple of minutes. But we feel proud of ourselves, satisfied to think that in the process we have become a little bit Neapolitan. Our friend reports satisfaction, so we are doubly pleased. I forget to ask him about the baby.

We also have temporary show-biz guests eating with us from time to time. One is Aida, a former Miss Greece, who is appearing in Naples' clubs. Tall, dramatic and classically proportioned, I think she sings, but if so, probably nobody pays much attention to her voice. Around the table, she is as haughty in her house dress as she is in her nightclub outfit, revealing and remote at the same time. She gives us postcards of herself in costume, one long taut leg thrust forward, and I keep her card on my bureau. We are also joined by the Sugar Sisters for a week or so, two innocent-looking dyed-blonde Italians trying to sing American songs they can't understand. They have been performing by trying to mimic as best they could the sounds picked up from the radio or records. None of us can carry a tune, but we undertake to tutor them in the meaning and pronunciation of the rock and roll lyrics that we know so well, and after lunch they rehearse with us. It's hard to get through a line without cracking up. We never catch their show at the nightclub, but we know it by heart by the time they leave.

Bianca, the maid who knows all, keeps no secrets. She is rosy-cheeked, cheerful and tiny in her blue uniform dress, wry and direct in her humor, shrewd and caustic in her observations. She skewers everyone—with the judicious exception of Mama Mia—but without malice. Thanks principally to Bianca, we know something about everyone's character, their quirks or preferred indulgences—especially sexual—and all this information is available to be used by anyone in conversation or in the frequent verbal jousting that goes on around the table. Bianca can be self-deprecating as well. One day she asks me if I would consider marrying her daughter. I say my Italian isn't good enough for me to talk to her. She tells me not to worry—all I have to say is 500 lire. Everyone—for this is at the table too—roars.

Antonio wears a white waiter's coat. He helps Bianca serve lunch and does the dishes afterwards. Antonio sashays as he serves, speaking in a high-pitched voice with the full range of exaggerated effeminate gestures. Everyone calls him Antoinetta, which he prefers. He seems to love his role; he adores being teased by the women and gives it back as fast and as strong as he gets it. His long brown hair is slicked back and held in place with bobby pins, and he hikes his apron like a skirt. For we Americans, this is our first brush with overt homosexuality. Antonio is a good twenty years ahead of his time. One wonders what it must be like for him out on the streets of Naples. But it is clear that Pensione Suisse is a sanctuary for him (as well as for us) and here he is free to be who he wants to be. His job is not dependent on pretending to be something he's not. In this environment, any pretense would be punctured quickly, most likely by one of Bianca's deft barbs. But more than that, he is frank about his preferences and, at Pensione Suisse he has an accepting audience in front of which he can discuss his love problems.

Antoinetta has fallen madly in love with a newly married man who just moved in with his wife across the narrow street. When their shutters are open, he can see into their apartment. He has taken to frequenting the balcony opposite their apartment hoping to be noticed. In a fit of desperate inspiration, he borrows a dress from Sonia and prances flirtatiously on the balcony in an effort to draw the newlywed's interest but to no avail. Unusual for Pensione Suisse, Antoinetta's desires remain unfulfilled.

In the afternoons we often go out to explore Naples, to sit and soak up the afternoon sun, to read and talk while we digest the meal and the events of the table. Two or three months pass, the pace of our lives has changed. We have glimpsed another world, one normally inaccessible to outsiders. We dream about staying in Naples, maybe going into business, maybe even running a place like Pensione Suisse where we could have all the pleasures of our own table and create our own family around it. We debate how best to do this but without any resolution. Finally, we decide we'll come back to Naples after we first visit some other places in Europe which we have wanted to see. With this agreed upon, we come to the decision to leave Naples in order to continue our travels. With great effort, we rouse ourselves and say goodbye to Mama Mia and all the others.

Our last lunch is like every lunch, wonderful, bountiful, entertaining. Leaving is sad for us, for we will miss them all, but we know that life at Pensione Suisse will go on as usual without much reference to us. Unlike for us, tomorrow will bring them no nostalgic memories of today.

*David Robinson is a photographer whose first book was a photo essay on
Italy. Since living at Pensione Suisse he has returned to Italy over twenty
times. He has published six books of his photographs plus numerous articles
on photography and travel. His two most recent books are on European
cemeteries:* Saving Graces *and* Beautiful Death. *After twenty-five years in
Boston, he and his wife now live in Mill Valley, California.*

⋆

Under current Italian legislation it is not punishable to make a living as
a prostitute (a business estimated by CENSIS to produce a yearly volume
of $4 billion), but exploiting prostitution is illegal. Accordingly, the courts
tend to define pimping broadly: A night concierge of the Cavalieri
Hilton Hotel in Rome was sentenced to a year and four months in
prison because he had allowed alleged call girls to visit hotel guests in
their rooms, charging double occupancy. Landlords who rent apartments
to prostitutes may also be prosecuted. At the same time, leading newspapers list the addresses or telephone numbers of "masseuses," "astrologers,"
"chiromancer," and "escorts" in their classified columns every day, and
nobody has any doubt about what the advertisements mean.

—Paul Hofmann, *That Fine Italian Hand*

TOM MUELLER

* * *

The Children
of Magna Graecia

*The ways of ancient Greece live on
in Southern Italy.*

ON AUGUST 16, 1972, ARCHAEOLOGISTS OFF THE SOUTHERN
Italian fishing village of Riace swung two muscular bronze men
out of the Ionian Sea and eased them to the deck. The Bronzes of
Riace immediately caused a worldwide sensation. Among the
most exquisite sculptures of classical antiquity, they are vivid
reminders of the glory of Magna Graecia, the necklace of Greek
cities that arose along the shores of southern Italy in the 8th century B.C., burned with a cultural brilliance that rivaled Athens itself, and faded while Rome was still young. Yet the Bronzes of
Riace, so handsome and lifelike, seemed more than sculpture. It
was as if two sexy inhabitants of a lost civilization had awakened
from a watery sleep of 25 centuries.

Few people who admire the Bronzes in the Museo Nazionale
of Reggio Calabria, the unofficial capital of the region, dream that
the real descendants of Magna Graecia are still very much alive. Just
20 kilometers inland, in the wild, wolf-infested Calabrian mountains, are a few isolated villages where the older inhabitants still
speak Greek. Not modern Greek, nor medieval Byzantine, but a
form of ancient Greek—the language of the Bronzes and their
sculptor, the language of Homer. The songs, customs, and religious

traditions of these impoverished farmers are a priceless cultural inheritance, unique in the world. They call themselves "Grecanici"
and are a living link to more than 2,500 years of uninterrupted history. A link that, barring a miracle, will soon be broken forever.

This is the Deep South, the extreme tip of the Italian boot, a
place known as Aspromonte, or "Harsh Mountain." At first glance,
the name seems to fit: steep, forbidding mountains advance almost
to the coast and rise away inland as far as the eye can see, a parade
of sun-scorched peaks and deep gorges of eternal shadow. For most
Italians, Aspromonte is synonymous with brigands and grinding
poverty. Yet driving south from Reggio along the sinuous Ionian
coastline down Highway 106, I begin to see that the landscape, at
least, is anything but harsh. To the right, smooth expanses of pebble and white-sand beaches are punctuated by steep-sided coves of
startling aquamarine. To the left, the lush mountain vegetation
spills down almost to the road: chestnuts, holm oaks, and quaking
aspen mingle with silvery olive trees and fruit-laden oranges above
a carpet of wildflowers. Here and there grow incongruous tropical
imports: date palms, banana, rubber, prickly pear.

At Bova Marina I turn off the highway onto a narrow road that
switchbacks its way up into the mountains, climbing 1,000 meters
in 14 kilometers. In the distance, set on a rocky promontory, is the
town of Bova, doorway to the Grecanico region.

Like other Grecanico villages, Bova occupies a perfect defensive
position. For very good reason—the Grecanici have been under
siege for the last 2,500 years. In the 5th century B.C., warlike Italic
tribes forced many inhabitants of Magna Graecia to abandon their
prosperous coastal cities and take refuge in mountain hill towns.
The domination of the Roman Empire brought a measure of sta-
bility, though Magna Graecia lost its freedom as well as its economic and artistic stature. When Rome fell a millennium later,
southern Calabria came under the control of the Byzantine
Empire. This ensured the continuity of Greek language and learning, but offered little protection from the wave upon wave of
Germanic warriors, Saracen raiders, Norman knights, Turkish crusaders, and Bourbon troops that ravaged the area. Other invaders

wielded not the sword, but a chalice and a cross. The Papacy systematically persecuted the Grecanici for their Greek Orthodox faith, driving them deep into the mountains to worship in hidden chapels. Bova, the last holdout of Orthodoxy, was forcibly converted to Roman Catholicism in 1573.

In the snug central *piazza* of Bova, I meet Carmelo Nucera, a native Bovese and the town's former mayor, who has agreed to be my guide in the Aspromonte. He leads me through the town's maze of cobbled alleyways and small cottages that seem to have sprung directly from the granite slopes. Street signs are bilingual, both in Greek and Italian, an initiative Carmelo took to emphasize the proud history of Bova—or "Vùa," the Grecanico name, which he prefers. He points out churches dedicated to saintly Greek Orthodox monks. From the 6th century on, these black-robed holy men from the East founded churches and monasteries throughout the area, in which they preserved intellectual treasures of the Byzantine Empire that had long since disappeared from Western Europe. The greatest treasure of all was their language, key to the knowledge of ancient Greece, which catalyzed the Renaissance. When Petrarch and Boccaccio wanted to learn Greek, they hired Calabrian monks as tutors. In those times, southern Calabria was rich in worldly as well as spiritual goods, renowned for its silks, honey, minerals, and fertile farmlands.

Now Calabria is the poorest region in Italy, and the Grecanico area is the most destitute of all Calabria. Though they have withstood countless hostile invaders, the Grecanici now falter before their most unforgiving enemy: the modern world. Mass media has steadily eroded the Grecanico language and culture, which the Italian government—despite Article 6 of the Italian Constitution that mandates the preservation of ethnic minorities—does little to protect. Since World War II, most young Grecanici have moved to Reggio and the North of Italy in search of work, losing touch with their past. Signs of this slow hemorrhage are visible in Bova.

Despite their current poverty and desolate future, the people are famous for their hospitality. Before heading back into the mountains, I get my first taste of Grecanico customs: lunch in a local home. When we arrive, the table is already laden with the appetizer, a smorgasbord of homemade salamis, ruby-red tomatoes dried in the sun, ugly little olives with a refined, complex flavor, marinated porcini mushrooms eaten one by one on a toothpick, and creamy *musulupo*, goat's cheese molded into five neat domes to resemble a Byzantine church. Then, riding on a luscious breeze from the kitchen, comes the main course: *capra alla pecurara*, a whole yearling goat slow-cooked in its own skin on a pit fire. Dessert consists of fresh figs, cottage cheese blended with orange blossom honey, and an enormous *'nugute*, a rich pastry with six boiled eggs cooked—unpeeled—inside. This last dish appears to have a long history: vases discovered in nearby Locri Epizephyrii, one of the capitals of Magna Graecia, portray women in graceful robes carrying trays of pastries with eggs imbedded in them. Certainly the *philoxenia* (sacred hospitality) of the ancient Greeks continues among the Grecanici.

With the bitterness of the crowning espresso on our tongues, we climb aboard a battered Fiat 4x4 and drive uphill out the back end of town. The gravel track loops and tightropes along sheer precipices. Carmelo stops occasionally to explain points of interest, which show the intimate tie between the Grecanici and nature. We encounter clumps of coarse green grass sprinkled with fragrant yellow flowers. This is *ginestra*, a species of broom that a few old women still

---

*I*talians do diet—but not quite as we do. For almost any ailment, one is told to go on a "white diet"—veal, chicken, rice (and, depending on your physician, white wine)—a low-cholesterol diet; but just as Italians don't have the same relationship to food that we have, they appear not to have the same diseases. Just as gout is an English ailment—everything is in the terminology—Italians (like the French, I am told) are forever having *crisi di fegato* (crisis of the liver).

◆

—Barbara Grizzuti Harrison,
Italian Days

weave at the *argalio* ("loom," a Homeric word), miraculously producing wedding dresses and silky soft blankets from its rough stalks. There are enormous rock monoliths with fantastical shapes, which are enshrouded in centuries of folk legend. We see Pentedattilo, Greek for "Five Fingers," a granite outcropping in the shape of a giant hand where, on the night of April 14, 1686, the noble Alberti family was ambushed in their castle by a rival clan and slaughtered. (Tradition has it that their bloody handprints are still visible on the stone.)

As we proceed, the gravel road deteriorates to clay, and the clay to mud. Tiny, precariously perched villages appear above us. Their names—Condofuri, Gallicianò, Ghorio—are pure Greek, for this is the heart of Grecanico territory. Though most residents speak Italian or the Calabrian dialect, their first language remains Grecanico, a close relation to classical Greek. We stop briefly in each town and climb a rutted track to the main *piazza,* under the watchful eyes of the villagers.

A small group of men is always waiting silently in the square. The Grecanici are solemn and reserved, with a hint of melancholy about them and a hesitance to make eye contact that at first seems mistrustful. Yet after Carmelo's slow, formal introductions, they flash a brief smile of unmistakable warmth and candor. Someone invites us to his home, and the village escorts us to the door. We all enter a cramped but immaculate dining room and find seats around a low table. Our host's family drifts in, and he introduces them one by one. Coffee and wine are served, and the family and village drink to our health.

Then our visit begins in earnest. Someone brings out a *tambureddu* (a drum strung with cat skin) and an *organetto* (a species of accordion), and people begin in pairs to dance the Tarantella. At my request they recite poems in Grecanico, shyly and reluctantly at first, then with a growing rush of confidence. It is a sharp, impenetrable language, with hidden melodies and gentle simplicity, like the landscape in which they live.

On the walls are images and icons of saints: San Rocco, San Pantaleone, and especially San Leo, patron saint of the

Aspromonte. The saints of the Grecanici are those of the Greek Orthodox Church, some of whom do not figure in the Roman Catholic calendar. The Grecanici remain fiercely loyal to their ancestral protectors, nonetheless. On feast days they hold elaborate processions, bearing three-ton reliquaries in silver and gold up and down the hilly streets. Some of their ceremonies have even older, pre-Christian origins. On Palm Sunday the Grecanici come to church with life-sized dolls woven from olive branches, evident holdovers of pagan fertility cults. During marriage rites, the women of the village proceed from the bride's house to the groom's, balancing the objects of the trousseau on their heads; identical scenes appear in *pinakes* friezes of the 5th century B.C. excavated in Locri.

The next village on our route is Roghudi, on the Amendolea River. We stop at a widening in the road that overlooks the town and the surrounding river valley. The broad stony bed of the Amendolea rolls through misty mountains to the coast, clearing a gap in which we glimpse the unearthly blue-green of the Ionian Sea. Beyond is the snow-covered cone of Mt. Etna, on nearby Sicily. Smoke trails from its active crater. Directly beneath us is Roghudi, whitewashed houses distributed along a knife-sharp ridge.

In the streets and squares there is no movement, no sound except the whistle of swifts, the lonesome bray of a donkey somewhere on the opposing cliff, the roar of the river.

Looking closer, I see that many windows are broken, their torn drapes flapping in the wind.

Carmelo explains that the village was abandoned in 1973 when a catastrophic flood put an end to a century-long battle against depopulation and the elements. We walk down into the town, past colorful doors thrown open to reveal scenes of domestic life suddenly stilled: tables set with dusty crockery, kettles rusting on the stove. Word is that someone still lives in Roghudi, an octogenarian who cannot bear to leave his native home. There is no sign of him, only swooping swallows, bats fluttering in the darkened houses, and a one-eyed sheepdog that watches us warily from a distance.

In the small main square, identical to the others we have visited, a grapevine climbs fresh and green up a rotting wooden trellis. Carmelo stops a moment to look. This is the fate that awaits all Grecanico villages, his beloved Bova included, unless something is done to halt the demographic decline of the region. In the last 30 years alone, five Greek-speaking villages have been abandoned. Though no one knows exactly how many native speakers remain, they cannot number much above 2,000.

We drive past the last village into the wilderness of Aspromonte, where even our sturdy 4x4 struggles on the crumbling grade. Eventually we come upon a lone house set back in a grove of chestnuts. A squat, powerful man with the face of a Renaissance *condottiero* emerges, his worn work clothes smeared with a glistening substance, and offers me a hand as hard as a horn. He is Don Domenico, who cultivates bees in these isolated mountains, continuing a tradition of apiculture that has existed here for thousands of years. He shows us his hives. Then, in typical local fashion, offers us copious quantities of homemade sausage, packs of honeycombs, and cupfuls of a delicious wine made from fermented honey that, he explains with a twinkle in his eye, will let us live 100 years. Afterward, we tour some of the ruined Orthodox monasteries and churches near his home. Some we enter, only to find moldering altars, battered and forgotten saints.

All around us stands one of the densest and most pristine forests in Europe, which is now a national park, the Parco Nazionale dell'Aspromonte.

*T*he farmer's daughter
arose early at dawn,
with her flock and her crook
took some wool to be spun.

She had in her flock
a sheep and a billy-goat
and a bull and a heifer.
An ass and a nanny-goat.

She saw a scholar sitting
underneath the tree.
"What are you doing, sir?
Come and play with me."

◆

—Carmina Burana, "Farmer's Daughter" (1150 A.D.)

We pass tall, silent groves of beech, fir, larch, and Phoenician juniper—the primordial vegetation that the Greeks and Romans would have found. Wild boars, otters, peregrine falcons, and Bonelli's eagles live here; in the winter, Don Domenico hears the lonely howl of wolves that descend from the peaks in search of prey.

As evening approaches, we take our leave and head for the sanctuary of San Giovanni Theristìs. Though it is only 40 kilometers to the north, no roads lead over the mountains, so we have to return to the coastal highway. We drive along in the failing light, the blue of the water shading slowly into purple, then dusky gray. Carmelo is less talkative now. When we turn back into the mountains at Monasterace, I ask about the church we are to visit. What makes it different from the others we have seen? Carmelo smiles faintly, then looks quickly away, Calabrian fashion. "This one is different—you will see," he says. "It is a new beginning." He does not explain further.

When we arrive, the full moon sits like a round of goat's cheese on the far mountains. In its milky light we see the ruins of a church. A figure in a full black gown and skullcap stands beside it, waiting. He is Father Kosmàs, a Greek Orthodox hermit who moved from Mount Athos, the spiritual heartland of his religion, to this secluded place two years ago. When I ask him why, he smiles and strokes his grizzled beard, his dark eyes amused, then glances wordlessly away—just as a Calabrian would do, evidence of enduring parallels between the two races. Instead of answering, he suggests a tour of the church, dedicated to St. Giovanni Theristìs, a Greek saint venerated for centuries in this area before the Vatican exterminated Orthodoxy. Once this was a dignified church in clean yellow sandstone, with an adjoining monastery housing dozens of monks. All that remains today is the ruined, roofless shell. Father Kosmàs steps through a hole in the east wall and turns into the apse.

It is like entering another world. In the shadowy bowl of the apse, which I now see has been carefully restored, candles burn beneath dozens of glowing golden icons, giving the church the warmth of a hearth. As we speak an owl watches with black liquid eyes from a nest it has made on the wall. Lighting another candle, Father Kosmàs holds it up to the central icon of Giovanni Theristìs. The priest-artist who painted this icon, he says, prayed and fasted for a week, then let the Holy Spirit guide his hand in successive applications of egg yolk, wine vinegar, ochre, and animal bladder. Greek Orthodoxy was restored in this sanctuary on February 24, 1995, and Father Kosmàs now worships here daily. I imagine the haunting polyphonic chorus of the Orthodox liturgy echoing once more in the rough stone apse after a silence of four centuries, then spiraling upward with the candle smoke like the incense and hymns of a Greek temple into the open sky above.

This is what Carmelo means by a new beginning. Despite the precarious condition of the Grecanici, a few determined people like Father Kosmàs have started to rebuild the Grecanico culture and are fighting to preserve it. Filippo Condemi, a successful big-city psychiatrist born to a poor Grecanico family in Gallicianò, has written a grammar of the language and is working to have it introduced in elementary schools. Bruno Casile, a farmer from Bova who became a self-taught poet, continues despite his advanced years to sing the rage and determination of his forgotten people in their ancient tongue. Carmelo Nucera himself has devoted his life to the Grecanici, among whom he grew up. He organizes music festivals, forges ties with Greek sister cities, and campaigns for legal recognition of the Grecanici as an ethnic minority.

Even a few of the younger people are beginning to take pride in customs and traditions that have long been a source of shame to them. Mimmo Cúppari and Pasquale Valle lead tours of the Grecanico region, during which participants stay with local families and learn about their crafts and foods. Leo Zindato heads a new agricultural cooperative that grows the prized mushrooms of the Aspromonte. Each of these lone defenders is working with desperate energy, knowing that the Grecanico culture is on the verge of extinction.

In the silence of the darkened church, Father Kosmàs speaks. "You asked why I came here. I came at the direction of my spiritual adviser, whom I assisted at his deathbed in a cell on Mount

Athos. For hours at a time he lay silent, his eyes closed, barely breathing. Just before he rejoined the Father, however, light returned to his eyes. He began to celebrate our glorious saints who lived and died in Calabria, the many miracles they worked here. Southern Calabria, you see, is a holy land for us."

Father Kosmàs is watching me now, with a look as searching as the owl on the wall, as powerful as the icons that surround us. His voice has a new intensity. "Suddenly he grasped my hand. 'Go!' he said, 'Return to the land of our saints. Begin a new life there. For darkness now reigns in Aspromonte, but it is from Aspromonte that the sun will rise again.'"

This is what Father Kosmàs believes. It is what the other people who are fighting for the Grecanico way of life, in one way or another, hope some day to see. Time will tell whether the sun will indeed rise once more for the Grecanici or whether they will slip, as they seem on the verge of doing, into a final, lasting darkness.

Tom Mueller also contributed "Underground Rome" in Part Two.

★

What opened Augustine's heart to Latin literature was Virgil's _Aeneid,_ the literary masterpiece of the Roman world, its Bible and its Shakespeare in one. The _Aeneid_ is a conscious literary epic, not a folk epic like the Greek _Iliad_. Picking up where Homer leaves off—with the fall of Troy to the Greek forces, who penetrate its impregnable walls by the "gift" of a huge hollow horse lined with armed men—Virgil recounts the exploits of his hero, Aeneas, son of Venus and a Trojan father. _"Arma virumque cano"_ ("I sing of arms and the man"), begins Virgil in a great trumpet fanfare. As all Virgil's readers could savor with thrilling foreknowledge, Aeneas will miraculously escape the certain doom of burning Troy, faithfully carrying his ancient father on his back and holding his little son by the hand. A wanderer, he is received with high celebration by the queen of Carthage, who is riveted by his tale. Dido and Aeneas are fated to fall passionately in love, but Aeneas always knows—as does the reader—that, though it will break Dido's heart and end her life, he must move bravely on to his destiny, the founding of the City of Rome.

Virgil wrote in the age of Caesar Augustus, the first emperor, and he conceived the *Aeneid* as a national epic (the only completely successful one in world literature), orchestrated artfully to evoke in the reader a wave of patriotism for the great empire's heroic beginnings. This younger, less seasoned civilization of the Latin west, having absorbed, both politically and culturally, the lofty civilization of the Greek east, needed to establish its own legitimacy to rule and to overwhelm.

—Thomas Cahill, *How the Irish Saved Civilization: The Untold Story of Ireland's Heroic Role from the Fall of Rome to the Rise of Medieval Europe*

LAURA J. AYMOND

✦ ✦ ✦

Sleepwalking in Italy

Discovering ties that bind.

HE COULD HAVE BEEN MY BIRTH BROTHER, SLOUCHED AGAINST
the wall of the ski lodge in the alpine sun. Eyes closed in apparent
oblivion, he strummed a black and white guitar and his voice quiv-
ered with longing to Italian lyrics that rippled over my skin like
golden olive oil. Although I couldn't understand the words, my
feet refused to move me further through the glittering sugary
snow, and I stood spellbound at the summit between two worlds.
At my back was France, a country I'd traversed with tunnel vision,
focused only on the winding road that led me up into thin air that
stung my lungs with pleasurable pain and left me teetering on the
brink of Italy.

He could have been my birth brother, but of course I knew he
wasn't. His features were nothing like mine—rounded cheeks and
nose, a head of fuzzy caramel-colored hair, the lopsided grin when
he saw me watching him and smiled. It was a fantasy I'd played out
in the theatre of my imagination for years, meeting my biological
family face to face. Realizing a connection I had never known,
seeing a face that mirrored mine, feeling in the motion of their
hands and fingers the others that had come before them and before them. A long rope of solidly twined humans whose feet had

328

moved them through the ages of the ancient turning earth. And here I was, in the Italy of my ancestors, my own feet walking the same ground theirs had walked.

He stood, motioned me to him and I suddenly felt ridiculous, felt my throat throb with heat under my turtle neck sweater. What would I say to explain away my transfixed posture, my unblinking dreamy stare, as if I had just witnessed the miracle of *The David* or the Sistine Chapel?

"Andiamo, Savino!" Two young men and a woman called to him from a tarnished and dented compact car in the parking area, where they clipped their skis on the roof rack. He shouted something over his shoulder at them and turned to me as I approached the stone wall of the lodge. His face was cherubic, cheeks flushed with sun and singing.

"Ciao!" he said, and pointed to the car with a hooked thumb and raised eyebrows. I accepted the ride. It was that simple. But the drive itself was another matter, as complex as the switchback turns, as confident as the driver of his inborn Italian ability to fly. How simple it all was, I thought, as we careened on two wheels around bends and bounced blithely over dips in the road. How simple it had been to come halfway around the world, to find myself in the back seat of a car with four Italians blooming with youth and high expectations, bound for a mountain village whose name held magic in its flowing name. Triana, Triana by the river roaring out the back door.

Their few words of English, plus my few of Italian, plus much miming was a formula for eloquent and meaningful conversation such as I had rarely experienced in my 23 years on the planet. Desire. That was the missing element in so many other conversations, I discovered. For if you truly needed to understand and be understood, and if the desire was mutual, conversation was a most creative and satisfying medium of exchange.

The tiny house was made of stone the color of golden beach sand, leaning slightly toward the river as if to more clearly hear its murmuring secrets. The village houses huddled like penitents about the skirts of mother church in the diminutive central plaza.

A cracked ancient fountain was set in its heart, lined with a lat-
ticework of plane trees. Old men slumped in folding wooden
chairs against the sienna-tinted wall of a cafe, absorbing the pale
mountain sunlight of spring. The voices of women and children
and canaries blended, trilling and bantering, laughing and wailing.
Banners of color flapped between houses like flags as women
draped in black hung out their wash. The air was scented with
crushed pine needles and the gunmetal smell of snow, thick sweet
coffee and baking bread.

As I walked, a sleepwalker in a joyful dream, the flowing cadence of my ancestors' native tongue flickered through me like
fireflies in the dark. Church bells tolled, their solemn voices vibrating my rib cage as they floated past me down the long valley,
notes dispersing like fragile ice crystals melting. I searched every
face for a glimmer of myself, spoke to every person I came upon,
and was rewarded tenfold. I found myself in their strong features,
in the shape of their eyes, on some mysterious level understood the
words rolling from their tongues like strains of mandolin music
that had always stirred me. It seemed I had always known these
things, as well as I knew the scent of my own skin. I had always
known them. By heart.

I stayed at Triana three days. Three blissful days of camaraderie
and fishing in the river, playing music together, singing Italian folk
songs that sent vibrations of buried memory skittering up my
spine. We turned the days and nights upside down, ate spaghetti for
breakfast and coffee and pastries for dinner. My friends taught me
some Italian phrases and I taught them some English folk song
lyrics. We had supper with Savino's parents and they accepted me
like a daughter.

Then it was time for me to move on, for my friends to return
to their work. We were resting from playing soccer at a park near
the train station in Torino. Suddenly Savino and Pietro jumped up
and ran to the ticket booth, then disappeared into a grocery on the
corner. A few moments later they emerged grinning and handed
me a bottle of wine and a loaf of warm bread. I should not travel

alone, they told me. They had friends in Florence, and would accompany me to their home.

We descended the spine of the country, rippling with hills studded with crow's nest villages the color of eggshell. We sang until the last ray of light glazed the terra-cotta roof tiles with gold. The train rocked us like a cradle with its metallic lullaby, and their eyelids flickered with dreams, their crossed legs stretched out on my lap. Like brothers.

Laura J. Aymond is a freelance writer who lives in rural Washington state. She has met one brother from the Italian side of her biological family, and has five more siblings and a birthmother she hopes to know. A pilgrimage to her birthfather's village in Greece will bridge her ongoing journey of the heart. She is currently at work on a collection of travel essays, short fiction, and a novel that traces a woman's quest for family and heritage.

✳

We walk
Between the high poplars
Along the banks
Shimmering emerald, opaque.
We have arrived at the island.
There is nothing
More beautiful than this:
Here it is
That the Fibreno opens
Like a bird's beak.
Here is my real home
And my brother's too.
From here we spring
From ancient stock;
Here all that we call holy,
Here our relations,
Here so many memories
Of our ancestors.

—Cicero, *De Legibus*

PART FOUR

IN THE SHADOWS

✳ ✳ ✳

Satyric

Satyrs still prowl Tuscany.

ART IS OFTEN A DISEASE THAT LIFE ACQUIRES BY CONTAGION. A month later, while Maro and I were down in Sicily taking part in a group exhibition, the agricultural helpmate beside whom I've worked for years assaulted Georgina, my second daughter's best friend.

He joined us six or seven years ago, replacing a bent old saint no longer able to keep the olive trees trimmed. As large and energetic as the former had been cowed, Furbuffo had the little terraces in order within a year.

He fired once more our torpid agricultural ambitions. Together we reclaimed a hillside gone wild thirty years before, cut the tangled broom to the ground, nourished the self-seeded oaks. Planted pine and ilex among the crumbled stones of fallen eighteenth-century walls. Recently he had grown ambitious about the dark wood itself, dragging the plough among the oaks, making harassed paths southwards through the trees.

Stones were his bane. His ambition was to clear the whole farm of them, lifting the jagged fragments of sedimentary limestone, *galestro* and *albarese*, into the cart, and creating a private pyramid in the corner of a remote field. From time to time we would hear

335

him, even in high summer, making a crash in the middle distance like a small building falling down a cliff.

In my studio he would lift heads of stone, and wooden figures six foot high, as if they were dolls. He told me where they would look good, and would take them in his arms to the ideal spot against a background of foliage.

Everything about him was on a Homeric scale, even his voice. Maro would point outside if ever he tried to talk to her in the house. At which he would shout, "*Si, Si,*" so that the whole downstairs boomed, then flinch and raise his hand to his mouth as if trying to grab the words in the air, even as they left his throat.

Georgina on the other hand was with us briefly for the first part of her year out. A substitute daughter for us, in a mood of self-absorption, doing nothing during the time of year that used to be term-time. The last sweet flavour of childhood before the ornate gateway of university, and beyond it the real world. A dreamer.

And then she was stumbling over the wet fields, hysterical, the mood of quietness shattered. He looking after her, pale eyes protruding from reddened features, a worried frown, making as if to follow, to explain. Gesturing after her with a hand like a clawless bear. Suddenly glimpsing him through Georgina's eyes, I could see Furbuffo as terrifying.

Maro and I had a day or two in which to run through this imagined movie in our heads, music-less and jittery, with no facts to go on but that she had abandoned the house in a thunderstorm and had been saved by a friend who happened to be passing by, after goodness knows what kind of phone calls for help, conducted publicly in poor Italian at the local bar.

I was furious with him. I cannot even call him by his real name, or choose an innocuous one. Furbuffo let him be, both tragic and crafty, feigning innocence and avoiding the direct confrontation, like the baritone of misfortune in an opera buffa.

I telephoned him late at night from the desk of a third-class hotel in Sciacca, the night the exhibition opened, drunk and inarticulate, staring wildly at the ceiling of stencilled cherubim. "Shame," I said. The night porter was used to such scenes and remained aloof. "Shame on you, shame on our household. What have you done? How dare you?" I let my accusations flash down the wires as imprecisely as possible, having nothing substantial to go on. Alcohol and disgust spurred me. It was two in the morning and far from home, with the bags of surreptitious weekenders hidden under the potted greenery in the hall, waiting for an early start.

I have never felt less English. There are things you do not do if you come from the frigid isle. You do not telephone an employee at two in the morning upon an unconfirmed rumour of rape, yelling your sense of grief and squalor out into the night. Some instinct must have told me that if I kept quiet, Furbuffo would take my silence as acquiescence. Any responsibility he might have felt would evaporate with the passing days. Incoherent chastisement at long distance was what he would have expected if his employer was, as for a moment I felt, Italian.

His voice quavered. Down the crackling telephone line I heard it echo about the concrete corridor of the council house on the outskirts of the little town, by the slaughterhouse, above the main road. "I never! Who has been telling lies about me? What has she said? Nothing took place—nothing, I tell you. What! I hold you in all possible respect, Signor Matteo. I would never permit myself..."

"*What has she said?*" That was enough to make me feel that something had in fact taken place.

Trembling, I smoked a cigarette with the hall porter.

A trace memory came back to me of an incident that occurred some years ago, on the Ponte Vecchio in Florence. As Maro and I were admiring the Christmas jewellery, I noticed that a young man near by had his hand deep in her bag. Now I consider myself a man of peace, so it was with surprise that I noticed that my left hand was around his throat, and that I was raising him slowly from the ground. Is it normal, I yelled, for you to put your hand in the pockets of others? Is it? My thumb was on his artery. A semicircle of curious people instantly made a theatre around us. His face changed from mild concern to incredulous fear, to panic. He realized he was about to be throttled.

At this point a thought went through my head. Am I overacting? Is this fascism? I dropped him, and he was gone. The crowd, mildly perturbed, returned to its earlier ebb. My wife and I fluttered at each other like poultry after a quick brush with the weasel. It took us some minutes to subside.

"My man!" said Maro comforting. "Now why can't you do things like that more often?"

I was shocked by my own violence, by the realization that I *enjoyed* the thief's fear. What qualities of reason of detachment in my soul could outweigh this reflex of pure violence?

So again I thought, why, this is fascism, as I turned from the hall and walked upstairs. The unclear accusation, the sense of large disaster, betrayal, *brutta figura*, my voice echoing in the foyer of a large hotel, his in *a casa popolare*, bound by seven years of agricultural cooperation now gone in a whisk, a whimper.

We came back by water, from Palermo to Viareggio across the inland sea. The air was sullen and milky as we docked, the port stacked with slabs of concrete as if the war were not yet over. We entered the long valley between the sea and Florence through a tangle of small industries that were gradually devouring the marshy land, with marine birds feeding among the sedge behind the wire periphery of future factories.

"Let us take the slow way back," said Maro quietly. "It is so much prettier."

Prettier, and ten times as long—that was the point. The slow road to postpone a showdown. O Christ! The late morning shuffled quickly in the pack, and it seemed to grow dark some few minutes after we penetrated the hills. The sky was deep blue over the pines above Poggibonsi. Slit eyes appeared in the windows of the new bank, illuminated by lights switched on automatically at dusk.

"Better step on it," Maro said after our subdued day's drive, "he might go home. I'll drive on to collect Georgina"—who was staying with a friend.

I caught him at the door, making for his gutted Fiat.

I sacked him immediately. No excuse, no explanation accepted. Out! There was no other way to discover what had taken place. Boil a small hard fact out of seething grandiloquence.

"I trusted you," I said, making as if to shoo him away. "I do not yet know, do not want to know, what you did to the poor girl. For me it is enough that within two days of leaving you in charge, you frighten her so badly that she runs away into the fields at night, runs to the village and telephones England. Phones England! Do you realize how frightened her parents must have been? What am I to say to them? What am I to say to her father? Her father! How can I look him in the eye, ever again?"

"*O Signor Matteo!* I cannot tell why she ran away like that! For me it is a complete mystery. Perhaps she suddenly felt ill!"

His eyes wet and protruding, the whole of him glazed with anxious sweat. He was trying to tell me that Georgina lied to me. I was so furious I could not speak. Seeing this, he changed tactics instantly.

"No, no! That is…Nothing happened! Nothing at all!"

"I only hope that this is true. I am sure it is true! You are at heart a good person and I am sure you would never do anyone any harm. I'm certain of it! Even now, I still would be glad to trust you, if I dared. But it is not for me to say. Do you realize how dangerous these things are? If her father asks for an explanation, what do I tell him? They know their daughter well, know that she does not imagine things. She showed no fear when we left her here in the house alone, the day we left."

And, with heavier overtones, "These are questions, Furbuffo which entail inquires by the authorities. These stories touch upon the jail!"

"Truly," said Furbuffo, shouting as quietly as he could, "I showed her only the greatest respect, of that I can assure you. Never in my life have I harmed another. Never. I have never done any wickedness towards anyone. Never!"

His brother came in from the fields. A remarkable pair in their way, working until a time of night when even an owl would find it hard to see, singing among the terraces in the dark.

An hour later Furbuffo sank to his knees.

"Ever since you shouted at me," he said, "I have not felt in good health. Ever since you woke me at two in the morning, the day afterwards. Woke the whole house! The whole *palazzo*! The children crying, my wife asking what the matter was—she knows nothing—why I was so upset. They could all see I was upset. That I was suffering. And now what am I to tell them?"

A mans iratus multa mentitur sibi.

An angry lover tells himself many lies.

◆

—Publius Syrius

"But Furbuffo," I said, fairly amazed, "we are surely not here to talk about your suffering."

"I have not slept! I come in from work and I sit by the fire, and I start crying because I am so uneasy, and the children ask me, "*Babbo*, why are you crying? Why are you so nervous?"

Eyes squeezed tight by red cheeks as meaty as biceps, limp hair cut short, curling like weeds in a current. Huge hands one held within another, stout fingers with broken nails; or waving them at me palm forwards, in some attempt to placate, to worship. He was begging me for forgiveness by showing me his wounds.

His brother unfolded his crossed arms and said calmly that at this point he might as well tell me exactly what happened. A look of mingled doubt and calculation came into Furbuffo's eyes: was this the winning strategy? "All right," he said at last, getting up and coming close, looking me in the eyes.

"I was changing the wine, right? And we needed a pot from the kitchen, something with a handle so that I could get the dregs in the bottom of the vat, right? So I came into the kitchen and asked the Signorina if I could take one. But she did not answer me. Maybe she did not understand. So I followed her, and I found her standing in the studio upstairs, and I asked her again, if we could take this pot, and she said finally yes. And then I saw her standing there, and she looked so pretty that—just to indicate that I admired her very much—so I asked her if I could give her a kiss. Well! The Signorina perhaps, you know, doesn't understand Italian very well, so she said again to me yes. And so I did. But no more than this..."

Stepping forward, he gave me a fairly chaste kiss on the cheek, perhaps a little near the mouth, but all the same a fairly straightforward buss.

Relieved, but also flabbergasted, I said, "But how on earth could you accept her yes as being sincere, *voluto*, when you yourself say that she could not speak Italian? Good God, she had only been in the country for about three days! What sort of a welcome—what hospitality! Of course she did not understand what you were saying!"

"Ah, but I meant it with all respect," he said. "And she did say yes."

A look of reasonable cunning, as of "I'm trying to help you," came over his face. Then seeing me getting really angry he mumbled, "But it was nothing, really nothing."

So saying he stepped forward and kissed me again.

"Do stop it," I said, wiping my face with the back of my hand. "Believe me, I can see your point!"

"Ah, so you see! It was really nothing!"

"Look," I said, trying to sum up for him, "the kiss may have been nothing special in itself, and you can thank all the saints that I believe you, and that it went no further than that...In fact we can all be incredibly relieved, it seems to me."

Then I tried to repeat the theme of having taken advantage of Georgina's lack of Italian. But it was hard to concentrate. In the back of my mind it occurred to me that a defence lawyer could make a lot of mileage out of her puzzled *Si*.

Half-hearted he took another step towards me.

"No, no," I said, "please don't kiss me again. I don't think I could stand a third."

Once again he showed his respect for my inviolable personage by showing me the palms of his hands, and stood there dumbly awaiting the word that all was right again.

"You both tell me that you are fundamentally a good boy, and I believe you," at which he nodded five times and repeated *Si*.

If it weren't for his size, looking at him standing there so hopeful and self-pitying, I could almost believe him innocuous. But it was not a question of uncontrollable desire, still less of calculation. He was a victim of something much more primitive: the incapacity to think forward, to imagine even a very immediate future. How easily it might have gone further, I thought. From one thing to another, via misunderstanding, smothered panic, in an upstairs room.

"So you see," said the brother as I stood silent, "now that you know, it's all over. There! That was simple wasn't it?"

"What do you mean?" I said, aware that in my reverie I had missed some important cue. "Not at all. I am very happy to hear that nothing serious took place, but this does not affect the betrayal of trust which you made to me, the moment my back was turned."

It took a moment or two for Furbuffo to realize that forgiveness was not inevitable, would never take place. With a huge shout he collapsed on to the floor again and to my horror started to beat his head against the tiles. The whole room boomed and echoed, his sinal cavity by chance awakening some sympathetic voice in the plumbing under the floor.

"I am finished," he said. "You might as well kill me right now, here as I lie at your feet. I am a man who has been utterly destroyed. *Un uomo finito*. How can I go home tonight and face my family? What will they say at work? What will they say in the village?"

"Good Lord," I said, "you don't mean to tell me you have been telling everyone all about it?

"No, no," he said quickly. "But, with all due respect, the Signora Maro won't be able to keep it a secret. O! With all respect, you know how she is."

"The Signora Maro will keep it quiet."

"But what can I say to the others, to explain that I have lost my job?"

"You say as little as possible, and put all the blame on us. Say we have lost millions on the stock exchange! Have to save our pennies for something else, some other luxury."

The brother and I exchanged glances. I took comfort from his calmness.

Furbuffo instead seemed unable to face up to it.

"But I enjoy working here!"

"I know you do, and it's great to have you here."

He brightened.

"But unfortunately it is just not possible...I don't know how to choose the words with which to tell you this."

Hearing himself rejected yet again, he set about banging his head on the floor again, at which I suddenly lost my temper.

"Oh, for the love of heaven stop breaking my handmade tiles with your forehead! Can't you understand? These are things which involve a denouncement, a trial, even prison. I am not going through all this confrontation because I dislike you or reject you or whatever. Surely you can see that there are some objective standards at stake?"

He flailed about on the floor, wailing.

"What about your own daughter," I screamed.

Face down, he mumbled, "But she's only thirteen!"

By this time a part of me was engaged with the fantasy of making out a denouncement in front of Tiripepe, the *Brigadiere di Carabinieri* down in the township, in formalese, including my mother's Christian name and the crime all in one long sentence. Identity and act between neat consecutive commas, sworn before the silver grenade in flames.

"Get up," I shouted. I felt like kicking him. "Get up off my floor! We've been here for over two hours—I arrived at five-forty and it's now ten to eight—and you still cannot see that you've done something wrong. You are just concerned about your job! There's nothing more I can say to you, save perhaps give you a good beating."

Instantly he was up. "Oh yes yes yes," he said, and went outside, coming back in a moment with what to him was a light wand, and to me was the trunk of one of the large olive trees that had died in the frost, one of the pile waiting outside the back door for the buzz-saw and the axe.

"Beat me," he said. "Beat me hard hard hard, and when you have beaten me we will leave, go home, sleep soundly and in the morning all will be forgotten. This terrible thing that has happened to us," he said, as if inflicted by fate from outside. "Beat me as hard as you like, I shan't complain."

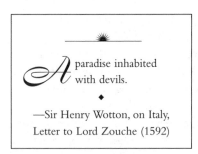

A paradise inhabited with devils.

♦

—Sir Henry Wotton, on Italy,
Letter to Lord Zouche (1592)

I told him I could not speak to him any further. Could certainly not beat him. That I was speaking ironically. I was joking, I said. An incredulous look came into his eyes, that I could be so heartless at a time like this, at his expense.

"Put it back," I said. I had to keep it simple. "Put back the log, please. Nobody here can lift it but you."

A moment of calm came over us as he came back into the room. He seemed finally to have accepted it.

"If I had known it would end like this," he said sadly, "I would have done much more."

I did not like the sound of this.

"I mean, if I was to lose my job anyway."

I thought swiftly that I had better not inquire quite what he meant, risking still murkier depths.

"After all," he mumbled, "the postman in Montecaio with that English schoolteacher who was here for the summer, the blond one…"

(Goddammit! All English girls are longing for it the moment they step off the plane, aren't they just?)

"And to think I took such care, during August, to treat all the young *signorine* with respect. I did not even look at them! Why, when they were sunning themselves by the pool, I would drive all the way around the vineyard with my tractor, a much longer way, so as not to observe them as they were lying there."

"Perhaps," I said, "you should refrain from telling me this."

"If only you knew how protective I was, when the Signorina Georgina was here alone. Why, the very afternoon you left, I came back at midnight to make sure that everything was in good order. The *signorina* was in the house, I could see her. She had not pulled the curtains, and I could observe her walking around inside, from room to room. And when a car came by with a hunter, I asked who he was, what he wanted, and sent him away, so that she would not be disturbed. I stayed until late, very late, all to make sure she was all right."

What extraordinary rooms had been opened in the primordial labyrinth of this man's mind by an act committed in my house? Whose person might I be risking in the future, by keeping the incident closed?

"Are you a religious man?" I asked him.

A devious look came into his eyes, down there on the floor below me. He admitted he was. "Why?"

"Because at this point I feel that the only thing that can be done is for you to confess everything to the priest. In fact I will make a deal with you. If your priest tells me that he thinks I have treated you unfairly, I shall consider taking you back."

Fair enough, I thought, given the circumstances.

Doubt still overcame him.

"But," he walked, "he's the biggest gossip in town!"

And so I had to give him a lecture about the secrecy of the confessional, and how the priest, if he betrayed it, would most certainly go to Hell, and roast. Him on his knees, and me talking about roasting in Hell...

With the help of his brother, he left at last, and I was able to telephone Maro and Georgina to say they could come back.

While waiting for them in the silent house, listening to the creak of the fridge and the birds on the roof settling down for the night, I suddenly became aware that Furbuffo was still out there, sitting in his car, perhaps trying to think of further things to say. This silent brooding touched me. I could imagine him, a huge man in a small dark car, trying to recapitulate the argument.

They missed each other by five minutes. The cars must have passed each other on the road. Don Bernabei telephoned us about four days later. I was delighted that Furbuffo had actually gone to see him, and arranged to talk with Don Bernabei himself a day or two later, taking Georgina with me.

She took great care in dressing for the occasion. Crisp white shirt with a small lace collar, suggesting a girl trained by adamantine nuns. This she starched to the consistency of transparent cardboard. Long black skirt, dark tights, shoes with a "sensible" bow. Tight black belt, so that the shirt stuck out. Her breasts alone below the hard creased linen were proof of immaculate innocence.

She kept me waiting, as the hour for the showdown with the priest drew near. At the upstairs mirror she removed with small white pads any trace of make-up that lingered from the urban day. Her lips needed no lipstick to improve their pinkness, her eyes required no lining. Then she changed mirrors, and I watched as with silent drama she combed her curly hair, in long persistent strokes.

Strange though this may seem, I had not yet asked for her own account of what had happened. Hesitantly I described to her Furbuffo's version of her recent experience. She looked at herself as I talked, kept combing, and gradually blushed.

I waited for her own account. None emerged. Georgina combed as I waited, and in the end I was left with nothing but the swish of the brush in her long curly hair, hypnotic, recurring, like waves ascending an estuary.

At length she gave herself a chaste centre parting and tied her hair in a tight knot behind, then pulled out one single curl as if it might have escaped from such severity all by itself.

Then to my amazement she removed from a small case an old rosary of mother-of-pearl and silver, with a diminutive crucifix at the end. This she twined around her neck and hid with the closed lace collar, to be perceived under the shirt, rather than seen. It had belonged to her grandmother apparently.

She turned to me and said, "How's that?"

Indeed, she seemed the very epitome of virginity.

We were late getting to Gaiole, and stood outside the church for a while in silence, listening to the evening Mass. The singing seemed weak and untuneful, the bare walls of the recent construction were unlikely ever to receive their marble facing. The Arizona cypress in the playground of the kindergarten had grown considerably since my children had been pupils there, and was crowding out the diminutive swing. There were new flats going up the hill.

We heard the service end, and the priest move from the sacristy to his private quarters without coming outside. Eventually Don Bernabei came to the door. He had intelligent eyes, and possessed a quality in common with certain saints that lie in glass cases beneath the altar, in that his teeth protruded.

He let us into a small room off the sacristy, with a large desk and some very full cupboards in the background. Faintly formal atmosphere, headmasterish. He seemed very pleased with Georgina, and stooped with an abrupt bow as we sat down, perhaps to see her better.

"This," Don Bernabei told me, placing his hand upon her knee, "this child is an innocent, as we can see."

Georgina nodded, sitting up straight.

"It is quite clear..." he said, and hesitated.

I would have thought it was quite clear that any red-blooded man would have had difficulty in keeping his hands off her.

"It is quite clear that this poor man has certain problems," he said, meaning Furbuffo. At which the conversation became serious, undistracted by the presence of Georgina, who continued to sit bolt upright on the hard-backed chair, eyes demurely down, nodding from time to indicate polite attention.

Sadness came over me as I listened to Don Bernabei. I had no idea that Furbuffo's background was quite so tortuous, or his family so beset by financial and emotional strains. The priest made a plea for Christian forgiveness, and for a moment I hesitated in my determination to be rid of a very valuable hired man.

That the girl herself had suffered, there was no doubt. That

Furbuffo was untrustworthy was irrefutable. There was not much that Don Bernabei could say that could move me. What made me hesitate was Georgina herself sitting quietly to my left, the innocent virgin dressed up as an innocent virgin. Her subtle revenge via starch and white linen. Perhaps she should not have made such an effort to dress the part.

When Don Bernabei had ended, I could do nothing but look at her, puzzled. The priest too seemed slightly mesmerized. At length I murmured, "A temptation."

He understood immediately what I was talking about.

And so I managed to make a small speech. I said that we were a family of artists, and that artists led lives which were in some ways unusual. In the summer the young lay about the lawn, dressed in very little, *con grande disinvoltura*, and now and again I would draw them, and they did not mind. Draw them, in a word, stark naked. A matter of studying anatomy and composition, of course, as he would surely understand. But that the atmosphere this created might be expected to confuse anyone whose background was more "traditional," so that a permissiveness might be felt where none existed. For in fact these young people, including this lady on my left, were in their way very serious (thank heavens!), brilliant in their exams, ambitious for their future.

All the time, I was thinking of the man in late autumn, ploughing the terraces in a biting north wind, cheerfully.

So that if we could by chance arrange this transaction between ourselves, as man to man, and little by little, I would be deeply grateful. By Christmas, he would have found something else, I was sure. For there was no question of him coming back before this young person (I gestured surreptitiously towards Georgina's white starched frontage) returned to her native land.

Don Bernabei looked down at the table and sighed.

Afterwards he insisted on giving her a bar of chocolate, from a small pile on a shelf in the kitchen. For me, a massive Vin Santo, causing instant hangover, even as it is drunk.

Georgina tried to refuse the chocolate, and looked so demure and pretty as she bowed to Don Bernabei, curls slightly falling forward around her face, that a viper would have turned sweet-toothed at the sight of her. Only later did it emerge that this was not more of her low-keyed mime, the innocent pretending to be innocent. She did, in fact, dislike milk chocolate. Another case of art and life intermingling.

A quiet six weeks passed by.

Furbuffo stayed away until the olive harvest, when, surrounded by peers in a far field, I felt I could not deny his presence without causing comment. It would be quite untrue to say we lived in a state of siege, even though there was something about the whole story which seemed to me never to have been brought into focus.

Getting the olives to the press coincided with a flurry of foul-weather, though the days were streaked with low sunlight in fine yellow bands. I slid across the road, crashed the car, remained alive. Rose at two in the morning to sit it out with the olives as they went under the press, while starting an eight-foot terracotta later the same day at the kiln in Castellina. Briefly, we came to one of those difficult moments in life when you are obliged to postpone inessentials, like sleep.

Maro went north, to Milan, and I was left alone with Georgina and the tanks of olive oil.

They were short of plastic tanks at the olive mill, so I tried to sell my oil in a hurry. One of the buyers was Franco, the man who supplied all the isolated houses like ours with gravel for the roads.

As we were bent over the scales together, pouring the green concentration of my fields into a small demijohn, he told me that up at his new job Furbuffo was telling everyone about his tussle with Georgina, in the hopes of gaining sympathy. What! And we'd tried so hard to keep it quiet, for his sake? "I know," said Franco. "He's mad. And of course his mates say he was completely in the wrong, shouldn't brood, should be grateful not to be in jail. But he keeps on about it!" (Franco, sniggering, made the bent column of oil wobble in the side of its plastic funnel.) "And so they have made a little song about it up there, you know, to tease him. When he comes in, in the morning, they sing it, and he gets angry. It is truly very amusing."

A song!

Two nights later I arrived back from a hard day at my statue to find the house dark, with no reply to my peremptory knock. Potatoes in one hand, stuffed pig's trotter in the other, the seasonal fare, abandoned at the woodstack as I tried to find a way in.

Brief panicky note on the scrubbed cypress table in the kitchen. The house dark and cold. "Gone to the neighbours. Come and get me. Furbuffo…"

My heart doubled up. Adrenalin, like a hailstorm at sea, crashed around my chest.

Telephone. Weak voice the other end.

"He looked in the window. I'm sure he did. I'm so sorry. Please come and get me."

Trace memory of Peter Pears in *The Turn of the Screw*, seen when I was twelve, staring in through the window, all fangs and ferocious desire. A sense of the unreasonable demands of life on a tired artist needing sleep. This rape we all fear; this child's anxiety. This menace. By what unfathomable chance had Furbuffo guessed that she was once again alone in the house, for half a day?

Light mist as I drove out again, among oak trees whose leaves had quite suddenly turned brown. Olive trees at the edge of the road, occasionally tatty, shorn of their fruit.

Georgina looked pale when I found her. It was no longer a question of dressing the part. She waited for me to speak, with a kind of tense vacancy, as if prepared to stand up to the most brutal interrogation.

Seeing her in such a state I felt could not, would not, try to get to the bottom of this new assault. The idea that Furbuffo was genuinely obsessed with her was terrible. I was fairly sure that it could not have been him she saw peering in the window. We talked of other things, and gradually she calmed herself, became more lively, less wan.

The house seemed large and remote at our return. A peasanty smell pervaded the ground floor, a phenomenon which strikes me whenever I feel tired or have been away for a while, as if the walls when left alone immediately revert to the ghosts which at some level must still inhabit them.

Georgina, I am sure, felt homesick for her parents, for home, for England. She went upstairs early, leaving me restless for a while, listening to the noises of the night. The imagined thrashing of a large man in the undergrowth. The night, the house itself, seemed to behave strangely. Observed with such attention, life can seem unfamiliar, your own self an intruder.

Yet when I went to sleep I did not dream of Furbuffo, but of a clump of strange scented cypress trees moving in a high wind, somewhere in the north of Japan.

Nymphs and satyrs have to make their own arrangements. To identify with them is not the business of mere humans. As in so many things, it is we who are on the outside peering in.

Matthew Spender also contributed "Seravezza" in Part Three. This piece was taken from his book Within Tuscany.

✻

> *Ahi serva Italia, di dolore ostello,*
> *Nave senze nocchiere in gran tempesta,*
> *Non donna di provincia, ma bordello!*

> Ah, slavish Italy! thou inn of grief!
> Vessel without a pilot in loud storm!
> Lady no longer of fair provinces,
> But brothel-house impure!
>
> —Dante, *Purgatorio*, c. 1310-21

⋆ ⋆ ⋆

Una Bustarella

A meditation on bribery.

THEY HAD SHOT GENERAL DALLA CHIESA, THE MAN WHO HAD defeated terrorism, the man the government had appointed to defeat the Mafia. About the same time a very close friend of mine paid his first bribe to a state official. These two facts are not perhaps entirely unrelated.

It's a complicated story, perhaps a little bit of a digression, but I'd like to tell it all the same because it shows how even the ingenuous foreigner who arrives here, as one arrives most places, more or less by chance can so easily run up against the dark side of Italy.

This was an extremely close friend of mine. Like me he had arrived in Italy some time before, like me he lived in a little village not far from a sizable town, like me he had slaved for a while with private lessons and commercial translations until good fortune had landed him one of the much-sought-after jobs teaching English at the university, a position offering a decent, steady income for work that is pleasant and not overly taxing. He was delighted. Now he could relax a little. No more the breathless hurry to get from one lesson to the next, only to find the student had canceled. No more the embarrassment of having to insist that patently rich people deign to pay one with a certain regularity. No more the smell of the correction fluid in the early hours while laboring over translations on the recycling of waste sludge in marble sawmills, the unsurpassable tourist attractions of the nearby town. He was home and dry.

But the contract they made him sign at the university was a strange one. Although to all intents and purposes an employee, in the sense that he had a timetable and certain well-established duties, he was in fact officially a free lance, the university retaining 18 percent of his income as tax (had he not had *residenza* they would have retained 20 percent), but paying no health contributions and requiring him to declare the money on a freelance basis.

Now, since this friend of mine had a VAT number, which he used for his translations, he went to the university accounting office to ask what exactly his tax situation might be. Complicated, they said, and went into great detail. Which he didn't entirely understand. Italian tax law might well be written in hieroglyphics, for all the average citizen can understand of it. Never mind a foreigner. Rather than on actual income, everything seems to depend on the category of worker you are (artisan, lawyer, doctor, plumber, farmer, shopkeeper...) and the nature of the work you do (regular, casual, occasional, for one client, for various, etc., etc.), with different rules applying for each different category, different tax brackets, different deductions, different percentages for national insurance, and so on and so forth. So that at the end of the explanation, which might also have been described with the much-used Italian substantive *mistificazione*, my sensible friend demanded to know the bottom line: could he retain his VAT number, do a few translations, and do the job at the university without paying VAT on it.

They said yes. And made him sign something. The usual *documento*. They also said that even if he did want to charge VAT on the job, they wouldn't pay it, but would deduct it from his salary.

Had any of the other thirty or so *lettori*, readers, opted for this alternative? he asked.

And was told, none. Because it wasn't necessary.

But being a cautious lad, my friend also had an accountant. And went to see him. To clear the matter up. The accountant, however, could do nothing more than offer a second equally mystifying "explanation" which simply defied comprehension, perhaps because, as the accountant readily admitted, the law in many areas was not only unclear, but frankly contradictory. It also changed with great regularity, and often government decrees, which were officially law, were not ratified by parliament and thus not only ceased to be law but were deemed never to have been law in the first place. Basically my friend could do what he wanted. Since everybody else at the university was doing precisely that, my friend took this wise advice. He worked, he got paid, and, at least in this regard, he was happy.

Four years later he received a small white card in his mailbox. From the VAT office. He was required to present himself with great urgency, indeed before a date already past, for the printed card had taken more than a week to travel the four miles from the center of town to his modest flat in the outlying village.

He got on his moped and rushed into town, found the VAT office, showed his card at reception, and was directed along a maze of corridors to a huge office whose walls were lined from floor to ceiling, door to door, with box files bulging with tax declarations. It quickly became apparent that the four mus-

---

One year my father overpaid his Italian taxes. He received a refund check from the government. My mother dutifully went to our bank to cash in the check. When she handed it to the teller, he began to laugh. He called over three or four of his associates and they all studied the check carefully and laughed, winking at my mother, giving her the thumbs up. Perplexed, she waited, until the teller explained. "We can't cash this. We'd never get the money back. Hold onto it. It's a souvenir." My parents never could get any bank to cash this government check.

◆

—AC

tached men behind four gunmetal desks were sorting through the VAT declarations of four years before.

My friend was breathing heavily, because he had made it just in time. Like most public offices in Italy, this one was open only in the morning, since, unlike employees in the private sector, civil servants enjoy a thirty-six hour week, six mornings, six hours a day. It was now ten to one.

He handed his card to an older, weary, dusty, bespectacled man behind a huge dusty heap of papers colored the kind of garish pink and yellow that forms can be. In parentheses, I find it is curious how coloring forms does nothing to make them more attractive. Rather, the colors themselves become, by association, somewhat frightening: those tissue blues, washed-out mauves.

He apologized for the delay, but the mail had been slow. The man said the date was a formality and of no relevance. He then proceeded to look for the English teacher's VAT return out of the thousands, perhaps hundreds of thousands, which not only lined the walls, but were arrayed in great barriers of box files between the desks.

When the document was finally found, it emerged that while my friend had been wise perhaps to realize he needed an accountant, he had been unlucky in his choice. For the accountant had made a mistake. In the declaration of four years before, he had mentioned the university income and stated that it was exempted from VAT, but without indicating the code that would explain this exemption. The dusty old man now wanted my friend to tell him which code it was, so that he could write it in the space and the completed form be filed away and forgotten.

In passing, it's worth pointing out here that had the accountant filled in that space with any code, even a nonexistent one, there would most likely have been no problem. For Italian tax inspection appears to be mainly involved in finding contradictory statements within any given declaration. Only very rarely do inspectors go out of their offices to see if the life-style of the taxpayer bears any resemblance to his declaration. Thus it is common and frequently repeated wisdom (in the bars in Montecchio, for example) that it is far better to make no declaration at all than an incomplete or even minimally incorrect one. A line made all the more attractive by the fact that in this case one doesn't have to worry about an accountant. When Franco Pazienza, a millionaire entrepreneur, was arrested in connection with the collapse of the Banco Ambrosiano and the death of director Roberto Calvi (hanged under Blackfriars Bridge), it emerged that he had never made a tax declaration in his life, nor even bothered with a tax code. He had thus never run up against the kind of problems experienced by my friend. And the same could probably be said of one or two people within striking distance of Via Colombare.

But the story that follows will offer a certain justification for that apparently antisocial kind of behavior.

For my friend now made a terrible mistake. Lulled into a false sense of security by the bland innocuousness of this man with dust in his wrinkles and along the rims of his spectacles and peppering his anyway gray mustache, he said, truthfully, that he didn't know what code it might be. The man kindly suggested that he go away, consult his accountant, and return with this information inside a week or two. But here the young foreigner was quite criminally ingenuous, a born victim. He didn't want, he said, to have to return over such a small matter, nor to have to go and consult his accountant. It took him more than half an hour every time he came into town. Surely if he told the old man the nature of the work, he in turn could produce the code; they could then write it down and all would be over.

On the desk there was a little carousel of rubber stamps of all shapes and sizes, some adjustable, some not. The old man tapped the thing with his finger and it began to turn, squeaking slightly. Perhaps this was a warning.

Unheeded. My friend told him the nature of the work. Indeed of all his work. As a person who has nothing to fear from investigation and authority.

The older man became more interested, licked the dust off his lips, said he couldn't say offhand what code that would be; they would have to go and talk to a colleague.

The maze of passages again, gray carpets, fluorescent light. Indeed, apart from the occasional crucifix hanging under the heating pipes near the ceiling, this could perfectly well be an unemployment office in some quiet London suburb. But it isn't.

In another gloomy but more private office the colleague is of an entirely different variety. He is young, sanguine, peremptory, and dust-free, despite the tomes and papers on his desk.

Such work, he pronounces, after hearing the story, should not have been exempt from VAT. There is no question of there being a code.

But my friend has a document provided for him by the university accountants, whom he consulted precisely over this question.

Already he appreciates what a mistake he has made. But it is too late.

A document from the university? The younger man is scornful. No accountant worth his salt would be working at the university, getting only a million and a half a month. Would he? How could they advise him? In any event my friend, as a resident and contributor, is personally responsible for paying his taxes regardless of any advice received—even, the man adds triumphantly, if such incorrect advice were to come from this very office.

The dusty man has stayed to listen. Warming his hands over the radiator, he looks out over the window at a building identical to the one the three of them are in, five, six stories, white concrete, regular square windows. In every room all the typewriters are supplied by Olivetti, as they should be.

"And you're still working at the university?" The sanguine inspector has assumed an interrogator's tone.

"Yes."

"So that this had been going on for four years?"

"Yes."

During which time your remuneration has been what?

My friend tells him. The other man's fingers are extraordinarily rapid on the keyboard of a calculator. "You have evaded VAT for around nine million lire," he says.

But as the English teacher gasps, makes to protest, the inspector has suddenly become friendly. "However, we should see this document you mentioned and your contract before we go into detail. Why don't you bring them in?"

He smiles, goes to pick up his coat. Is it because he's realized that it is time for him to go home for lunch? Or is there some other reason?

"When?"

"Oh, when you like. But don't forget."

Leaving the building, my friend reflects that this kind of vagueness is more disconcerting than comforting. As was the unexpectedly chummy smile on the young man's previously severe face. Extremely anxious as he is, he wants the matter settled at once, not left hanging over his head. And so he rushes things. When perhaps he might have been wiser to do what Orietta would no doubt have advised: had his blood pressure checked, wait till it had fallen.

In any event, he calls his accountant immediately, from a phone box outside the tax office, and tells him the story. At no point does the accountant apologize for his original mistake. If his client wishes, he says, he will go and talk to the tax office about it himself, but perhaps before he does so, it would be better if my friend got the document in question and the contract, took it to the inspectors, stressed his ingenuousness, and insisted on his good faith. He has not, after all, pocketed any money in VAT and then avoided paying it to the state, as perhaps a shopkeeper might. He has merely omitted to charge the client VAT on top of the regular price, always assuming he was in fact supposed to do so. In this way he has not profited from the situation at all. Nor will the state have lost through the university's having detracted from their own VAT payments any monies supposedly paid to him.

My friend, however, is losing his nerve. He positively flaunts his anxiety by returning to the tax office with his documents the very next day. First there's the dusty man again, then the sanguine man, the one dryly polite, apologetic, apparently innocuous, the other tougher, dismissive, immediately assuming the attitude of one who is fed up with hearing cock-and-bull stories.

Allora?

Here is the document.

The younger man looks at it; the older is window-gazing again. The document quotes three or four different laws, sections, paragraphs, amendments—convincing pomposity.

"*Incompetenti*" is the comment, and the VAT man opens a tome on his desk, finds a page, begins to read rapidly out loud from one of the laws cited. My friend, who is actually a whiz at translating complex commercial insurance documents, can't quite follow it. Somehow it all depends on whether his nonuniversity jobs are *continuativi* (regular) or *saltuari* (occasional). He earns, he says, about ten million a year from translations from a variety of clients, some new, some old, but he would be hard pressed to say if this added up to *continuativo* or *saltuario*. The words surely require more precise definition.

The sanguine man undergoes one of his mystifying changes of behavior. He smiles, he is relaxed. "*Sí, Sí, sono d' accordo*," he agrees. And adds: "Five in ten people would probably feel you were in the right."

"After all, given that I've made nothing out of it, no one can deny I'm in good faith."

"*D'accordo, d'accordo.*"

The dusty man turns from the window to watch. My friend is smiling, seeing lights at the end of the tunnel. The accountant seems to have advised him well.

Then the younger man lifts a hand to his face, touches his cheek, and says very politely: "Though good faith is no defense under law, only a mitigating circumstance."

"But..."

"And my interpretation remains that you should have been paying VAT, that you have evaded VAT for a sum of approximately nine million lire, and that you are thus subject to repayment of that sum, plus further payment of a fine."

Flabbergasted, my friend can barely get out: "How much?"

"Fines are usually equal to the amount evaded. A further nine million, with some reduction if you pay immediately, of course."

A total of eighteen million lire, or about eight thousand pounds.

With his back to the window now the older man doesn't bat a dusty eyelid.

"But only a moment ago you said interpretation could go either way."

"Naturally you could appeal against this, and the judgment could indeed go either way. Which would clarify the law most usefully in situations of this kind. In the meantime you would be obliged to pay thirty-three percent of monies due as a first install-ment. You would also lose any possible reduction for immediate payment."

My friend and the inspector are of about the same age and build. They stare at each other across the desk. One in disbelief, the other almost quizzical. And at last my friend makes his first smart move, even though his original idea is merely to gain time. He explains that some of his colleagues have recently fought and won a case to be recognized as employees of the university, not freelance workers; this means that the job cannot be considered subject to VAT. And recognition was retrospective. It would cover this period.

The sanguine man caresses his chin, narrows his eyes. He re-minds my friend that in Italy the decision of a court does not establish precedence. It merely offers one interpretation of the ex-isting law. The verdict in favor of his colleagues, if such a verdict exists, thus refers exclusively to those who fought the case, not to him. A second judge could perfectly well decide differently in his case. His status thus remains the same, and as far as he, the inspec-tor, is concerned, VAT has been evaded to the tune of nine mil-lion. As an employee of the government he has a duty to collect evaded taxes and to punish those who evade them.

For the first time my friend lies, and this is another step forward. "But I have begun my own case too," he says. He is trembling.

"Ah?"

"So at present, in a way, everything is *sub judice.*"

There is a long hard pause, much eye contact. The dusty man pouts, coughs dryly. Finally the younger inspector politely invites my friend to come back once again, this time with a copy both of the sentence of the case won by his colleagues and of his lawyer's presentation of his own case to the Tribunale di Lavoro.

Which, of course, he hasn't got. Looking back at the building as he leaves, my friend remembers *The Castle*, the courtrooms of *The Trial*. Immediately he phones his accountant. The avuncular man, in yet another cluttered office complete with crucifix, is kind and genuinely concerned. He hadn't initially wanted to go and speak to the tax people personally, since "*finora io e te abbiamo sempre collaborato in modo amichevole*," i.e., "so far you have paid me under the table and I haven't given you a receipt for my services or in any way indicated in my books that you are a client of mine." However, at this point he agrees it is time he went to talk to these people. Yes, he knows who it must be.

A nail-biting week. During which, to pass the time, and then because once there's an itch you have to scratch it, my friend goes to the university accounting office and again inquires, as if merely to reassure himself, about his tax position. Again he hears, as he did four years ago, that there is no need for him to pay VAT on his university income. He then tells the accountant, a forty-year-old man with the dress style of someone determined to stay young, an expensive mixture of Armani, Gianfranco Ferrè, and Benetton, that the VAT office thinks otherwise and is at this very moment asking him to pay a heavy fine. To which the other man replies with great promptness that he can in no way be held responsible for the advice he gives. A brief slanging match follows, since this is one person, my friend feels, he can give a piece of his very worried mind to with impunity. As always Christ is looking on from his own particular cross. Plastic in this case.

Finally the accountant phones. He has talked to the VAT people. Could my friend come into his office. They can't discuss it on the telephone.

And in the office he says: "They want a Christmas present."

"*Prego?*"

"*Una bustarella*." A little envelope. A bribe.

"Did they say so?"

"God forbid."

So how does he know?

He knows. And this burly accountant with thick bushy eyebrows now proceeds with nostalgic revelry to launch into the story of the very first time he offered a bribe. Oh, twenty years ago.

He simply became so exasperated with the obtuseness of the official he was dealing with that he said, "Okay, how much do you want?" and then fell silent, stunned by his own rashness. What if he had read the signals wrong? But he hadn't.

Later he learned the trick of dropping an envelope on the floor and asking the other if he had dropped it there. Another important indicator was if the official invited you out for a coffee.

It occurs to me, writing this down, that this sort of breath-taking breaking of cover—the dropping of the envelope, the invitation to coffee—is not unlike one's first declaration of attraction to a possible lover; there's sudden intimacy and self-exposure. It's exhilarating.

And, my friend tells me, his accountant was indeed exhilarated. In this case, the man began to explain, he had understood that they wanted a bribe, because otherwise they would have already proceeded to fill in the document requiring him to pay the fine. After which there could be no turning back, the matter would be officially registered. And had my friend really evaded so much VAT, they would almost certainly have proceeded with the matter and nailed him. As it was, appreciating he was merely a victim of circumstance, they were inclined to let him off the hook in return for a small Christmas present.

"How much?"

Two days later the accountant phones to say the matter in question would cost 800,000 lire. My friend should come to his office in a couple of days' time to say whether he intends to pay.

My friend is still very English. Though less than he was a month ago. In the past week he has joined a group of colleagues bringing a case against the university to be recognized as employees. So he now has a lawyer. An attractive young woman six months pregnant. And finding the idea of paying a bribe somewhat offensive, the kind of awful initiation into a different way of life, a different state of mind that theft or adultery might be, he phones this lawyer to discuss the problem. She is polite and patient, listening to the complex story. Until he gets to the bit about the little envelope, at which she suddenly becomes frantic. "*Per l' amore di Dio* we're talking on the phone." Anyway, she will consult her accountant and ring back.

Which she duly does. Indeed, it's surprising how kind and helpful and civilized everybody is being. On the phone she's calm, matter-of-fact: "The manner," she says—and my friend has written her circumlocutions down because he finds them so amusing—"in which your accountant has chosen to resolve the particular difficulties in which, through no fault of your own, you find yourself, although perhaps not immediately attractive, and you do have my sympathy here, is nevertheless not so mistaken as you appear to think. If you follow his advice to the letter, I am sure you will be able to arrive at a *soluzione felice* without my help."

But another anxious week has definitely Italianized my friend that little bit more. For rather than simply shelling out the 800,000, as it now seems he will have to, he points out to his accountant that since the VAT office's complaint is based only on that one declaration of four years ago, they could perfectly well pull out the next declarations one by one, year by year, and have him over a barrel for the same amount again.

The accountant accepts this. It is agreed the 800,000 will be paid only if the VAT office can dig up the other declarations and allow the accountant to change them; otherwise the sum must be renegotiated. The VAT men, whom my friend never saw again, and whose names he does not know, are likewise reasonable. No, they can't dig out the other declarations; yes, they do appreciate the problem this represents; they will bring their request down to 400,000.

Pride satisfied, my friend pays.

"And a hundred thousand for me for negotiating the deal," the accountant says, with still no apology for his initial mistake. And no receipt.

Before leaving the office, in the state of exhilaration that every initiation, every surrender of self brings once one has decided to go through with it, my friend asks the accountant, "But it's so little. Why would anyone corrupt himself for so little?"

"No accountant worth his salt," the burly man explains, "would work in the VAT office. How much can they be getting—two million a month? They have to supplement it. A hundred thousand from you, half a million from me, it all adds up. And the rules are a lot simpler than the written ones." Reflectively, as if this has occurred to him for the first time, he adds: "There's only one person I know of in the VAT office who won't take something sometime. Lucky it wasn't he who picked up your problem."

My friend walks out into the bright street with the feeling of one waking up from a nightmare. In the end he's only lost 250-odd quid. Not much to pay for a significant experience.

Tim Parks also contributed "Facciamo le Corna" in Part One. This story was excerpted from his book, Italian Neighbors.

⋆

The man in front of me [at the post office] got into a heated argument with the teller because she wouldn't accept his torn fifty thousand lire note. Italian notes have a metallic strip sewn into them to distinguish the real from the forged; in this man's case, the strip was not intact.

Discussion quickly escalated to the level of a fight. Not that it needed to—the man brandished a billfold stuffed with fifty thousand lire notes; the problem was that he was determined to pay his bill with this *particular* fifty thousand lire note.

Oh great, I thought, and eyed the other lines, running smoothly. Customers who'd arrived just when I had were already leaving. I started to fume. And then a strange thing happened. As the voices of the man and woman rose to a pitch just below shouting, I found myself becoming increasingly hypnotized by their elaborate—almost arcane—rhetoric. Something primal, historical, was being fought out here. Perhaps he was Guelf, she Ghibelline; he black, she white. It occurred to me that argument could be a form of intimacy, a ritual as elaborate as the mating dances performed by exotic birds. Vendetta—the settling of a score—was not its purpose; its purpose was the brandishment of rhetorical epées; the venting of spleen.

As is inevitable in such situations, a supervisor was soon demanded, produced. While he listened to the man's plaint a finger of ash formed on the end of his cigarette. A lady near the back of the line interjected that just yesterday the post office had accepted a bill of hers that was in worse condition. (The teller's eyes narrowed: traitor.) The man started shouting at the supervisor. The supervisor shouted back. Then, just when blows seemed certain to ensue, the tension, as it were, deflated; the protagonists, descending from icy heights, reached sudden and complete accord. A new note was produced (the old one to be turned in at the bank). Good wishes were offered round like after-dinner mints. The customer was *molto gentile* ("very nice"), the teller *troppo gentile* ("too nice"). The supervisor prayed that should the gentleman have any further problems he would come directly to him, and the gentleman, promising to do so, wished him a *buona giornata*, as if to say, rest assured: this argument was just a game; all the days and evenings will puddle into a happy and profitable life.

—David Leavitt and Mark Mitchell, *Italian Pleasures*

✦ ✦ ✦

The Italian Mistress

Love always has a price.

EUROPEAN CHILDREN TOOK FOR GRANTED, YEARS AGO, THAT there were two kinds of women: women like one's mother, aunts, grandmothers, sisters, cousins, family friends; and the others. The others were habitually called "them"; "one of them," *une d'elles, una di quelle*, were the common euphemisms. When one absent-minded grown-up started talking about "them" in front of children, the other grown-ups winked, coughed, and pointed with their chins to the little tots. The topic changed abruptly. Young ladies were asked to leave the room when "they" were mentioned.

There was, children knew, something mysterious about them which nobody, not even chauffeurs and waiters, who were generally reliable sources of illicit information, would reveal. One studied "them" whenever one could. One saw them at a distance (or imagined one saw them) in the city, during the winter, but one could really observe them at close quarters and at leisure only in summer hotels, the huge and stuffy *palazzi* in the Alps, by the foaming sea or a flat green lake, where guests changed every night but Sunday and the music played Schumann among the potted palms after dinner.

These particular women were more beautiful, wore better

clothes and bigger jewels than mother and mother's friends, walked more elegantly, turned their chins up and closed their eyes when they laughed. When they were alone, they sometimes had a bored or melancholy expression, like actresses after the show. They were often fond of children (they never had any of their own) and sighed deeply when caressing a little curly head.

Father was the only one of the family who sometimes talked to them. Waiting for his wife to appear in the morning at the beach or, in the evening, dressed for dinner in the lobby he would fill a few empty minutes exchanging polite pleasantries. When mother appeared, he would stop the conversation cold, without a concluding nod. Mother looked calmly through the woman as if she were a ghost, as transparent as the air itself.

I must have been eight or nine when grandmother took me and my little brother and sister to visit "one of them." Grandmother was a widow who lived alone, traveled frequently, and despised stuffy prejudices. I was old enough at the time to know what the woman was, but pretended I knew nothing. She was the mistress of a famous Milan jeweler, a small and dapper man with impeccable shirts, whom I had seen around town.

It was the Christmas season. The woman lived on a quiet side street by the Park, in a tiny flat. It was very romantically furnished with bric-à-brac, Oriental incense burners, brocades strewn everywhere, exotic plants and old church paraphernalia. In this dimly-lit and perfumed ambiance she had set up a little Christmas tree and an elaborate *presepio* just for us. There were gay packages, ice cream, pastry and chocolates enough for a whole school, all waiting for us.

She embraced all three of us hysterically, laughed loudly for no reason at all, continually thanked my grandmother, and tirelessly wound up the Victrola to fill the shy silence with music. She was on the verge of tears when she watched us unwrap our gifts. They were splendid gifts: military uniforms, trains, dolls, construction sets. Nobody had ever given us such expensive things before. She wept when we left.

Luigi Barzini is the author of The Italians *and* Memories of Mistresses: Reflections from a Life, *from which this story was excerpted.*

★

In a country where the local prostitute is as visible a presence in many middle-class neighborhoods as the butcher or the baker, the Italians have always known how to separate sex from marriage. Some conventions of Italian life seem designed to encourage extracurricular sex. The obligatory summer exodus from the cities, when almost all Italian wives and children go off to the sea or the mountains, is considered a time when husbands who stay behind are let off the leash to cavort with their mistresses or with enterprising American coeds on their junior year abroad. Tradition of more recent standing allows vacationing wives discreet encounters with tennis and aerobics instructors and the ever ready *bagnini*— the muscular men who rent beach umbrellas. The rule for women is: Don't get caught. The rule for men is: Get caught or not, but don't even think about breaking up your marriage. Floating in the background is the very Latin idea that for a man having lovers is a sign of virility that even his wife can learn to value. "My husband only has gorgeous girlfriends," a Milanese woman says, as if somehow the fact reflected well on her.

—Andrea Lee, "For Better, For Worse," *The New Yorker*

GARY PAUL NABHAN

✦ ✦ ✦

Sagra di Polenta

*The discovery of the Americas led
to an unusual problem.*

I COULD NOT BELIEVE MY EYES WHEN GINGER AND I FIRST DIPPED down into the Etruscan valleys. They were thick with summer crops laid out in long rows, the same crops that I had seen in most Native American farming villages from the Rio Grande pueblos of New Mexico through the Mayan highlands of Guatemala. There they were, my old neighbors: maize, tobacco, and sunflowers in the fields; beans, amaranths, and finches erupted out of the thorny mass of one hedgerow; hooded crows cawed and cackled above us as we crossed the Tiber floodplain and approached Cittá di Castello. We failed to notice such birds and weeds only in the manicured to-bacco fields that were swarming with poor farm workers, stomp-ing down the aisles, stooping to cut the rank growth by hand, and stashing the odorous leaves on portable drying racks. There, the human presence overwhelmed us, and our eyes were not fixed on the ground.

By the time we limped into sight of the stone walls of Cittá di Castello, I felt awed by the tenacity of the weeds that stain and fla-vor everything in the Italian countryside. There were amaranths and grasses rooted in the sheerest of stone walls and doves wher-ever a space was found large enough for a nest. Even along the roadside—regardless of how narrow, how frequently mowed, how incessantly sprayed—the flowering herbs were indomitable: filaree and gypsywort; comfrey, chicory, and timothy; butter-and-eggs, cheeseweed; hawkbit and foxtail; sow thistle, lamb's-quarters, and hogweed; mustards, false basils, borages, and sages. When I took off my socks and jeans that evening in a small room above a café, I found barbed and bristly seeds, sticky leaves, and stains of golden pollen coating my clothes from my calves to my ankles.

In 1648, Ovidio Montalbani explained that such weeds were not at all peripheral to Mediterranean culture but had been and would continue to be essential to human welfare: "Hundreds and hundreds of different roots, buds, fruits, and seeds of herbs are edible and can well pass into the diet with little artifice." Between 1600 and 1650, when Italy's population dropped by almost two million due to the plague, the distribution of food supplies was periodically disrupted by regional epidemics; to get by, survivors found themselves turning to foraging beyond their fields and gardens. To help the unacquainted, many of them on the verge of starvation, Montalbani offered instructions on how to gain sufficient sustenance from the wild herbs in the rural landscape.

It turned out that many people soon needed to heed his words. Suddenly, price controls on grains triggered a collapse in the bread market, and increasingly oppressive sharecropping policies kept peasants from having either the buying power or the land to grow much food to feed themselves. The poor had been left poorer, forced to give the bulk of their cultivated produce to their landlords and to glean whatever nutrients they could from the spontaneous vegetation left around them. They began to live outside the formal economy; in much the same manner, Francis and his followers had survived in the woods and swamps four centuries before.

Then, in the hundred years following 1650, Italy's population grew by four million, and there were nearly 50 percent more mouths to feed off the same amount of land than there had been in 1492. By the 1740s, cold snaps and other climatic fluctuations had reduced the quantity and variety of food crops being produced in Italy, and agricultural yields could no longer keep up with population growth. Hungry peasants again turned to wild greens and starchy roots as mainstays during the warmer seasons. During the winter, they were forced to rely on rustic breads made from stale or larvae-ridden flours and meals.

To extend their grains as far as the resource could go, they added to the batter herbs or their seeds, some of them bitter, mildly toxic, or potently psychotropic. Folk historian Piero Camporesi explains this survival strategy in *Bread of Dreams*: "Through operations of simple magic, the camouflaging and metamorphosis of flavors, the denaturing and recycling of herbs—even the most unpleasant—provided for the neutralizing of poisonous herbs and...[rendered] pleasing the taste of those which were repulsive. The artifice derived from 'natural magic' would extend bread miraculously: a saving demon for a starving populace."

It was a "saving demon" because the hunger was masked more than it was quelled; the poor remained exploited and undernourished, but the narcotic herbs buffered them from this reality. This dark tradition of escaping from hunger through drug-laden meals is what has come down to us in the diluted forms of dill-laced loaves of rye bread and of poppyseed cake. But the narcotic white poppy seeds sown for centuries amid the fava bean fields of Tuscany were not the only psychoactive seed kneaded into the dough. Among the poor, *poppyseed bread* came to mean any bread "disguised and flavored, and in addition spiced with coriander seeds, anise, cumin, sesame-seed oil, and all the possible delectable additives available in the vegetable kingdom, with which man dwelled in a close intimacy, today unthinkable. In areas where it was cultivated," Camporesi adds, "even the flour of hemp seeds was used in the kitchen to prepare doughs and breads which 'cause the loss of reason' and 'generate domestic drunkenness and certain stupidity.'"

It is no shock that such plants were used by the peasantry; what is startling is that Camporesi believes that for several centuries, many of the poor of southern Europe were immersed in general states of domestic drunkenness and delirium, conditions induced "with the help of hallucinogenic seeds and herbs, arising from the background of chronic malnourishment and hunger…the simplest and most natural producer of mental alterations and dreamlike states."

Knowledge about such mind-altering herbs was no doubt ancient in southern Europe, but dependence on them probably resurfaced whenever social or environmental stresses ravaged the poor. If Saint Francis did indeed live and eat as the poor of his times lived and ate, he was inevitably exposed to these herbs and influenced by their qualities. Camporesi does not let this possibility slip by unnoticed; instead, he suggests that Saint Francis was, in all likelihood, an "eccentric wizard of ecstasy in a body consumed by penance and privation, his mind altered by fasts, like certain hermits kept alive by roots and herbs [that] stimulated the same sense of the real and the impossible as experienced by those who, suffering and subdued by an involuntary poverty…fell into shocking hallucinations and stupefied contemplations."

Perhaps Francis himself was a voluntary victim of hunger and herbal hallucination, for we know that he suffered as well from the oozing wounds of leprosy, the incessant pain of arthritis, and four dozen other maladies and degenerative diseases by the time he died.

It may sound like blasphemy for Camporesi to attribute the "vision" and "saintly wounds" of Francis to the same dream-inducing diets and diseases that the poor of his times experienced, but young Bernardone set out to experience fully the "immeasurable treasure of most holy poverty" that he had not experienced while growing up in a privileged family. His meditative powers may have moved him into sublime trancelike states at times, but spoiled breads and narcotic herbs may have enhanced Francis's reputed capacities to talk with animals, to endure unspeakable pain, and to survive freezing nights or red-hot coals. We retell the stories of when he soared like a hero but forget the many times he suffered the same insults that any poor European must have suffered. Father Roy Gasnick has quipped, "Americans gravitate not to Francis the sufferer but to Francis standing in the birdbath," despite the fact that during the last six years of his life, the saint could hardly stand as upright as his statues now portray him.

As Italians multiplied and their population recovered after the plague, there was only one thing that staved off hunger and herbal hallucinations for the bulk of them: maize. Word of this productive summer crop from the Americas may have arrived in Italy as early as 1494, via letters from Guglielmo Coma, who accompanied Columbus on his second voyage. A pamphlet written in Latin and published in Pavia in December of that year told of "a prolific kind of grain, the size of a lupin, rounded like a chick-pea. When broken, it produces a fine flour, and it is ground like wheat. A bread of excellent flavor is made from it." The pamphleteer, Nicoló Syllacio, added a comment that tells less about corn's presumed use in the Americas and more about how it would be consumed in times of stress in Europe. Speaking from fourth-hand knowledge of Native American farmers, Syllacio claimed that "many who have little food simply chew the grains without preparation."

Some European historians claim that maize had arrived in Florence and was being grown in botanical gardens there within ten years of Syllacio's pamphlet being distributed. What strikes me is that by the 1530s and 1540s, it had spread beyond the botanical elite of Europe and was being grown by the masses, many of whom assumed that it had been brought from Asia Minor. Like many items introduced from foreign lands through Islamic traders, it was attributed to the "Turks," or Moors, and was commonly

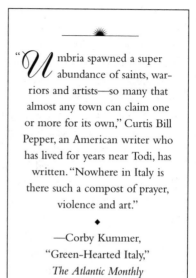

"*Umbria* spawned a super abundance of saints, warriors and artists—so many that almost any town can claim one or more for its own," Curtis Bill Pepper, an American writer who has lived for years near Todi, has written. "Nowhere in Italy is there such a compost of prayer, violence and art."

♦

—Corby Kummer,
"Green-Hearted Italy,"
The Atlantic Monthly

called *frumentum turcicum* or *granoturco*. Of its true origin, Italian herbalist Petrus Matthiolus knew better, and said so in 1565: "This type of grain, which they wrongly called *turcicum*, can be numbered among the varieties of wheat. [They have named it] incorrectly I say, because it ought to be called *indicum* not *turcicum*, for it was brought from the West Indies, not out of Turkey and Asia."

By the time Matthiolus wrote these words, maize had already come into widespread cultivation among the peasants in the Venetian states, Lombardy, and north central Italy. Within another three or four decades, *granoturco* had even begun to appear prominently in economic production summaries for northern Italy. Because it could be planted in the warm season after the harvest of wheat, barley, and buckwheat, it complemented rather than competed with the traditional winter cereals, allowing farmers to double-crop the same piece of land and to produce grain year round. By the end of the eighteenth century, maize had eclipsed wheat and other winter grains in total yields in many of the northern and central Italian provinces.

When it came to keeping the poor fed, maize, it appeared, would make all the difference in the world. Arthur Young, an English traveler to the Mediterranean, summarized the situation in the 1780s: "Where there is no maize, there are fallows; and where there are fallows, the people starve for want. For the inhabitants of a country to live upon that [maize] plant, which [prepares the ground] for wheat and at the same time keeps their cattle fat...is to possess a treasure."

It may come as no surprise that such a treasure would inspire the Italian populace to glorify and praise their adopted miracle crop. One such cultural celebration of maize is the Sagra di Polenta, a festival still celebrated near the border between Tuscany and Umbria. Ginger and I decided to stay over an extra day in the Valtiberina Alta near Città de Castello so that we could participate in this pageant in honor of cornmeal mush.

After accepting a ride from Città de Castello to Monterchi, we walked across a bridge and through corn-adorned gates at the base of the hilltop village. As I looked at the ears and stalks decorating the arc across the road, it dawned on me that hybrid dent corn from the midwestern United States was the icon of the day. I was perplexed, I guess, because I had read somewhere of at least eight heirloom varieties of maize in Italy, ranging from white and red late-maturing races to beaked and dwarfed early varieties. After several hundred years of maize cultivation near Monterchi, the farmers should have accumulated their own races that would be favored over recently introduced midwestern dents. Ginger patiently waited while I asked elderly Monterchi residents if they had favorite kinds of corn that they grew here year after year.

"Oh, certainly, I can show you," one man said to me enthusiastically. He then pleaded with me to stay put so that he could bring me evidence of the range of maize they grew on the bottomland surrounding the town. He returned a few minutes later with a stack of brochures from multinational hybrid maize breeding firms.

"Look at all the kinds of *granoturco* that are accessible to us! We don't grow all of them in this area each year, but I've tried some from nearly every one of these companies!"

I read aloud the company names and the hymns of praise by their agronomists who had put the hybrids through last year's variety trials. In slick, color-printed handbills, Italian farmers were offered a cadre of seven hybrids from DeKalb; fifteen from Asgrow; eighteen from Pioneer Hybrid; and

*M*aize, which is ground into cornmeal for *polenta*, like wheat, is grown in small quantities on farms all over the country. In the Friuli region, even more than the neighboring Veneto, *polenta* is central to the diet. It is so popular there that it is even eaten for breakfast, dipped in milk. (Coffee is rarely taken at breakfast in Friuli.) In both Friuli and Veneto, grilled or broiled slices of *polenta* accompany the main course in place of bread.

◆

—Giuliano Bugialli,
Giuliano Bugialli's Foods of Italy

finally, fourteen dents from Agrigenetics, including new releases named Las Vegas and Dragon, for those farmers who loved gambling and fantasy.

The maize varieties were recent immigrants, but there was nevertheless something profoundly traditional about this folk festival. The *sagra* pays homage to a food of the poor and celebrates polenta in all its forms: grilled, baked, or fried, glorified by spices, embellished by savory sauces, served side by side with sausage, truffles, or calf livers, swallowed down with local wines or with draft beers.

While Ginger wandered the streets, I went to watch and talk with six white-haired men in equally white smocks and chef's hats, decorated with husklike green bandannas; all of them were slightly drunk. Between slapstick routines that recounted their shared exploits, these polenta pros were dumping cornmeal into twenty-gallon cauldrons, where it was being mechanically blended with boiling water at the bottom and churned with wooden spoons by hand at the top. The batter of one part cornmeal to three parts water belched and blistered over a small wood fire.

Every twenty minutes, three of the old men would pick up the cauldron to ladle the steaming mush out into a wooden box six feet long by three feet wide and four inches deep. Using their huge wooden spoons, the polenta chefs spread the mush flat like an enormous cake of butter, smoothing its surface, then letting it cool. Once the haze of steam had cleared its surface, it had lost enough heat to allow the chefs to work with it, simply scooping heaps into bowls for waiting customers or preparing more elaborate dishes for later sale. According to the customer's request, a vendor might add a sauce of fresh and pureed tomatoes, olive oil, carrots, onion, sausage, garlic, or dill seed, or sprinkle on Parmesan cheese. Other cooks let the corn cakes harden longer so that they could be cut into squares and grilled next to juicy sausages and livers, whose grease sprayed and saturated the corn with their taste.

Once Ginger and I rejoined to talk with the old men, they handed us bowl after bowl of the polenta, soon forgetting to charge us, then refusing our offerings of lire. They began to ask us as many questions as we asked them. While we leaned against wreaths of wild sunflowers and dried ears of dent corn, Ginger nudged me and whispered, "Ask these local farmers, and I'll bet they'll tell you that corn is a native here."

I did, and they did. They pushed forward one of the oldest, most drunken cooks, who took another sip of his beer before offering me their official testimony on the corn's antiquity.

"Maize has been here always, as long as we as a people have been here. It is what has always fed our village," he said, turning for confirmation to his cronies. They solemnly agreed, but one of their sons winked at me. Later, this son leaned over the counter and offered another perspective.

"My father does not know world history as I do, but maize has only been grown here since it was brought from Native Americans. Of course, some of us know that its Indian name is maize, not *granoturco* like most of them call it here."

The elders were innocent of any understanding of American Indian contributions to their crop. Nevertheless, I sensed that many of my Native American friends

*T*he true test of your Italian adoption arrives with *polenta*. A whole world of moral, social and political values is contained in a single dollop. I can't look at the stuff without thinking of that particularly inglorious period of the nation's history which followed unification in 1870 and culminated in the seizure of power by Mussolini and his fascist squadrons: the age of anarchist assassins, daredevil aviators, prancing Futurists, saintly Queen Margherita and gerrymandering Prime Minister Crispi, dubious colonial forays into Abyssinia and Tripoli, the first Fiat cars, *verismo* opera and the works of Gabriele D'Annunzio, whose massively fraudulent personality, specially constructed out of nothing very much in particular so as to gratify other people's overblown fancies, sums up the gimcrack, pinchbeck, penny-trumpet-and-twopenny-drum quality essential to the epoch.

◆

—Jonathan Keates,
Italian Journeys

would have felt at home with the festival itself. It had many of the components of traditional celebrations found anywhere in the world: the crowning of a queen; a race between the men; a social dance; plant decorations in praise and thanks for an abundant harvest; plenty of rich food and hearty drink. And it seemed to me that corn, among all crops, was particularly likely to become laden with cultural expressions wherever it traveled from its Neotropical birthplace—expressions that were remarkably similar to those of the Mesoamerican cultures that had first nurtured it. I simply cannot imagine the Italians, Mayans, Tarahumara, or Hidatsa making a comparable fuss over alfalfa, soybeans, or rapeseed.

Whatever cultural elaborations Italians had independently evolved in their nurturing of corn, they did not, until this century, rediscover one of the essentials of using maize as a staple; processing it with ash, calcium bicarbonate "lime," or other mineral salts as a means of releasing its essential nutrients in forms that would be available to the human metabolism.

This oversight had grave consequences, for until maize is processed in such a manner, its niacin remains bound. The amino acid tryptophan cannot be converted to niacin until it is made available by hydrolysis with either lime water or other sodium solutions, which is exactly what Native Americans did in making hominy or ash breads wherever maize was their mainstay. Sadly, Italians received the Mesoamerican maize without knowledge of the native processing techniques that would render it most nutritious. As a result, the regions where Italians were most dependent on maize suffered from an epidemic called pellagra, which is a severe nutritional deficiency rather than an infectious disease. This affliction further crazed the poor and hungry, pushing them over the brink into delusions and hallucinations far worse than those that the spoiled, herb-laden breads of previous centuries had given them.

Pellagra as an affliction was described relatively recently and appears to have been entirely absent in American lands where corn was native. But by 1730, a Spanish physician, Gaspar Casal, was noticing an undescribed mania and delirium setting in among the corn-eating poor of his country. He noted that the common folk called this affliction *mal de la rosa,* for the reddish spots and horrible scabby crusts that appeared on the skin of those who later lost their minds. By 1740, the same disease had been described by Italian physicians, who called it *pelle agra,* or "sour skin." A 1771 treatise by Dr. Francisco Frapoli described how truly terrible pellagra becomes:

> *The disease rages recurrently until at length the skin no longer peels, but becomes wrinkled, thickened, and full of fissures. Then, for the first time, the patient begins to have trouble in the head: fear, sadness, wakefulness and vertigo, mental stupor bordering on fatuity, hypochondria, fluxes from the bowels, and sometimes, mania. Then the strength of the body fails...[and the patient becomes] most resistant to all remedies, consumed with a ghastly wasting, [until it reaches] the last extremes.*

By 1784, five percent of the population of certain Italian provinces suffered from the malady, and twenty percent of the inhabitants in some hill-country farm towns were debilitated. Tuscany was fifth in the severity of the pellagra epidemic among the Italian provinces, while Umbria was third. In Tuscany maize had become the major agricultural product on 65,000 acres of land, and it was clear that the farmworkers who ate polenta as their mainstay were the most susceptible. The malady became so widespread that the first large insane asylum was established in Milan in 1784 to serve as a *pellagrosario,* and even a quarter of a century later, nearly two-thirds of those confined in this hospital were deranged by pellagra. Asylums were soon established in other regions as well, but all pellagra sufferers could not be so contained; many remained on the land. When Goethe crossed into Italy from the north in 1786, he not only found the disease commonplace but related its presence to the consumption of polenta:

> *I noticed as soon as it was daylight a definite change in their [northern Italians'] physical appearance. I thought the sallow complexion of the women particularly disagreeable. Their fea-*

*tures spoke of misery and their children looked as pitiful. The
men looked little better...I believe that their unhealthy condition is due to their constant diet of maize and buckwheat, or as
they call them, yellow polenta and black polenta.*

*These are ground fine, the flour is boiled in water to a thick
mush and then eaten. In the German Tirol they separate the
dough into small pieces and fry them in butter, but in the
Italian Tirol the polenta is eaten just as it is or sometimes with
a sprinkling of grated cheese. Meat they never see from one
year's end to the other.*

Despite such early intuitions that pellagra was due to a lack of
dietary variety, it wasn't until 1905 that the key factors were clari-
fied. At first, social reformers gained some success in reducing pellagra by increasing the food choices available to the poor, even
when poverty itself could not be eliminated. Clinicians, on the
other hand, chose to provide vitamin supplements of niacin in
order to reduce the dominance of leucine over tryptophan in the
amino acid balance of the overall diet. European health workers
ignored an equally effective solution first proposed by a Mexican
physician, Ismael Salas, while lecturing in Europe in 1863; he
wanted to teach the peasants to eat corn as lime-soaked tortillas instead of as polenta—in other words, to introduce to Europeans the
niacin-releasing food preparation method of Mesoamericans that
had not arrived with the maize itself centuries before.

Nevertheless, Italy lagged behind Spain and France in control-
ling pellagra. Some historians claim that this is because the Italian
government was not as effective in changing the food habits of its
polenta eaters, but more likely, it was unwilling to tackle the causes
of poverty and oppression that kept many peasants on the verge of
starvation. Instead, it launched huge sanitation campaigns to keep
corn from being spoiled by "pellagra-causing microbes." Worse
yet, some public health workers claimed that pellagra was heredi-
tary, so that the poor could not be helped.

Elsewhere, other health workers treated the disease as if it were
infectious, a fear that generated racism against Italians in the

United States. A U.S. commission on pellagra reported that an American woman died in 1894 after contracting the disease from immigrant Italian farmworkers. In American cities, a common turn-of-the-century rumor took another twist: immigrants had carried with them from Italy foods contaminated with a pellagra-causing fungus. Perhaps mycophobic Anglo-Americans thought that Italians were so recklessly indulgent with edible fungi that they would let the fungi spread.

By 1930, pellagra victims could be found in only a few Italian hospitals, and the Italian sanitation programs to eradicate it had been dismantled. When Daphne Roe visited Italian hospitals in the 1950s—half a century after a 1904 Italian commission enacted a law to eliminate pellagra permanently—he found that "It had virtually disappeared from northern Italy. I was not innocent enough to believe that this change was due to a law. Rather, the *mezzadria* [sharecropper] system had died out, the tenant farmer had gained independence, and the poor could for the most part 'inherit the earth.'"

Nevertheless, there was something in Roe and the Italian physicians she visited that still blamed the peasants for the persistence of the disease, as if their allegiance to "primitive" food traditions had kept them from being helped earlier by scientists. Dr. Ferdinando Serri could show Roe only one "prematurely old woman, clothed in old-fashioned black garments, who bore the classic traits of the disease on her skin...Here was a [sole] case to show foreign visitors; I was having a demonstration of a condition which persisted only among the people of the backwoods, who through a combination of ignorance and poverty continued to follow their traditional food customs."

Ignorance, poverty, and traditional foods—if we are to dismiss all food customs of the poor and uneducated as being maladaptive and based on ignorance, then we have to account in some other way for the absence of pellagra during thousands of years of traditional maize processing in the Americas. It is easy to dismiss the uneducated as ignorant; on the other hand, it was the educated European elite who failed to bring the secret of maize pro-

cessing along with the corn seed that they obtained in the
Americas. It took educated European doctors two centuries from
the time of pellagra's first clinical description to understand the
chemical, biological, and social context of niacin deficiency. In the
meantime, poor peasants continued to suffer the most as professional health workers tried out one faulty solution after another
to quell the epidemic.

At its root, the pellagra problem emerged precisely because educated Europeans disregarded the traditional knowledge of native
maize processors. They did not pay sufficient attention to it when
they first extracted this miracle crop from its traditional setting;
neither did they heed the words of Mexican health worker Ismael
Salas when he alerted the European medical profession to the
value of the lime-soaked tortilla in preventing pellagra in 1863,
seventy years before the disease was finally curbed.

As I looked around at the faces of people, rich and poor, attending the Sagra di Polenta, I could not bring myself to dismiss
their affection for polenta as retrograde or ignorant. If they could
have gone with Columbus to encounter maize farmers in the
Americas, their attention to the details of food processing probably would have allowed them to learn of lime soaking and adding
ash to maize. We cannot now turn back the clock, but we can
learn to respect surviving ethnic food traditions for the hidden
knowledge they may contain. And we can celebrate the gifts—
native or other—that have been bestowed on us, learning from
the mistakes made in the past that kept us from fully appreciating
such gifts.

Bellies full, Ginger and I finally abandoned our places in the po-
lenta-cooking arenas. We gravitated toward the dance floor, where
it was plain to see the anomalous mix of custom and modernity
that rural Italy embraces.

I watched rows of teenagers, dressed to kill, in outfits ranging
from bib overalls and black high-top sneakers to fantasy gowns as
bizarre as those in Milan fashion shows. They flirted and looked
bored or pained, as hormonally impaired juveniles do anywhere in
the world. What pained them the most was when the piped-in-

rock-roll music was turned off so that a polka band could take the stand.

A motley crew of middle-agers brought out accordion, alto sax, bass guitar, and bar-relhouse piano. To the teenagers' disgust, the band played a brand of polkas, mazurkas, waltzes, and schot-tisches that would have been welcome from Lithuania and Romania to the Mexican and Indian villages in my desert homeland. A couple in their eighties took the dance floor; the teenagers glanced away, while everyone else looked on with interest. The arena to themselves, the elderly pair el-egantly turned a waltz through its cycles before bowing and inviting other couples to share the floor with them. As the band beat out the tempo of a vigorous polka, younger married cou-ples felt obliged to take up the old-timers on their invitation.

By this time, six kinds of draft beer were coursing through bloodstreams, and the kegs were nearly empty. Tired but upbeat farmwork-ers appeared, ones who had toiled all day cutting tobacco

My mother was brought to live in Italy by my father, but she was raised and bred in Oregon. She grew up on abundant corn-on-the-cob and strict Lutheran morals. One time, after a decade of doing without, her craving for corn got the best of her, and overrode her morals. We were driving past a luscious cornfield in July. Mom abruptly pulled over and said, "I've just got to get some. You stay in the car." Astonished, I watched my moth-er run to the edge of the corn-field to begin stripping away ears of corn. Unfortunately, the farmer seated in his high tractor saw her. A chase ensued. My mother leapt into the car, throwing corn ears hither and thither, driving off at high speed. I watched the gesticulat-ing farmer grow smaller and smaller. That evening, she boiled the corn for 15, 20, 30 minutes but the kernels remained hard. It turns out she had stolen hog corn, unfit for human consump-tion. "God got me," Mom mused. She hasn't been seen stealing corn since.

◆

—AC

leaves. They had downed several mugs of beer or glasses of wine as soon as they arrived. Now they were moved by the music and began to find their spouses and in-laws among the tables of peasants congregated off to the side. The dance floor filled as the shadows of the late afternoon descended on the stone walls of Monterchi.

I remembered a man from a nearby village who had told me stories of Sardinian sheepherders coming to these *sagre*, using them as their only release after weeks of twelve-hour workdays. He recalled how one massive Sardinian danced a mazurka without ever letting his dainty partner's feet touch the ground. Others would show their prowess by balancing two wooden chairs on each of their outstretched arms or by stacking up bricks to see who could carry the largest pile.

Ginger and I descended from the village as the last glints of sunlight stained the cornfields below. Our eyes drank up the saturated colors: umber brown soils, terra-cotta roofs, beige and cream stuccoed walls, and yellow splotches of wild sunflowers amid the dark greens of well-fertilized corn.

But these calming tones and textures were juxtaposed with lead-colored antennae, concrete telephone poles, metallic loudspeakers, and electric signs. Ginger and I rode the last bus heading back to the vicinity of our inn in Città di Castello. We talked about "purity" and how it infects landscape photography, high-brow literature, and gourmet cooking. Why, we wondered, do the purists feel the need to edit out the delightful incongruities, the ironies that wreak havoc on idealized landscapes?

God bless the Sardinian transplant to the Tiber floodplain, dancing in high-topped sneakers to the beat of polkas played on electric accordions hooked to wah-wah pedals. And God bless the New World crop, *granoturco*, which has been in the Valtiberina Alta since the beginning...or at least since the Turks brought its *siciliano* seed from Mexico.

And if God can't bless them, then perhaps Saint Francis can, for he is rightfully the patron saint of contradiction and paradox. He inspired grain farmers to leave their fields to become monks, only to tell them later that they could stay and be brothers to the crops. He inspired Columbus to go across the ocean to discover the Garden of Eden, and Columbus brought back to Europe maize seeds to prove he had been there. The Native Americans mission-ized by the Franciscan friends of Columbus claim that the saint is still wandering among them, out in the desert scrub where they live. He is probably looking for a good bowl of polenta, lime or no lime, and a few pungent herbs to help get him through the night.

Gary Paul Nabhan has published numerous books, including Gathering the Desert, *which won the Burroughs Medal for nature writing, and over 100 technical articles on ethnobotany, nutrition, and plant conservation. This story was taken from his book,* Songbirds, Truffles, and Wolves: An American Naturalist in Italy, *in which he traces the footsteps of St. Francis of Assisi.*

*

For some time now, our country walks had been interrupted by bursts of gunfire, as huntsmen endeavoured to wipe out the local bird population, taking pot shots at anything with wings bigger than a butterfly. This had always struck me as a gruesome exercise, mitigated only by the relish with which the poor little victims were later eaten. The local men defended their right to hunt so keenly that they claimed there would be a revolu-tion if this basic right were taken from them. Imolo was one of the few men in the village who didn't take part in these excursionary massacres. As the guns popped over the hills, bringing down wild pigeons, black-birds, and larks, he shook his head sadly and said it was a pity to take the life of anything so free. In this, we of the *palazzo* agreed, but all attempts to make this point to the huntsmen were in vain. They argued that this was something that their ancestors had been doing for centuries and it was their God-given right, in a country riddled with bureaucracy and regulations, to gain the freedom of the woods every year and complement their diet with the birds of the air. After the birds, it would be the turn of the wild boar, and then anything else that roamed the wood on four legs.

—Lisa St. Aubin de Terán, *A Valley in Italy: The Many Seasons of a Villa in Umbria*

MARGARET GREEN

The Nicholas Effect

One family's heartbreaking story
riveted a nation.

WHILE TOURING SOUTHERN ITALY, WE VISITED AN ANCIENT GREEK temple in Paestum. The children scampered up and down the worn steps. Taking my eyes off them for a moment, I spotted four doves perched on top of a column. Two of the birds suddenly flew away, disappearing into the golden sky. *Someday, our children will be gone too*, I thought.

Glad to be reminded of how much I loved my children, I gave seven-year-old Nicholas a big hug. Four-year-old Eleanor ran from the temple and let me hug her too.

It had been a dream trip, especially for Nicholas. Entranced by ancient history, he was thrilled to see the Roman Forum and Colosseum, the ruins of Pompeii and now these beautiful temples. Recalling his mythology, he had announced in a mock-serious voice from the steps, "I'm Zeus!" And then remembering how the Romans had referred to the same god, he ran onto Italian soil and said, "Now I'm Jupiter!"

"We'd better be going," Reg, my husband, said, glancing at his watch. We headed back to our rental car.

We planned to drive all night to the southern tip of Italy and take a ferry to Sicily. The sun hung low when we finally got under way. Reg was behind the wheel while Nicholas and Eleanor settled against pillows in the backseat. Soon they dozed off and, sometime after ten o'clock, so did I.

Angry voices shouting in Italian woke me up at 11:00 p.m. "Something is going on," murmured Reg. A car was keeping pace with ours on the dark *autostrada*. From the passenger side a man with a black bandanna over his face pointed a gun in our direction.

Worried that we'd be at their mercy if we stopped, Reg floored the accelerator. There was a loud crack, and the backseat window shattered. I heard more angry shouts. "It's too dangerous to stop," Reg said. He pushed the car faster. A moment later another shot blasted his window. But now a gap was opening between the cars, and the attackers dropped farther and farther behind.

Cold night air was rushing in. I unbuckled my seat belt and leaned over the seat to check on the children. Nicholas lay on his pillow, his eyes closed. He had always been a heavy sleeper, so I assumed he was still dozing. Eleanor sat up, complaining, "I'm cold, Mommy." Relieved that both of them seemed unhurt and had slept through the worst of the ordeal, I brushed away granules of glass and covered the kids with extra clothes. Eleanor settled in her seat.

I strained my eyes, looking for help, occasionally glancing into the backseat. Finally we spotted flashing blue lights. Two police cars and an ambulance were stopped at the scene of an accident. We pulled over. An officer tried to wave us on, but Reg gestured to our damaged car.

As we opened the car door and the dome light glowed over the children, I noticed that Nicholas's tongue was protruding slightly. Then I saw blood on his hair. *Dear God, he's hurt. Is he cut from the glass?* Trembling with fear, I looked closer and found a small round bullet wound in his head.

The officer yelled for the ambulance. A medic raced over and lifted Nicholas's limp body into the ambulance. Reg picked up our son's blanket, a small patch of sheepskin, and put it on the stretcher. If Nicholas woke up in a strange place, it would comfort him.

As the ambulance headed toward the nearest hospital, I begged to follow. We tried to explain to the officers what had happened.

We still couldn't understand it ourselves. A young Italian man who had stopped his car when he saw the commotion translated for us. We would have to go to the station to make a report. *But what about our son?*

Reaching into his coat pocket, out translator pulled out a string of blue plastic rosary beads. He kissed them and handed them to me. "For you." I gripped those beads so tight they left indentations in my palm.

When we arrived at the hospital, a swarm of medical personnel was standing around the ambulance. Nicholas would need special care, we were told. They wanted to take him to the hospital in Messina, more than an hour away on the island of Sicily. We gave our approval and then made our report at the police station.

I felt as dark and empty as the streets we were driven through. Escorted by police cars with flashing blue lights, we were put on a ferry to Sicily. At the hospital in Messina we could only view Nicholas from outside a window in the intensive care unit. Electrodes were patched to his forehead. He was surrounded by wires, tubes and hospital equipment. I hugged Eleanor close as the neurologist explained slowly and carefully, "The bullet is lodged in an area where it is impossible to operate. Your son is in a coma. All we can do is wait."

As we were taken to a hotel, I longed for home. If this tragedy had happened there, we would have had the support of our family and friends. We would have been better able to understand what the doctors and nurses were telling us.

The hotel lobby was empty except for a desk clerk. We wearily made our way to our room and tossed and turned for an hour or two.

The next day I felt as though we were living in another world. I tried to remain hopeful. When we were not sitting on the hard plastic chairs in the waiting room, we hovered helplessly by the hospital window or waited at the hotel for a phone call that would bring some news. I could be with Nicholas only once, and then for just five minutes. The doctor said I might be able to sit with him the next day—perhaps for twenty minutes.

But the following morning the doctor ushered us into a

conference room. The team of physicians looked grave. With the help of a translator the head of the intensive care unit explained that Nicholas's brain had died during the night. The respirator was the only thing keeping his small body going. He was gone.

I held Reg's hand, barely able to comprehend the horrible truth. Was there nothing more we could do? "Shouldn't we give his organs?" one of us said (we don't remember which one). "Yes," we agreed.

"We would like to give his organs," Reg told the doctors. *Maybe this way his death can make a difference*, I thought.

That afternoon, when we returned to the hotel, a crowd of people waited by the front desk. Some stepped aside, too shy to intrude, but wanting to comfort us. The hotel clerk gestured to one young mother who wished to see us. She turned to us with a tear-stained face, and we hugged each other and cried. A perfect stranger but she understood.

We were flooded with kindness until we left Italy. On the street in Messina an old man pressed a stuffed animal into Eleanor's arms. When I asked if I could bring some clothes for Nicholas's body, the head of a department store invited me to pick out anything I wanted for free—I chose a blue blazer, gray slacks and a tie with Goofy on it. The day I wanted to walk Eleanor to get some ice cream, a policeman drove us to the best spot in town and bought it himself. The president of Italy arranged for us to be flown home in an Italian Air Force jet.

Bringing Nicholas's body back home to California for burial, we faced our loss all over again. Little things set me off, like going to the grocery store and grabbing Nicholas's favorite cereal. Or the day a package arrived in the mail with all his toys we had left behind in the rental car. Or when I opened his closet and saw the tricorn hat for his George Washington costume for Halloween—a costume he would never wear.

But the letters and telegrams kept pouring in. Newspapers and TV stations throughout Italy had carried our story. The country grieved for the boy. Schoolchildren wrote stories and poems. Towns small and large named streets and schools after him.

We had been home for only a few months when we were invited to Italy for a ceremony honoring Nicholas. *How can we go back?* I wondered. *How can we face the pain again?* But I realized we had to go for his sake.

The morning of the ceremony, Eleanor, Reg and I got dressed in our hotel in Messina. We went to the lobby, and a beautiful young woman came over to us and introduced herself as Maria Pia Pedala. Only 19 years old, she had been near death when she received Nicholas's liver. She was alive, thanks to our son.

Next we met fourteen-year-old Anna Maria Di Ceglie. She had received one of our son's kidneys. At the ceremony, we greeted, one after another, the people whose lives had been changed by Nicholas. There was an eleven-year-old boy who had been on dialysis for a year until he was given a new kidney. We met a schoolteacher and a salesman who had each received a cornea from our son. We shook hands with the thirty-year-old woman who had received cells from Nicholas's pancreas to help her body produce insulin. The only one missing was fifteen-year-old Andrea Mongiardo, who was still recovering from a heart transplant operation.

More important were those who had simply been affected by our story. An Italian specialist told us he had done only one transplant every four months, but ever since our son's death, the number of organ donations had risen dramatically. Doctors said Nicholas had changed the entire country: Italy, which has one of the lowest rates of organ donation in Europe, reported the willingness to donate went

*M*aggie and Reginald Green donated the money that they had saved for Nicholas's college fund to the National Association for Gifted Children. "They believe, as we do, that the public schools should treat each child as an individual," Maggie explains. For more information write to 1707 L Street, Suite 550, Washington, DC 20036.

♦

—AC

up 400 percent since Nicholas died. They called this the Nicholas Effect.

Of course, I would have done anything to have my son back, but the fact that his young life had made this much difference was overwhelming.

On the last night of our stay, after an exhausting day of visits and speeches, we returned to our hotel at midnight, only to find a man who insisted that Reg come to a disco with him. "Two musicians have written a song about your son," he said. Reg didn't have the heart to turn the man down.

Filled with loud music and youngsters dancing, the disco came to a stop when Reg walked in. In the silence two young musicians started strumming guitars and singing a song. The only word Reg could understand was Nicholas. At the end, the people erupted into cheers and hugs for my husband. Everybody wanted to give him their blessings.

"It was like a church," Reg told me later. "There was that much love in the place." All because of a seven-year-old boy.

Maggie Green lives in Bodega Bay, California.

✦

Sunt lacrimae rerum et mentam mortalia tangunt.
Here are the tears of things; mortality touches the heart.

—Virgil

IVO JOHN LEDERER

* * *

Are the Germans Gone?

Recollections of a special day.

June 3, 1944. I have not gone into the streets of Rome all day and am aching to do so. I know better. It won't be safe. The Germans are pulling out. We are glued to the lace curtain, through which we watch troop carriers, an occasional shiny staff car, standard and all, a light tank now and then. The heavy ones have already moved north, leaving the pavement of the Viale del Parioli a mess. The few officers in the staff cars look very smart. The soldiers in vehicles and those walking on the opposite side of the Parioli look tired. And fierce.

8 p.m. Daylight is turning to night. There is an odd air about the street. Some German soldiers, in twos and threes, are walking slowly on the other side, carrying arms and light equipment. My father whispers, "They are from special units—probably mining buildings." Two boys emerge from the building opposite. A German grabs one—about my age, thirteen—by the scruff of his neck, puts a satchel in his hands to make him carry it north, toward the Tiber. The boy tries to object, gets a kick in the rear and moves on, stumbling. The other boy runs back into the building. My mother pulls me away from the window.

10 p.m. No one out there. Nothing. Are the Germans gone?

Are the Allies on their way? My lucky Jewish family has been waiting for this day since we narrowly escaped the Ustashis and Nazis in Yugoslavia in June 1941, through two years of internment in northern Italy and the endless eight months of hiding in the apartment of a courageous Italian friend in Rome.

We have false Italian identity cards, but my parents have not ventured out much because of their foreign accents. Nor has my sister, because she is eighteen, and some German or Italian could get nasty ideas.

My father has sometimes gone out after dark to sell something on the black market. My mother has gone to the market to buy what could be gotten without ration cards, like turnips, which I hate.

I speak Italian very well and go to a Catholic school off the Piazza di Spagna—something my father arranged with the Vatican. Every second day or so, my sister and I go with buckets to fetch water from a pump a block away. The lines sometimes are very long.

2 a.m., June 4. An eerie silence out there in the dark. You can hear a mosquito sneeze in Sicily. When will they come? Hurry up! For weeks, we have listened for the distant sounds of artillery from the advancing Anzio front. When we hear nothing, we know the Allies are being driven back. By now, everyone is a nervous wreck.

5 a.m. We doze by the window on our feet. Daylight is beginning to crack through the darkness. Outside, nothing. Then, with the speed of lightning, an incredible noise. An open truck whizzes by, filled with wild-looking men wearing bandoliers, some without shirts, several swirling Italian and red flags, all shouting: "*Roma é libera! Viva l'Italia! Abbasso il Fascismo!*" The Partisans. Within seconds, the truck is out of sight. I look up at my parents. They are tense. Both caress my head.

5:30 a.m. Suddenly, the strangest apparition I have ever seen: a Jeep, rolling down the Parioli at a leisurely pace. A driver; next to him a British soldier; behind them, an enormous man with a black beard, a turban on his head; next to him, another soldier, bandaged, with blood showing through. A zoo, I think to myself. I focus on the Jeep. A metal box on four wheels, as if from an Erector set. These can't be the famous Allies, not in a cheap toy like that.

German cars are solid, beautiful. "We are going to lose the war," I declare. My parents smile.

Early morning. A deep droning rumble, like an approaching drum roll, begins to be heard from the direction of the Piazza Ungheria, to our left. We crane our necks, all four faces flush to the window panes. I ask permission to go out. "Better not. How do we know it's not the Germans coming back?"

The avenue is empty. The rumbling grows louder and louder. Moments later, the procession begins, a parade of vehicles to stagger the mind: Jeeps, troop carriers, armed vehicles, closed military cars. "The Americans," my parents whisper. Their eyes are moist. The four of us embrace, for a long, long time. I don't believe what I see. Heavy tanks on long flatbeds with rubber wheels, towed by trucks. Soldiers on all over the tanks, broad smiles, a V-sign on every hand.

"Now I am sure we'll win the war."

"Oh?"

"If the Americans are so caring and rich to put their tanks on beds with rubber

---

*I*n August 1942, whilst serving with the SBS, I was captured during a raid on a German airfield in Sicily, a year before the Allied landing took place.

In September 1943, the Italian armistice was announced and the following day, on 9 September, together with all the other inmates of the camp in the Po Valley near Parma, I absconded in order to avoid being sent to Germany, as did thousands of other prisoners-of-war in camps all over Italy.

The one thing that most of these escaping prisoners had in common in the course of the succeeding months was the unstinting help they were given by all sorts and conditions of Italians who risked their lives in doing so without any thought of subsequent reward. One of these, a girl called Wanda, subsequently became my wife.

◆

—Eric Newby,
A Small Place in Italy

wheels, not to ruin the streets of Rome, we'll win! Now I know. Can I go out now?"

Peals of laughter. My mother and my sister are weeping from happiness. The avenue is invaded by shrieking humanity. I run off into the crowd. Girls kissing soldiers, everyone embracing everyone else.

Some men shout, "Down with Fascism!" "*Fascismo, pfui!*" as they spit on the pavement. Several remove their Fascist Party lapel pins—a green, white and red enameled shield—and throw them on the ground. I pick one up, put it in my pocket and turn to catch some of the chocolates, chewing gum and cigarettes (for my parents) that the GIs are giving the crowd. This day never ends.

June 6. Word of D-Day and the Normandy landings spreads like wildfire. Still exhilarated by the liberation of Rome, I am back out into the fray to celebrate this second special day!

July 21. My family and I sail out of Naples for America. A few years later, I become an American citizen and add John as my middle name. It means the same as my given name but symbolizes the transition from the Old World to the New.

June 2, 1994. I have just returned to New York from a business trip to Rome. (A pity I could not stay until June 4.) In my home, I open a small box of childhood mementos. It's still there—the little enameled Fascist pin I picked up on the Parioli 50 years ago.

Ivo John Lederer, a former history professor at Yale and Stanford, is director of the global business policy council of A. T. Kearney, a management consulting firm.

✳

It might be objected that the Italians survived World War II precisely because they did not fight as stubbornly as the more "serious" Russians and Germans did, because they eventually changed sides when they knew who was winning, and because they surrendered instead of holding out and thus suffered few casualties. By not being all too serious about World War II, Italy got out better than did its erstwhile allies, Germany and Japan, even though those two "serious" nations eventually caught up with the Italians on the road to recovery and became economic superpowers.

A 1988 poll in Japan ranked the Italians as the "most stupid" among the major nations because of their perceived lack of seriousness. The poll was received with incredulity and mirth in Italy. The popular reaction was "Doesn't everybody know we are smart? The stupid ones are the Japanese because they work too hard and never have a good time."

—Paul Hofmann, *That Fine Italian Hand*

PART FIVE

THE LAST WORD

H . V . M O R T O N

The Waters of Clitumnus

Drink from the well of History.

ON ONE OF THOSE HUSHED MORNINGS IN EARLY AUTUMN
when the grapes, the olives, and the chestnuts are nearly ready for
the harvest, I left Assisi with the idea of reaching Rome that night,
for Rome is only a hundred miles away. I had packed some sand-
wiches, to which a kind friend had added a basket of ripe figs
picked that morning; and so I set off down the hill and across the
valley. I had made to myself the most difficult of all promises in
Italy, that I would not pause or dawdle on the way, that I would
not be lured by hilltop towns, or be beguiled for any reason at all,
with one exception: the Waters of Clitumnus.

I was soon travelling south along the Via Flaminia, which was
the Great North Road of the Romans, and I saw the old towns
standing high in sunlight upon the hills, echoing their Latin
names—Spello, *Hispellum;* Foligno, *Fulginium;* Trevi, *Trebia*—and I
had the feeling, not easy to explain, that I had been here before;
that some tree or rock or some river or bend in the road might
unlock the gates of memory and resolve the mystery. Of all the
Regions of Italy, Umbria is the most subtle, the most tranquil, and
the most mysterious. One has the feeling that the roots go down
even deeper than usual, beyond the Etruscans to unknown people

speaking a lost tongue, and that the mountain-tops have seen stargazers of whose existence history has no record. It was no accident that S. Francis was an Umbrian. A chain of religious faith and speculation links the *Canticle of the Sun* with the Eugubian Tablets of Gubbio; and as the pagan world revered the Umbrian Schools of Divination, so the modern world finds at Assisi the shrine of the greatest of all the Umbrian seers. It is curious that the augurs saw the will of the gods in the flight of birds in that same countryside where many centuries later S. Francis loved birds as a manifestation of the divine spirit.

When I came to the Waters of Clitumnus I saw a beautiful, rich and well-watered valley, lying between two ranges of thirsty hills. The little river went sliding on its brief course to join the Tiber, and I soon arrived at its source. A path led from the road to a farm-house where I asked permission to go down to the Waters, for they are private property. The farmer's wife nodded pleasantly towards the gate that leads to the Waters—*fonti* she called them—and I came to a scene of entrancing beauty.

The "Fountains," or Waters of Clitumnus, look at first sight as if some landscape gardener of great talent had designed perfect surroundings for the clearest water on earth, water so limpid and translucent that it appears as if it had been filtered in some underground laboratory. Then you notice that it is not ordinary water: it is strangely alive, not with the ascending bubbles of mineral gas but with a slow, curious, and gentle quivering for which there seems no explanation until you look into the depths. There, upon beds of silver sand and clean gravel, you see the "eyes" of hundreds of springs welling up out of the earth. The water is rarely more than two or three feet deep and it is fascinating to look down, as through a sheet of glass, and see the "eyes" bubbling, each one agitating a little wisp of the finest sand. Tall poplars grow round the pools and are reflected in the glassy water; willows bend above them, and anyone at all sensitive to atmosphere would recognize, and rightly, another Umbrian shrine.

Virgil, Juvenal, and Propertius (who was born near Assisi), are among those who mentioned the Waters of Clitumnus and their strange quality of whitening the cattle that bathed in them, and their more than curious habit of reflecting not a person's physical appearance, but his nature. This must have changed since Pan died for, looking down rather fearfully, I saw myself! The Emperor Caligula paid a visit to the Clitumnus, so did Honorius, who turned aside to see the Waters when on his way to Rome. No doubt they saw the special breed of white oxen dedicated to the gods which grazed upon the banks of the Clitumnus in Roman times. They were never broken to the plough or mated, but were fattened on the rich pastures until the time came when they were led garlanded to the altar.

I looked into one of the springs and saw that the sands were covered with silver coins. So the old pagan custom of casting an offering to the river god still continues, as it does at the Fontana di Trevi in Rome. I do not know why this particular spring should have been selected for the offerings, and I wondered if it were the same in which nineteen centuries ago Pliny noticed a shower of coins. When he was there many shrines had been erected to the various deities who presided over the pools, and he read inscriptions on walls and columns written by visitors who wished to testify to the virtues of the presiding gods. "There are many of them," he wrote, "you will greatly admire, as there are some that will make you laugh." The chief deity of the pools was the god Clitumnus whose statue, says Pliny, stood in a shrine near by, clothed in a toga.

While walking along the bank of the river I came upon this shrine, or one remarkably like it, standing higher up near the road. It is a small temple with just room for a priest and a few visitors who had come to consult Clitumnus, who was an oracular god. I saw that the place where the oracle once stood in his toga is now occupied by a disused Christian altar.

I returned to gaze again into the crystal pools, fascinated as men have been for thousands of years by their furtive and mysterious movement. I have never seen any place in which the pagan world seemed nearer. I thought of Pan and the Naiads, and I wondered about the local people. An old man came from the farmhouse and dipped a kettle in one of the pools. Yes, he said, it was good water;

and that was that. I wondered what he really thought about it, and whether he liked wandering out to fill the kettle after dark. I wondered too, if at times when the moon is full, he has ever heard the white oxen going down to drink.

I continued my journey through the enchanted land, a land so warm with life and so rich in experience, and late that night I slept in Rome.

H. V. Morton also contributed "Mediolanum" in Part One.

★

Glossary

abbasso	down
albergo diurno	day hotel
aliscafo	hydrofoil
andiamo	let's go
architetto	architect
autostrada	highway
avvocato	lawyer
bambina	little girl
bell' appartmento	pretty apartment
bella pallazina	pretty building
bella zona	pretty neighborhood
bene, allora	good then
bruschetta	bread slices, lightly toasted in olive oil
buon giorno	good day
buona sera	good evening
carabinieri	branch of the police department
casa popolare	government-funded low-income housing
centro	center
coincidenza	coincidence
Colpo Grosso	Popular Italian soft porn TV show
commercianti	local business people
complimenti	compliments
con gran disinvoltura	with great ease
cornetto	pastry similar to a croissant

cucina	kitchen
d'accordo	agreed
divieto di pesca	no fishing allowed
dormire	to sleep
drogheria	drugstore
farmacia	pharmacy
fegato	liver
festa	celebration, party, feast
finalmente	finally
formaggio	cheese
frutteria	greengrocer, fruit market
geometra	surveyor, also a contractor
giornalista	journalist
incidenza	incidence
ingeniere	engineer
isolotto	small garden island
la poverina	poor thing
la dolce vita	Idiomatic expression meaning "the good life"
latteria	dairy store
letto matrimoniale	double bed
medici	doctors
mi hai tradito	You have betrayed me
mistificazione	alteration from the truth
molto bello	very pretty
motorino	moped
non toccare	do not touch
Orario Generale	Daily Train Schedule
padrone	owner or landlord
palazzo	large, usually residential, building
pancetta	hand-rolled Italian bacon
pane	bread

panificio	bakery, bread store
panino	sandwich
partenze	departures
pasticceria	bakery, pastry store
pensione	small hotel with some meals included
per l'amore di Dio	for the love of God
permesso	May I please? Is it permitted?
Porca miseria	mild expletive
porti d'incontro	meeting places
prego	please
presepio	crêche
professore	professor
prosciutto crudo	cured ham
restauro	restoration
ribollita	Tuscan bean soup
salumeria	Delicatessen meats store
sciarpe	scarves
scopa	a card game
Sempre avanti	Idiomatic expression meaning "No turning back" or "Onward and upward"
soluzione felice	a happy solution
stracotto di asinello	deep-cooked baby donkey
stronza	shit
tabaccheria	tobacco store
tiamo	I love you
trattoria	informal, local restaurant
trenino	little train
ufficio postale	postal office
va bene	it's okay
vicoli	side streets
viva	hooray

Index

Index of Contributors

Acknowledgments

I would like to thank Raj Khadka for making the Travelers' Tales connection and reviving the past, James O'Reilly for his instinct in trusting me and his passion for all things Italian, Larry Habegger for his calming wisdom, Susan Brady for her dynamic efficiency, Sean O'Reilly for his love of ancient Rome, ribald humor, and for the historical perpective he brought to the book, and Arwen O'Reilly and Tim O'Reilly for their continuous source of materials. I am ever grateful for DePaul University's University Research Council and College of Liberal Arts & Sciences grant support, which enabled me to hire Nellie Greely and Patrick Hanrahan, DePaul students, as editorial assistants. *Travelers Tales: Italy* would not be what it is without Nellie's superlative mind and her editorial and organizational acumen. Her astute and enduring eye for narrative is in every page of this book. Patrick, too, lives on in this book as an unseen maker, which is the editorial role. His unerring falsehood detector and his enthusiasm and demand for all things finely written were so important. I thank Gretchen Rhode for searching out Travelers Tales, and jumping aboard as an editorial assistant, when Patrick and Nellie were gone, the ship in full sail and moving fast, needing so many final parts to get us to shore, which she did ably and enthusiastically as is her want. Thanks also to Michael Reilly, Deborah Greco, and Trisha Schwartz.

My mother and father and sister, in Italy, searched high and low to locate memories, books, and articles for me; I thank them for always helping me to cross the Atlantic. Finally, I thank my husband, Leo, for holding all things Italian in the highest esteem, so that I could work long hours away, coming home just to pile up books in bed. Dearest soulmate, he has always known we would return to Italy again and again.

Introduction, "The Idea of Italy," by Jan Morris copyright © 1998 by Jan
    Morris. Published with permission from the author.

"Big Butts and Walnuts" by Doug Rennie published with permission from the author. Copyright © 1998 by Doug Rennie.

"Indirections to Rome" by Donald Gecewicz published with permission of the author. Copyright © 1998 by Donald Gecewicz.

"Rocking the Gondola" by Jan Warner published with permission from the author. Copyright © 1998 by Jan Warner.

"The Errant Steps of Wooden Shoes" by Adria Bernardi published with permission from the author. Copyright © 1998 by Adria Bernardi.

"Vacationing with Mom" by Henry Alford originally appeared in the May 1995 issue of *GQ.* Reprinted by permission of the author. Copyright © 1995 by Henry Alford.

"The Visible Man" by Trey Ellis reprinted from the December, 1988 issue of *Travel & Leisure.* Copyright © 1988 by Trey Ellis.

"Lunch at Pensione Suisse" by David Robinson published with permission from the author. Copyright © 1998 by David Robinson.

"The Children of Magna Graecia" by Tom Mueller reprinted courtesy of the author and *Hemispheres,* the magazine of United Airlines. Copyright © 1996 by Tom Mueller.

"Sleepwalking in Italy" by Laura J. Aymond published with permission from the author. Copyright © 1998 by Laura J. Aymond.

"Satyric" by Matthew Spender excerpted from *Within Tuscany* by Matthew Spender. Reprinted by permission of Penguin Books Limited. Copyright © 1992 by Matthew Spender.

"Una Bustarella" by Tim Parks excerpted from *Italian Neighbors or A Lapsed Anglo-Saxon in Verona* by Tim Parks. Used by permission of Grove/Atlantic, Inc. and William Heinemann Publishers. Copyright © 1992 by Tim Parks.

"The Italian Mistress" by Luigi Barzini reprinted with the permission of Simon & Schuster from *Memories of Mistresses: Reflections from a Life* by Luigi Barzini. Copyright © 1986 by Ludina Barzini.

"Sagri di Polenta" by Gary Paul Nabhan excerpted from *Songbirds, Truffles, and Wolves: An American Naturalist in Italy* by Gary Paul Nabhan. Copyright © 1993 by Gary Paul Nabhan. Reprinted by permission of Pantheon Books, a division of Random House, Inc. and The Spieler Agency West.

"The Nicholas Effect" by Margaret Green reprinted from October, 1995 issue of *Guideposts.* Reprinted with permission from *Guideposts Magazine.* Copyright © 1995 by Guideposts, Carmel, New York, 10512

"Are the Germans Gone?" by Ivo John Lederer reprinted from the June 4, 1994 issue of *The New York Times.* Copyright © 1994 by The New York Times Company. Reprinted by permission of The New York Times Company.

Additional Credits (arranged alphabetically by title)

Selection by Angelique Syverson excerpted from *Gutsy Mamas: Travel Tips and Wisdom for Mothers on the Road* by Marybeth Bond. Copyright © 1997 by Travelers' Tales. Reprinted by permission of Angelique Syverson.

Selection from "The Universal Primate Does Rome" by Sean O'Reilly published with permission from the author. Copyright © 1998 by Sean O'Reilly.

Selection from "Valentines to Venice," by Paolo Lanapoppi originally appeared in the February 1988 issue of *Travel & Leisure*. Copyright © 1988 by American Express Publishing Corporation.

Selections from *A Valley in Italy: The Many Seasons of a Villa in Umbria* by Lisa St. Aubin de Terán. Copyright © 1994 by Lisa St. Aubin de Terán. Reprinted by permission of HarperCollins Publishers, Inc.

Selection from "Venice: A City of Love and Death" by Erica Jong originally appeared in *The New York Times*. Copyright © by The New York Times Company. Reprinted by permission of the author.

Selection from *Within Tuscany* by Matthew Spender. Reprinted by permission of Penguin Books Ltd. Copyright © 1992 by Matthew Spender.

Selection from *The World of Venice* by Jan Morris copyright © 1993 by Jan Morris. Reprinted by permission of Harcourt Brace & Co.

About the Editor

Anne Calcagno was raised in Milan and Rome, and is both bilingual and a dual national. She came to the United States to attend Williams College, and remained. She now lives in Chicago, where she is an Assistant Professor of English at DePaul University. For her short story collection *Pray For Yourself*, variously set in Italy and in the U.S., she won the James D. Phelan Award, a National Endowment for the Arts Fellowship, and two Illinois Arts Council awards. She is currently at work on a novel about Italy and Eritrea during World War II. Her travel writing has appeared in *The New York Times*.